Diving
Southeast Asia

A guide to the world's
most diverse marine environment

Beth and Shaun Tierney

Contents

Introduction

Indonesia

Malaysia

Philippines

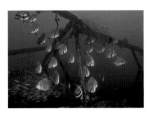

Thailand

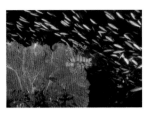

Singapore

Resources

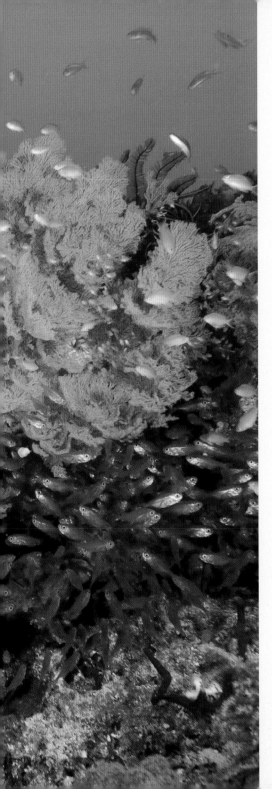

Introduction

And so the addiction continues. This is where it all started. This is the place we will always love most. The dive drug that we are most heavily reliant on. The one we won't give up, no matter what anyone says, or whatever the treatment might be. Southeast Asian waters.

It's not just the things we have seen in these seas, it's the entire experience of being there: sitting moments from the equator staring down at colours so intense you simply can't describe them; the sensation of falling into a rainbow, of being swallowed by this other world; emerging from the warm water to find balmy air, the scent of the tropics, a smiling face. Wishing, desperately, to be down there just one more time, before we know we have to give it all up and go home.

No more encounters with a minute pygmy seahorse, no more heart-stopping moments with a manta ray, never again to experience being watched by the curious eye of a cuttlefish or to glance at a sponge and realise it is actually a frogfish. Well, not until next time. We will be back...

About this book

One of the best things that ever came our way was the invitation to write *Diving the World*, to be able to share our experiences of all the wonderful places where we have explored the incredible underwater realm. However, we soon realised that a guide book had to be much more than just a collection of stories so we researched long and hard to ensure we included places that everyone wanted to see.

We sent out questionnaires to as many people as we could, bored our dive buddies senseless and asked a million things of as many dive professionals. This became a hit-list of worldwide where-to-dive destinations.

The divers hit-list

When the time came to choose a single diving region, we did it all again, then just to be sure, we took the research a stage further and ran some public opinion polls. With so many places to dive – the choice is almost endless – we asked "which of the world's regions do you want to see the most"? The one that came up on everyone's list – the clear majority – was Southeast Asia. This area has always been a personal favourite, so imagine how delighted we were to discover that for many other people it either already is on, or is at the top of their aspirational list.

Diving Southeast Asia

Aside from our work commitments, we dive in Asia every year, but this new guide gave us the chance to revisit places we hadn't been to since we were trekking many years ago. We rediscovered the joy of diving on some easily accessible reefs, the ones that more experienced divers scoff at, but where novices go to train. We spent time with those novices too: it was like a time warp to share their first-ever experience of dropping onto a brightly coloured reef, meeting a turtle, seeing a shark. Then we headed off to some new and unexplored destinations, ones that currently only attract serious divers who are looking for new experiences. No doubt these will be the on the wider hit-list in the future.

Every diver has a list of destinations that becomes their personal hit-list so how do you decide which one to visit first, which is the number one priority and which one remains a dream? Read on – our hope is that you find inspiration here rather than definitive answers. The world is a small place these days, and the seas cover most of it. Explore, dream, discover.

Image © Suzanne Turek

About the authors

Our love of all things underwater first developed whilst snorkelling in Mexico during a round the world trip in the late 1980s. By the time we reached Indonesia we were completely hooked by what we were seeing beneath the surface.

As soon as we returned to London, we gained our BSAC qualifications and headed off to do our first open water dives in the Maldives. It was a heart-stopping moment when we came face to face with a whitetip reef shark and the start of a love affair that has influenced our lives ever since. As a photo-journalist team, we went off around the world again in the 1990s, this time specifically to dive. During this incredible year we explored many of the exotic locations that are now in this new guide and in *Diving the World*.

Since then we have become increasingly involved in the dive industry, and have been lucky enough to have revisited, photographed and written about many of the best dive destinations in the world.

Using this book

It's not our intention to claim this is the 'absolute' in dive guides, rather we hope to give divers and divers-to-be enough information to feel secure about choosing and booking that all-important trip.

Everything in this guide has been based on our personal experiences. Over the years, we have dived each and every one of the sites listed: some dives were a few years back but we have managed to revisit most. Sometimes, we would ascend thinking we had been there before so it was a case of working back through our old log books to check. Where we couldn't visit a new destination, we have asked those that have for their personal views: check these tales from others, they are great for making comparisons.

When it came to deciding which destinations to include, we asked both dive professionals and ordinary divers for their opinions, listening to their often very emotional responses. We've mentioned up-and-coming places for those who like to be more adventurous and have done our best to ensure that information is up-to-date, unbiased and, more importantly, first hand. However, things change in a heartbeat so regard what is written in these pages as reference rather than gospel. And more than anything, bear in mind that If you go at a different time of year, chances are your experiences will be very different to ours. And that, of course, is the fun of dive travel.

❝❞ **Our hope is that you find inspiration here rather than definitive answers. The world is a small place these days, and the seas cover most of it. Explore, dream, discover.**

Dive logs Descriptions of dives are as we found them when we did them. We have tried to ensure names for dive sites are both correct and consistent, but these vary according to individual operators as do modes of transport: many sites can be reached by day boat and liveaboard. More than anything else conditions change season by season. These logs are not definitive, nor are the descriptions: after all, fish swim away.

⌄7 Three Caves Slope		
Depth	45 m	The name of the site when we went
Visibility	good	Our depth, not necessarily recommended
Currents	mild to strong	Visibility on the day and season dependant
Dive type	day boat	Currents on the day and tide dependant
		How we travelled to the site

Images The photos used in each chapter – and against the dives – are what we saw on the day we were there. We have not taken images in Sulawesi and used them in the Similans. If a dive site is famous for manta rays but we haven't shown one, it's because we missed out. And that as we all know, is the way of things when you play in the sea.

Maps Dive area maps are not to scale and are only intended to be an indication of a sites location in comparison to the nearest landmass and dives nearby. Dives will often have several names as different operations use a traditional or a pet name. Sea depth and drop-offs are indicated by colour changes to give a loose indication of reef locations and surrounding sea conditions.

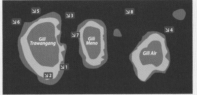

Drying out At the end of each geographic region are recommendations for resorts, liveaboards, restaurants and things do to when you are not diving. Listings with reviews are those we have first-hand experience of; those listed under *Other options* come recommended by trusted friends and colleagues, or when someone we have worked with in the past has moved on or perhaps started their own operation.

🛏	**Sleeping**	$$$	150+ double room per night
		$$	US$75-150
		$	under US$75
🍽	**Eating**	$$$	US$40+ 2-course meal, excluding drinks
		$$	US$20-40
		$	under US$20

Resorts and liveaboards To the best of our knowledge all operators listed hold PADI, BSAC, NAUI or similar affiliations, but always check, especially if you are taking a course.

Sleeping and eating What makes some people happy will not be to someone else's taste. We target hotels in the three star range as these are more likely to be comfortable, safe for you and secure for all your expensive dive kit. However, star ratings don't exist everywhere and some remote destinations have only minimal or basic accommodation options. These are noted on the Drying out pages along with a few up-market hotels, ideal for special events or honeymoons. Meal costs are subjective, but will give a general idea of how much cash to take out.

Marine species names When it comes to naming creatures, there are many and often conflicting common names. In general, we have used what seems to be most frequent. Likewise, the spelling of common names for marine animals varies considerably so we chose to set a standard based on some well trusted, scientific sources which are listed in under Resources on page 299.

Planning a trip

Inspiration for the ultimate dive trip can come from this book, from magazine articles or tales from friends. Wherever you plan to go, specific details of getting there, and what to do once you've arrived, are covered in the respective chapters. But before you rush into booking, take a look at the bigger picture. Does your dive destination have all the elements that you're looking for?

It's not enough to know that someone else had fun – if you don't get what you personally want, you'll be disappointed. To solve this, define your requirements before you start the booking process. Think about what time of year you can go and the prevailing weather conditions; how much you can afford including the cost of the trip itself plus the cost of any extras; and most importantly, what type of diving you want to do and what you want to see.

On land or by sea

First, ask yourself, do you want to be on a liveaboard or on land? Being on land is perfect for people who are happy with fewer dives, have a non-diver or family with them or want to enjoy the local culture. There's more flexibility – you can go where you want, when you want, but there is usually a limit to the number of dives you can do. Liveaboards, in comparison, are perfect for serious divers who like to do as many dives as possible in their time away, or those who just like floating about an idyllic location with no need to do more than eat, sleep and dive. You will have access to more remote, uncrowded areas with fewer divers and often better reefs.

Weather and seasons

For any dive holiday, this is the next consideration. Are you going at the best time of year or the cheapest? If you go in low season and save some money don't be surprised if it rains or the seas are choppy. That's why it's the low season. Marine life is seasonal too: be aware that even if a destination is promoted as year round, its most famous attraction may not be. Pelagic species in particular move great distances and can often only be seen for a few months. Also consider if you want to combine diving with land-based attractions. A cultural experience or rainforest trek may be ruined by rain while underwater it's not such an issue.

66 99 Diving holidays are not like other holidays. They are not about lazing around in the blistering sun, waving at a passing cocktail waiter and spending hours over a three-course lunch. They are instead a series of all-action, adrenaline-rush days interspersed with balmy nights, waiting for dawn. Just so you can go and do it all again.

On land or by sea

Consider these options before making a final decision:

Land-based diving
- ▸▸ Hotel standard: luxury versus rustic, large and lively or small and quiet
- ▸▸ Hotel location: near a beach, restaurants, bars and shops
- ▸▸ Is the dive centre on site or will you need to travel there each day; if so, will they pick you up?
- ▸▸ Is the dive centre PADI, NAUI or BSAC regulated?
- ▸▸ Check for specific needs like nitrox or course availability
- ▸▸ Distance to the dive sites – is it shore or day boat diving?
- ▸▸ How many divers and guides will be on the boat?
- ▸▸ Are you expected to dive as a group or in buddy pairs?
- ▸▸ Camera facilities on the boat
- ▸▸ Other activities for the kids, a non-diving partner and drying out days
- ▸▸ Are there other options for bad weather days?

Liveaboard diving
- ▸▸ Boat standard: luxury versus budget
- ▸▸ Cabins: en suite or shared bathrooms, air-con or fan?
- ▸▸ Meals are always included but ask if special diets can be catered for and what drinks are included
- ▸▸ Maximum number of passengers
- ▸▸ How many dives in a day?
- ▸▸ Is nitrox available if you want it?
- ▸▸ Boat policy on buddy pairs, solo or group diving
- ▸▸ Are land visits scheduled?
- ▸▸ If you are travelling with a non-diver, are sites suitable for snorkelling and are there other activities available?
- ▸▸ Camera and computer facilities, battery charging stations, specific rinse tanks for non-dive equipment
- ▸▸ On bad weather days can the boat shelter or be re-routed?
- ▸▸ Boats rarely accept children but you may want to check

Costs

There is no doubt that diving is an expensive sport. As a rule of thumb, a land-based diving day worldwide averages at around US$120, which includes transport to the site, two dives with tanks, weights and a light lunch, although this will vary depending on local staff costs and expenses. Training courses average in a similar way with a PADI Open Water course costing around US$375. Liveaboard rates vary more as they reflect the calibre of vessel in much the same ways as a hotel may be two-star or four.

When you are budgeting for your trip look at all the angles to see if you are getting good value for money. Many people reject liveaboards as the initial price can seem prohibitive, yet as this often includes unlimited diving and extras like soft drinks, the cost in real terms may not be as high as it seems.

To work out a value-for-money comparison, try looking at the cost per dive. Add the cost of your flights, accommodation, dive packs and any extras you can think of (marine park fees or visas) together and divide by the number of dives you expect to have. Use this as a benchmark to see if your trip will be good value. In the comparison below, both packages are available for the same period and include flights and transfers. However, the liveaboard includes all meals and soft drinks while the hotel package only includes breakfast. Essentially, you are getting free meals and double the dives on that option. Of course, this scenario won't always come down in favour of the liveaboard and much depends on the cost of flights, time of year and what you want out of your holiday.

Thailand liveaboard
Deluxe 10 day trip with four dives per day   US$3900.00
Cost per dive (3900 ÷ 40 dives)   *US$97.50*

Thailand resort
10 days/3 star resort with two dives a day   US$2018.00
Cost per dive (2018 ÷ 20 dives)   *US$100.90*

Budgets

So how long is a piece of string? When it comes to guessing how much to take for extras, it's good to know that all Asian countries are fantastic value for money compared to those in the west. Of the four in this guide, Thailand could be considered moderately more expensive and Indonesia the cheapest. Some examples in US$ of local prices of goods in a shop at time of writing follow:

	Litre of water	Can of coke	330ml beer	MnM's	Litre of petrol	Internet 30 mins
Indonesia	0.25	0.15	1.00	0.50	0.52	1.00
Malaysia	0.30	0.50	1.50	0.65	0.75	1.00
Philippines	0.44	0.30	0.75	0.65	0.87	1.00
Thailand	0.35	0.40	1.50	0.65	1.00	1.80

Fees, taxes and surcharges

When you are planning and budgeting for your trip, allow a 'slush fund' for all those little extras you never quite know about until you arrive. These can be marine park fees, diver taxes that are ostensibly intended to support local recompression chambers or rescue services. Fuel surcharges are becoming ever more common. Individually, these costs are quite low but can add up.

Filling up in Indonesia; the Bunaken Marine Park fee disc is issued to all divers and lasts a full year

It has become a worldwide standard for US dollars to be the currency of choice with dive operators although more and more are quoting and accepting Euros. All rates in this book are US$. Travelling with currency is much the same: US dollars are easy to exchange no matter where you go, in fact many resorts accept them rather than local currencies.

Depending on current world politics, you may find it advantageous to have some cash in a second currency as well. Traveller's cheques are secure but can be hard to exchange. An option is to take your bank cash card with you. Most countries have cash machines and although your bank may charge a fee, it's not going to be far different from that of a foreign purchase. Hotels always charge a premium to change money so it pays to know the going rate in advance. Check rates inside your arrival airport. These may be slightly lower than with a local exchange office but the airport is more secure and less hassle. Singapore Airport can be a good place to change cash, rates there are often better than at your arrival destination.

Insurance

Travel insurance is an absolute necessity. Don't ever consider trying to save a few bucks by not covering yourself properly. You need a policy that will cover travel and flight delays, cancellations, baggage and diving equipment, money, cameras and other valuables and, most importantly, medical emergencies. Ensure that any policy you take out covers repatriation home or to the closest recompression chamber. Note that even some dive specific policies have a depth limit. DAN (The Divers Alert Network) has thorough dive accident insurance but they do not automatically cover travel related issues (diversalertnetwork.org). Other worldwide insurers offer policies that may suit personal needs just as well. Check diveassure.com, scubasure.com, diveinsure.co.uk and divinginsuranceuk.com. A special note is to check any other insurance you may have. Many life insurance policies, for example, specifically exclude scuba diving as a high-risk sport.

Paperwork and disclaimers

There you are, just arrived and settling in to your room or cabin, and along comes a whole raft of paperwork. You feel like you are signing your life away: first, acknowledge that your operator is in no way liable for any harm that might come your way. Second, promise that if anything does go wrong, and it was someone else's fault, you won't take action against them. Third, accept that even if there is a complete blunder, you will only ever blame yourself... then sign the papers regardless as you know, deep down, there is no choice. And in reality there isn't.

If you question a disclaimer, or refuse to sign it, it's likely you won't be able to dive. Where disclaimers may once have been a declaration of fitness and training levels, they have since become a reflection of a society inclined to sue at the drop of a hat. There is nothing the average diver can do about this, except ensure that you choose reputable operations that will take all the necessary precautions to guarantee your safety.

✷ Reasons to be insured

Apart from the obvious one for divers, a diving accident, there are many other reasons to ensure you are completely insured. Loss of baggage, missed flights, camera flooding, getting pregnant and so on. We are well and truly covered for all that and any other eventuality – or so we thought – until recently when we got caught out. Yes, even travel writers blow it occasionally.

We had booked flights on a low-cost carrier that went bankrupt two days before our due departure. Thank heavens for insurance we thought! Until we rang up and the fine-print was quoted: not covered for bankruptcy of any provider used in the formation of the trip. The lesson to be learned: pay by credit card. Although rules vary by country, generally a card issuer is liable for your purchase and with sufficient evidence, will refund your cost. This will apply to nearly all purchases made using a credit card, but not a debit, or cash card. Many companies charge a premium if you pay by credit card, but really, it is worth it.

Another reason to be insured!

Tipping

It's hard to be definitive about such a sensitive subject. Individual attitudes to tipping depend very much on where you grew up. In America it's an accepted way of life to tip generously for every service as staff rely on their tips to make a living wage. In Europe, the attitude is more likely to be a considered sum for good service while in Australia and Singapore people tip less, if at all, as these countries have higher minimum wage structures.

When it comes to tipping your dive crew, consider how much work they do behind the scenes, whether their actions ensured your trip went smoothly – or better than smoothly – and what their likely wage is. Although they will have been paid in line with local standards, a tip will reward those who often work very long hours for meagre salaries. Liveaboard crews, in particular, are often on call 24 hours a day to cater to your every whim. And always remember that these are the people who ensure you come back safely from every dive.

There is no magic formula but for land based diving, a starting point could be US$5 per day. If you did three days shore diving and had a guide and driver looking after you, consider US$15. If you are a couple, US$25 might suffice. However, if you are on a liveaboard where a crew of 15 saw to your every need for 10 days, US$50 would be far too low. In these circumstances, $10 per day would be a better starting point. Bear in mind too, that over-tipping in certain countries can be an insult. If you need advice, ask your cruise director or resort manager.

There is a growing trend among higher-end liveaboard operations to formally request that guests leave 10% of the trip cost as a tip. At US$3000 a trip that would be US$300 – which may well be appropriate, but many divers find this approach offensive, regarding it as an extra charge. In the end, only you can decide what the service was worth but always remember that it was worth something and being generous is a good thing.

Just a dozen of Archipelago Adventurers' wonderful crew of 18

✪ Booking a trip

Although this is probably the first thing on your mind, it should be the last thing you do. Once you are confident that you know what you want, you can either contact a specialist dive travel agent or book the trip yourself.

Agents With access to information and systems not available to the public, these can be a mine of information. A dedicated dive travel specialist will not only understand divers' needs but also be incredibly knowledgeable of the regions they promote. They will have suggestions, up-to-date information on local situations and often first-hand experience. They will also take the flack if things go wrong – very important these days – rearrange flights when schedules change or re-book you to another destination if there is a political or natural disaster. In some countries, they are also bonded or registered with government backed bodies. This may not always be a failsafe but it really can help.

DIY Becoming ever more popular as the internet continues to spread its web, booking your own trip can have advantages: you might find a product that is not available in your home country and direct rates are sometimes discounted. However, if you book direct you assume complete responsibility for your own trip. You have to ask all the right questions, ensure you have the right papers and co-ordinate every aspect involved – flights, accommodation, transfers, diving, meals, sightseeing. It can be a hefty job but if you like a sense of adventure it can also give you the flexibility to make on-the-spot changes.

There are many specialist dive travel agents around the world. Everyone will have their favourites, just as we do. The following are ones we can personally recommend:

▸▸ **Dive Discovery**, divediscovery.com. Based in San Francisco. Plenty of first-hand experience of Asian and worldwide waters; personally tailor-made diving holidays; organizes group tours and can issue flight tickets for unusual regions.

▸▸ **Dive The World**, Dive-The-World.com. Offices in Phuket and Kota Kinabalu. Highly knowledgeable and informative European run booking service offering impartial advice on all regional diving in a range of prices.

▸▸ **Dive Tours**, divetours.co.uk. Based in Chester, UK. Very friendly and helpful agent with well selected dive trips across Southeast Asia and worldwide.

▸▸ **Dive Worldwide**, diveworldwide.com. Based in Hampshire, UK, this full service company promotes a broad range of destinations and has very knowledgeable staff.

▸▸ **Ultima Frontera**, ultima-frontera.com. Office in Madrid, Spain, this experienced agent is especially helpful for Spanish speaking divers.

Air travel

That saying 'getting there is half the fun' was obviously coined by someone who had never spent 18 hours in the rear economy class cabin of a jumbo – with two screaming kids behind and the person in front's seat resting on their nose. Nothing will ever convince most people that flying is a good way to spend time, but it is a means to an end. The trick is to minimise the difficulties and discomforts.

Airlines

Delays, overbooking, stray luggage – airlines seem like a law unto themselves. Some treat their passengers as honoured guests while others bring a new meaning to the term 'cattle class'. Some airlines are so much better than others that paying a little extra really can make the difference between a miserable long haul flight and a pleasant one. Ask yourself if you really want to save US$75 on a 12-hour flight and not have seat-back TVs with on-tap entertainment and free drinks?

The ever expanding number of low-cost carriers is making this type of comparison even more obvious. Try booking a cheap flight with one of those and half way through the booking process you realise that the bargain of the year has just skyrocketed. Do you want a meal (click, $10 extra) to book the seat beside your partner (click, $10). Do you want to check your bags into the hold (click)? Are you overweight (excuse me? click, more money). The only positive result from this is at least it's clear what you are paying for. Until you get on board and it's, 'Headphones?' $10. Plus the plane is freezing, so you ask for a blanket, and guess what?

If you have a choice of airline, go to **skytrax.com** for airline reviews then take a look at **seatguru.com** which has advice on what seats are best so you can request your favourite.

Baggage

All divers bemoan their lot when it comes to airline baggage allowances. It can be very hard to pack your dive kit plus the usual holiday necessities and remain under the limit. The good news is that most scheduled airlines will waive a couple of kilos. However, that does mean a couple, not ten or twelve! It is now internationally accepted that all bags must weigh under 32 kg for health and safety reasons.

In general, airlines flying to or from Europe or Australasia allow 20 kg in economy, while American airlines will sometimes (but not always) allow two bags of up to 23 kg each. If you know you will be over this, call in advance for current excess rates but whoever you fly with, if you exceed the limit be prepared to be charged. If you are faced with having to pay at check-in, keep cool and try to negotiate based on being a sports person. Bear in mind that the standard complaint that 'golfers can take their clubs for free' is rarely true. Nor can surfers take their boards. Instead they both get a dispensation to take oddly shaped items. The few airlines that do allow free golf clubs also allow free dive kit so beware – if you use this type of complaint at the desk, you are likely to get less sympathy as they have heard it all before. Charter and low-cost airlines allow less and are quite strict but have introduced clearer and more affordable excess rates.

Another item of note, always lock your bags. There is a trend of not doing so because "if security wants to check, they'll break the lock". This is true but it is better than having a stranger sneak a look at the contents. There have been several high profile cases of people being arrested for drugs offences after leaving unlocked bags in hotel foyers and airports. Carry spare miniature padlocks or use plastic cable ties to secure your luggage, or if you are travelling from or via the USA, you can get special padlocks that can be opened by security at the airport.

Andrew, Shaun and Sue checking in at Manila airport; In transit at Changi airport

Packing

Unfortunately one of the biggest problems for most divers is that they have non-travel-friendly dive kit. No one ever considers the weight if an item before they buy it and if you hope to do a lot of travelling, you should. Simply compare the weight of two pairs of fins. They can range from 600 grams per fin to well over a kilo. That extra weight per item really adds up. If your current kit is heavy, consider having a second travel-friendly set and before you get negative on the additional purchase cost, remember that excess charges at check-in can be as much as 1½% of a full economy fare. To Bali that might be as much as $900.

▸▸ Reduce the weight of your luggage. A hard case can weigh as much as five kilos more than a soft bag, which is much the same as your BCD.

▸▸ Reduce the weight of your kit by buying travel BCD's, or at least ones without integrated weights, lightweight regulators and fins.

▸▸ Buy a safety sausage rather than a reeled SMB. Invest in small, lightweight torches; get a small multipurpose knife.

▸▸ Do not take scuba toys – or other toys – away with you unless they serve a purpose.

▸▸ Do not take doubles of major items. Any dive centre that's worth diving with will have a spare if yours breaks down.

▸▸ Take a small repair kit for minor emergencies. Include duct tape, superglue, a multi-tool, strong cord, plastic cable ties and a spare mask strap.

▸▸ If you only intend diving for a few days consider hiring your equipment, but book it in advance.

▸▸ Get out what clothes you think you need and halve them. Then halve it all again. Really, no one cares if you wear the same t-shirt every other day.

▸▸ Reduce toiletries by getting mini-bottles, take medicines out of packets and write instructions down.

❝❞ We are often asked how we manage to pack all our kit and include our working kit while we are researching abroad. It's not easy and we have to be very disciplined. And we can honestly say that there is at least one good natured argument every time...

Rental equipment

We are all taught how important it is to be both familiar and comfortable with our equipment so are encouraged to buy our own. This is a valid standpoint, but in light of recent airline restrictions, may need to become a more considered decision. A full set of gear can be 12 or 15 kilos, which at 65% of your total allowance, means you need to you think carefully about what you can take and what you have to leave behind.

Another resolution is to consider renting all or some of your equipment. For some people this simply won't work: if you are over two metres tall, you will never get an off-the-rack wetsuit; if you are a very petite lady, it's unlikely you will find a BCD small enough. However, it may be worth renting fins, which average 1½-2 kilos a pair, or a regulator with octopus, which may be 2-3 kilos. Email in advance and find out what is available. Many dive operators now offer complete kit packages purely for this reason. Remember that any operator that is worth diving with will maintain their kit well. On the same note, never take spares of bulky items like regulators with you. If you trust this operator to find you floating in an ocean after a dive, it's fair to assume you can trust them to supply you with a decent regulator.

Luggage handlers at Indonesia's Berau airport; dive equipment ready and waiting in Gili Trewangan

Wetsuits

Countries covered by this book have similar, tropical climates with water temperatures averaging 27-28°C. Exceptions are noted in each chapter. For these conditions you should only need a 3mm full wetsuit. However, a hood, rash vest or fleecy-lined skin is worth poking into a corner of your bag and will allow some layering up. You may appreciate this on the fourth dive of the day, where there are known thermoclines or if you stay still like photographers do. However, some will shiver in 3mm suit while others swelter. It's a personal issue that only time and experience will resolve.

Other equipment

When it comes to smaller items of dive equipment you need to weigh the pros and cons of safety versus enjoyment. Torches, for example, are useful for night dives and dark spots on wrecks, but keep them small, so they fit in your pocket, and lightweight: huge ones are heavy and annoy other divers at night. Likewise, you must have an SMB (safety sausage) but a simple tube that rolls up in your pocket is as good as one with a reel.

One way to keep 'extras' to a minimum is to have multi-use electrical accessories. For example an iPod can be used for photo storage, recording notes and playing music and is much lighter than a laptop. Rechargable items mean you don't have to carry as many batteries and that is also better for the environment. As you buy items, aim to get all one battery type, AAs are the most common, then look for a single recharger that is small and light. However, you will need to ensure you bring the right power adaptors: common types are in the table below and referenced in the Fact files at the beginning of each chapter.

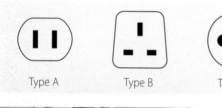

| Type A | Type B | Type C |

✪ Trouble-free travel

▸▸ Make sure your passport has at least one free page and six months to run after your departure date

▸▸ Check visa requirements well in advance

▸▸ Take out travel insurance that specifically covers diving as well as transport problems but check the fine print for depth limitations

▸▸ Take a copy or record of your passport numbers, travel insurance, qualification card, credit cards and any documents; pack separately to the originals

▸▸ Tell someone at home where you are going to be and when you are due back

▸▸ Take copies of booking forms and correspondence from your agent, hotel or dive centre

▸▸ Research your destination; check health requirements and updates on government advisory sites

▸▸ Ensure your dive gear is working and you have the appropriate kit for your intended location

▸▸ When you arrive obey the law and respect local customs and traditions

Suz and Linda at the camera table; Jill, Beth and Carole squeeze into neoprene one more time

MANADO - INDONESIE

Experience North Sulawesi with Seaside Resort Santika & 5* Dive Center Thalassa

Come as a guest, leave as a friend!

WWW.THALASSA.NET - INFO@THALASSA.NET

Indonesia

Green turtle, *Chelonia mydas*, nestled on Maratua's Mid Reef.

▶▶ Discovery zone

Hunt for rare and unusual animals off Lembeh or Ambon

▶▶ Distant Horizons

Get off the beaten track in Kalimantan or sail to far away West Papua

▶▶ Total immersion

Dive till you drop in the world-famous marine parks in Manado and Komodo

South China Sea

Celebes Sea

MALAYSIA

□ KUALA LUMPUR

□ SINGAPORE

BRUNEI

MALAYSIA

Berau

Maratua
Kakaban
Sangalaki

Sangihe Talaud

Bunaken
Manado

Bangka

Lembeh

Gorontalo

HALMAHERA

Kapuas

M a h a k a m

Pontianak

Balikpapan

K A L I M A N T A N

SUMATRA

SULAWESI

BURU

Bangarmasin

Ambon

Banda

Gunungan Barisan

Java Sea

Makassar

Banda Sea

Bandar Lampung

N

D

O

N

□ JAKARTA

JAVA

Surabaya

E

S

Bandung

Bali

Komodo

Alor

WETAR

Denpasar

SUMBAWA

FLORES

Lombok

N U S A   T E N G G A R A

TIMOR

SUMBA

EAST TIMOR

▶▶ Above and below

Dive all day then satisfy a craving for culture in Bali or Banda

▶▶ Take the plunge

Learn to dive in novice heaven, the Gili islands, off Lombok

0   100   200 km

0   50   100 miles

Indonesia is the largest archipelago on the planet and by far the biggest of the Southeast Asian countries. Her extensive arc of islands forms the southern edge of the Coral Triangle, reaches up past Malaysian Borneo and abutts the Melanesian nations to the east.

Not only is this a physically immense country, Indonesia is also where the world's marine biodiversity rankings are at their highest, and these factors combined mean that there are more opportunities to explore the underwater realm than anywhere else in the region, if not the world.

Every inch of water has the potential for mesmerizing diving: some is up-tempo and adventurous, some just as calm as you could wish for. Many marine animals that are rare elsewhere are common here. No matter what it is you look for, chances are you will find it.

Despite the massive changes the country has seen in recent years, Indonesia has completely retained her sense of tradition. On land there are almost as many religions, cultures, arts and cuisines as there are islands. Diversity is not confined to Indonesia's world beneath the seas. From peace-loving Bali to the outer reaches of Raja Ampat, this water-bound land is one of the world's most fascinating places to experience.

Essentials

Getting there

Travelling to Indonesia is simplicity itself. Flights to both Jakarta and Bali arrive from almost everywhere. Airlines include Eva, Qantas, Qatar, Singapore Airlines, Thai and United amongst many others. Garuda, the Indonesian national carrier, has a nominal long-haul network but Singapore Airlines (singaporeair.com) and their regional subsidiary Silk Air (silkair.com), have flights to diver-orientated destinations including Bali, Balikpapan, Lombok and Manado. Singapore is also an ideal city to use as a stopover (see page 273).

There are several low-cost regional options like AirAsia (airasia.com) or Jetstar (jetstar.com) that connect Bali and Jakarta to Australia and other Asian countries.

Visitors can buy a visa on arrival at any of the above airports. These are required by most nationalities except those from neighbouring countries. Queues can be long and slow, so if you are able to get a visa in your home country it will save time. Also bear in mind that only main entry points issue visas so before planning an arrival via an unusual land route, for example, check with the nearest embassy.

Getting around

As this is such a widespread country, there are endless internal travel options including masses of local airlines: Garuda, Merpati and Lion Air (garuda-indonesia.com, www.merpati.co.id, lionair.co.id) are the most reliable but as online booking is not easy, ask your dive operator to handle this for you. Don't be too concerned if they book you on an unheard of airline: new ones appear almost by the minute. What won't work by the minute though are schedules, which are permanently on 'Indonesian' time. Internal flights run like buses, hopping from one island to another, and delays can have a knock-on effect. There are also ferries and buses, which you are unlikely to need, and fun local options like horse and buggies.

Airport to hotel transfers will almost always be included but taxis are reasonably priced and usually metered. If you fancy a day or two to explore land-based sights, ask your hotel or dive centre to arrange a driver and car to escort you around. Alternatively, simply wander up the road until someone asks, "Transport, mister?" This is one of Indonesia's most universal sayings. You'll hear it along every street, on the beach or in a restaurant. It's the way a lot of people earn a living and, as long as you set a price first, you're unlikely to have any problems. Car hire is easy enough and cheap, especially in Bali, but is not highly recommended due to the state of the roads, the traffic and many less than clear road rules. Anyway, it's much nicer to let a local do all the work while you sit back and enjoy the view.

Indonesia	
Location	5°00'S, 120°00'E
Neighbours	Australia, Malaysia, Philippines, Papua New Guinea
Population	237,512,352
Land area in km²	1,826,440
Coastline in km	95,181
Territorial sea in km²	3,205,695

Transfers

It is normally possible to transfer straight to your final destination. However, if you are heading to one of the outlying islands, an overnight stop near the airport is a good idea. If you are taking an internal flight, ensure you allow enough time – in both directions – to connect. Internal flights rarely keep to schedule although they are also rarely very late. Some good news for divers is that excess baggage rates are low. At US$10-12 per kilo you can afford not to worry too much but be sensible. If your bag is really heavy, and the flight is full, it may get left behind.

Jakarta the nation's capital has many flight connections but this very busy airport isn't one to linger in. Travel via Bali or Manado is just as expedient and, if you do get a delay, they have nicer airports.

Bali Denpasar airport sits near Bali's southwestern tip. There are no internal flights, which is a shame for those heading to the far northwest about six hours away by road. Other diving areas are two to three hours drive and you will be collected by the resort.

Lombok Fly direct with SilkAir from Singapore or fly to Bali and transfer by road to Padangbai (1½ hours) then: by ferry to Lembar (five hours); by speed boat direct to the Gili islands (the Gilicat, gilicat.com, is a superb and safe service, three hours). Fly from Bali to Mataram Airport (one hour) where you will be collected.

Nusa Tenggara For Komodo, Flores and Alor fly to Bali and take an internal flight (up to three hours). Resorts arrange pick-ups or if you are on a liveaboard, the operator will arrange all transfers.

Manado and Bunaken For coastal resorts, the transfer is usually 30-45 minutes by road; for Bunaken Marine Park and the other offshore islands, allow 1½ hours by car and boat.

Lembeh The drive from Manado airport to Bitung port and the resorts on the east coast of Sulawesi takes around 1½ hours. Allow another 10-30 minutes to reach the island resorts.

West Papua Flights land in Sorong on West Papua. You can leave from Bali, usually with a transit in Makassar on Sulawesi (around three hours), or fly direct from Manado in two hours but the flight departure times are often highly unsociable.

Ambon and Banda For Pattimura Airport on Ambon, fly from Bali with a transit in Makassar (around three hours) or from Manado, via Sorong, it is 2½ hours. Ambon to Banda is just 30 minutes.

Kalimantan The resorts in Kalimantan are reached via a direct flight from Singapore to Balikpapan or with connections from Manado, Bali and Makassar. You will then need a connecting flight to Berau (one hour) followed by a three or four hour transfer by boat to the resort, which will make all arrangements for you.

 Tourist information → the government website can be found at my-indonesia.info; other webistes include indonesia-tourism.com; Bali: balitourismboard.org, Komodo: komodonationalpark.org, West Papua: diverajaampat.org Sulawesi: divenorthsulawesi.com, north-sulawesi.org.

Fact file

International flight	Air Asia, Eva, Jetstar, Malaysian, Qantas, Qatar, Singapore Airlines/Silk Air, Thai, United
Departure tax	International 150,000 IDR; Domestic 20,000 IDR
Entry	Visas required for most nationalities, US$25 on entry
Internal flights	Garuda, Lion Air, Merpati
Ground transport	Plenty but use private rather than public
Money	US$1 = 11,000 rupiah (IDR)
Language	Bahasa Indonesia, English is widely spoken
Electricity	220v/110v, plug type C
Time zone	GMT + 8 (Bali/Manado) GMT + 9 (Irian Jaya)
Religion	Muslim, Hindu, Christian, Animist
Phone	Country code +62; IDD code 001; Police 110

Language

There are many indigenous languages right across Indonesia but government education policies have ensured that the national language, Bahasa Indonesia, is spoken everywhere: people just love tourists who greet them in Bahasa. It's easy enough to learn and pronunciation is straightforward. The only confusing issue is getting to grips with variations within a simple saying – the way you say hello varies by the clock!

good morning (until 1100)	*selamat pagi*
good day (until 1500)	*selamat siang*
good afternoon (until dusk)	*selamat sore*
good evening	*selamat malam*
welcome	*selamat datang*
goodbye (if leaving…)	*selamat tinggal*
…and if you are staying	*selamat jalan*
yes	*ya*
no	*tidak*
please	*tolong*
thank you	*terima kasih*
sorry	*ma'af*
how much is...	*berapa harganya...*
you're welcome	*kembali*
good	*bagus*
great dive!	*menyelam yang bagus!*
one beer/water	*satu bir/air*

Local laws and customs

Religions in Indonesia are equally varied so it's difficult to define a behavioural pattern for tourists except to say that anywhere divers are likely to go will be 'tourist tolerant'. Take local advice if you are unsure.

Much of the country is Muslim but there are substantial Buddhist, Christian, Hindu and Animist communities. The Indonesian version of Islam is strongly influenced by these other religions, which in turn influence each other. However, the religion most people encounter is Balinese Agama Hinduism which is not the same as Indian Hinduism. Its calming presence is strongly felt in day-to-day life from the ever-present woven baskets offering flowers, rice and fruit to the gods to the almost daily island-wide festivals.

Safety

Indonesia has experienced more than its fair share of trouble and strife over recent years. Terrorist actions, natural disasters and racial tensions in out-of-the-way regions have all hit the headlines creating a mood of concern. It's worth taking advice from those on the ground (your dive centre or resort) who will have the most up-to-date information and views. Also check your government's travel advisory website for the official view. That said, crimes against tourists are rare, except in highly populated towns which may have been affected by an economic nosedive. Sadly, it is budget travellers who bear the brunt of this as they tend to use public transport and stay in cheaper, less secure hotels.

Divers travelling to a suitable resort and using private transport are unlikely to encounter trouble. If you are out at night take only what you need and always keep valuables concealed. Lone women should be aware of the mixed message they are sending to a society that regards sexual openness as taboo, yet is inundated with Western culture that promotes sex as a selling tool.

Health

Malaria and other mosquito-borne diseases occur in some areas. It depends on who you talk to as to how much of a risk this is. For some time Bali was declared malaria free but occasional cases are now being reported. Get up-to-date advice and always use a repellent. Many hotels have purified tap water or supply bottled. There are plenty of medical facilities but these vary depending on the relative wealth of

🍴 Feeding frenzy

Indonesian cuisine is one of Asia's great masterpieces, although it is less well recognized than the flavours of Thai cooking. It's not dissimilar though, with an equally strong use of the main taste sensations: sweet, sour and spicy. The country has absorbed much of the various cultures that have influenced its growth so sometimes the uniqueness of the food is lost behind a front of simple Chinese influences. The country's most famous dish is satay, so well known that it has been adopted by all neighbouring nations. Barbecued slivers of meat are served with a spicy sauce based on ground peanuts and chilli. This sauce is also used on *gado-gado*, a vegetarian salad and a staple of menus across the country. *Redang*, a rich curry that originated in Sumatra, has also spread across the region. Of course, it should never be forgotten that modern-day Indonesia is the location of the famed Spice Islands, the only place in the world where nutmeg is indigenous.

Eating out can be an incredible experience right across the country and while you can live easily on satay, *nasi goreng* and *mie goreng* (fried rice or noodles), look out for local specialities. Also ensure you try as many local fruits as you can: salak, mangosteen, rambutan, langsat and jackfruit are unfamiliar but stunning. The same cannot be said of the ever-pungent durian. Words cannot describe this seasonal fruit, but locals love it.

a particular locality. Medical consultations are costly for locals and many simply can't afford it. For a visitor, a trip to the doctor is just a few dollars but rest assured that for minor illnesses doctors are well-trained and know their stuff.

Costs

Of Southeast Asia's destinations Indonesia consistently provides the best value for money. You can spend a fortune on an all-singing all-dancing hotel room with a private pool and maid, but it will still be only half of what it would cost elsewhere. The variety of accommodation is incredible, from ultra-modern to quietly traditional; a small, simple bungalow will be as little as US$30; spend over US$100 and you can have luxury; over $200 and you will feel like you have a palace. Where you are limited to a lone resort, these will be of a good standard and reflected in the price. Food is much the same: a delightful meal in a small, local restaurant may be less than US$10 a head or visit an ultra-trendy affair a mile along the bay and pay much more. Drinking is cheap too; a large bottle of the local brew, Bintang, will be US$2, or more in resorts which add their own mark-up. Tipping is the done thing and, in general, about 10% on meals and similar services would be reasonable. Bear in mind that salaries are very low by Western standards so you can afford to be generous. For dive crews, see page 11.

Dive brief

Diving

Indonesia is the largest of Southeast Asia's countries with an estimated 18,000 islands that stretch east to west for over 5000 km. Compare that to continental America at only 4400 km wide and realize just how big this archipelago is. As her myriad land masses sit surrounded by six different seas and two oceans and include around 18% of the world's coral reefs, you can take it for granted that there is some pretty impressive diving here. What's more, Indonesia's southern islands mark the edge of the Pacific Ring of Fire and the country falls completely within the Coral Triangle, the most diverse marine region on the planet. There are many localized features which go even further to ensuring that no matter which part of Indonesia you visit, there will be a fantastic ecosytem to explore.

The incredible number of diveable regions is only outdone by the number of dive sites at each. However, what makes this such a special destination is the growing recognition that this is also an important business. A couple of decades ago there were few formal dive facilities but that is no longer the case. Areas that are easy to get to have many professional dive operators catering for all budgets and tastes, while for those with an adventurous spirit there are distant areas that can be reached only by liveaboard. Conditions and dive styles vary region by region and sea by sea according to which monsoon season is prevailing. Surprisingly, this is good news, as you are not restricted to visiting in specific months like in some countries. Simply choose a destination according to when you can go.

Snorkelling

With so many coral reefs the options for snorkelling are endless. On Bali, reefs reach right into shallow bays; the tiny Gili Islands north of Lombok are a favoured haunt as is Bunaken Island off Manado. More distant, adventurous regions have fewer options as currents can be strong, but that should not put non-divers off. Good liveaboards always ensure the dive tender stays nearby whenever someone is in the water. And what could be more alluring than snorkelling over a reef in Irian Jaya so remote that the closest island doesn't even have a name?

Discovery

Another particularly attractive feature of diving Indonesia is the way that, year on year, somewhere completely new gets 'discovered'. Some research, a few articles, and suddenly there is an exciting new

❝❞ If there was only one country in the world we could dive, Indonesia would be it. We have seen it develop and change; we have been there both in peaceful and troubled times and we still love it the most. The marine realm is superb and there is something about the people and their incredible integrity that keeps it at the centre of our affections.

Dive data

Seasons	May to September, SE monsoon (dryer); November to March, NW monsoon (wetter)
Visibility	5 metres inshore to infinity in open water
Temperatures	Air 19-36°C; water 23-32°C
Wet suit	3 mm full body suit, add 2 mm extra for Komodo
Training	Look for PADI 5-star (or equivalent) training agencies
Nitrox	Generally available on land. Limited on liveaboards
Deco chambers	Bali, Manado, Jakarta, Singapore

Diversity
reef area
51,020 km²

CORALS	602
FISH SPECIES	3277
ENDEMIC FISH SPECIES	111
FISH UNDER THREAT	105
PROTECTED REEFS/MARINE PARKS	40

All diversity figures are approximate

destination that everyone flocks to. These areas can go in and out of favour due to political events or natural disasters: the waters around Maumere in Flores were breathtaking until the devastating tsunami of 1992 but over the intervening years the reefs have started regenerating. Whichever way you look at it, there is always somewhere exciting to go.

Diversity

It is important to recognize that this country is regarded as the world's most biodiverse marine environment. Research studies have found more species in Indonesian waters than in other Asian countries although new research is pushing the Philippines closer to taking that accolade. However, a recent survey in Indonesian Papua recorded the Raja Ampat islands as having 950 fish species, 450 corals and 600 molluscs. Four new fish species and seven new corals were discovered and the area is being proposed as another World Heritage Site. Likewise the Bunaken National Park, Banda and Derawan Islands are all on the tentative list for World Heritage status while the superlative Komodo National Park already is.

Of course, this is not to say that all reefs here are pristine. Like much of the region, fishing isaa major source of income and not all practices are how you would like them to be. However, in line with research and education programmes by the likes of WWF and the Nature Conservancy, things are definitely improving.

Making the big decision

It isn't easy to recommend one area of Indonesia over another as they all have something to offer. One way to choose would be to decide what else you want to do. Bali is by far the most developed island, with everything you would expect from a major resort destination including incredible land attractions. In comparison, a liveaboard trip to Banda or Irian jaya won't suit if you like to have all the mod cons (no mobile phones or TV way out there), while Manado would sit somewhere in the middle of all that. Or you could choose by dive style: big open waters with pelagics in Kalimantan or the ultimate in muck diving in the Lembeh Straits.

Bottom time

Bali

This tiny volcanic island is one of the world's most stunning. Even the Balinese call their home the 'Island of the Gods'. The combination of a balmy climate, unique culture, great facilities, delightful people and superb diving all adds up to one supremely good dive destination.

Bali's diving is defined by its position to the west of the Wallace Line. This invisible marker, between Bali and Lombok, was noted by British naturalist Alfred Russel Wallace in the 1860s. He recognized that islands to the west of the Lombok Channel displayed Asiatic species of flora and fauna while those to the east were more in tune with Australia. The line sits on the edge of the Sunda Shelf, which links Borneo, Bali and Java to the rest of Southeast Asia, while Australia and New Guinea sit on the Sahul Shelf. The deep waters in between are subject to the Indonesian Throughflow current pattern, which has a substantial effect on dive conditions (see page 54).

Bali is a vaguely triangular shape with the southwestern shore leading into the Indian Ocean; beaches are white sand and surfers arrive in droves to catch the waves. The east coast at its southerly tip is not dissimilar: shallow fringing reefs are affected by currents and surf. However, start heading north and things improve.

By the time you reach the easternmost point – beneath mighty, active Mt Agung – the reefs are flourishing due to the rich nutrients supplied by both the volcanic soil and upwellings from the Lombok Channel. On the north coast, the environment changes again. The soil here is volcanic too, but less dark. This is good agricultural land, where high mountains drop to flat coastal plains which lead to shallow bays with patchy reefs.

Locations

Bali is often overlooked by divers who use it as a staging post en route to distant marine parks, yet these reefs are simply too good to miss. Walls, wrecks, muck – it's all there. Novices are fascinated by training dives on the *Liberty* wreck or in the shallow waters near Padangbai while experienced divers are captivated by unusual and rare marine creatures.

Choose where to stay by defining how much moving around you want to do. Diving is land based: there are a few liveaboards but you would miss the joys of Bali's many land attractions. You can stay in the popular south but that means long hours on the road to reach the best diving. A better idea is to have a few days for the nightlife and retail therapy, then go elsewhere. Some operators arrange round-the-island diving tours that visit all the major dive sites.

Destinations

Southern tip

This is Bali's most popular tourist area. Heading west from the airport are **Kuta**, **Legian** and **Seminyak** – beach areas riddled with shops, bars, restaurants and every type of hotel you could wish for. There's no diving but plenty of dive centres who organize day trips and courses. Just south of the airport is the **Nusa Dua** peninsula, location of the most pricey resorts. There is a little diving but it's not worth the money as the shallow reefs suffer from currents, surf and boat traffic. **Sanur**, northeast of the airport, also has plenty of facilities and is less lively than the Kuta–Legian stretch. The reefs are a little better but are really only good for a training dive or two.   *Distance from airport: 5-30 mins*

Central east coast

The towns that sit around Bali's easternmost point provide access to some of her best diving. The first is **Padangbai**, a bustling bay that is also the ferry port for Lombok. A tiny lane leads along a lovely beach. Just behind is a row of small hotels (mostly catering for budget travellers), some restaurants and tourist shops. Diving inside the bay is excellent, as are the dives around the smaller bays and tiny offshore islands that lead up towards **Candidasa**. This peaceful one-road town is an ideal base as it has access to sites both north and south: it's 20 minutes from Padangbai and an hour from Tulamben. There are a lot of good hotels and restaurants: this is the best place to get actual Balinese food. After Candidasa, the road turns inland, passing some stunning scenery, then back to the coast where you can head a few kilometres south to **Amed** where a few small villages are interspersed with occasional hotels and restaurants. The shallow offshore reefs can be good dives when the tides are right. Only 20 minutes north, **Tulamben** is without doubt the location of Bali's finest dive and thought by many to be one of the best wreck dives in the world, the *Liberty*. The village itself is small, attracting only divers, but the bay can be very busy with day trippers. By night, residents have it all to themselves. Nearby bays are becoming well known as muck dives.   *Distance from airport: 1½-2½ hrs*

North coast

Much less touristy than the south, this area is quieter than the east and still relatively undeveloped – a reminder of how the island was 20 years ago. Singaraja and Lovina are the main towns. Both are pleasant enough but a little removed from the best diving although there is some great muck in the shallow bays to their west. However, the best access and facilities are in **Pemuteran** with its lovely beach and uncrowded feel. The bay has an award-winning reef eco-project plus a handful of good hotels and dive centres. From here, it's a short hop to the offshore **Menjangen Marine Park** where the diving is very different to the surrounding coast, with deep walls and clear water. On the western tip of the island is **Gilimanuk**, where ferries leave for Java, and just to the side is Bali's most famous muck dive, Secret Bay.   *Distance from airport: 6 hrs*

Nusa Penida, Lembongan and Ceningan

These three islands dissect the Lombok Channel and are about an hour by speed boat from Padangbai or Sanur. Most people travel across on day trips and dive along the Penida coast or in the channels between the islands. Because of their location these dives are renown for strong currents which in turn attract impressive, but seasonal, pelagic life. If you fancy a real get-away-from-it-all break **Lembongan** has great accommodation and a very peaceful atmosphere.   *Distance from airport: 2 hrs*

Places to stay and things to do at all these destinations are listed in Drying out on page 38

Ubud temple; The Watergarden, Candidasa; Tulamben tank lady; Bali festival; Padangbai; Jimbaran

Padangbai and Candidasa

These two villages sit on either edge of six-kilometre wide Amuk Bay. Just below Bali's easternmost point, and beneath active Mt Agung, the coastline here faces the Lombok Strait, location of the Wallace Line.

Padangbai is a deep-water harbour and the ferry port for Lombok to the east. Inside this horseshoe-shaped bay there are several good and easy dives. It can get murky when a ferry is on the way in or out, a strange sensation if you are diving as it gets very noisy and can turn the water dark and green. It feels like you're in a disaster movie, which amuses the dive guides no end! On the outer edges of the bay, and in bays along the nearby coast, the water is clearer and the reefs more varied. To the north, closer to Candidasa, there are several rocky islets. The scenery is dramatic, which is reflected below the water. Currents, surges and cold water upwellings are common. Dive trips rarely leave from Candidasa as the water is too shallow for boats and there is some surf.

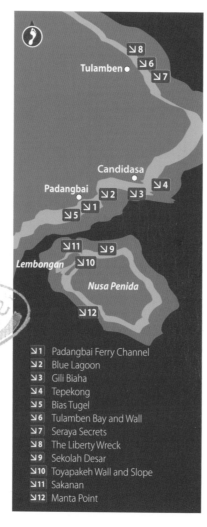

↘1 Padangbai Ferry Channel
↘2 Blue Lagoon
↘3 Gili Biaha
↘4 Tepekong
↘5 Bias Tugel
↘6 Tulamben Bay and Wall
↘7 Seraya Secrets
↘8 The Liberty Wreck
↘9 Sekolah Desar
↘10 Toyapakeh Wall and Slope
↘11 Sakanan
↘12 Manta Point

↘1 Padangbai Ferry Channel

🕙 **Depth**	18 m
◐ **Visibility**	poor to good
〰 **Currents**	slight
⛵ **Dive type**	day boat

This dive starts just beyond the beacon marking the ferry route and is scheduled for when they aren't passing by. After descending down a steep slope to about 15 metres, you find a series of small caves and crevices. These are known refuges for sleeping whitetip sharks but if the current is running – and this is mostly a drift dive – they will be out patrolling the wall. Up in the shallower sections, the coral cover is good so turtles and cuttlefish are seen, while rubble areas reveal nudibranchs.

Rhinopias eschmeyeri in Blue Lagoon

⬐2 Blue Lagoon

🕐	**Depth**	22 m
◑	**Visibility**	fair to good
〰	**Currents**	slight
⬭	**Dive type**	day boat

A short ride north of the main bay, this white-sand beach extends down to a pale seabed, interspersed with small patches of coral. They aren't all that prolific but are a haven for many animals: one bommie has a whole gang of leaffish on it – white, pink, brown and green. There are blue ribbon eels, tiny juvenile sweetlips and masses of blue-spotted rays. This was recently noted as a residential area for the rare rhinopias: the least well known of the scorpionfish family is getting a lot of attention as new species are being discovered.

⬐3 Gili Biaha

🕐	**Depth**	26 m
◑	**Visibility**	good
〰	**Currents**	slight to strong
⬭	**Dive type**	day boat

Sailing to this small island outcrop takes about 30 minutes from Padangbai. As the crescent of land emerges from very deep water, the sea temperature here can be much lower than other dives nearby and is likely to take your breath away as you drop in. There are currents and surge but the dive is well worth it. At one end you drop onto one of Bali's most impressive walls, encrusted in the most incredible amount of coral and, because of the current, there are swarms of fish. The current then pushes you to the wall, where a small cave on land opens up to a big cavern below the water. There are baby and adult whitetip sharks swinging in and out. Further along the wall another small cave is a riot of life: three different coloured leaffish, two blue ribbon eels, a mantis shrimp and mating nudibranchs with freshly laid, lacy egg rings all in a small space.

⬐4 Tepekong

🕐	**Depth**	29 m
◑	**Visibility**	good
〰	**Currents**	slight to strong
⬭	**Dive type**	day boat

A little south of Biaha, Tepekong Island also emerges from the depths and is equally well known for its cool water and currents. To the west of the island are some rock pillars that break the surface and a canyon lies between them. Depending on the conditions on the day, there are several dives here but the most spectacular route is to go from the pillars, over the canyon to the main island – or vice versa. In between there are extensive sloping beds of hard coral with masses of pelagic fish hovering over them. They at least seem to enjoy the moving water. You can also swim down through a chimney and out onto the lower reef where the water is much cooler, then back up over the coral beds which are interspersed with lots of anemones with their resident clownfish and porcelain crabs. A small cave here often has groups of juvenile whitetips too.

⬐5 Bias Tugel

🕐	**Depth**	30 m
◑	**Visibility**	good
〰	**Currents**	slight to strong
⬭	**Dive type**	day boat

Just south of Padangbai, this site is in front of a lovely white-sand beach, its very broad sweep continuing underwater. There are few topographical features but the entire bottom of the bay is carpeted with small corals and many different coloured crinoids so it's really very pretty. At 28 metres there is a ridge where a row of pink fans grow and divemasters search on these for pygmy seahorses. This section is in a thermocline so it can be very chilly when the currents pick up. Under other outcrops are juvenile pinnate batfish and cuttlefish.

Indonesia Dive log Bali: Padangbai and Candidasa

☺ What's a mola-mola?

He had warned us it would be cold... "21°C so wear a hood if you have one," he said. "We are going deep. But if the sun gods are smiling you just might see a mola-mola. "OK," we said, "but what's a mola-mola?" Ketut smiled and said, "you'll see."

After waiting for almost an hour onboard our boat for the current to be just right, Ketut our dive guide, motioned for my wife and I to drop in and head for 90 feet. Clearing my ears every 10 seconds to eliminate any chance I would miss an encounter with a mola-mola, I followed Ketut less than 10 feet away. Then suddenly I glance over at him and focus on his eyes. They are as large as sand dollars and he is pointing in all different directions… Up, down, behind, in front of us. One, two, three, four, five, six, seven, eight, nine, ten mola-mola surround us. He indicated for us to hold still and not move.

We leveled out at 94 feet and remained motionless for almost 15 minutes watching these magnificent creatures being cleaned by hoards of moorish idols. A cleaning station for the oceanic sunfish, a gigantic 15 feet long oval fish with no tail and eyes the size of your favourite DVD.

At the surface, our excitement was equal to Armstrong landing on the moon or Hilary scaling Mt. Everest. Never had Ketut seen more than three together… but 10 mola-mola had made even this 15 year veteran of diving around Bali's coast excited.

Phil Tobin, diamond broker, Portland, Oregon

Tulamben

Driving north from Candidasa, the road veers inland along shady hillsides, past lush rice paddies, until you are beneath towering, imposing Mt Agung. This 3000-metre high active volcano is Bali's most significant landmark. The volcano last erupted in the 1960s but its presence affects the island daily by influencing the climate. As clouds move in from the west, Agung grabs their moisture – Bali's west is lush and green while the east is dry.

As you emerge from Agung's shadow you find the coastal landscape is rather barren in appearance but this doesn't extend below the waterline. The bays punctuating this coast are prolific marine ecosystems, with good coral and a high density of both pelagic fish and unusual bottom dwellers. Dives are seasonal, although only in the sense that during some months you will find huge schools of jacks on the wreck, in others, the mola-mola – or sunfish – arrive. A little to the south, Amed has some good diving that is shallow and excellent for novices or trainees but the sandy bays tend towards low visibility.

▼6 Tulamben Bay and Wall	
🕐 **Depth**	17 m
🔵 **Visibility**	fair to good
🌀 **Currents**	slight to strong
〰 **Dive type**	shore

Often eclipsed by the famous wreck 20 minutes walk up the rocky beach, Tulamben Bay is a good dive in its own right. Directly in front of the hotels and dive centres, the black sand and pebble slope drops gently to 15 metres or so before heading into deeper waters. There, a patchy reef consists of small corals, sponges, crinoids and anemones plus leaves, coconut husks and other detritus. There's a phenomenal number of nudibranchs; ornate ghost pipefish shelter in crinoids and even blue-ringed octopus can be caught prowling about. What's more, if you walk – or fin – a little way south over the shallow river mouth there is another dive which centres around the rocky headland dividing Tulamben from the next the bay. At the eastern end the sand slope leads to a sharp wall that drops from about 5 metres to well over 50. The wall is coated in an amazing variety of life, from huge barrel sponges to fans with longnose hawkfish in residence. This is also a favoured snorkelling spot.

▼7 Seraya Secrets	
🕐 **Depth**	25 m
🔵 **Visibility**	fair to good
🌀 **Currents**	slight to strong
〰 **Dive type**	shore/day boat

Seraya Bay is about 20 minutes by *prahu*, the local outrigger boat, south of Tulamben. The diving here is becoming very popular due to an easy shore entry and a wealth of unusual critters. The seabed is black sand with a few outcrops of rock and some small coral heads, but very little reef topography. The lone dive resort located on the bay has started building some interesting artificial reef structures: one is a woven cane dome that has attracted a school of batfish. Past this and down over the gently sloping, patchy reef there is a lot of life: nudibranchs and shrimp are prolific. A lone harlequin shrimp lives on the side of one rock, which is odd as they always live in mating pairs. On the other side of the rock a miniature cave houses a moray and cleaner shrimp. Across the rest of the site there are large seahorses in a variety of colours, plus red and yellow striped pipefish, pink frogfish and juvenile cuttlefish. In the shallows, if you look up, are small schools of squid.

On Tulamben Wall, the yellow banded pipefish is a cleaner that will approach divers; juvenile batfish at Seraya Secrets

8 ★ The Liberty Wreck

❂ **Depth**	30 m
◐ **Visibility**	fair to stunning
≋ **Currents**	none to medium
⬮ **Dive type**	shore

The *Liberty* is part of diving folklore. Lying just 30 metres from shore is the broken hull of a Second World War US supply ship.

Torpedoed in 1941 by a Japanese submarine, she lay beached for 20 years before Mt Agung erupted and pushed her down the sloping seabed. She broke into several sections with her top facing towards deep water and is one of the best artificial reefs you will ever see. Divers come from all over the island – and the world – to trek slowly up the rough, pebble-strewn beach. Conditions are not always easy: if the winds and surf are up, getting in is a real struggle. Visibility varies depending on the season and run-off from the nearby river mouth yet despite that this dive is always magnificent. Finning towards the hull you pass a gang of resident oriental sweetlips (they've been in the same spot for nigh on 20 years) then the wreck quickly materializes from the blue. Start at the stern, circumnavigate the structure to the deeper bow then finish up on the hull. Every inch is covered in life of some sort, so much so that it can be hard to pick a gun, winch or boiler from the corals, sponges and crinoids. You can't penetrate the holds but you can see ladders, parts of the engine and the anchor chain. There are jacks swirling above, Napoleon wrasse in amongst them and, on rare occasions, a bizarre mola-mola visits.

Every feature is surrounded by fish and more fish: leaffish, dragonets and more nudibranchs than you thought possible in one dive. At the bottom, a little past the bow are some gorgonians that are known to have pygmy seahorses on them.

❝❞ **Time after time, we return to the wreck and it's never been the same twice... mola-mola, vast schools of jacks, pygmy seahorses and clusters of nudibranchs.**

Nusa Penida, Lembongan and Ceningan

These three offshore islands sit in the middle of the Lombok Channel and can only be reached by sea. Dive boats take an hour or so to whisk people across from Sanur or Padangbai to dive what can be the most challenging sites on Bali.

Nusa Penida is the largest island with Ceningan and Lembongan sitting on her westerly corner. Currents rush down the Lombok Channel and hit Penida's north coast, splitting both east and west, then forcing themselves into the narrower channels between the two smaller islands. The pattern reverses depending on the seasons so at times, these dives can be difficult. They are mostly drifts yet currents can swap and change mid-dive. Plus the water here can be cool: it's always colder than Bali and with some chilly upwellings. The good news is that all this oceanic activity means the reefs are impressive with lush soft and hard corals and sometimes some very large animals. Both mola-mola (or sunfish) and mantas can be seen, but you need to know that the season for those is short and you certainly won't be the only person on the dive.

N9 Sekolah Desar	
Depth	34 m
Visibility	fair to good
Currents	none to ripping
Dive type	day boat

If life was simple you could drop into the water at one end of Nusa Penida's north coast and simply drift along until you reach the opposite corner. But things are never simple here and chances are you will dive several sections of this coast but in stages. The Sekolah Dasar (primary school) sits in the middle and in front of it is one of the most popular sections of this reef. The reef scenery is a gently undulating slope that leads down to a short wall where there are some very large barrel sponges and a few nice fans. In some sections, hard corals form a flat carpet across the topography while in others there are patches of sand punctuated by outcrops with gorgeous soft corals. There is some damage – from the currents more than anything else – but also a little evidence of past destructive fishing. Tuna, jacks, mackerel and turtles are seen fairly often but the highlights are just as likely to be small: orang-utan crabs, porcelain crabs, clownfish on anemones and mantis shrimp, providing the currents allow you time to look.

N10 Toyapakeh Wall and Slope	
Depth	24 m
Visibility	fair to good
Currents	slight to strong
Dive type	day boat

Like Sekolah Desar, this site has multiple dives. Located near the corner of Penida but inside the Ceningan Channel, the currents here are slightly less aggressive than outside. The wall itself is covered in masses of small crusting corals and soft corals, and there are plenty of outcrops coated in fish life. All this is interspersed with tunicates and sponges so it's quite a colourful area. There are some unusual fish, like shy and skittish soapfish, and many queen angels being cleaned. Morays are also common but have taken to hiding in interesting places, like winding up inside a large barrel sponge or in the rear of a cave. A second, shallower dive takes place close to a rather unattractive pontoon frequented by banana-boat loving holiday-makers. Although that rather spoils the view, beneath the water are large swathes of staghorn coral. As you drop down the slope there are coral bommies decorated with crinoids and lots of magenta anthias that seem to be diverting attention from the masses of curious nudibranchs and a giant black frogfish.

Flourishing soft coral tentacles emerge with the currents at Toyapakeh; Emperor angelfish being cleaned at Sakanan on Nusa Ceningan

🌀11 Sakanan

🕐 Depth	23 m
◐ Visibility	fair to good
🌊 Currents	slight to strong
⬍ Dive type	day boat

This sloping site sits off the edge of Nusa Lembongan but is close to the corner of Penida. Although the reef profile is similar to nearby dives, things at this one all seem a little bigger: bigger fans, larger soft corals and a surprising quantity of queen and Emperor angelfish. These were unusually docile and stayed near one cleaning station waiting their turn. A bit further along you may come across a banded seasnake: they can be up to two metres long. Unperturbed by divers, this impressive creature just keeps nosing about in the bommies looking for tasty morsels. Living amongst the corals are all sorts of smaller animals from nudibranchs to flatworms, mantis shrimp to minute whip coral shrimp and many pretty coloured starfish. There are also lots of scorpion and lionfish, and in the shallows where there are extensive beds of healthy staghorn coral, there are large schools of butterflyfish and damsels.

🌀12 Manta Point

🕐 Depth	14 m
◐ Visibility	fair to good
🌊 Currents	slight to strong
⬍ Dive type	day boat

Nusa Penida is heavily promoted as the best place in Bali to see big stuff – manta rays and mola-mola being the most popular. Some people do see these beautiful creatures, but this is seasonal diving and you have to take your chances along with the huddle of other dive boats that all arrive at the site hoping for the same. There are several spots along Nusa Penida's dramatic southern coast that have manta cleaning stations – and very little else. The plan is to enter near to one and wait until these majestic creatures arrive to enthral the divers. If they don't there is very little else in the area to look at.

66 99 **This is a classic reminder that the sea is not a zoo. We have dived here more times than we care to think. Mantas? Never, not once. Mola-mola, no, but we have seen those on the Tulamben wreck!**

🌊 Conservation

An apparent contradiction in Bali diving appears with commercialism versus conservation. The island is a major player in the tourism stakes, attracting a wide variety of visitors. Divers, sunbathers, spa groupies, trekkers, culture vultures – all arrive to take advantage of one feature or another. For all though, the marine realm is a favourite and there are many options for non-divers like the massive pontoon moored off Toyapekah dive site. Divers are unlikely to be impressed when a bevy of banana-boat babes turn into try-divers and disturb the peace (and reefs) of this once pretty bay. However, on the positive side, the masses who are not genuinely interested in the marine environment are funnelled into a small area and damage caused by such activities is contained. Another plus is that some operators who profit from this activity are also well known for supporting other more positive ones. There are some strong conservation projects on Bali: two in Pemuteran Bay near the Menjangen Marine Park include a Biorock project and turtle rescue centre and hatchery. To ensure the continued survival of these beautiful creatures, tourists can take part in a hand release programme for a small donation. There's nothing quite so satisfying as returning a fledgling turtle to the sea.

Hungry seasnake hunting for dinner; fan coral hovering over the sloping reef at Sekolah Desar

Menjangen and the northeast coast

Around the top edge of Bali, the northern shore is dotted with small and extremely shallow bays which attract many fascinating marine creatures and are substantial nursery grounds. Regarded as the ultimate by underwater photographers these contrast strongly with the open waters and deep walls of Bali's only marine park.

Pulau Menjangen, or Deer Island, sits off Bali's northwestern corner and is about 10 km from the coast. The Menjangen Marine Park is part of the Bali Barat National Park. The island is home to barking deer, which live wild here, but very little else. There is only one resort allowed on the island so most divers stay in nearby Pemuteran where there is an award-winning artificial reef project and a turtle hatchery programme.

⇘13 Anker Wreck

🜚 Depth	45 m	
🜛 Visibility	good	
🜜 Currents	mild to strong	
🜝 Dive type	day boat	

Anker is the name of a local beer but this wreck has nothing to do with the brew: it's said to be an old slave boat. The wooden hull sits on a gentle, sandy slope at about 40 metres. There is little left to see as the timbers have decayed almost beyond recognition, but they are heavily encrusted with beautiful soft corals and small fans. The surrounds are thick with barrel sponges and flitting fish. On the gradual ascent back up and along the wall, more fans and whip corals grow from cracks and crevices in the reef until you reach shallow beds of hard corals with masses of swarming fish.

⇘14 Eel Gardens

🜚 Depth	27 m	
🜛 Visibility	good	
🜜 Currents	mild to strong	
🜝 Dive type	day boat	

On the western end of Menjangen, this wall dive is full of colourful soft corals. As you enter, you are likely to be met by a huge school of batfish that like to follow divers but always stay off in the blue. About two thirds of the way through the dive, you hit a small point – and there are often currents here – so you can see larger animals like Napoleon wrasse, which sweep past beneath, and the occasional whitetip. There are also many other fish including enormous lionfish feeding around the fans and soft corals and, obviously, a bed of garden eels.

⇘15 Secret Bay

🜚 Depth	10 m	
🜛 Visibility	fair to good	
🜜 Currents	slight	
🜝 Dive type	shore	

Just beside Gilimanuk harbour, where the enormous ferries depart for Java, is a shallow bay, that has entered the realms of dive legend. The sand is pale and fine so it's easy to stir it up, the depth is under 12 metres and the seabed is protected by an offshore reef. Currents that sweep up the narrow Bali Strait are funnelled into the cove, bringing all sorts of animals. Some start life here as plankton then grow and breed in the protected environment. There is little in the way of coral, just detritus: cans, branches and other rubbish interspersed with patches of seagrass and algae – a classic muck dive, where your log book ends up reading like a who's who of unusual marine creatures. There are gold seahorses living on a rotting tree branch, lots of filefish and puffers, juvenile batfish, many colourful and unusual nudibranchs and many an octopus squeezing its way into a can or coconut shell. Really lucky divers might spot the lime green Ambon scorpionfish, a very small and hairy member of this family with lacy wings.

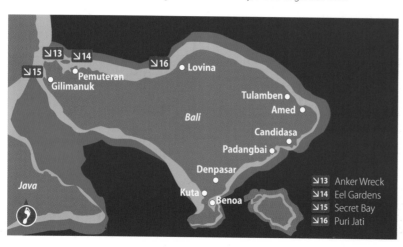

⇖16 Puri Jati, Siririt Bay

⬙	**Depth**	25 m
◑	**Visibility**	fair to good
≋	**Currents**	slight
⬓	**Dive type**	shore

Where Secret Bay has already passed into diving folklore, Puri Jati is the latest 'in-thing'. About an hour by car to the east of Menjangen but on the coast, this is an absolutely marvellous muck diving site that gives Secret Bay a run for its money. Its geography is similar: a very flat, sandy bay that stays at under 10 metres until you are a very long way offshore. Then there is a shelf that drops quite steeply to depth, although the principal interest is in the shallows. The bay is covered in almost nothing, just little patches of seagrass and some large leaved halameda algae. There's not even very much rubbish, but when there is, it harbours plenty of stuff. A list of critters over a few dives is outstanding: coconut octopus in cans, mimic octopus, seahorses, juveniles of frogfish, lionfish, and filefish. Then there's cockatoo waspfish, slipper lobsters, lots of imperial shrimp on sea cucumbers, squid eggs, seasnails and cowrie shells – even cowries with imperial shrimp sitting on them. Nudibranchs crawl up blades of seagrass and as you stare you realize there are tozeuma shrimp, ghost shrimp, harlequin crabs, sand divers, dart gobies, shrimp gobies, snake eels, garden eels, jellies, tiny white faced stone fish, tiny crab on a fire urchin and most exciting, if it's possible to define that here, a frogfish that was five milimetres long.

Introducing some of the residents of Secret Bay and Puri Jati, clockwise: hanging on a branch, the common seahorse; a baby lionfish sitting on halameda algae; harp shells extend their mantel to graze on the sand; juvenile frogfish at less than 5 mm long; mother and baby imperial shrimp on a sea cucumber; juvenile filefish at 15 mm long, sheltering under a soft coral; the tiniest of pipefish in the seagrass; and a juvenile white razorfish at 10 mm.

“ ” The beauty of a harlequin shrimp masks its murderous nature. They are usually seen eating starfish alive, from the tip of each arm to the centre.

Temperatures rising **Wakatobi**

❝❞ Recently I spent 10 days at this incredibly popular resort just an hour's flight north of Bali. After six Indonesian liveaboards and a trip to Lembeh, it was time for a different Indonesian dive experience.

Wakatobi did not disappoint. The trip had all the lovely quirks that make diving and visiting Indonesia such a pleasure. After a smooth transfer from Bali on the resort charter, we arrived to find a boat grounded on the harbour sandbar, blocking access to the dock for the resort ferry. Into the dinghies we went. Very Indonesian. And still the start of a great vacation.

Wakatobi is a quintessential Indonesian resort. Our wooden beach bungalow was clean, spacious, comfortable with a large front porch, a foot wash, more than enough hot water (usually), and towels large enough even for Americans. For those like me who look for such things, there were reading lights on both sides of the bed. The entire resort was immaculate (except for the new villas under construction – if I can afford them, I will stay in one if I return. Although the resort is already big enough as it is).

Food was plentiful and delicious, served from the largest and cleanest kitchen I have seen in Indonesia. Taking a tour of the kitchen was almost like a land dive, entering a world different from the one that I live in.

The diving operation was exactly like the resort – well-run, and complete. Our gear was well cared for. Markus made sure that any kit problems for any guest were fixed before they got in the water. The photo gear area is roomy and made for the photo pros that often visit the resort. Diving here really is a vacation. There is little work for the guest – except getting in and out of the water. It's ideal for a beginning/intermediate diver – advanced divers may find it a little dull. Especially after the fourth day of diving at highly appealing, but indistinguishable, walls.

Animal and reef life was abundant. Alex found us all three types of pygmy seahorses – the clear blue water made it easy to tell one from the other. Each dive site had a surprisingly healthy reef. Pairs of ghost pipefish, egg-laying nudibranchs and egg-carrying jawfish, coral, coral everywhere of every size and species, turtles munching, the occasional shark or ray seen in the depth or the blue, sea snakes, ribbon eels. My big gripe was the vigilance of the dive guides in limiting the interaction of divers with the animals on the reef. While totally understandable in the cause of conservation, the trip to Wakatobi was my first Indonesian adventure without a cuttlefish kiss.

Bruce Brownstein, VP Business Development, Los Angeles, USA

Wakatobi dives

Wakatobi has 43 named dive sites, but there really are only two – the incredible house reef and the already mentioned wall/drift dives everywhere else. But don't misunderstand – each dive site has its own charm and beauty.

House Reef One of Wakatobi's claims to fame. It lies just in front of the jetty and goes down to over 40 metres. Spend an hour in one spot or pick an end and drift back to the resort jetty. Critter check: mantis shrimp, blue-ringed octopus, squat lobsters, every shrimp and crab you can identify, plus some you can't. During the length of the house reef, I stopped counting fish species at a couple of hundred. Pipefish, eels, gobies, blennies, etc, etc.

Everywhere else The wall dive sites have what you can't see at the house reef. Canyons and drop-offs, huge sea fans, barrel sponges, napoleon wrasse, barracuda, Moorish Idol schools. The list goes on and on. Write down the name of each site – you may not be able to tell them apart after a few days of diving.

Drying out

Bali has an extensive number of dive centres and operators. Most target divers of a specific nationality and some also operate as more general watersports companies. It's worth checking these points before booking to ensure you get a suitable operator. Bear in mind that all dive centres will take you to any location on the island. Likewise, there are hotels at every level and many have several grades of room to choose from. Some have on-site dive operations or are affiliated to a specific company, but that doesn't obligate you to dive with them.

South coast
Dive Centres
AquaMarine Diving – Bali, T+62 (0)361 730107, aquamarinediving.com. Bali's only British owned and managed dive shop is in Seminyak. First-class service, full client insurance and great dive guides who are particularly good with photographers. They organize accommodation as well as diving including tailor-made land excursions and round-island dive tours.
Blue Season Bali, T+62 (0)361 282574, baliocean.com. Spacious boat and a good location in Sanur for easy access to Nusa Penida. PADI training programmes at all levels and customized safaris around the island. Also located at Zen Resort in North Bali, zenresortbali.com. Dive then luxuriate in an Ayurverda spa treatment.

Sleeping
$$$–$$ **Patra Bali Resort**, Kuta, T+62 (0)361 751161, patra-jasa.com. Villas with pools or spacious 2-roomed suites. Only 5 mins from the airport but there is surprisingly little aircraft noise. Good for stopovers.
$$$ **The Elysian**, Seminyak, T+62 (0)361 730999, theelysian.com. At the far end of the Kuta-Seminyak beach strip in a quiet location and 20 mins from the airport. Fantastic boutique-style villas, each with a private pool. Just back from the beach but near many higher-end facilities so perfect for pre- or post-trip relaxation.
$$ **Tamukami**, Sanur, T+62 (0)361 282510, tamukamibali.com. Charming, small hotel in Sanur a short walk from the beach. Large rooms in delightful tropical gardens that surround a free-form pool. On-site is **Alise's Restaurant** with delicious and well-priced local and international food.
$$ **Villa Casis**, Sanur, T+62 (0)361 270521, villacasis.com. Beautifully designed luxury villa with 6 bedrooms near Sanur beach. Can also be rented by smaller groups.
$ **Poppies Cottages**, Kuta, T+62 (0)361 751059, poppiesbali.com. Great value, traditional bungalows in pretty gardens. Located in the lively heart of Kuta.

Eating
$$$ **Ku De Ta**, Seminyak, T+62 (0)361 736969, kudeta.net. Fabulously trendy and horribly expensive, incredible fusion food with the very best views of posers and breathtaking Balinese sunsets.
$ **Tekor**, Legian Beach, T+62 (0)361 735628. Right at the end of Double-six lane, on the beach, this truly excellent restaurant has genuine Balinese food and is favoured by residents as much as tourists.
$ **Jimbaran Seafood Café**, Jimbaran Beach. For exquisite, unbelievably cheap seafood, ask a taxi to drive to the Italian consulate then turn towards Jl Raya Uluwatu and Jl Kenanga Jati. This café is in the middle of a row of 8 open-air cafés on the beach.

East Coast
Sleeping
$$$ **Alila Manggis**, Candidasa, T+62 (0)363 41011, alilahotels.com. Stylish, upmarket hotel in a quiet, beachside location a few miles before Candidasa. Very peaceful location plus they run a cooking school.
$$ **The Watergarden**, Candidasa, T+62 (0)363 41540, watergardenhotel.com. Peaceful and charming hotel; each room has a deck that sits over a magnificent koi carp pond and is surrounded by private 'jungle' gardens. Great restaurant as well.
$$ **Mimpi Resorts**, in both Tulamben and Menjangen, T+62 (0)363 21642, mimpi.com. The original divers' resort in Tulamben and just south of the *Liberty* wreck. Their resort at Menjangen is opposite the National Park. Both have good restaurants on-site.
$ **Anda Amed**, Amed, T+62 (0)363 23498 andaamedresort.com. Stylish, small hotel overlooking the Lombok Channel. Spacious rooms, lovely views and a good restaurant.

Eating
$ **Dewata Agung Lagoon View**, Candidasa, T+62 (0)363 41204. Great food and views over the Candidasa lagoon. Also has evening dance performances.

North coast
Sleeping
$$$–$ **Taman Sari Bali**, Pemuteran Bay, T+62 (0)362 94755, balitamansari.com. Garden hotel with both budget cottages and high-end villas. The restaurant is very good. Bali Diving Academy are on site and have full, local dive programmes (dive link on website above).

Lembongan
Sleeping
$$ **Waka Nusa Resort**, T+62 (0)361 484085, wakaexperience.com. This small resort (and island) has a laid-back style that harks back to the days before Bali became so popular. The resort organizes diving for guests using local operators. Waka also manage Waka Nusa, the only resort in the Bali Barat National Park opposite Menjangen island.

🛏	**Sleeping**	$$$ US$150+ double room per night	$$ US$75-150	$ under US$75
🍴	**Eating**	$$$ US$40+ 2-course meal, excluding drinks	$$ US$20-40	$ under US$20

Sightseeing

Although much developed in the south, Bali has an incredibly beautiful landscape, distinctive culture and is world-famous for its arts, crafts, dance and music. Take a day tour to get a feel for the island, which will include a few of the sights below. They can cost as much as US$100 per person, and you may also find yourself squashed into a minibus with a group of strangers. As an option, make enquiries with your hotel or dive centre who will recommend a reliable guide, often a staff member, with a private vehicle to escort you about for a day. This way the rate will be more like US$75 for the whole minibus.

Ubud The artistic and cultural heartland of the island – the town is full of artists with galleries, dance, music and retail therapy to die for. Surrounding villages specialize in handicraft production while gorgeous hotels are of the spa variety.

Barong and Kris dances These impressive dance dramas represent the everlasting struggle between good and evil. The best performances, accompanied by traditional gamelan music, can be seen in Ubud. Abridged versions are held in Batubalan.

Kintamani A cool mountain region of volcanoes and crater lakes surrounded by deep green rice paddies.

Bedugul Mystical Pura Ulun Danau on the shore of Lake Bratan is one of Bali's most beautiful temples. It was built in 1633 and honours the goddess of water, Dewi Danau. Note that to enter any Balinese temple, a sash should be worn around your waist. These can be hired or bought for very little.

Tanah Lot Bali's most important temple is built on a rocky outcrop overlooking the sea. It is just half an hour from Kuta and is breathtaking – if busy – at sunset.

Bali Aga Village, Tenganen Bali Aga were the island's inhabitants before the arrival of Hindu Javanese. The village retains its ancient customs by allowing only minimal contact with outsiders.

Bali Barat National Park This extensive area on the island's western side covers woodlands and coastal areas and houses some of Bali's resident wildlife including rare birds, monkeys and iguanas.

Festivals

The Balinese are Agama Hindus, a religion developed long ago and influenced by many things including Indian Hinduism. There are many differences though, and it is said that even Hindus are confused by them. For travellers, Bali's religion is ever present, interwoven with daily life through offering rituals. These are conducted everywhere: in doorways, in homes and hotels and at temples scattered across the island. Festivals are just as prevalent: it is said there is one every day of the year – somewhere – as they are the essence of Balinese life, regarded as the balance between order and disorder. If you hear of one, go: etiquette requires you to stand politely back, but tourists are not resented. There are festivals dedicated to the arts, the birth of a goddess, parades to the sea to cleanse villages, special prayer days for the dead and harvest festivals. The Balinese calendar is only 210 days long, so actual dates vary.

Galungan The most important holiday symbolizing the victory of virtue over evil.

Nyepi Balinese New Year is a day of total silence. No activity whatsoever is allowed, no walking anywhere, even electricity is banned in hotels. On New Year's Eve, purification and sacrificial rites are followed by dancing through the villages. The men carry *ogoh-ogoh* (demon images) and make as much noise as possible. This wakes up all the evil spirits and on Nyepi, Bali is so quiet the spirits can't find anyone and leave the island for good.

Balinese cremation Regarded as a sacred duty as it liberates the deceased soul, allowing it to enter a higher world and be free for reincarnation. If you're invited to a ceremony, don't miss it – this is a joyous celebration.

Balinese festival; Pura Ulun Danau Bratan temple; in the monkey forest at Ubud; Balinese dancer

Nusa Tenggara

A chain of islands stretch east from Bali all the way to Timor. Collectively known as Nusa Tenggara, the Southeastern Islands, these are stepping stones in a sea full of intense dive opportunities.

Nusa Tenggara lies west of the Wallace Line (see page 26) so her islands are far from typical tropical idylls. Arid landscapes with sparse foliage, active volcanoes and black-sand beaches contrast strongly with Bali's lush shores. To the south lies the Indian Ocean and north is the Flores Sea; the two bodies of water are connected by many deep channels that carve watery highways between the islands. Cold water upwellings and strong currents impact on the diving. The conditions are not always easy but the whole area is a haven for all sorts of unusual creatures both on land and in the sea.

Directly opposite Bali is **Lombok**. Much the same size, but rural where Bali is developed, Sasak rather than Hindu, this was long the haunt of the backpacker set who discovered the charming Gili Islands just off her north coast. These coral-ringed cays are designated marine parks. Diving is land based and often touted as best for novices and trainees yet even hardened divers would be mad to miss some of these easy-to-dive reefs. Lombok's south coasts couldn't be more different. Diving is still a developing industry with much to explore from shallow bays full of tiny creatures to wild, deep-water pinnacles for advanced divers only.

Further east, dive facilities are minimal: this becomes liveaboard territory. Next along is **Sumbawa**. The reefs bordering the north coast sit beneath dramatic hills and are always included on liveaboard routes. The diving tends to be more about small creatures but surprises happen.

Just past Sumbawa is magnificent **Komodo** Island and her World Heritage Marine Park. This is a dream location with many reef-ringed islands sitting in the deep channel between Sumbawa and Flores. However, conditions can change in a nano-second: currents go from washing machine to speed demon and often do both on the same dive. However, Komodo's resources have been preserved better than some: the island has a minimal number of humans but the world's biggest population of the $3\frac{1}{2}$ m long, monitor lizard known as the Komodo Dragon.

At the far end of the chain, **Alor** may seem like a poor, distant cousin but the diving here can be highly impressive. Liveaboards often include Alor in their routes, (and even parts of Flores which was damaged by a tsunami in 1992) but there also a few land-based resorts.

Locations

Lombok is purely land based, perfect for a pre or post liveaboard stop as well as a destination in its own right. Further east, it only makes sense to go by liveaboard to cover greater ground in comfort and without having to take extra flights.

Destinations

Lombok

Mataram, the capital, is actually an amalgamation of four towns: Ampenan, Mataram, Cakranegara and Sweta. The airport is currently just north (a new one is being built not far away to the south) but apart from flying in or out there is no real need to spend time along this busy stretch. More popular and just a 30-minute drive north is **Senggigi Beach**, a cluster of sandy beaches with safe swimming and a small reef that's nice for snorkelling. There are shops, restaurants and mostly large hotel complexes although there are some charming smaller ones as well. From here, many dive centres organize day dive trips to the Gili islands although it makes more sense to stay on one or at least on a closer beach, like Mendana. **Gili Air, Meno and Trawangan** can be reached by slow boat from Bangsal or Teluk Kode a little further north of Senggigi, taking 15, 30 and 45 minutes respectively. Each of these has a distinct personality: Air is closest to the coast and mid-range. Meno, in the middle, is quietest and furthest away is lively Trawangan. On this, the largest island, there are hotels, shops and restaurants. Even so, this is still a small place with a typical island atmosphere. What all three have in common though – apart from no cars – is that they are ringed by sandy seabeds interspersed with coral mounds and pinnacles which create some very interesting diving. *Distance from airport: 30-90 mins*

Heading to the south of Lombok, the pace is quite different with three smaller, very quiet, developing resort areas. **Kuta** sits in the centre of the south coast on a broad bay with a beautiful, white-sand beach and just a couple of hotels. To the west is **Belongas Bay**, a truly undiscovered area that has access to some of the most challenging diving on the island (but little else) while due north of that is **Sekotong**. The town here sits in a mostly rural area that faces back towards Bali, creating a large protected body of water dotted with many small islands. *Distance from airport: 1½-2 hours*

Sumbawa to Komodo

Once you move east from Lombok, and this cannot be stressed enough, it's liveaboard territory. Vessels depart from Bali plying the waters to Komodo and some keep going all the way to Alor. Others fly passengers to Labuanbajo on the western tip of Flores and sail back to the marine park, even more start and end in Bima on eastern Sumbawa. Bima and Labuanbajo are the locations of the closest airports to the Komodo Marine Park. As to hotels and land-based diving – not really. You could stop at the breathtakingly expensive Amanwana on Moyo Island ($900 a night) and there are hotels in Bima but these are not set up for divers. A few in Labuanbajo are but day-trip diving is restrictive. Interesting though all these options may seem, you just won't get the best of diving in the marine park unless you are on a boat. At least there are boats for all budgets.

Alor

Diving in this most easterly part of Nusa Tenggara is both impressive and undersubscribed. Access was difficult in the past but new flights are opening up the area. Always part of occasional liveaboard routes, more boats are coming this way although not as frequently as some might like. There are a few small resorts for those looking for absolute peace and quiet. Either way, diving takes place around the islands in the channel that cuts between Alor and Pantar. Conditions here are more suitable for experienced divers than complete novices as there can be some ripping currents. *Distance from airport: 2-3 hrs*

Places to stay and things to do at all these destinations are listed in Drying out on page 60

The Oberoi; Komodo bay; Alor teenager; sunset in Flores; Gili Trewangan dive lesson; Moyo fishermen

The Gilis, Lombok

Small and sandy, no roads, no cars, just horse-drawn carriages: there is no doubt why the three Gilis (meaning island) are so popular with long-term travellers. While the locals leave every morning to work on the 'big' island, these tiny specks of land are inundated with travellers and divers.

All three are ringed by reefs and bordered by white sand encapsulating a green interior. Only Gili Trawangan, furthest from the mainland, rises more than a few metres above sea level. At her centre is a small hill and lookout from where you can stare back to Bali – and on a good day see Mt Agung. Face the other way, and you see the equally imposing Mt Rinjani on Lombok.

Perhaps it's the geography that has made Trawangan the most popular of the coral cays, and the most developed. There isn't much to do apart from enjoy the sea and, at night, the lively party atmosphere. Plus it's definitely the hub for dive centres. Meno and Air are just as beautiful and somewhat more relaxed. There are a couple of small turtle sanctuaries on Meno and a new bird park, while days on Air are about total relaxation .

As the islands are so close to each other, you can easily dive around all three from whichever one you are based on, or for that matter from the nearby coastal resorts. Dive sites are hardly ever more than 20 minutes away. The conditions are usually easy. Strong currents occur around the full moon but these are not the type that compete with the high drama of those in Komodo.

The straightforward conditions, and the proximity of the reefs, makes these waters ever popular with novices – many people come here to train – and local fishing fleets. In the past there was a lot of fishing, along with some bombing, and the evidence of this is clear. However, the birth of the Gili Eco Trust and its strategy to encourage sustainable practices are resolving this. No matter what some will try to tell you, there is some impressive diving here.

Deeper reefs have vast areas of pristine coral while the shallower reefs, despite exhibiting lots of rubble patches, are just teeming with life. Divers who take their time are rewarded with all sorts of unusual animals, like both species of mantis shrimp and more turtles than you are likely to see anywhere else.

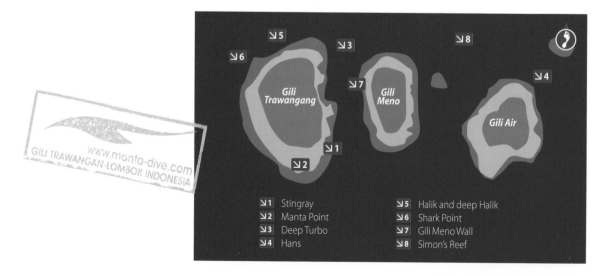

↘1	Stingray	↘5	Halik and deep Halik
↘2	Manta Point	↘6	Shark Point
↘3	Deep Turbo	↘7	Gili Meno Wall
↘4	Hans	↘8	Simon's Reef

⌖1 Stingray

◈	**Depth**	18 m
◑	**Visibility**	poor to fair
≋	**Currents**	slight
⬯	**Dive type**	day boat

A testament to the work done by the Gili Eco Trust, this site is a wealth of embryonic artificial reefs. The site runs along the edge of Trawangan's southeast tip. A sandy beach and lots of boat traffic means that visibility can be pretty low. The gently sloping drop falls from about 5 to 12 metres, then has a slightly steeper fall. Small ridges project at right angles to the beach and as you fin along you encounter both patches of coral and the various Biorock projects. Several are already well established with new corals coating the various struts and frames. A little further north but down at about 17 metres, a larger one has been built. Formed of enormous organic shapes, it is starting to show good signs of growth. The animals taking refuge here include white clown frogfish and very friendly octopus. There are lots of fish, nudibranchs, cuttlefish and, of course, the omnipresent turtles, a feature of every dive in the Gilis.

⌖2 Manta Point

◈	**Depth**	24 m
◑	**Visibility**	good
≋	**Currents**	slight
⬯	**Dive type**	day boat

Not true to its name, this dive is more likely to produce a gang of sharks than a mass of mantas. Just south of Stingray, the terrain here has the most extensive corals around Trawangan with swathes of pink and beige hard corals that feed in the current. Large patches of healthy staghorn host flitting schools of anthias and lined snappers amongst others. Passing over this section and dropping, you reach a plateau that had once seen some damage but is now a favourite resting spot for whitetip sharks. Fairly docile considering how many people visit, they only move off when divers get too close. Nearby, a baby whitetip is tucked right under a low-growing table coral; a little further down the reef, there are more turtles including one brave soul that was with a queen triggerfish to completely devastate a hard coral for dinner, the turtle snapping up the scraps as the trigger ripped away.

♒ Conservation

The dive operators on Gili Trawangan have achieved something very special, the sort of co-operation you often wish you saw in more countries. Aware of the need to preserve local reefs, the Gili Eco Trust was established in 2001 to try and resolve some of the less than ideal fishing practices occurring on local reefs.

They set up a system where each diver pays a one-off fee of US$4 and a percentage of these funds are used to pay local fisherman to use sustainable fishing practices: currently only line fishing, surface nets and spear fishing are allowed. Other funds, combined with assistance from local businesses, have also been used to create a series of Biorock projects off the beach. These consist of steel rods that have an electric current running through them. Live coral is attached to the structures and the energy stimulates and supports their growth creating a new reef, which in turn, attracts a variety of marine species. The Trust is also looking at setting a series of mooring buoys along the shoreline so that boats no longer need to drop anchor.

An octopus on Stingray; fiery reef corals at Manta Point; part of the Gili Eco Trust artificial reef system

Life in the deep
Hitchhiking on a fire urchin

The first time you discover a sea urchin, you know all about it. Usually it's a nanosecond after you've put your foot on one and the needle sharp spines have inserted themselves deep into your skin. Absolute agony follows along with all sorts of traditional remedies for removing the broken spines. Peeing on your foot always comes up, as does vinegar, lemon juice and hot water.

Just imagine the extra dose of ouch factor when you learn that certain urchins also harbour venom in those spines. One of the most impressive members of the family is the fire urchin, which is both incredibly beautiful and incredibly toxic. So it may come as a surprise that this hazardous little bundle also hosts a group of much smaller creatures. It has five house guests that live with it in varying degrees of harmony.

There are just two types of fire urchin, *Asthenosoma varium* and *Asthenosoma ijimai*, which are only found in tropical and subtropical waters. At about 25 centimetres across, their flattened dome shaped body has a flexible, soft skeleton and is covered in needle sharp spines an inch long. Each spine is beautifully striped in tones of red, yellow, blue and white and just below the tip is a rounded bump that houses a poison. Should you be unlucky enough to put your hand on one, the pain can last from fifteen minutes to several hours. Some reports even state that it can take a week to get back full use of the affected limb.

↘1 **Asthenoma varium** Despite its in-built defence system the *asthenoma varium* is the favoured form of housing for these diminutive, and often hard to spot, critters.

↘2 **Coleman's shrimp** Living exclusively on fire urchins, *Periclimenes colemani* nestle on a patch of skin surrounded by a ring of spines like a military fortification. The shrimp clears this patch for itself yet does so without causing any substantial damage to the urchin, nor does the urchin inflict any harm on the hitchhikers. The Colman's are usually found in mating pairs with the female being substantially larger than her mate.

↘3 **Wentletrap Snails** Beneath their bodies, fire urchins have tube shaped feet which are important for feeding, movement and clinging onto surfaces. These feet are attacked by colonies of the white-shelled snail, *Luetzania asthenosomae*, the only parasitic hitchhiker. Their bodies have a reduced tongue in favour of a protruding trunk which allows them to feed on the urchin by nibbling at their feet and external soft tissues.

↘4 **Zebra crabs** Futuristic looking, dark brown and white striped, *Zebrida adamsii* are an inch or so across their carapace. They have specially adapted legs where the last segment forms tiny hooks that ensure them a safe ride on their host. Mostly seen alone, sometimes in pairs, they use the toxic spines for shelter but give nothing back to the urchin. Unlike the Colman's shrimp, zebra crabs are seen living on other types of sea urchin.

↘5 **Commensal shrimp** Of all the critters that live on fire urchins, the *Allopontonia iaini* shrimp is the hardest to spot. Its almond shaped body and pointy head are marked by a single white stripe, which camouflages him amongst the spines. At first glance he is a dead ringer for a squat lobster. Completely protected by the urchin, he lives on its base where the mouth is located and scavenges the scraps from the urchins' meals.

↘6 **Urchin cardinal fish** Generally urchins are nocturnal, but they are often found on sandy patches at depth. Whole colonies emerge to graze and groups of tiny cardinals take shelter around their base. The reason for this isn't clear but it is thought the 20mm long adult fish gain protection although their host gains nothing for its hospitality.

☷3 Deep Turbo

🕑	Depth	32 m
🔅	Visibility	good
🌊	Currents	slight
🌊	Dive type	day boat

Located to the north of Trawangan but sitting midway in the channel between it and Meno, this dive has really interesting topography. The visibility is better in this vicinity so as you drop in over a large flat area – where the seabed is covered in several beds of garden eels – you can see a series of low ridges or mounds going in all directions. These are interspersed with clumps of whip coral and enormous fans in incredibly bright shades of orange, red and pink. Swimming up a gentle slope to shallower waters there are some bommies that were recently affected by a storm, turning one huge hard coral on its side. The bottom is now exposed and many fish are sheltering beneath. Further up the slope, a really lush bommie is masked by sweepers and anthias while a marble ray hides beneath, then further along a high sponge has a resident giant frogfish nestling on one side.

☷4 Hans

🕑	Depth	23 m
🔅	Visibility	fair to good
🌊	Currents	none
🌊	Dive type	day boat

This fabulous muck dive is located off the northern rim of Gili Air. Entry is over a white sand and coral rubble slope with very little in the way of reef structure, just a few rocks and patches of coral. This environment is a haven for critters and you can hop from one curious animal to another every few seconds. A crinoid reveals a baby cuttlefish, next it's the spearing mantis shrimp, followed by the most tiny Emperor angel, then several leaffish, blue and black ribbon eels and a huge black frogfish trucking across the sand. If you have the chance to do this dive more than once you can head a little deeper to where a small outcrop is covered in cardinalfish. This rocky area is known to harbour flounders and flatheads so the divemasters will search those out, while small cracks and crevices are packed full of cleaner shrimp and hingebeaks. Elsewhere there are juvenile sweetlips, moon cowries, pufferfish and filefish.

☷5 Halik and Deep Halik

🕑	Depth	18 m
🔅	Visibility	poor to fair
🌊	Currents	none
🌊	Dive type	day boat

Another advanced dive, this involves a drop into the blue then descending until you find a series of ridges and canyons. At first, the terrain seems quite stony – it's not very lush as currents here restrict growth – but this site is favoured for the larger life it attracts. In a sandy gully three whitetips rest but they seem quite skittish and move off quickly. A little further on you are likely to encounter a turtle hiding under a shelf. Another ridge along and the view changes to lots of small corals and huge numbers of fish. One outcrop has massive schools of sweetlips sheltering on it and as you swim past, you find more whitetips sitting to the side. The dive then requires a long swim back to the reef wall and up a slope densely covered in pale *Xenia* corals which smother old rubble, rejuvenating the reefs and attracting ever more turtles. Every full moon, a school of bumphead parrotfish appears.

Indonesia Dive log Nusa Tenggara: The Gilis, Lombok

Almost invisible frogfish at Deep Turbo; mantis shrimp seem playful, but the 'thumbcracker' strikes with the speed and force of a .22 calibre bullet

⬂6 Shark Point

🌀	**Depth**	32 m
◐	**Visibility**	fair to good
〰	**Currents**	slight
🌊	**Dive type**	day boat

⬂7 Gili Meno Wall

🌀	**Depth**	18 m
◐	**Visibility**	fair to good
〰	**Currents**	slight
🌊	**Dive type**	day boat

An underwater tongue extends from Trewangans west coast at about 30 metres deep. The dive involves dropping into the blue over this, then descending onto a plateau. The surface is stony and broken by a series of depressions followed by ridges of corals. These aren't very lush – there is too much current – but the growth is fairly good. In one sandy gully are the whitetip sharks. They are fairly skittish, and move away quite quickly but a third soon appears. Moving on, there is a turtle hiding under a shelf. The next ridge across has more small corals and incredible numbers of fish: one outcrop has a huge school of sweetlips sheltering around it and another whitetip sitting to the side. To finish the dive, there is a long swim back to the reef wall, then up a slope covered in swathes of pale pink corals until you encounter more of the Gilis turtle population and there are certainly plenty of them.

The area's most popular night dive runs along the west coast of Gili Meno where a rubble slope leads to a small wall of rocky outcrops with sponges and crinoids. There are a lot of crustaceans here, from crinoid and saron shrimp to spider crabs, decorator and hermit. All very beautiful. Along the wall there are a lot of sleeping parrotfish. Turtles swim about, disorientated by torchlight, while tiny cuttlefish and snake eels patrol the bottom. There are spanish dancers here too, including the imperial shrimp nestling in their gills.

Baby cuttlefish are wary of divers at night; Simon's Reef is loaded with large swathes of *Porites species* coral surrounded by dancing anthias

Indonesia Dive log Nusa Tenggara: The Gilis, Lombok

↘8	Simon's Reef	
☻	**Depth**	24 m
◑	**Visibility**	fair to good
☰	**Currents**	slight to strong
☁	**Dive type**	day boat

Possibly the best dive in this area, Simon's Reef sits above the channel that divides Gili Air from Gili Meno. Descending to the bottom at 28 metres, you swim across to a maze-like structure of gullies and reef mounds. The raised sides are coated in masses of fans and huge barrel sponges obviously thriving in the strong currents that flow around and feed these lower sections of reef. Everything here is in pristine condition. Amongst the oversize corals there are several muricella species fans which are known homes for minute pygmy seahorses, if you can spot them – stay near your guide! There are also plenty of angelfish and morays (amongst other things) living here. Passing over another sand channel the reef starts to rise to probably the highlight of the dive: a circular section of *Porites* hard corals has grown into what is almost a pinnacle. It extends for some distance and in the centre is a deep cut that you can carefully swim through. This area dances with the most amazing numbers of anthias – it's really a spectacular sight.

66 99 The barrel sponge was so huge I thought Beth would drop inside before I managed to press the shutter.

South Lombok

This island's second dive region is as far south as the Gilis are north. And it's a long way distant: Lombok is as big as Bali and you can spend a whole day going from top to bottom, but don't be put off by that. The far south borders the Indian Ocean, which makes some of the diving here extremely adventurous and full of potential.

The drive along the north side of Lombok's southwest corner winds past a flat sea dotted with masses of tiny offshore islands. There main town is Seketong: there are many small villages and very few hotels, however, diving options are plenty. Conditions can be variable, depending on currents and due to the shallow waters visibility is never crystal clear. However, this doesn't affect the calibre of the dive sites, which are full of life and colour.

    Things change dramatically along the south coast, which borders the Indian Ocean. Kuta Beach has been on the dive map for some time. It could hardly be described as busy although this sandy bay also attracts surfers. There is a hint in that: conditions here vary from very rough outside the bay to much calmer inside, and of course, diving is scheduled around that. Nearby Belongas Bay is fairly similar and gaining a reputation as the adrenaline rush destination, which is certainly justified. Reaching the bay requires a long bumpy drive on an unmade road to Teluk Sepi then a boat ride. Here, conditions can be extreme and dives are not suitable for the inexperienced, but can be highly rewarding. In season, roughly June to September, the offshore pinnacles attract many larger species.

are the most incredible number of crinoids in an array of colours and these sit on every available surface. The first section of this dive slopes down to the seabed. Whip and soft corals protrude from the sand, gobies and shrimp living on them. As you approach a slight wall, there are more substantial outcrops which are worth inspecting for smaller critters: shrimp on anemones, lion and scorpionfish, moon cowries hiding in crevices and juvenile pinnate batfish at different stages of their development. There are also the most amazing swathes of tiny colonial tunicates forming brightly coloured carpets.

↘9	Medang	
🌀	**Depth**	16 m
◐	**Visibility**	poor to fair
🌀	**Currents**	slight to strong
🌀	**Dive type**	day boat

Sailing east from Sekotong towards the tip of Lombok, you pass some really gorgeous island scenery. Gili Gede, one of the larger islands, is ringed by dives revealing a riot of brightly coloured crinoids, sponges and corals. The sandy seabed is dotted with lively outcrops although the animal life tends towards the small stuff. Nudibranch species include flabellinas and halgerda plus the stylish funeral jorunna. The top of reef is smothered in yellow sea cucumbers, which looks like nudibranchs but are of the few sea cucumbers that live is groups.

↘10	Gili Gede Wall	
🌀	**Depth**	18 m
◐	**Visibility**	poor to fair
🌀	**Currents**	slight
🌀	**Dive type**	day boat

Dives like this are closer to the Lombok Channel and can be subject to slightly stronger currents. These no doubt supply plenty of nutrients to the reefs nearby and although quite shallow, they are smothered in small soft corals and hard corals. There

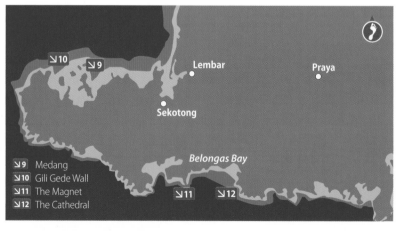

↘10   ↘9   Lembar   Praya

Sekotong

Belongas Bay

↘9   Medang
↘10   Gili Gede Wall
↘11   The Magnet
↘12   The Cathedral

↘11   ↘12

⌖11 The Magnet

🕐 **Depth**	32 m
◑ **Visibility**	fair to good
🌊 **Currents**	strong
🛥 **Dive type**	day boat

To the far west of Belongas Bay in open water and marked by a lighthouse, this circular pinnacle rises up from about 80 metres. The dive is known for currents and strong surges: the surface waves can be daunting – a quick negative entry is needed. The sides of the pinnacle are punctuated by several caverns which are known to attract sharks, amongst other things, and you will see whitetips at least. One cave at 30 metres has fan corals and sheltering snapper while another a little higher hosts large numbers of lionfish. Further around on a ledge, you are likely to find more sharks. The outer walls are covered in a rich variety of corals and tunicates so it's all quite colourful, but the growth is flat, restricted by the sea conditions. In the middle of the year this site is known to attract schools of pelagic fish, manta rays and hammerheads.

⌖12 The Cathedral

🕐 **Depth**	32 m
◑ **Visibility**	fair to good
🌊 **Currents**	strong
🛥 **Dive type**	day boat

Located on the far side of the bay, this second pinnacle is marked by two rocks that break the surface. Entry is on the east side where, near the bottom, a small cavern has large black coral bushes in it. The dive route then turns south, where you encounter the most incredible number of fish travelling up and down the wall. They seem to be playing in the surge and are obviously coping with it far better than the divers! There are jacks, batfish, snapper, Indian Ocean triggers, sweetlips, rainbow runners and many more species. Even when conditions are good you are likely to hit some current somewhere on the dive and the surge can drop as much as 5 metres. Despite this, the dive is well worth it as the walls are coated in lots of colourful small corals, tunicates and plenty of macro life.

◉ Strange creatures?

The first time I came to Kuta I had mixed feelings as its reputation wasn't so spectacular. I was pleasantly surprised to find a friendly and happy community at one of the most scenic places on Lombok. Witnessing big reef breaks, and having been told about strong currents, I thought to myself, "Ok, now let's see about the diving." Crossing the bay on a local outrigger boat we came to a massive sheer cliff and dropped into one of the most amazing underwater scenes I've ever seen. Descending down along a steep slope lined with massive, coral rich, boulders we were joined by giant trevally and massive grunts. Down further, towards where some shadows were moving about, I was amazed by the abundance of macro life and huge lobsters. At 30 metres, I realized that the shadows were huge potato groupers zipping in and out of the many crevices. A slight current carried us toward the mouth of the bay, and as we slowly ascended a giant school of mobula rays darkened the sky above. They just wouldn't stop circling, and it seemed like the school had no beginning or end. We continued ascending right through the mobulas, and they weren't at all bothered by our presence. On the contrary, it seemed more like they were enjoying the sight of the 'strange creatures' they had encountered. This day ended for me with a huge smile on my face and a certainty that this was the place to set up a new dive shop in South Lombok.

George More, owner of DiveZone-Lombok, has dive centres in Kuta and Sekotong

Sumbawa

One of the greatest liveaboard adventures has to be the trip from Bali to Komodo. Cruises depart Bali at night, reaching Sumbawa waters at dawn. Each boat's itinerary will be slightly different, with operators choosing likely spots along this well-trodden path to see if they can discover something new. However, there are several islands that are on most lists – Moyo, Satonda and Sangean – as well as dives around Bima, eastern Sumbawa's main port, a busy yet traditional Indonesian town.

First stop en route to Komodo is likely to be at one of the small islands bordering Sumbawa's western tip, before heading on to **Moyo**. Boats stop here not because the diving is spectacular, but it makes a good break in a long journey. There are a few good dives in this region but the reefs around Moyo show signs of illegal fishing. All the same, it is good to get wet.

Satonda, a little further west, is actually a volcanic island with a magical crater lake at its heart. The dive sites here hold some magic too, as this is a great place to see some of Indonesia's unusual, small marine creatures. Sailing further, you pass under the shadow of active, Mt Tamborah before reaching the narrow body of water that leads due south to **Bima** harbour. Diving here is understandably of the muck variety so is less frequently included in schedules, which is a bit of a shame. Last stop on this route is another volcanic island, **Sangeang**, sitting right on the edge of the buffer zone to the splendid Komodo National Park.

◹13 Pulau Panjang

🕐 **Depth**	27 m
◐ **Visibility**	fair to good
🌀 **Currents**	slight
🌊 **Dive type**	liveaboard

Sitting in the strait opposite Lombok, this small, flat island, is currently uninhabited (there are rumours of a resort) and ringed by thick mangroves around her coast. Beneath the water, a small wall drops to around 28 metres and at it's base are some very nice fan corals are used by damsels, anthias and other small fish for protection. In fact, there are rather a lot of small reef fish along this wall, like triggerfish and butterflies. As you come back up to the shallows, it becomes more interesting to look for smaller critters living amongst the hard corals. These include flatworms and shrimp, mushroom coral pipefish, sangian crabs on sponges, moray eels and lobsters hiding in crevices and giant cuttlefish.

◹14 Angel Reef, Moyo

🕐 **Depth**	25 m
◐ **Visibility**	fair to good
🌀 **Currents**	slight to strong
🌊 **Dive type**	liveaboard

One of Moyo's healthier reefs, Angel lies off the west coast. Entry is over a vertical wall with reasonable soft corals, fans and tunicates. Drifting along, you will see a variety of nudibranchs. The fish species are typical: butterflies, redtooth triggers and occasional angelfish pass by. There are also a few small schools of batfish in the blue. In the shallows on the top of the reef, the corals become quite patchy and there are, sadly, some signs of damage. However, the rubble areas are also home to flatworms, blue ribbon eels and sea cucumbers often with tiny crabs living on them.

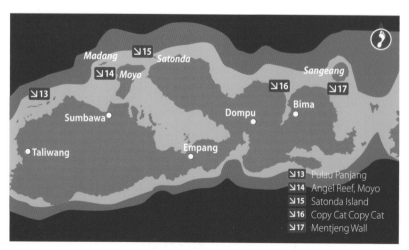

Madang
◹15 Satonda
◹14 Moyo
Sangeang
◹16
◹17
◹13
Sumbawa
Dompu
Bima
Taliwang
Empang

↘15 Satonda Island

🌀	**Depth**	30 m
◑	**Visibility**	fair to good
〰	**Currents**	none
🌊	**Dive type**	liveaboard

There are two contrasting dive types on Satonda: a steep wall on the northwest side and a shallow, sheltered dive on the diagonally opposite coast. The wall has good coverage of hard corals and sponges, the panorama broken up by some small caves. These house interesting fish like sailfin gobies – who wave their dorsal fins at divers – along with shrimp and cowrie shells. In the southeast, there is a sandy bottomed sheltered bay. It has far less coral but plenty of unusual critters living alongside what is there. Jewel anemones are covered in whole families of commensal shrimp while feeding mushroom corals disguise mushroom coral pipefish. In the sand you can find the spearing mantis shrimp, a variety of nudibranchs and, at night, pastel-toned seapens emerge from the sand as well.

↘16 Copy Cat Copy Cat, Bima

🌀	**Depth**	19 m
◑	**Visibility**	poor to fair
〰	**Currents**	none to medium
🌊	**Dive type**	liveaboard

Not far from Bima harbour, this is a classic muck dive, one of those sites that at first glance makes you wonder why you pulled on your wetsuit. A patch of flat reef leads to a seagrass bed then slopes away to a fine silt sea floor. Boat traffic and currents ensure visibility is never great here. Looking down at the seabed though, this is all about focusing on the small creatures that latch onto any available bit of detritus and mimic it as much as possible. Pipehorses act like sticks, brown frogfish blend into decaying bits of timber and ghost pipefish pretend to be blades of seagrass. A large log is a haven for hingebeak shrimps and crinoids disguise ornate ghost pipefish. Seapens emerge from the sand and reveal tiny crabs and gobies on their stems. This site actually gained it's name from the mimic ocopus which lucky divers may spot.

↘17 Mentjeng Wall, Sangeang

🌀	**Depth**	45 m
◑	**Visibility**	fair to good
〰	**Currents**	none
🌊	**Dive type**	liveaboard

On Sangeang's southern point a small, nondescript beach disguises a fantastic dive site. The upper levels of the shallow bay have good coverage of hard and soft corals and plenty of small fish. However, the real excitement lies in the wall to one side. Descending along it you see such curiosities as colonial anemones, then the wall bottoms out at around 20 metres into a black-sand seabed. Around the base of the wall are masses of unusual critters: crinoids house ghost pipefish, sponges with crabs, sea whips with gobies and tiny commensal shrimp. There are frogfish, saron shrimp and, for the eagle-eyed, tiny, tiny boxer crabs hide under small rocks, but the biggest attraction here are the nudibranchs. Nicknamed 'butterflies of the sea', at the last count nearly 40 different species had been logged on a single dive.

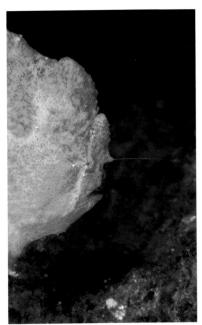

Frogfish with his fishing lure extended; Satonda reef wall, smiling moray

Komodo

Once, people came to Komodo only to see her famous dragon: a huge monitor lizard that must be one of the ugliest creatures on the planet. The Komodo National Park was established in 1980, originally to conserve the dragon and its habitat. However, its marine biodiversity was recognized as equally important and, in 1986, the Park was declared a World Heritage Site and a Man and Biosphere Reserve by UNESCO.

Komodo's incredible diversity is coupled with equally incredible currents. Lying at the centre of Nusa Tenggara, which separates the Indian Ocean from the Java Sea, currents are unpredictable to say the least. At times they can be a rapid drift, at others they will toss you about like a washing machine. What's more, the cold water upwellings can be breathtaking. It's not like that all year but the harder conditions often correlate with the best animal spotting seasons. This is some of the most challenging diving in Indonesia, yet the reefs are spectacular, with a mixture of large and small animals on every dive.

66 99 Dive Komodo and you will never again question the wisdom of diving with a reef hook.

↘18 Tanduk Rusa, Gili Banta

🌀	**Depth**	32 m
◐	**Visibility**	fair to great
🌊	**Currents**	mild to ripping
🌀	**Dive type**	liveaboard

Gili Banta is the first island you encounter as you approach the marine park from the west. It's located just inside the park buffer zone and is a great taste of things to come. In particular, it's a test of your mettle with Komodo's ever changing, raging currents. One dive will be as still as a mill pond, the next in the most breathtaking washing machine currents. Despite that, this is a dive of note. Sitting on the northwest peninsula, the underwater scenery outside the bay consists of a pinnacle with steep slopes dropping off to depth. Large rock formations are shaped by the up and down currents which attract plenty of big stuff: sharks, barracuda, tuna, Napoleon wrasse, schooling jacks and batfish. Inside the bay, which makes a good night dive, things are sometimes calmer and you can see crabs, shrimp, nudibranchs and gobies.

↘19 It's a Small World, Gili Banta

🌀	**Depth**	45 m
◐	**Visibility**	fair to good
🌊	**Currents**	slight
🌀	**Dive type**	liveaboard

On the opposite side of Gili Banta and just inside the northeast point, this sandy bay is a haven for macro life. There is a quite a decent small wall that runs towards the west. This area has some good hard corals and is patrolled by a handful of small whitetip sharks. Scrawled filefish hide on the reef and on the pale coloured sponges there are likely to be frogfish. They can be hard to spot as they blend perfectly with their backgrounds. Back on the sand patch there are garden eels, seapens and lots of small soft corals. Other life includes carpet anemones with porcelain crabs sitting on their rim while clownfish and tiny juvenile sweetlips flutter beside them. This is a great night dive too. You can spot lined clingfish and tiny trumpetfish hiding inside crinoids and there is always the possibility of finding a stargazer grinning at you from the seabed.

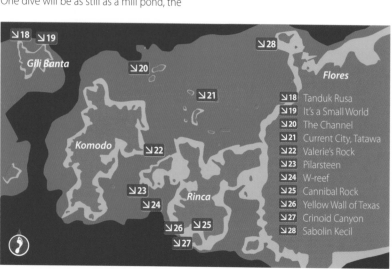

↘18	Tanduk Rusa
↘19	It's a Small World
↘20	The Channel
↘21	Current City, Tatawa
↘22	Valerie's Rock
↘23	Pilarsteen
↘24	W-reef
↘25	Cannibal Rock
↘26	Yellow Wall of Texas
↘27	Crinoid Canyon
↘28	Sabolin Kecil

Tatawa reef and corals

↘20 The Channel, Gili Lawa Laut

🐢	**Depth**	24 m
🔵	**Visibility**	fair to good
🌊	**Currents**	none
🌀	**Dive type**	liveaboard

Gili Lawa Laut sits just spitting distance from her sister island, Gili Darat Laut. These two islands mark the upper edge of the Komodo Marine Park and the dive in the channel between them is another classic example of Komodo conditions. Although there are sites here where you can avoid the currents, this one is all about taking advantage of them. The rapid movement ensures that the fan corals are in pristine condition as they take advantage of the passing plankton to feed. There are also large schools of fish: you can see mackerel, grouper and bumphead parrot fish while smaller fish that hug the walls include butterflies, clown triggerfish and angels.

↘21 Current City, Tatawa

🐢	**Depth**	16m
🔵	**Visibility**	fair to good
🌊	**Currents**	none
🌀	**Dive type**	liveaboard

Although the hint is in the name, there are times when there aren't any currents at Current City – it just depends on when you dive. And if you go twice, it may have all changed anyway. However, no matter whether the water is ripping or almost still, this is a great dive. At slack times, you can see the walls are thick with soft corals and fans. Masses of brightly crinoids hang on to them for dear life (they know what will come later) and curious morays poke their noses out from the wall. You might even spot a crocodile fish on a ledge. An hour later and it's all changed. As you drift at speed along the wall, you can see the huge barrel sponges are now quivering in the current, and an eagle ray passes so quickly you almost miss it, as does a small turtle. Schools of trevally and rainbow runners keep pace.

↘22 Valerie's Rock/Pantai Merah

🐢	**Depth**	45 m
🔵	**Visibility**	fair to good
🌊	**Currents**	none
🌀	**Dive type**	liveaboard

This pinnacle, rumoured to be named after Valerie Taylor, is just off Pantai Merah – Pink Beach – and not far from the entrance to the Komodo National Park, where you can visit the dragons. The shallow bay encloses a sloping reef and a tower of rock rising from 30 metres to reach the surface at low tide. The site seems like perfection from the boat but once in the water you may find Komodo at its most temperamental.

Temperatures can drop from a previously comfortable 28°C to a brain-numbing 20°C. The currents can rip and if you're not careful you will be over the site and out the other side before the rest of the group has even managed to enter. At other times, however, it can be the most impeccable dive in the world: calm, warm water and all sorts of weird and wonderful creatures such as leaffish, scorpionfish and sea hares. Bits of detritus turn out to be the solar-powered nudibranch and even the pretty stuff that makes an appearance is worth being careful over. You can see toxic sea urchins here or a dozen mobula rays as they sail over your head – provided you're looking up at the time, of course.

The incredible *Phyllodesmium longicirrum* nudibranch uses the sun to create energy; Scrawled filefish

ⓘ23 Pilarsteen	
🕐 **Depth**	30 m
◑ **Visibility**	fair to great
🌀 **Currents**	mild to strong
🌓 **Dive type**	liveaboard

Not far from Padar Island, Pilarsteen is a submerged rock pinnacle with a very impressive wall. Starting from the south, the currents send you along the western side where, between 30 and 40 metres, there is a series of caverns and rocky outcrops. These have created fun swim-throughs. After exploring them, you can ascend back up the wall, where the steep slopes are well covered in yellow, orange and red toned soft corals, sponges and fans. Tunicates and hydroids punctuate the scene with paler tones. If the current is up there will be schools of trevally and bumphead parrots while up in the surge zone, a gigantic, lone barracuda watches the struggling divers below.

ⓘ24 W-reef (aka Three Sisters)	
🕐 **Depth**	32 m
◑ **Visibility**	fair to great
🌀 **Currents**	mild to strong
🌓 **Dive type**	liveaboard

Originally named after one of Indonesia's finest sea captains, Wesley's Reef is a series of three long, oval-shaped underwater pinnacles that run parallel to each other and almost break the surface. Their positioning makes for a fantastic zig-zag swim between each of the channels they create. Every surface is painted with colour and there is a fantastic quantity of life on the pinnacle walls – this site is almost as diverse as Cannibal Rock. There's a small cave jam-packed with lionfish, anthias dance in every crevice and moray eels poke about. Small creatures include orang-utan crabs, imperial shrimp on cucumbers, mating nudibranchs and the tiniest of clown frogfish, though it's hard to keep your eyes down and focussed on them with gangs of batfish or huge tuna passing overhead. Even manta rays sometimes flit by. Once you have located all these fascinating animals during the day, it's worth returning at night to watch their nocturnal activities.

🌀 The Indonesian Throughflow

To understand why Komodo dives have currents like nowhere else, you need to know a little about the Indonesian Throughflow. This term describes the major current that transports water from the Pacific to the Indian Ocean by pushing south past the myriad islands of the Indonesian Archipelago. In the north, the current enters via the Makassar Strait (between Kalimantan and Sulawesi), until it reaches the Nusa Tenggara chain. Here it splits around the various land masses, forcing its way through any available channel – especially the Lombok Channel. Currents on either side of Komodo island are also highly affected by this hence all those nasty drift dives that hit five knots, sometimes much more.

The direction of the flow is seasonal but is principally south bound. A northerly flow was last recorded in 1998 which was regarded as a post El Niño effect. The western equatorial Pacific Ocean is also warmer than the Indian Ocean and it has lower salinity. This means the Throughflow transports warmer and fresher water south where it is swiftly diverted towards Africa by the Indian South Equatorial current, eventually joining the Agulhas current around South Africa before travelling to the Atlantic Ocean.

Of course, this simplified explanation doesn't do justice to the importance of the Throughflow nor its impact on diving right across Southeast Asia. It influences all weather patterns – for example, it is the seasonal change in the Indonesian Throughflow that triggers rainfall in the Andaman Seas between May and September.

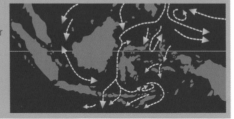

25 Cannibal Rock

⊗	**Depth**	33 m
⟐	**Visibility**	fair to good
≋	**Currents**	slight to strong
⬭	**Dive type**	liveaboard

Horseshoe Bay is within the Komodo Marine Park, at its most southerly point. Nestled between Rinca Island and Nusa Kode, the bay is now world famous for its incredible diversity. You name any small critter and it's bound to have been seen here. There are several dive sites but Cannibal Rock is the most famous for its all-round variety. The site is a sloping, submerged sea mound that can just about be seen from the surface. Rolling in over the rock feels a bit like rolling into a rainbow: the entire mound is luminescent, smothered in bright soft corals, olive green tubastrea corals, many-coloured crinoids and iridescent sea apples. These animals are a member of the sea cucumber family, their round shape having a vague resemblance to red apples – until they poke their yellow and white tipped tentacles out to feed. They are extremely rare elsewhere. Then there's the macro life. Amongst the corals you can find frogfish, mushroom coral pipefish, seasnakes tiny shrimps in bubble coral and orang-utan crabs. A lot of the more bizarre life is at great depth so it's easy to go into deco if you're not careful. Tiny pygmy seahorses are seen on pink gorgonians at 32 metres and toxic sea urchins cluster on the slopes beyond 30 metres. Night dives are a treat, where every tiny crustacean seems to come out and hitch a ride on another animal – squat lobsters sit on urchins and zebra crabs on fire urchins. There is some pelagic life here too but visibility is variable so you may only see passing tuna. Minke whales are said to pass through the bay: you might only see a fin or fluke, but you'll certainly hear them calling.

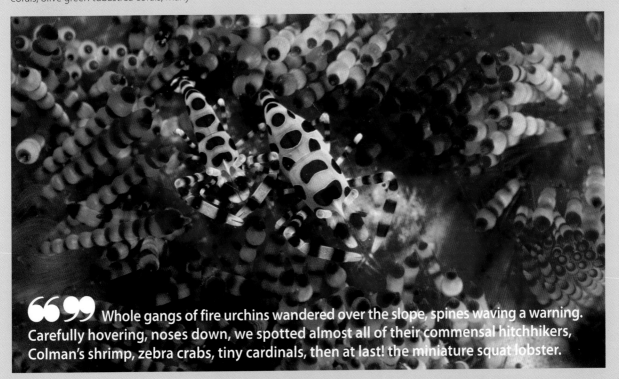

" Whole gangs of fire urchins wandered over the slope, spines waving a warning. Carefully hovering, noses down, we spotted almost all of their commensal hitchhikers, Colman's shrimp, zebra crabs, tiny cardinals, then at last! the miniature squat lobster.

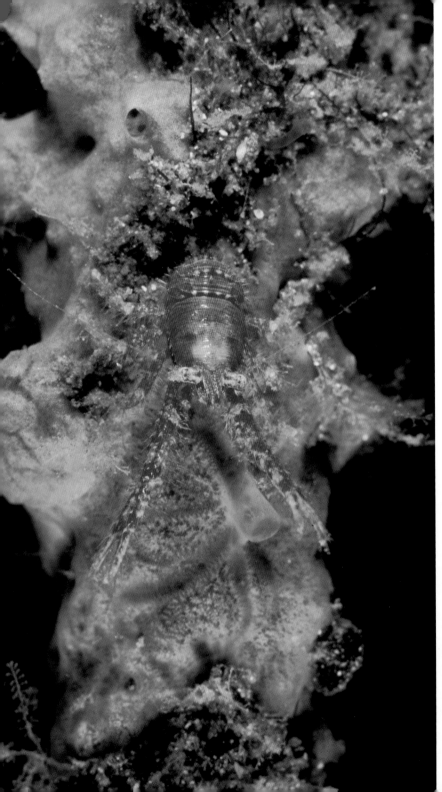

🌀	**Depth**	22 m
◐	**Visibility**	fair
〰	**Currents**	can be strong
⬱	**Dive type**	liveaboard

This dive was named in honour of the legendary divemaster Larry Smith as a play on the *Yellow Rose of Texas*, the unofficial song of his home state. The dive is on the eastern side of Nusa Kode and, apart from being a wall rather than a mound, is not all that different to Cannibal Rock. Surfaces are equally well painted by masses of crinoids and soft corals, although here they mostly display tones of yellow and orange. The population of bright red sea apples is just as prolific so the whole dive takes on a rather sunny countenance even on a cloudy day. On a bright afternoon, this dive is really something – simply floating over the reef is a calming experience. However, taking time to look closely inside the crinoids is likely to reveal one or more of their inhabitants, such as crinoid shrimp, while wandering amongst the tunicates and sponges are many types of nudibranchs, juvenile fish, squat lobsters and tiny flatworms.

Crinoids and critters on the Yellow Wall

↘27 Crinoid Canyon

Depth	28 m
Visibility	fair to good
Currents	slight to medium
Dive type	day boat/liveaboard

Almost opposite Yellow Wall but in a small cove, this long wall drops from just below the surface in an almost vertical line until nearly at the sea floor where it slopes off and levels out. There isn't as much current here as its location inside the cove means the site is a little more protected than some. There are obviously rather a lot of crinoids here as well, and these ensure this wall is pretty, but at the bottom, swim a little way out into the canyon. You may encounter a little current but it's worth a look to see what bottom-dwellers are about. There are bluespotted rays and more crinoids that grip onto anything they can. If you look closely at these you may even spot a seagrass ghost pipefish hanging inside for protection.

↘28 Sabolan Kecil

Depth	26 m
Visibility	good
Currents	slight to medium
Dive type	liveaboard

Outside the marine park and just a short distance from the port of Labuanbajo on Flores, this site is often visited by liveaboards extending their trips along the top of Flores. The best section is a sandy channel, that sits between the coastal fringing reef and a submerged plateau. On the sand are some great critters: this is a good place to spot the spearing mantis shrimp, which are very active here, even coming right out of their tubular burrows in the sand. There are plenty of seapens too, and you can watch their tiny crab residents climbing up and down their branches as if on ladders. Back over on the reef slope there are tiny frogfish and orang-utan crabs nestled into corals and at night you might spot an unusual cleaner pipefish.

☯ Flores after the tsunami

We first dived Flores way back in 1990. It was part of our honeymoon trip and we were amazed: the clearest of clear waters, warm and calm, the sharpest walls, that incredible feeling of flying, launching from the reef top and out into the blue. Two years later, we booked to go back. We were just getting over the jetlag in Bali when the news came. A huge tsunami had hit Maumere with 30-metre waves washing over Pulau Babi, a short way offshore. The loss of life – and livelihoods – was extreme. Prior to this terrible event, marine tourism here had been so very important. The area was known to have one of the highest biodiversity figures in Indonesia, yet divers naturally stopped coming.

The area has since struggled to regain its reputation. We dived nearby from liveaboards in 1998 and again in 2000. Our log books note we were saddened that the divemasters hadn't managed to find a site without signs of damage, yet we also noted there were signs of coral regrowth and that we saw mantis shrimp, blue ribbon eels, morays, octopus and nudibranchs. By all accounts, things are now improving even more. The two original resorts in **Maumere** are open and a new one indicates an upswing for the area, no matter how small. The offshore islands create a barrier around the outer edge of the broad shallow bay which has sloping seabeds near the coast, walls and channels offshore. Several liveaboards are also including stops here so it seems that in nearly 20 years, the sea may have won the struggle.

Blue-spotted ray; check out those eyes on the orang-utan crab; cleaner pipefish, *Doryhamphus janssi*

Alor

Just about as far east as you can go before reaching Timor, Alor is the last of the dive destinations in the amazing Nusa Tenggara chain. Alor and Pantar are the main islands while the Pantar Strait which divides them is a superb marine environment.

Strangely, it's an area that has gone in and out of favour, mostly due to the vagaries of getting there. Until recently there were no flights, except to Kupang on Timor to the south. Now though, two airlines connect Alor to Kupang daily. And it's well worth it. Lovers of complete isolation, peace and incredibly undersubscribed dive sites will enjoy this isolated destination. Ecotourism and conservation programmes work in tandem with local communities and the strait is virtually free of destructive fishing practices although you will encounter occasional traditional bamboo traps nestling on the reefs beside the extensive beds of coral.

↘1 Cave Point

🕐 **Depth**	26 m
◑ **Visibility**	good
🌀 **Currents**	mild
🌊 **Dive type**	liveaboard

This dive off the bottom of Buaya Island is fairly easy. You can drift along a wall that drops from 20 to 35 metres and explore the small caves that appear along its expanse. These house the usual fish, from scorpions and lions to tiny gobies. The wall itself is coated in barrel sponges, fans, crinoids with their resident shrimp and some black coral bushes. You may see Napoleon wrasse or a gang of bumphead parrotfish.

↘2 The Boardroom

🕐 **Depth**	18 m
◑ **Visibility**	good
🌀 **Currents**	mild
🌊 **Dive type**	liveaboard

With absolutely no resemblance to a dull corporate boardroom, this great dive has a variety of things to discover. You can drop down the wall past barrel sponges and lush corals, watching the blue for pelagic fish, or stay up in the shallows to look for the animals that live in the hard corals. There are octopus and catfish in their rolling balls. Leaffish sit on the staghorns and tiny clown frogfish nestle into the reef.

↘3 Sea Apple Slopes

🕐 **Depth**	24 m
◑ **Visibility**	good
🌀 **Currents**	slight
🌊 **Dive type**	liveaboard

This aptly named site starts with a sloping wall that bottoms out at about 25 metres, where, on the sandy seabed, you can find masses of bright red sea apples. This filter-feeding cucumber seems to enjoy the slight currents but divers need to take care as there are lots of toxic fire urchins here too. You might also find Coleman's shrimp on these although they aren't as prevalent as in Komodo. The seabed is also a good spot for seeing lots of seapens popping up from the sand. They usually have small crabs nestled in their fronds.

↘4 Clown Valley

🕐 **Depth**	45 m
◑ **Visibility**	fair to good
🌀 **Currents**	none
🌊 **Dive type**	liveaboard

Copious, extensive, lavish: words can't quite describe these anemones. Drop in and that's what you see, as far as you can see. There are a variety of different ones and they all house various clownfish species. In between there are other things like mantis shrimp and nudibranchs. At the end of the dive a group of large boulders are covered in orange cup corals and if the current is running these create a wall of bright orange. If not it's a good place for spotting small shrimp, more nudibranchs and – for the really lucky, the utterly gorgeous and equally lethal blue-ringed octopus.

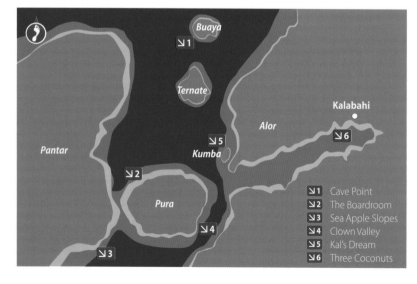

↘1	Cave Point
↘2	The Boardroom
↘3	Sea Apple Slopes
↘4	Clown Valley
↘5	Kal's Dream
↘6	Three Coconuts

↘5 Kal's Dream

🕐	**Depth**	26 m
◐	**Visibility**	excellent
🌊	**Currents**	mild to rip-your-mask-off
🌊	**Dive type**	liveaboard

Alor's most famous dive is Kal's Dream, a heart-thumping, jaw-dropping rush of big animals in fearsome currents. The site sits smack bang in the middle of the open sea between Alor and Pura islands. Divemasters usually look down at the swirling eddies and say 'No way' but when the tides are just right, you can drop to the top of the pinnacle. Dives often start peacefully and you get the chance to spot mantis shrimp, moray eels, barramundi cod and some large groupers while sitting in the lee of the pinnacle. When the currents start to lift you crawl up the side, hook on in the flow and wait for the action to start. Grey reef sharks move in to keep company with the fusiliers, triggers and surgeons, as do tuna, whitetips and schooling snapper. You might see some barracuda, or even a hammerhead. After watching the show for a while, ascent is a slightly risky game of releasing your hook from the rocks and ensuring you don't fly to the surface.

↘6 Three Coconuts

🕐	**Depth**	18 m
◐	**Visibility**	fair to good
🌊	**Currents**	slight
🌊	**Dive type**	liveaboard

The channel that leads to Kalabahi town on Alor is fairly protected so dive boats moor overnight to take advantage of the easier conditions. There are several sites along the shores, often known by names personal to the operator, but most are fascinating muck dives. The sandy sea floor will have hermit crabs, flatworms and nudibranchs, pipefish and many types of urchin including pencil urchins with their commensal shrimp partners. Up in the shallows, a crack in the wall has a special treat for those in the know. As soon as it gets completely dark, hoards of flashlight fish emerge for their evening run, winking the light cells behind their eyes – a sparkling effect like fireworks going off.

Traditional bamboo fishing basket; clownfish in their anemones; our first ever blue-ringed octopus

Drying out

Lombok has a broad selection of dive centres, hotels and restaurants. Hotels range from extremely luxurious to tiny guesthouses, restaurants are plentiful and good. Dive centres in the Gilis tend to cater to the novice and trainee market so if you are a more experienced diver, check that arrangements can be made to do the more advanced dives. In South Lombok, you are likely to dive, sleep and eat with one operation. Heading east from Lombok, except perhaps in Alor, you will need to choose a liveaboard.

The Gilis and North Lombok
Diving and sleeping
$$$ The Oberoi, Medana Beach, T+62 (0)370 638444, oberoilombok.com. On the Lombok coast opposite Gili Air; rooms are quiet, gorgeous and huge – the ultimate in luxury at reasonably affordable prices. Look back to Bali's Mt Agung from the lovely garden, chill out in the spa or eat at a choice of 2 good restaurants. A perfect spot for honeymooners and romantics. The resident dive centre is **H2O Divers**, diveh2osportz.com/lombok.

$$-$ Manta Dive and Bungalows, Gili Trawangan, T+62 (0)370 643649, manta-dive.com. Extremely friendly operation near the dock with excellent dive facilities, cute bungalows and a café. Full training programmes from try-dive to instructor level. Also caters for more advanced divers. The bungalows are based on a traditional Lombok style. They are small but perfectly formed (with air-con and hot water) and surrounded by pretty gardens. Also the owners of **Gili Villas**, swish 2-bed villas with private swimming pools a short walk away. Great value for groups of four.

Other options
Vila Ombak Diving Academy, on Gili Trawangan, hotelombak.com.

Eating
$$ Scallywags, Gili Trawangan. On the south of the beach in the waterside 'strip' of restaurants and bars. Barbecued seafood and Mediterranean-inspired dishes at ridiculously good prices. Great menu with imported wines and beers means this place gets very busy but is worth waiting for a table – or go early.

$ Juku, Gili Trawangan, T+62 (0)81 237 83208. Just a few steps north of Manta and the dock for well cooked and very tasty traditional Indonesian fare.

$ Coco, Gili Trawangan. The best lunches on the 'strip' with freshly baked bread, juices and delicious salads.

South Lombok
Diving and sleeping
Dive Zone – Lombok, T+62 (0)370 661 3585, divezone-lombok.com. Welcoming owner whose company focuses on South Lombok including the advanced dives off the southern coast. Very personal service at centres in Kuta Beach and Sekotong. Also facilities in Belongas Bay and an office in Senggigi Beach. Great value packs include dives, accommodation and local transport. Will also arrange comprehensive land and dive tours in the south and around the island.

$ Bola-Bola Paradise, Sekotong, bolabolaparadis.com or via Dive Zone. Charming, small resort with simple rooms and breezy balconies that look over the gardens to a sandy beach. Restaurant with good quality local meals under $10.

Komodo
Liveaboards
Archipelago Adventurer II, T+62 (0)361 282369, archipelago-fleet.com. Top class vessel with British-American management. Trendy, extra-spacious cabins, with large picture windows, smart ensuites and desks for the all photography and computer kit. Highly knowledgeable guides and a variety of regional routes. Great meals too.

Kararu, T+62 (0)361 282931, kararu.com. This company has a long-standing pedigree in the region, with a great crew, food and management team. They now have a new boat, a phinisi schooner, which is, by all accounts spacious, comfortable and with good facilities.

Other options
As Indonesia's most sailed route, there are many operators from budget to luxury. Remember that vessels that cost more will be of a higher quality – ask enough questions to ensure your choice has the right facilities (see page 8). Check out:

Baruna Adventurer, komodo-divencruise.com
Bidadari, kmbidadari-cruises.com
Komodo Dancer, peterhughes.com
Mona Lisa, monalisacruises.com
Seven Seas, thesevenseas.net

Alor
For many years, most divers reached Alor on a liveaboard but the following resorts are available:

Diving and sleeping
Alor Divers, Pantar Island, alor-divers.com.
Dive Alor, Alor Island, divealor.com.

The Oberoi, Lombok; Manta, Gili Trewangan

	Sleeping	$$$ US$150+ double room per night	$$ US$75-150	$ under US$75
	Eating	$$$ US$40+ 2-course meal, excluding drinks	$$ US$20-40	$ under US$20

Lombok

The name Lombok is a derivative of the Indonesian word for chilli – and you will see plenty if you explore this rural island – but its size and the often poor roads mean you may not manage to do all that much.

Mataram Lombok's capital is actually a long string of towns that merge together. Mataram, Ampenan, Cakranegara and Sweta are worth a visit but the centre is busy and noisy. You can stop in at the Museum, which explains island history as part of the Balinese Kingdom.

Mayura Water Palace Part of the old Balinese royal court, this open-sided pavilion floats on an artificial lake. Built in 1744, it was both a court and a meeting place for the Hindu rulers. In 1894 the Dutch fought the Balinese for control here.

Pura Meru Built in 1720 by a Balinese prince, this is Lombok's largest temple. Opposite the Water Palace, Pura Meru is dedicated to the Hindu trinity of Brahma, Vishnu and Shiva.

Mt Rinjani Towering over the north of the island, this active volcano has the second highest peak in the country at 3,726 metres and last erupted in 1995. You can climb through the lush National Park until you reach the rim and caldera lake, but the round trip takes three days.

Tanjung village Not far from the Gilis or Medana Beach, this traditional village is worth visiting to see the daily farmers' market and at weekends, the wheelings and dealings at the lively cattle market.

Rembitan and Sade In the far south, these villages are Sasak, the main religion on Lombok. Derived from basic Islamic beliefs with some Hinduism and a dose of animism thrown in, it is known as the Wektu Telu religion and was influenced by the Islamic Makassarese in the late 16th century and later by the conquering Balinese in the 18th century. These two villages are a small reflection of Sasak style with authentic thatched houses and *lumbung* (traditional rice barns).

Sumbawa

Sailing along the northern coast you pass under the vast shadow of Mt Tambora. It exploded in 1815, spewing 100 cubic km of ash into the air. Worldwide, 1816 became known as the year without a summer. Satonda is uninhabited except for fruit bats. Every sunset, millions of these creatures appear from the island's tree-clad hills, taking off for their evening activities and turning the sky dark. You can also visit the crater lake, a short walk from the beach, where hundreds of stones hang from tree branches on scraps of rope. Local people come here to make a wish. They believe that when the rope breaks, their wish comes true. Some boats stop in at Bima, a typical Indonesian port town. It's not particularly attractive but the market is colourful.

Komodo

Everyone goes to the National Park to see the Komodo dragons. These enormous, ugly beasties are not to be trifled with so you will be met by a park ranger who takes you along to a feeding station. The world's largest monitor lizard grows to over three metres and weighs up to 165 kg. With huge jaws, squat muscular legs and sharp claws they prey on live deer, goats and wild pigs. Youngsters spend most of their time in trees but adults cannot climb so hunt from the long grass. You may see one wandering along the beach so solo treks are not encouraged.

Market on Padar; wishing trees on Satonda; fishing community at Labuanbajo; commuting in Alor; the world's largest monitor lizard, *varanus Komodoensies*

North Sulawesi

The bizarrely shaped island of Sulawesi sits in the centre of the Indonesian archipelago but it's the tip of the far northern arm reaching towards the Philippines that has captured the hearts and minds of both scientists and divers. Way up on this narrow stretch of land are two destinations with the most incredible diving. Their styles are diametrically opposed yet complement each other perfectly.

This entire island is ringed with coral reef systems so it may seem odd that most dive centres are based around the northern city of Manado. However, there are good reasons why Manado Bay, the offshore islands and the coast that leads around to the Lembeh Straits have become diving hotspots.

For a long time scientists believed that this small area contained the greatest marine biodiversity in the world and was at the heart of the Coral Triangle. Although research wasn't conclusive, exceptionally high levels of certain species had been noted. There are substantial communities of extremely rare animals and recently live coelacanths were caught by fishermen. Until 1938, these were thought to be extinct. Newer research indicates that other parts of Indonesia are equally prolific and, as time goes on, it has been noted that parts of the Philippines have similarly prolific marine environments.

The underlying causes are, as always, location and sea currents. This top end of Sulawesi is swept by strong northeasterly currents that originated in the Pacific Ocean. In addition, many smaller counter currents influence this region bringing in rich nutrients that feed and sustain the coral reefs which in turn sustain all the fish and marine life.

Locations

Perhaps the most famous and certainly the most favoured destination for many divers is the Bunaken Marine Park, sitting just off Manado. Coral gardens are a big feature of these islands and several others just outside the park to the north, while the shallow coastal plateaux are more volcanic and great for spotting small animals. The Lembeh Strait, across the peninsula to the east, is distinctly volcanic. Corals take a back seat to the wealth of rare animals that are almost guaranteed to be seen. There is also a third player in this area, the little known Sangihe Talaud island chain which runs away to the north. This has been dived for quite some time but is only now gaining popularity as divers visiting Manado look for extra experiences to add on to their trip.

Destinations

Manado

The lively, thriving city of **Manado** seems an unlikely destination for gorgeous diving resorts, yet there are plenty in the coastal suburbs to the north and south of the city. Only 20 years ago facilities here were minimal. A couple of well-known local dive pioneers worked hard to protect and promote the reefs and the expansion process escalated from one resort to three and then suddenly, in the late 90s, dozens of seaside resorts emerged onto the scene. Apart from price, there is little to choose between them. Accommodation standards vary a little but are generally quite high. Most sit in small, quiet coves with few local facilities other than those in the resort itself. Resorts to the north are closer to the marine park and the airport. It is easy enough to get into town or head up into the mountains for some sightseeing. *Distance from airport: 20-60 mins*

Bunaken Marine Park

There are four islands inside the Bunaken Marine Park, but there are resorts only on **Bunaken** and **Siladen**. Here too, standards have risen dramatically. The resorts on Bunaken tend to be cheaper, simpler and have retained the castaway feel despite it being a comparatively crowded place. A number of small resorts are clustered onto the same beach, but at least there are other places to go at the end of the day. Siladen has just two resorts, one budget and one upmarket. *Distance from airport: 60-90 mins*

Bangka and Gangga

The islands to the north of the marine park are quieter. There are several small resorts on **Bangka**: these come in a variety of sizes and budgets and are scattered across the island so it feels peaceful, while **Gangga**'s lone resort is more upmarket. Once you are on the islands you are pretty much there for the duration, which is no great hardship as they are all fairly typical of your average tropical idyll. *Distance from airport: 90 mins*

Sangihe Talaud

These islands mark the very top edge of Indonesian territory. Sangihe is just about as far as you can go before finding yourself in the Philippines. As such, this is still a strictly liveaboard destination and a fairly unexplored one at that. For a long time there were just one or two boats that would sail around these under-dived waters, but now the numbers are on the increase with a variety of vessels in all budgets.

Lembeh Straits

The port town of Bitung sits due east of Manado and although this is an important commercial centre, it's not one that attracts tourists. There are markets and shops, but this is definitely a working port town with the type of atmosphere that engenders. However, to the north of the city and on the island of **Lembeh** opposite are a handful of resorts that have as much as a diver will ever need. Originally, and for many years, there was just one resort in this area, at **Kungkungan Bay**, which earned a respected reputation for their development of the local dive scene. However, it was very expensive and its position was challenged, first with the addition of a resort on **Lembeh** island then with several more opening right across the area. Like those near Manado, there are few facilities outside the resort itself – no shops or restaurants to wander around, no nightlife, bars or discos. All resorts are self contained. Prices and standards vary so even divers on a budget can experience what has become the best muck diving destination on the planet: probably. *Distance from airport: 1½-2½ hrs*

Places to stay and things to do at all these destinations are listed in Drying out on page 86

Cocotinos Resort; hill farmer; Manado Tua; Lembeh Resort; children in Sangihe; Bunaken at sunset

Manado Bay

While the majority of divers are attracted to this region to dive the justifiably famous Bunaken Marine Park, many more spend an equal amount of time in the waters of the surrounding bay. The coastline here, even where the city of Manado runs right to its edge, is a fascinating place.

Diving the 'city limits' is not what you would expect of a tropical holiday but where the suburbs reach the coast there are a variety of dives: small reefs, a wreck and for those who don't have the time to get to Lembeh, there are a couple of great muck sites.

↘1 PohPoh	
⬙ Depth	28 m
◑ Visibility	fair
≋ Currents	none
⬓ Dive type	day boat

↘2 Murex House Reef	
⬙ Depth	8 m
◑ Visibility	fair
≋ Currents	none
⬓ Dive type	shore

On the southern fringe of Manado Bay, this area is nicknamed Little Lembeh as many unusual critters are found on the barren seabed. Visibility can be low due to the silt but drop below six metres and it improves. Critters regularly found include a bright yellow *Rhinopias frondosa*, gold and brown-toned ornate ghost pipefish and seahorses. Swimming up the slope on the slopes you find clownfish and porcelain crabs in pretty anemones, many types of shrimp and frogfish, then in the seagrass beds at 10 metres there are cockatoo waspfish, leaffish, a Pegasus sea moth, seagrass pipehorses and fingered dragonets.

All the resorts that nestle on the edges of Manado Bay have great potential for shore based night dives. At Murex Resort, you simply wander off the beach to find a mix of animals living on the small fringing reef. Boulders and other detritus are havens for lion and scorpionfish. Common octopus come out at night to hunt. There are several blue ribbon eels in residence as well as some unusual nudibranchs like the *Chelidonura Hirundinina*. This pretty chap is usually called a twin-tailed slug. Juvenile and teenage stage pinnate batfish are also fairly common but can be hard to spot in the dark.

↘1	PohPoh
↘2	Murex House Reef
↘3	Molas Wreck
↘4	Tanjung Pisok

Montehage

Siladen

Manado Tua   Bunaken

↘4

Molas

↘3

Manado Bay

Manado

↘2

Tateli

↘1

PohPoh

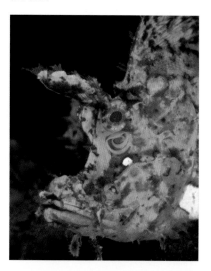

◢3 Molas Wreck

⏱	**Depth**	39 m
◑	**Visibility**	fair to good
〰	**Currents**	ripping
⬯	**Dive type**	day boat

Named the *Molas* Wreck after the nearest village, the history of this ship is not clear although it is thought to be a Dutch cargo vessel that sunk in 1942. Regarded as an advanced dive due to the depth, what really makes this a hard dive are the often extreme currents. You can go down the mooring line in perfectly still water only to find a complete change within minutes. The bow is at 24 metres, but it's best to head straight down to the propellers which are at 42 metres. These are heavily encrusted in coral and small sponges. The sides of the hull display good soft coral growth as does what remains of the cabin. There is too much coral cover to make swimming through it easy plus it is occupied by lots of young batfish. Many are being cleaned at the bow where they can shelter from currents.

Above the cabin of the Molas Wreck

◢4 Tanjung Pisok

⏱	**Depth**	20 m
◑	**Visibility**	fair to good
〰	**Currents**	slight
⬯	**Dive type**	shore

A fairly typical coastal dive, this small wall is quite pretty with a sharp drop to about 18-20 metres. There are a lot of soft and black corals dotted along it, interspersed with whip corals and some absolutely enormous barrel sponges. Schooling fish patrol the edges of the reef with Indian Ocean triggers, butterflies, angelfish and coral trout all in abundance. Damselfish keep their babies in tiny caverns on the wall not far from tiny lobsters. Part way along there is some significant damage but the corals are starting to regenerate well. The rubble area seems to attract scorpionfish which are hard to spot.

🌀 So many things to write, so few words

When I was asked to write about my one favourite Manado dive site, I was completely lost and stumped. Just one? I think. Only 400 words? Oh man, so many things to write, so few words. With a skip of a heartbeat I remembered – my all-time favourite. I asked my girlfriend and best dive buddy what she thought and we agreed: this is what we will share.

A mere five minutes away from Cocotinos Resort, the boat glides quickly across to our happy place – Aba Point. A site which combines, muck, reef and wall all into one dive. Patience is a requirement when it comes to the playground of the dark bottom. All is still at first then out pops an eye and feeler from nowhere, and we are confronted by a mantis shrimp. Then it all comes to life, a school of razorfish sliding sideways to the right, a patch of anemone in the desert of black sand guarded by a small family of clownfish. Never belittle these cuties, they bite!

After we frolick for a good 15 minutes at 20 metres, it's time to progress up to 16 metres and the warm welcome of colourful reef activity. Hawkfish perch cautiously on a coral, cuttlefish are suspended in mid-water slithering slowly backwards: this is a great place for a novice photographer. So much to shoot but we always try to save some battery for what may come our way. As far as our eyes can see, the pantones of yellow, red and orange splay out like paint on a canvas. Soft corals sticking from the reef wall from all angles, length and size. This sight never fails to surprise us. We wonder how they got there in the first place; the landscape of corals is simply amazing. By now, the dive has shifted to a comfortable five or eight metres. Sunrays stream through the clear waters. Along with some other divers we suspend ourselves comfortably for this safety stop, enjoying the sights of the marine life below.

The only gripe I have is the amount of rubbish we sometimes witness after an episode of rain. It comes from the villages that are dotted along the river and it is never pleasant to see trash, no matter the amount, in a pristine area like this. Though the good thing about this site is divers don't have to be strapped for too long to reach the dive site in their stifling suits and there is plenty to see without having to go too deep or too long.

Muck diving, reef diving and wall diving are good for all levels, novice and experienced. Many of our underwater photography friends mark this site as mandatory, and needless to say night dives are always a surprise. Yes, Aba is still the all-time favourite.

Andrew Lok, Managing Director, Singapore, & Carlene Cheong, Project Manager, Hong Kong

Bunaken Marine Park

Lying northwest of Manado City is the Bunaken National Marine Park. Established in 1991, the park covers nearly 90,000 hectares of which 97% is sea. The remainder is made up of the islands of Bunaken, Manado Tua, Montehage, Nain and Siladen.

The reefs around all these islands are relatively untouched despite the area being so busy. This is due partly to the steep wall formations that drop rapidly to extremely deep water (1566 metres in Manado Bay). There is good year-round visibility, consistently warm water and some of the highest levels of biodiversity in the world, with impressive levels of coral and fish species. The eye towards conservation is strong and what is within the park boundaries is protected.

↘5 Mike's Point

🕐 **Depth**	17 m	
◐ **Visibility**	good	
〰 **Currents**	slight	
⚓ **Dive type**	day boat	

On the northern side of Bunaken, this long, crescent-shaped wall is decorated by fans and some enormous sponges. The top of the reef breaks the surface at low tide and the current is gentle although it can get strong at times. Adult blacktip sharks pass by in the blue and are followed by masses of schooling fish. Both rainbow runners and pyramid butterflyfish are incredibly common in this area as are Napoleon wrasse, two appearing together at times.

↘6 Sachiko Point

🕐 **Depth**	31 m	
◐ **Visibility**	good	
〰 **Currents**	strong	
⚓ **Dive type**	day boat	

A little way east from Mike's, this wall drops sharply to a few small caves where you can sometimes spot young whitetip sharks or bluespotted rays at rest. Drifting along the wall you pass masses of hard corals and quite a lot of nembrotha nudibranchs. In fact, one minute you spot something really big like a tuna or barracuda then the next it's the opposite as you focus on a much smaller animal such as a coral banded shrimp or even a frogfish.

↘7 Bunaken Timur

🕐 **Depth**	19 m	
◐ **Visibility**	good	
〰 **Currents**	none	
⚓ **Dive type**	day boat	

Around the bend to the east but still on the north side of Bunaken, this long reef has a pretty, flat top that drops off to about 35 metres. The life on the wall is quite similar to Sachiko, but the move around the point seems to attract bigger animals so you need to keep an eye on the blue. There are passing green turtles, a few more whitetips, a Napoleon wrasse and even some eagle rays in the distance. The shallows are very pretty with broad swathes of leather coral that attract dancing anthias and chromis, damsels and juvenile angelfish.

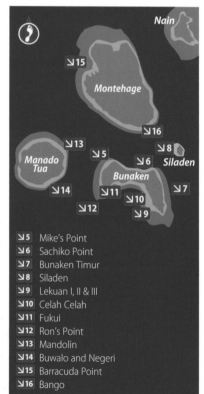

↘5 Mike's Point
↘6 Sachiko Point
↘7 Bunaken Timur
↘8 Siladen
↘9 Lekuan I, II & III
↘10 Celah Celah
↘11 Fukui
↘12 Ron's Point
↘13 Mandolin
↘14 Buwalo and Negeri
↘15 Barracuda Point
↘16 Bango

8 Siladen

◈	**Depth**	17 m
◐	**Visibility**	fair to stunning
≋	**Currents**	none to mild
◡	**Dive type**	day boat

This small island sits a little way north of Bunaken and seems to represent the best of the marine park. It may not be the most exciting of the dives here, it may not get the biggest of the pelagic animals, but the dive is consistently excellent and incredibly beautiful. The sloping reef wall is thick with both hard and soft corals of all species. Out in the blue you might spot a passing eagle ray or a small turtle while the wall itself is coated in ever-present schools of pyramid butterflyfish.

The currents are rarely strong so there is time to pause on the wall and

66 99 It is always great to come back to Siladen. It was our favourite on our first trip here – we have done it many more times over the years – and it still is.

look for smaller creatures. Inside the blue vase sponges are tiny white crabs that are impossible to spot, so stick with your divemaster who will point these out along with other crabs that hide in the folds of soft corals. Scorpionfish hide in these too, their skin textures mimicking the surfaces

around them. A variety of nudibranchs crawl over the wall and can be seen munching on tunicates.

Back up in the shallows, there is hardly a single patch of reef uncoated by the garden of corals. Huge swathes of leather corals compete with brain and staghorns. There are a lot of pink stinging hydroids (shame they're so pretty), untold numbers of anemones and clownfish and many anthias and chromis. Aubergine-toned leaffish appear brightly coloured once photographed.

A big plus for Siladen is that the main resort supports the village and the villagers, who in turn protect the reefs.

Life in the deep
Not even a pretty face

Blobby. Hairy. Lumpy. Prickly. Frogfish come in many shapes and sizes and varying degrees of ugliness. Yet there is something about them that makes them incredibly cute: perhaps it's the way they nestle on the reef then seem to play peek-a-boo with you; or the way they sit up on their little bent arms and legs with their toes splayed? Whatever it is, frogfish are definitely fascinating, if not exactly pretty.

The frogfish family, *antennariidae*, has 12 genera, at least 41 species and one very special feature – their modified dorsal spine which acts as a lure for prey. Mostly referred to as frogfish, 'anglerfish' would probably be a more accurate description of the way they live, act and feed, but that title is reserved for the deep-sea variety of these critters.

Adult frogfish are found right across the tropics and even in Australia's subtropical waters. Ranging in size from just a few centimetres up to 40 cm, they tend to dwell on or close to the sea floor preferring an environment with rocks, coral, seagrass or anything that affords them some sort of camouflage. They are masters of disguise, adapting to whatever is around them. Spotting a tiny orange froggy nestled on an orange finger sponge is hard enough but trying to locate a spotty spotfin frogfish amongst a mess of coral polyps is even more difficult. Others species use their hairy status to wander the seabed looking like nothing more than a bit of flotsam or have skin patterns that mimic a toxic nudibranch to avoid attention.

They also prefer locations that supply a passing array of suitable food. While most fish lie in wait until their prey swims close enough to be grabbed, frogfish strategy is to lure prey into striking range. Their first dorsal spine has adapted into a movable fishing rod (*illicium*) and is tipped with a lure (*esca*). The rods comes in varying lengths while the lure's shape mimics worms, shrimps or small fish. When they see a morsel, they extend their rod, wiggle the lure enticingly until a target comes within striking distance, then, with the fastest 'gape and suck' of any fish, they sucks the prey in whole. This lightening fast action takes just one six-thousandth of a second. Froggies can catch a single fish out of a school without the rest noticing its disappearance and, as they have an expandable stomach, can digest prey that is much larger than themselves.

Frogfish usually sit motionless, waiting for a meal to pass by but the real reason you are unlikely to see one swimming is because most lack a swimbladder. To get around they actually walk or gallop across small distances by sucking in large quantities of water through their mouth then forcing it out through tiny gill openings.

Little is known about mating habits, but it appears that once the female is ready to breed, she will stay with her partner long enough to mate several times. About eight hours before spawning takes place, the female begins to fill up with eggs, swelling to double her normal body size, with her tail up in the air. The male follows her around, nudging her in the abdomen until they make a mad dash to the surface. Thousands of eggs, encapsulated in a buoyant mass of mucus, burst from the female and form an 'egg raft'. For most tropical frogfish parents, their role is over and they return to the seabed. However, some species, including those in cooler waters, show a degree of parental care by guarding their eggs. Meanwhile, the egg raft drifts for several days before sinking back to the sea bottom as the embryos hatch.

Frogfish have descriptive common names ⬊1 painted, lure extended ⬊2 hairy ⬊3 unknown juvenile yawning ⬊4 warty ⬊5 coinbearing ⬊6 and giant frogfish

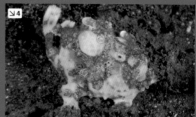

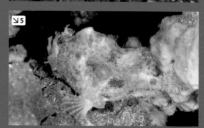

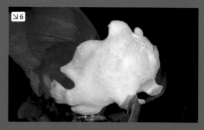

↘9 Lekuan I, II & III

🕐 Depth	25 m
🔅 Visibility	fair to good
🌊 Currents	mild to strong
🌊 Dive type	day boat

The three dives at Lekuan sit along the inner curve of Bunaken's south coast. You could say this is all one dive – if you hit it on a day when the current is really running – but you could just as easily divide it up into the three dives as named. Lekuan means 'curves' or 'bends' and refers to the winding nature of the wall. Dive operators all seem to have a favoured starting point although the topography is quite similar all the way along. The wall consists of a straight drop downwards and is coated in plenty of fans, sponges and soft corals. As you drop towards the bottom there are small caverns where turtles take a break. They often have huge remoras sitting on their shells. After spotting your first one, you seem to keep coming across them, as they swim up and down the wall, rising to the surface for a breath, then coming back down. These guys are in great condition, with pristine, healthy shells. Eagle rays pass by beneath the divers and there are huge schools of midnight snappers. Napoleon wrasse are always about. along with blacktip and whitetip sharks, tuna and pufferfish. When it comes to smaller fish, it's the usual suspects like anthias, damselfish and butterflies.

↘10 Celah Celah

🕐 Depth	21 m
🔅 Visibility	fair to good
🌊 Currents	slight
🌊 Dive type	shore

This wall dive is a little further along from the Lekuans. The name means 'the caves', referring to a series of deep crevices and channels in the reef. The geography is quite impressive and attracts lots of life. Bunaken-based dive centres use this for night dives although all the twists and turns can be quite disorientating in the dark. It can be pretty hard to remember all the things you see: moray eels, lionfish, slipper lobsters, normal lobsters, all sorts of crabs, saron shrimp, sea spiders and seahares. This site is also a known home for the latest pygmy seahorse discovery, the *Hippocampus pontohi*.

↘11 Fukui

🕐 Depth	24 m
🔅 Visibility	fair to good
🌊 Currents	slight
🌊 Dive type	shore

Fukui stands apart from the rest of the sites along Bunaken's southern coast because it actually doesn't have a wall. Instead, the topography here is a more gentle slope leading to a sandy seabed, which is broken by some patches of hard corals and a few short, sharp drops. The site is most famous for five giant clams near the base of the slope. These sit in a row and are much admired, hence the lack of coral that remains around them. Heading back up the slope you pass a colony of garden eels before reaching a series of cleaning stations that attract some big animals: turtles and grouper wait patiently for a spruce up. Giant cuttlefish are seen as well, often in pairs as they use the staghorn coral branches as a safe place to deposit their eggs.

One of Fukui's giant clams; turtle speeding past on Lekuan I

↘12 Ron's Point

⊙ Depth	26 m
◐ Visibility	fair to good
≋ Currents	none to ripping
⊜ Dive type	day boat

Off the western point of Bunaken, Ron's is a sloping wall that leads beyond the corner of the island to a promontory. Dotted with sporadic coral bommies, it is swept by strong currents. The further out you go, the stronger the currents get, and this attract some impressive pelagic action including huge schools of batfish and small schools of jacks. Returning to the slope, an even more exciting find is the *Hippocampus pontohi*, a newly discovered pygmy seahorse. This cute little chap is so small only the best eyes will see him well. Other critters include the false stonefish and a boxfish in turquoise with yellow spots.

❝❞ **More exciting was the *Hippocampus pontohi*, one of the newer pygmy seahorses. Cute little chap, but why is it you always have the wrong lens on the camera?**

↘13 Mandolin

⊙ Depth	34 m
◐ Visibility	good to excellent
≋ Currents	slight to strong
⊜ Dive type	day boat

Situated in the passage between Bunaken and Manado Tua, this is one of the area's more impressive dives. A sharp drop-off leads to a wall completely covered in soft corals and tunicates. It is a riot of colour that almost makes you forget you are underwater. In the depths, there are big gorgonian fans and barrel sponges. Narrow shelves display long whip corals growing out in parallel rows to the light. (Rumour has it that someone once thought these whips looked like mandolin strings.) Turtles and Napoleon wrasse swim past and you find masses of interesting smaller animals such as balls of catfish and white leaffish at the top of the reef. If you spend some time hunting around the bommies, there are orang-utan crabs, robust ghost pipefish, squat lobsters in a crinoid, shrimp in bubble corals and several moray eels including the very beautiful, spotted whitemouth moray.

↘14 Buwalo and Negeri

⊙ Depth	20 m
◐ Visibility	fair to good
≋ Currents	slight to medium
⊜ Dive type	day boat

The conical shape of dormant Manado Tua hovers over the Bunaken landscape and can be seen from almost everywhere in the park and surrounding areas. Its sides lead sharply down to what is possibly the best wall diving in the area. The north coast is swept by strong currents but on the southeast are two fantastic sites: Buwalo and Negeri are beside each other and are more or less the same dive, but both are absolutely stunning. A narrow strip of flat reef drops off to unfathomable depths. The wall is coated in masses of corals and gorgonians. Off in the blue are occasional sharks plus a few small schools of pelagic fish such as jacks and rainbow runners. Up in the shallows you might encounter a sea snake or three, while the very top levels of the reef have blue ribbon eels, red fire gobies, arrow dart gobies, several frogfish, leaffish and even a wary octopus.

Residents of Mandolin: a whitemouth moray and balls of catfish

◥15 Barracuda Point

🔽	**Depth**	25 m
◑	**Visibility**	fair to good
🌊	**Currents**	slight to strong
⬤	**Dive type**	day boat

Less frequently visited than the Bunaken sites, Montehage has a mixed diving reputation. When, it's good it's very, very good, but when it's not, well, draw your own conclusions. On the very top of the island, the reef at Barracuda Point is flat and swept by strong currents. At times these become aggressive up and down currents which attract a variety of pelagic species. If the currents are running, divers fin madly out to the point to see them and it can be quite an effort. At times, there are schools of barracudas accompanied by reef sharks and jacks. At other times, the reef can seem uninteresting but there are still some good things to see as long as you poke around a little. Under the small hard corals may be cowrie shells, a pair of lizardfish, bluespotted rays, blue ribbon eels, a wary cuttlefish laying eggs and even a young whitetip or two.

◥16 Bango

🔽	**Depth**	24 m
◑	**Visibility**	fair to good
🌊	**Currents**	slight to strong
⬤	**Dive type**	day boat

The village of Bango is on the southern tip of Montehage. The sloping reef that runs away from the village is a surprise as it is so very different to the dive at Barracuda Point. Completely covered in soft corals, this is a very lush reef and very colourful. At times, the top is exposed but that doesn't seem affect the growth adversely and, as current is usually mild, you can spend time hunting about for smaller critters. The *Chromodoris kunei* nudibranch is often spotted in gangs of half a dozen or more.

A jack on a mission; hard corals at Manado Tua

Bangka

At the very top of Sulawesi, just a short distance from Bunaken, is another cluster of gorgeous, coral-ringed islands. Bangka and her neighbours, Gangga and Talise, are now popular dive destinations despite being outside the marine park boundaries.

The diving here can be a little more challenging as these islands lie in an exposed position and are in the direct path of currents that rush down the north and in from the Pacific. This attracts some bigger pelagic species and both hard and soft corals are outstanding. However, there are some protected dives that extend from pretty, white sand beaches that are good for gentle drifts.

Indonesia Dive log North Sulawesi: Bangka

↘17 Sahaong

Depth	33 m
Visibility	good to excellent
Currents	mild to strong
Dive type	day boat

On the southeastern side of Bangka, this site is marked by an underwater pinnacle that dramatically breaks the surface. The surge and currents can be highly challenging but the landscape beneath the water makes this dive unmissable. Dropping down to the wall, you pass a phenomenal number of schooling fish. The current is doing a bit of a dance up and down the wall attracting a school of midnight snappers in from the blue until a whitetip shark buzzes the base of the column and they take off only to be replaced by some rainbow runners. After

some time on the pinnacle watching all the schooling fish, you swim upwards to a plateau covered in huge step-like boulders with everything carpeted in the most stunning soft corals. The whole thing is a riot of colour, glowing in tones of red, orange and yellow. A little further around the bend, you encounter a whip coral, thick with waving razorfish, then a tiny fan, which has an even tinier pygmy seahorse on it. The smaller creatures add a bit of scale to all the big things around. The ledge is great for a safety stop and down on the surfaces there are scorpionfish, rays and morays tucked into crevices.

↘18 Tanjung Sepia

Depth	18 m
Visibility	good to excellent
Currents	mild
Dive type	day boat

True to its name, this shallower and calmer site is home to many cuttlefish. As soon as you enter the water you are likely to find several of these delightful, shy creatures as they hover over the corals, adapting their body colours in an attempt not to be seen. Adults and juveniles live on the fringes of the reef, a slope marked by ridges of coral followed by depressions with sandy bottoms. The dive is also known for its resident frogfish. In one section a green frogfish sits within a few feet of another in pure black. The green chap was disturbed by the divers and took off from his perch, lurching through the water before finally settling on another sponge that was a perfect match to his skin. It was fantastic to see the lumbering movement, especially when he got to his second home and did a few circuits, like a cat fluffing up a pillow.

↘17	Sahaong
↘18	Tanjung Sepia
↘19	Batu Gosoh
↘20	Lehaga

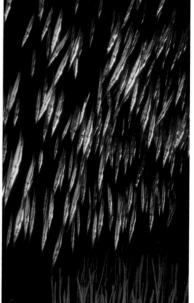

Soft coral clad walls at Bangka; razorfish huddled in a throng

↘19 Batu Gosoh

🌀	**Depth**	20 m
◑	**Visibility**	good to excellent
🌊	**Currents**	mild to strong
🌓	**Dive type**	day boat

Not dissimilar to the Sahaong, this site is a series of pinnacles with lots of angular rock formations. The currents can be strong here too, but the dive is a little easier as there are more places to shelter. Again, all the surfaces are covered with small, colourful soft corals although these are interspersed with tunicates and small sponges. Along with the usual schools of snappers and Indian Ocean triggers; there are a lot of sweetlips and lionfish – even the spotfin lionfish.

↘20 Lehaga, Gangga

🌀	**Depth**	45 m
◑	**Visibility**	good to excellent
🌊	**Currents**	mild to medium
🌓	**Dive type**	day boat

On the western side of Gangga island, this dive is quite a contrast to those around Bangka. A completely flat reef runs parallel to the island and drops away to sand on either side. The current can be strong but mostly this is a gentle drift dive spent looking for the smaller creatures. There are plenty of anemones demonstrating their commensal nature: you can find shrimp, porcelain crabs and clownfish in most. There are more commensal relationships to observe:, gobies with their partner shrimps on the sand and sea cucumbers with little crabs beneath.

Porcelain crab nestled in an anemone

66 99 After lurching across the bay, this frogfish jumped onto his new perch and did a few circuits, just like a cat fluffing up a pillow.

Sangihe Talaud

This is real frontier territory: the Sangihe Talaud islands stretch away from Indonesia to clutch at the Philippines and, despite being first colonized back in the 1670s by the Dutch, foreign tourists are still novel enough for every child – and a good number of adults – to turn out and greet visiting divers. Wander around a village with an assortment of 7-8 year olds in tow: the younger ones are too shy and the older ones too cool for that sort of thing, but barriers soon tumble when bags of sweets come out to be shared.

The landscapes and welcome are typical of Indonesia but what distinguishes these dives from the rest of Northern Sulawesi is the islands distinct volcanic formation. The chain is part of the Pacific Ring of Fire and has several very active volcanoes. Plus it sits right at the top end of the Indonesian Flowthrough current pattern (see page 54). These waters can be as very challenging to dive as the dramatic, rocky underwater vistas reflect those of the landscape above. Pinnacles and slopes are carpeted in a colourful display of marine life, all fighting the odds against such relatively harsh conditions.

Most liveaboards target the stunning islands of Biaro and Ruang. Schedules are tailored to the conditions of the day. If you manage to reach the top of the chain there is even a dive site at a bubbling underwater volcano.

⬐21 Bomb Rock

◷	**Depth**	33 m
◑	**Visibility**	good
≋	**Currents**	strong
⬲	**Dive type**	liveaboard

The topography of this site is as dramatic as they come. Dropping into the water beneath the cliff wall of Biaro's northeast face, you discover a steep pinnacle that is painted in the most incredibly colourful array of life. Small cup corals compete with tunicates for space. It's all so tightly packed you can't find a space for a finger in between, but if you look closely there are plenty of colourful nudibranchs lurking there. The pinnacle can be swept by strong currents, but you can hide on the lee side. Its sloping base is covered with hard corals that attract Napoleon wrasse and whitetip sharks.

⬐22 Sweetlip City

◷	**Depth**	21 m
◑	**Visibility**	good
≋	**Currents**	strong
⬲	**Dive type**	liveaboard

True to its name, this shallow site is home to many sweetlips. Just a short sail north of Bomb Rock, the dive is also subjected to strong currents and is often done as a drift. However, it is a very beautiful site, loaded with swaying softs corals and giant gorgonians that are swarmed by masses of schooling fish. Moray eels poke noses out of the reef. Turtles are common and truly enormous reminding you that these are senior citizens of the ocean. Many have remoras attached to their shells. More Napoleons arrive on the scene and you wonder if they have followed you up from the previous dive.

⬐25 Pasige · Tagulandang
⬐24
⬐23
Biaro · ⬐22
⬐21
Talise
Bangka

⬐21	Bomb Rock
⬐22	Sweetlip City
⬐23	The Labyrinth
⬐24	Old Lava Flow
⬐25	Serenade's Secret

↘23 The Labyrinth

🕐	**Depth**	55 m
🌓	**Visibility**	fair to good
🌊	**Currents**	strong
🌊	**Dive type**	liveaboard

Although billed as a shallow dive for the end of the day, it's easy to head a little too deep on this one because the nature of the Labyrinth leads you down deeper than you intended. The site lies off the northern tip of Biaro and the topography is quite unusual: a series of volcanic flows are divided by a maze of channels that rise and fall by around two metres. As you drop to the seafloor, you avoid some of the currents that rush around and can spend more time investigating the sections with plate and staghorn corals. These are interspersed with long whip corals and pastel-toned fans. Small fish flit about, using the fans for protection, while morays seem to enjoy swaying in the currents and perhaps waiting for a meal to snap at. Groups of batfish, jacks and tuna make occasional appearances in the blue.

↘24 Old Lava Flow

🕐	**Depth**	25 m
🌓	**Visibility**	fair
🌊	**Currents**	slight
🌊	**Dive type**	liveaboard

After the lively dives around Biaro, it can be a relief to head up to Ruang: usually if one island is swept by currents the other is reasonably calm. The most popular site is Lava Flow, but there are now two sites that bear this name, new and old. Ruang is an active volcano about four kilometres across and rising 725 metres into the air. There have been 14 eruptions recorded since 1808, the most recent in the mid-90s and then again in 2002. You can see the swathe of devastation left when lava poured down the side of the cone and into the sea below. Old Lava Flow is the dive beside the 1996 eruption and is quite something to see: on one side there is nothing but stark black sand and rocks, while the reef to other side is completely undamaged. The marine life seems to thrive on this, corals are good and there are orang-utan cabs, clownfish in their anemones, moray eels, masses of schooling butterflies and gorgonians decorated like christmas trees by crinoids.

↘25 Serenade's Secret

🕐	**Depth**	21 m
🌓	**Visibility**	fair to good
🌊	**Currents**	slight
🌊	**Dive type**	liveaboard

Named after, and by, the first liveaboard in this region, this dive soon becomes a favourite. Although the currents can chop and change the conditions tend to be less aggressive and there is time to enjoy the pretty underwater landscape. A gentle slope drops down to a small wall and the entire area is covered in an almost pristine reef. It's a stark contrast to the dive at Lava Flow. One moment you will see a large pelagic like a Napoleon wrasse, then a substantial school of barracuda, the next it's focusing on the incredible numbers of reef fish – lionfish, titan triggers, large and small scorpions and lizardfish. Then there are crustaceans – lobsters, mantis shrimp, crinoid shrimp and, in the sand, goby and shrimp partnerships – before you move on to large golden morays and the tiniest of white stonefish. This also one of those rare dives where you are likely to see the *Notodoris minor* nudibranch. This chap comes in sunflower yellow and grows to 14 centimetres long so is hard to miss.

Reef residents in Sangihe vary from unusual nudibranchs to sweetlips and lionfish while curious cuttlefish try to remain unseen

Lembeh Straits

While many places like to claim they are best of this or that, world famous, world class, there is no doubt that this small stretch of water is actually the best at what it is: a muck diving paradise. The Lembeh Straits deliver what they promise. This is the destination for seeing the weird, unusual and normally unseen marine critters.

KUNGKUNGAN BAY RESORT

The dark waters that divide Lembeh island from the Sulawesi coast have become a must for marine biology enthusiasts and underwater photographers. This narrow channel is riddled with dive sites fed by rich volcanic nutrients. It is by no means pretty diving –visibility is always low – but it is one of the few places where you can be guaranteed to see of some of the world's most unusual animals. You really can say "seahorse" to a divemaster and they will ask "what type?" Although muck diving made the area's reputation there is also some nice wall diving and a handful of Second World War era wrecks.

Many of these sites were discovered by legendary divemaster Larry Smith. He believed in this region and it's people, so ensured that a group of local young men were trained to be divemasters. Many of his original team still work in the area and

their fantastic spotting skills are a credit to their mentor. Look out for these guys: some are mentioned in the dive descriptions because they will make your diving day.

Dive sites have a recurring theme of dark sand bays that sit below coastal walls. Occasionally, the topography is different, which is noted in the following dive logs, but otherwise take it for granted that most of your time will be spent hovering over a black, sloping seabed that shelves gently down to around 30 metres. Sometimes there will be a short wall, but mostly you will be inspecting old cans and coconut shells, lengths of rope or tree trunks for whatever gem they are hiding.

For many years there was just one resort but, with the region's ever growing popularity, there are now several first-class resorts as well as a few that are aimed at those on a more restricted budget.

⬂1	**Police Pier**	
🌀	**Depth**	21 m
◐	**Visibility**	fair
〰	**Currents**	slight
⬭	**Dive type**	day boat

As its name implies this site lies below the pier used by the police. A gentle slope is covered with alternating patches of algae, sponges and piles of rubble. It is one of the best dives for thorny seahorses which use finger sponges as their home patch. Likewise, masses of frogfish utilize small rounded sponges. It's hard to remember how many small froggies you have seen, as there are so many different shapes and sizes. At night, there is a variety of shells, snake eels in the sand, decorator crabs, squat lobsters, dragonets, tiny bobtail squid or banded seasnake. Banggai cardinalfish are common too, despite being indigenous to the Banggai islands some way south. The story goes that a fisherman had a cargo hold of them bound (illegally) for the aquarium trade. The police got wind of this and pulled the captain over to the pier. He moored up and promptly dropped his cargo into the sea, and of course the Banggais colonized right where they were dropped.

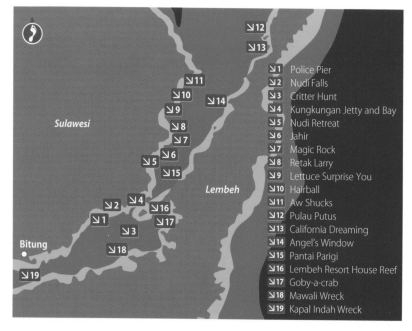

⬂1	Police Pier
⬂2	Nudi Falls
⬂3	Critter Hunt
⬂4	Kungkungan Jetty and Bay
⬂5	Nudi Retreat
⬂6	Jahir
⬂7	Magic Rock
⬂8	Retak Larry
⬂9	Lettuce Surprise You
⬂10	Hairball
⬂11	Aw Shucks
⬂12	Pulau Putus
⬂13	California Dreaming
⬂14	Angel's Window
⬂15	Pantai Parigi
⬂16	Lembeh Resort House Reef
⬂17	Goby-a-crab
⬂18	Mawali Wreck
⬂19	Kapal Indah Wreck

Sulawesi

Lembeh

Bitung

Adult Banggai cardinalfish

N2 Nudi Falls

🌀	**Depth**	27 m
🌓	**Visibility**	fair
🌊	**Currents**	slight
⬯	**Dive type**	day boat

Named after the plethora of nudibranchs found here, this site consists of a small wall sitting beneath a coastal cliff which leads down to a sand and rubble slope. The descending seabed can seem fairly barren until you reach a broad swathe of soft corals in lots of pretty pastels. Nestled in amongst them is a rhinopias. He's a well known resident and appears to be a lacy, displaying all the incredible patterns and markings of the *Rhinopias frondosa*. There are masses of other animals as well, like pygmy seahorses, sangian crabs, winged pipefish, dendronephthya crabs, filefish, porcupine pufferfish, the tiniest ever cuttlefish (about the size of a pea) and, of course, there are masses and masses of nudibranchs in all shapes and sizes.

N3 Critter Hunt

🌀	**Depth**	26 m
🌓	**Visibility**	fair
🌊	**Currents**	slight
⬯	**Dive type**	day boat

The tree-covered mound of Sarena Kecil, or Small Island, sits between Lembeh and the coast and is home to one of the straits' best night dives. Entry is over a bare sandy slope that leads down to a rubbly area. This is a surprisingly prolific dive for sand dwellers and creatures that slide over the seabed in search of their early evening meal. Seahares, which are rarely seen by day, are out and grazing, as are a variety of unusual urchins, like the pretty but poisonous flower urchin. All sorts of decorator crabs freeze under the beam of a torch. Tiny black corals protrude from the sand and should be inspected for the *Tozeuma armatum*, a tiny shrimp that lives on their branches.

N4 Kungkungan Jetty and Bay

🌀	**Depth**	12 m
🌓	**Visibility**	good
🌊	**Currents**	slight
⬯	**Dive type**	Shore

This most celebrated of dive sites was the first in the area and is still one of the most fascinating. It is unlikely you will get to dive it unless you stay at the resort though this hardly matters as all the animals can be seen elsewhere. However, the fun thing about being under this jetty is the way that it is a microcosm of much the Straits' life. The list of finds is never-ending, every surface is home to something amazing and, because it is so shallow, dives can seem almost endless. Most divers will have a favourite tale and ours would be the day that we watched our divemaster, Wilson, tapping a rock against his hand. Back on the jetty we asked why he was so upset with the rock and he replied with much frustration that he had seen a blue-ringed octopus crawl inside and was trying to get it out for us to take a photograph.

N5 Nudi Retreat

🌀	**Depth**	32 m
🌓	**Visibility**	good
🌊	**Currents**	slight
⬯	**Dive type**	day boat

The reef inside this small, protected cove is a very pretty one and, because it has a mix of coral and muck diving, is one of the most popular. All the divemasters like to ask for your 'critter order' in advance as the chances of finding most stuff here is very good. The dive starts by a small wall which is covered in masses of coral, both hard and soft. Some of the boulders that have dropped down from the cliff face are smothered in tiny soft corals. The area in front is known for its resident pegasus seamoths and you can see them mating at times. Descending down the sand slope there are minute cockatoo waspfish, the very ugly inimicus (devilfish), harlequin crabs and orang-utan crabs, morays and nudibranchs. At the top there are leaffish, clown frogfish, fingered dragonets and fire flame shells nestled into the cracks in some of the rocks.

The *Rhinopias frondosa* is often seen at Nudi Falls

6 Jahir

Depth	16 m
Visibility	fair
Currents	none to medium
Dive type	day boat

Jahir is one of the divemasters' favourites – in fact the name is made up of the initials of those who found it and is one amazing dive. It's a fabulous hop from one 'pet critter' to the next; so much so that a dive log report is very likely to look like a fish ID list. Here is just one of ours from a single dive: cockatoo waspfish, juvenile cuttlefish, dwarf scorpions, juvenile scorpions, tiny stonefish, thorny seahorses, mating crabs, hairy crabs, decorator crabs, flying gurnards, flounder, frogfish in many hues and varieties, *Inimicus* (or devilfish), robust ghost pipefish and a Pegasus seamoth.

All these are seen regularly and on most dives. At night the site gets even better as you see creatures you met in the daylight plus nocturnal ones that have emerged – free-swimming snake eels, moon snails and tiny shells trucking across the sand, and masses of crabs.

There are also a few special events. This is a known nursery site for flamboyant cuttlefish. You can see newly laid eggs inside discarded coconut shells and eggs: even a just-hatched baby. Jahir is also a good spot for the mimic octopus. As you catch it in a torch beam it will go into party-trick mode and become a flounder, a crinoid or a snake eel.

66 99 Much of what is great about the Lembeh Straits can be summed up in a dive such as this one.

☑7 Magic Rock

🕐	**Depth**	23 m
◐	**Visibility**	fair
〰	**Currents**	can be very strong
⊖	**Dive type**	day boat

Sitting in open water in the channel, this site was one of Larry Smith's favourites as it was the one where he could position his guests on the sand and point out critter after critter, watching the amazement on their faces. Larry called it the 'Mermaid's Manicure'. His list of sightings included ornate ghost pipefish, banded pipefish, crocodilefish, flounders, masses of shrimp (including those cleaner's that will hop on any hand held out to them and clean the fingernail), squat lobsters, mantis shrimp, clownfish on anemones, seapens with tiny swimming crabs sitting on them and so much more.

☑8 Retak Larry

🕐	**Depth**	18 m
◐	**Visibility**	poor to fair
〰	**Currents**	none
⊖	**Dive type**	day boat

This dive is another of Larry's discoveries. Entry is over a patch of coral with two frogfish sitting there awaiting admirers. As you head down over the slope there are robust ghost pipefish. At the bottom, where it gets murky, a ball of catfish add to the lack of visibility by stirring up the silt. However, it's still easy to spot masses of critter life: a flying gurnard, fingered dragonets, a bright yellow seahorse, a snake eel with a load of shrimp around him, then another. If you start the dive from the other side you will probably run into a resident seahorse or two, some pufferfish, more frogfish – both hairy and non – pairs of inimicus, loads of peacock flounders, the incredible solar powered nudibranch and even lizardfish eating a butterflyfish.

☑9 Lettuce Surprise You

🕐	**Depth**	16 m
◐	**Visibility**	poor to fair
〰	**Currents**	none
⊖	**Dive type**	day boat

One of Larry's favourite dives, this bowl-shaped bay is completely covered in delicate lettuce corals. Layer upon layer of these leafy, pale green hard corals deny visual access to the seabed so this site is unique in the Straits. A few enormous clams break through the 'foliage' to display their beautifully coloured and patterned insides. There are some fish flitting about, including filefish and cardinals, but what makes it so interesting is that it is also a fantastic site for spotting breathtaking, elusive mandarinfish at dusk. The channel that leads away from the bay also has beautiful hard corals.

☑10 Hairball

🕐	**Depth**	25 m
◐	**Visibility**	poor to fair
〰	**Currents**	none
⊖	**Dive type**	day boat

Perhaps the muckiest of the Straits' muck dives, and one that has the reputation for being most surprising as the animals have developed many ways to remain hidden – except from the divemasters. The seabed is fairly level with only black sand in every direction. There is a lot of fine silt (watch your buoyancy!) and almost no landmarks but it is the place to go to find hairy critters. Some grow skin filaments so they can hide in small patches of algae; others use the muck or each other. Fire urchins reveal zebra crabs while other crabs carry urchins on their backs. A tiny octopus will have his eyes poking out of a tin, a snake eel has a shrimp living on his nose and a coconut crab will be wrapped in three clam shells. And then there are the hairy creatures: frogfish that are fishing constantly, the small Ambon scorpionfish who is even harder to spot and hairy ghost pipefish.

☑11 Aw Shucks

🕐	**Depth**	18 m
◐	**Visibility**	fair
〰	**Currents**	slight
⊖	**Dive type**	day boat

Although just above Hairball, this site is quite different, with a small, patchy coral reef that leads along the coast. There are some very good corals which supplied another of our favourite tales. Semuel, our divemaster, came rushing over, indicating how excited he was and that we must follow. Two cuttlefish were performing some mating rituals, while a secondary male was trying to muscle in on the act. He moved away when disturbed by the voyeuristic divers and we settled to watch the now calm couple. A few moments later the female decided to release her eggs, gently swimming in and out of the staghorn and carefully positioning each egg case deep in the branches. The three of us sat at six metres till our tanks were out of air. Of course, there is much more here: mushroom corals have tiny commensal white pipefish, there are clingfish nestled in crinoids and masses of fantastic nudibranchs crawl on the sand.

Our first ever ornate ghost pipefish, Magic Rock

↘12 Pulau Putus

Depth	18 m
Visibility	fair to good
Currents	slight
Dive type	day boat

Heading to the top of Lembeh to dive is a bit of a hit and miss affair as the seas at the northern tip of the island are often rough. This site though is usually reliable as it is inside a small bay on the tiny island of Pulau Putus. The bay is protected from stronger currents. Dropping in over a bed of hard corals, you can fin along the wall, which is equally well covered in coral and barrel sponges. Sometimes, after a few minutes, you will glimpse eagle or manta rays but they don't stay around for very long. Back at the boat you find a lot of inquisitive young batfish.

↘13 California Dreaming

Depth	18 m
Visibility	fair
Currents	slight to strong
Dive type	day boat

Just south of Putus is this open water seamount. It can be choppy here but the underwater scenery is worth it as there are two peaks to explore that are linked by a flatter area. Dives usually start on the steeper wall that drops to over 40 metres and shelves back to 20. The soft corals are very impressive, covering the surface with rainbows of different shades: reds and oranges through to mauves and pale blue. There are a lot of pristine hard corals too and some nice fans all surrounded by plenty of fish. Near the end of the dive, you come across the cut through the reef and about halfway along a giant froggy sits in a pale blue elephant's ear sponge.

↘14 Angel's Window

Depth	24 m
Visibility	fair to good
Currents	slight to strong
Dive type	day boat

This is such a pretty dive, with so much variety you can understand why it is one of the most popular. Also based around a pinnacle with two peaks, and linked by a sandslope, the visibility can be around 15 metres, which is not bad for the Strait. At times the currents can become strong, especially across the sandy area, but there are plenty of places to get away from it. The plan is always the same: descend over the wall then go down to the cave – the Angel's Window – and through to the base of the pinnacle. There are fans on either side of the exit and these have the barbiganti pygmy seahorse on one and the miniature Denise pygmy on the other. Ascending past these, you can spend some time on the slope. There are small patches of coral and some rocks so look around these for leaffish, orang-utan crabs, imperial shrimp, whip corals and their resident gobies and crabs. There are even squid eggs on the sand. Around the bend of the reef there is another small wall where the corals are really pretty. This leads to a rocky section that is covered in a purple hue – this is made by sergeant major eggs and there are untold sergeant majors trying to defend their eggs against the onslaught of butterflyfish. (Curiously, this has been happened on every dive we have done here across a period of 12 years). Huge scorpionfish also perch on these boulders.

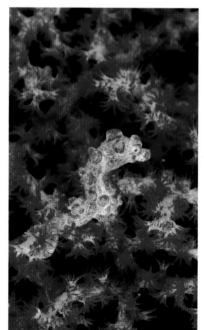

Whip coral shrimp and pygmy seahorse on a fan at Angel's Window; California giant frogfish

Ⓢⱼⱽ15 Pantai Parigi

🌀	**Depth**	18 m
◔	**Visibility**	fair to good
≋	**Currents**	slight
⬯	**Dive type**	day boat

Well Water Beach is another great dive that stands out a little from the others in the Straits as the sand here is actually a pale beige rather than volcanic dark grey. The bay extends from the beach down to about 18 metres, with few topographical features other than a tangle of ropes and some logs. However, every tiny feature has something of interest: a squat lobster sits on the fronds of a lonely crinoid, and seapens are smothered in crabs and shrimp. A tube worm about 10 centimetres across manages to shelter five dwarf lionfish. A small hollow in the sand has some corals in it, and beneath that is a ball of catfish and a moray trying to remain hidden. Another large brown frogfish sits nearby on the seabed and then you spot another tiny black one sitting alone in the middle of nowhere. The tangled ropes are covered in new sponges and tiny crusting corals, and the dive guides hunt between them to find more frogfish that are so small you wonder how they spot them. They are various colours: orange, beige and cream. Once your eyes adjust to this, you can swim along the rope watching for more, even smaller, ones. Pantai Parigi is also the site where divemaster, Abner, performs his party trick of enticing Wonderpus out of his whole in the sand . What a gorgeous little octopus this is – all long gangly legs and beautiful stripes that he uses as best he can to appear invisible, and not even faintly succeeding as there is nothing to hide in or mimic.

Wonderpus sliding across Pantai Parigi; the soft coral crab, *Hoplophrys oatesii,* which lives on *Dendronephthya* soft corals, California Dreaming; playful mantis shrimp on the sandslope at Angel's Window

Indonesia Dive log North Sulawesi: Lembeh Straits

↘16 Lembeh Resort House Reef

🕐	**Depth**	12 m
◐	**Visibility**	fair
〰	**Currents**	none
⬳	**Dive type**	shore

Just in front of Lembeh Resort, this house reef is as impressive as Kungkungan's, and like it, is mostly reserved for residents. You can wander in off the shore at any time of day as a system of buoys directs divers past all the highlights of this magical reef. In the shallows are some seagrass beds that are alive with small critters like filefish and nudibranchs. Then, descending slowly to around eight metres, you encounter some patches of coral. These include a lot of staghorn, and depending on what time of day you go, there are some truly fantastic residents in and beneath their branches. Most popular are the mandarinfish, which can be seen by day and at dusk when they emerge from the shadows of the coral branches to feed and mate. Large males flit to and fro to find a female, and when they do, they commence their mating ritual. Another unusual find is the sailfin waspfish, but even more exciting are the pairs of tiger tail seahorses who wrap their tales around the staghorn. At 15 metres there are now some reef balls which are attracting more creatures.

↘17 Goby-a-crab

🕐	**Depth**	19 m
◐	**Visibility**	fair to good
〰	**Currents**	none
⬳	**Dive type**	day boat

Named after the proliferation of crab-eyed gobies found here, this site surrounds a small rocky point that juts out from the coast of Lembeh. The reef is typical of the area, with a small wall dropping to the sandy slope. There is quite an impressive spread of corals and sponges with lots of good critters: a tiny scorpion fish, sangian crabs, dendronephthya crabs and both the thumbcracker and spearing mantis shrimp. The sand slope at the beginning has crabs on whip corals, squat lobsters and shrimps on crinoids and, of course, there are many, many crab-eyed gobies. The most popular highlights include several pygmy seahorses on fans and the huge schools of razorfish that hover over the corals in the shallows.

↘18 Mawali Wreck

🕐	**Depth**	30 m
◐	**Visibility**	fair
〰	**Currents**	can be strong
⬳	**Dive type**	day boat

Named after a nearby village, this Second World War Japanese cargo ship lies on her side at 35 metres. At 75 metres long, she is a substantial vessel with lots to investigate as she is intact and heavily overgrown. A typical dive involves dropping down to the propeller then swimming around the hull, up to the engine rooms then finally through a couple of the holds to the top facing side. The surfaces are completely smothered in life, mostly soft corals and sponges, but some huge hard corals have grown in on the edges, facing into the current. Around the hull are loads of fans, schools of batfish, plenty of schooling fish, barramundi cod, mantis shrimp, large scorpionfish, small cuttlefish and more nudibranch varieties than you will ever have time to admire.

↘19 Kapal Indah Wreck

🕐	**Depth**	27 m
◐	**Visibility**	fair
〰	**Currents**	can be strong
⬳	**Dive type**	day boat

This cargo boat is about 45 metres long and lies upright on its keel just off the coastal reef. Not much is known about the boat but it has been underwater for close to 50 years and is now completely overgrown with marine life. Because of this, the focus tends to be as much about what you see on it as the vessel itself. There are simply masses of critters hiding out in the corals: ghost pipefish, leaffish and all the critters found on whip corals. Colourful crinoids are full to bursting with their commensal friends and there are nudibranchs everywhere you look. The small reef is a good spot for a safety stop as there are also plenty of other things to discover there too.

Mating mandarins on Lembeh Resort's House Reef; the Mawali wreck

The biggest footprint
In memory of Larry Smith

When we first met Larry, we were just baby divers, arriving at brand new resort in an unknown area. We had no idea what to expect. He sat us on his arms – one on each side – swam along the channel to Magic Rock and, with that classic Smith twinkle, nodded towards a crinoid. There it was... our first ever ornate ghost pipefish.

We dived with Larry many times after that. He is there amongst our best ever dive memories: introducing us to our first zebra crabs and pygmy seahorses; teaching Shaun how to talk to cuttlefish to get that perfect photo; taking me on a special night dive for my birthday to see a whole firework explosion of flashlight fish. And as time went on, he stayed with us, looking out for us as we travelled the world, introducing us to people, helping and advising as we wrote our first book.

He was the world's best spotter, able to cruise around a reef and point out the most amazing critters to whoever was close by. It was such fun to see a diver's mask raised to his, full to bursting with astounded eyes. He would just know that the diver was thinking, "how the hell did he see THAT!" And you could pass by smirking, knowing you had been exactly the same the first time he took you on a dive.

Then there were the times when he used to gather the group onto a patch of barren seabed, get out his radio aerial and start tapping the ground. Did anyone ever know you could tame a mantis shrimp before you saw Larry getting them to do cartwheels?

He was also a consummate professional, running dive centres and liveaboards like clockwork, managing crews and guests with a firm hand but a friendly one.

Taking time to reflect on the man though, we have started to see past these obvious memories, delightful though they are. What sits strongest for us was seeing his amazing capacity to look at the people he came into contact with and turn that moment into something special. Larry had a singular capacity to instinctively know where the dive, the day, lay for them.

For me, it was all about the reef. He recognized my drive to understand the sea even before I knew it myself. He was an amazing teacher, the person who instilled in me the deep love for knowing what makes a reef work.

For Shaun, it was his willingness to understand the requirements of a fledgling underwater photographer, taking the time to encourage, looking out for the best of subjects and helping to ensure that moment was captured.

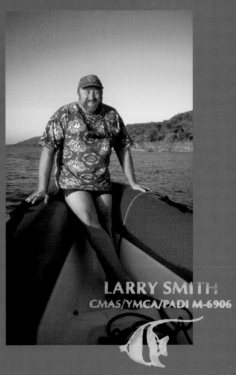

As time went on, he was instrumental in our joining the ranks of dive journalists, always keeping tabs on us, introducing us to people he knew we could work with. Some of our dearest friends came from this relationship and it's funny to think it all comes from just one accidental moment in time – when we were passing through Manado and heard about a new resort. Kungkungan Bay wasn't even properly open when fate took us there and we crossed paths with this one incredible man.

We saw Larry and his lovely wife, Dewi, shortly before he died. We gossiped for ages, caught up, compared notes. We joked how our mutual red locks were heading towards grey and realized we were starting to look like siblings! As he was leaving, he took hold of our book and said, "Wow, guys, just look at you now". He said he was so proud of us and to have had a small part to play in our lives and careers. Larry, you played a huge part in our lives and we hope we thanked you enough.

LARRY SMITH
CMAS/YMCA/PADI M-6906

Temperatures rising **Gorontalo**

❝❞ Among Gorontalo's unique sights are massive Salvadór Dalí sponges with their radically carved surfaces.

The distinctive and unusual shape of Sulawesi island was created by four peninsulas: the Semenanjung Minahasa, the East, South and Southeast. Manado sits at the very northeastern tip of the island in North Sulawesi province, but head westwards along the arm-shaped peninsula to Gorontalo province and you will find a whole new – and barely explored – dive region.

If you are looking for somewhere away from the diver crowds, head to the city of Gorontalo. This small city sits on the edge of picturesque Tomini Bay, where deep blue waters drop to over 4,000 metres. The coastal landscapes are of towering limestone cliffs which rise vertically from the sea. These walls are highly eroded and lead beneath the waterline, past a narrow coral shelf, to some highly complex underwater rock formations. There are dramatic walls full of holes and crevasses, buttresses and deep chutes all falling to a depth of 30 metres or so. The walls stop at a second sloping shelf which then leads to another sharp drop that goes far beyond dive limits.

For divers there is masses to see along these little-dived walls. Diversity is typical of the region and fish life is similar to the Manado area, but one of the most unusual features of the bay is said to be the diverse varieties of sponges including what has become known as a Salvadór Dalí sponge – *Petrosia lignosa* – for its surreal carved surface. The sponges from this species seen locally are far more distinctively patterned than those in other parts of Indonesia. Tomini Bay also contains more than 500 species of hard corals including an estimated 77 species of *Acropora* corals, three of which are endemic. Other endemic species include a little white mantis shrimp and the beautiful Orange-back wrasse, *Cirrhilabrus aurantidorsalis,* which was only named in 1999. The newly discovered Togean dottyback, *Pseudochromis sp.,* is also endemic to Gorontalo and the Togean Islands due south, while a new Coleman's coral shrimp *(Vir colemani),* named in December 2003 is common.

There are plenty of large animals too. Because of the depth of the sea, many cetacean species are known to pass along this wall within a short distance of the coastline. Bryde's whales, False killer whales and pods of ghostly Risso's dolphin have been seen.

Gorontalo was once a long bus ride from Manado, but is now easily reached with flights to the new Jalaluddin airport from both Manado and Makassar. The majority of dive sites are all within 15 minutes or so of the coast and the farthest site is just one hour away.

The Gorontalo season is November to April. In the other months, winds make surface conditions unreliable, see miguelsdiving.com.

⊘ Tales from the deep

The scenario before me seemed wrong. A colourful deep sea Nautilus shell appeared strikingly out of place against the dull muck bottom in Gorontalo. In jerky motions, it moved not backwards as expected, but forwards away from me. My computer read a depth of only eight metres, so hallucination from narcosis was ruled out. The logical answer would be an injured Nautilus having trouble returning to its deep ocean home. As I approached, its movements halted and the shell collapsed onto the sand bottom. I couldn't help bursting into laughter after a closer look – a different Cephalopod, namely a coconut octopus, had taken residence in a discarded Nautilus shell and was towing this trade-up home wherever it went.

Rantje Allen, the operator of Miguel's Diving, was quite right when he told me that Gorontalo has a bit of everything. Where else can you explore a mysterious cavern or a historic wreck, tour multiple pinnacles and then dive a dramatic coral wall or do muck – all in the same day? Each of my four trips holds special memories: a cleaner shrimp groping clumsily for parasites inside the jaw of a female ribbon eel, a squadron of mobula rays passing in the blue, eight pairs of rare bumblebee shrimp found in a single dive. A number of my images include unknown creatures and unheard of behaviour patterns that baffle scientists.

Among the unique sights in Gorontalo are massive Salvadór Dalí sponges with radically carved surfaces, the pulsating polyps of the dainty powder-blue fan at the edge of a deep blue abyss, the plumes of Foxtail tunicates in gloomy overhangs. New discoveries and tales of annual visiting whalesharks and beaked whales that swim close to shore to feed on nike minnows and yellow-fin tuna make me eager to return to this newfound diving paradise.

William Tan, Musician, Singapore

Drying out

North Sulawesi is a fairly sophisticated region with good facilities and many accommodation options. Standards vary from budget to top class. Most resorts are self-contained meaning they have a dive operator, restaurant and recreation facilities inside the complex. Packages include all meals and diving, so generally people do not venture beyond their resort unless it's to tour the highlands or rainforest. The number of liveaboards are increasing but this tends to be a land-based region.

Manado
Dive resorts
$$ **Cocotinos Resort**, T+62 (0)812 430 8800, cocotinos.com. Located in a picturesque bay and right beside lively Wori village,

this new resort has charming, beautifully decorated rooms, good food and incredibly personal service from the staff and the crew in the dive centre. From the moment you hand over your kit, everything is done for you. Opposite the Bunaken Marine Park, it's only a short ride to the majority of dive sites. Great value packages.

$$ **Seaside Resort Santika & Dive Centre Thalassa**, T+62 (0)431 850230, thalassa.net. Located on the mainland just opposite Bunaken National Park, this 4-star resort hotel has modern rooms with views over the marine park. On site is 5-star PADI **Dive Centre Thalassa**, a highly professional Dutch-run operation with both fantastic facilities and friendly, professional guides. This is a great place to do a course.

$ **Murex Dive Resorts**, T+62 (0)431 826091, murexdive.com. Founded by Dr and Mrs Batuna, pioneers of diving in this area, and still run by their family. The Manado resort has charming bungalows in a pretty water-garden setting just south of the city. Also with a small resort on Bangka. Good value packages include all meals and diving.

Other options
TwoFishDivers, TwoFishDivers.com. Operations in both Bunaken and Lembeh.

Lembeh Straits
Dive Resorts
$$$-$$ **Kungkungan Bay Resort**, T+62 (0)438 30300, kungkungan.com. The

American-owned resort that 'discovered' diving in the Lembeh Straits. Now larger and busier but still in a charming and with great shore diving. Rooms are spacious, some are in a traditional local style. Diving is run by **Eco-divers** who have a fantastic pedigree and lovely staff.

$$ **Lembeh Resort**, T+62 (0)438 550 0139, lembehresort.com. Sitting on the slopes of Lembeh Island, this relaxed, friendly resort is beautifully landscaped. Bungalows are built onto the hillside to capture the cool breezes and have fantastic views of the strait. Dive operations are run by **Murex**. Very knowledgable guides plus great dive and camera facilities.

Other options
Black Sand Dive Retreat, blacksanddive.com
Kasawari Lembeh, kasawari-lembeh.com
NAD-Lembeh, nad-lembeh.com

Sangihe Talaud
Liveaboards
MV Serenade, T+62 (0)431 838774, manado-liveaboards.com. For many years only *Serenade*, and sister-boat *Symphony*, ventured into Sangihe waters. Owned and operated by Murex, these boats are good value: cabins are air-con and ensuite.

Other options
Paradise Dancer, peterhughes.com
Ocean Rover, ocean-rover.com
Liburan, diveliburan.com

Left: Lembeh Resort; Kungkungan Bay Resort

> 66 99 It takes a lot for me to miss a dive but once, in Lembeh, I came down with a bad case of something. After missing three dives, the hotel decided I was off to the local doctor in Bitung, sending the bookkeeper along to translate. As a foreigner (read VIP) I was shunted past all the local ladies with their grumpy babes and straight in to meet the Lady Doctor. Then the fun started, trying to convey the problem: sore throat, swollen glands, a bit dizzy, can't dive! I was asked to lie down so Doc could examine my tummy. For a bad throat? Next came a long series of giggles, pokes and exclamations until we realized it was all about comparing the colour of my skin (pale), hair (red) and nose (freckled) before we were invited in for a cup of tea and cakes with the family. An hour later, we excused ourselves (all those waiting babies!) and left with a bag of pills. It cost just a couple of dollars, so we were glad to donate a little extra for the local ladies. Doc was delighted, but she was also very professional and the unnamed illness cleared up promptly.

 Sleeping $$$ US$150+ double room per night $$ US$75-150 $ under US$75
 Eating $$$ US$40+ 2-course meal, excluding drinks $$ US$20-40 $ under US$20

Sightseeing

Not as culturally rich as Bali, there is still plenty to explore in this area. Day trips are available from any of the resorts and usually include several features of the Minahasa Highlands. This extremely mountainous area is covered with spice trees and rice fields. Tours also visit villages that specialize in pottery making or traditional house building.

Airmadidi A fascinating historical site just half an hour from Manado. Near the town of Airmadidi, an ancient cemetery is full of Waruga – Minahasan tombs dating back to the ninth century. Carved from rectangular stones, the chambers are hollowed out and corpses placed inside in a sitting position. The triangular lids and exteriors were carved with motifs indicating the sex and status of the occupants. Some of the 144 sarcophogi held whole families as indicated by notches on the side of the lid. There is a small museum on site.

Japanese Caves Carved by prisoners into the mountains during the Second World War and mainly used as storage for supplies, these dark and deserted caves can be explored from the road between the villages of Kiawa and Kawangkoan.

Lake Tondano 2,000 ft above sea level, this scenic lake lies in a valley surrounded by the Lambean Mountains. The area is lush with paddy fields. Stop for lunch at a traditional Minahasa restaurant which serves barbecued fresh fish from the lake.

Lake Linow A beautiful but strange lake, which changes colour from red to green and sometimes blue. There are hot springs and and many birds in the park surrounding this very peaceful stop.

Bukit Kasih Centred around a steaming, sulphorous series of hot springs, the 'Hill of Love' is a billed as spiritual epicenter where followers of different faiths can commune and worship in open air. There is a cluster of temples and monuments for each of Indonesia's different faiths:

Christianity, Hinduism, Buddhism and Islam. You can climb all the way to the top of the mountain passing the Stations of the Cross on the way.

Pinawetengan A carved, table-shaped stone around which ancient chieftains of Minahasan tribes discussed unification, peace and war against enemies.

Lokon and Mahawu Volcanoes These have smoking crater lakes. Lokon, the prettier, requires a 45-minute climb but can be done by the reasonably fit.

Tangkoko Rainforest The tip of north Sulawesi is covered in tropical rainforest. Tangkoko Batuangus National Park sits beneath Mount Dua Saudara and covers 9000 ha from sea level up to 1000 m. This spectacular area is home to several rare species of monkeys, birds, butterflies and tropical plants. The main attraction is the tarsius – the smallest primate in the world. Walking tours are best at dusk when you are more likely to see one. Beware of the mosquitoes.

Clockwise from top left: the tarsius, children at Lake Tondano, Bukit Kasih, Waruga and Lake Linow

West Papua

One of the newest Indonesian regions to come under diving scrutiny is the western end of New Guinea. Officially known as West Papua but often called Irian Jaya, these waters are as remote as anywhere can be, yet are surprisingly easy to reach.

The eastern tip of West Papua is the Bird's Head Peninsula and lying offshore are a group of islands known as Raja Ampat, or the Four Kings. This lovely archipelago consists of over 1,500 small islands, cays and shoals. The four principal islands are Waigeo, Batanta, Salawati and Misool. When the reefs around them were surveyed a few years back by a group of Australian scientists, their research registered the world's highest counts of corals, molluscs and crustaceans.

Not long after their reports hit the press a whole new dive industry developed. However, the momentum didn't stop with that one survey. The Raja Ampat reefs have been monitored frequently since and the numbers appear to rise with every new report. One of the most recent noted some 1,200 species of fish plus dozens of unrecorded species. These included new wrasse, a mantis shrimp, reef building corals and the headline hitting 'walking' sharks. Almost 600 species, around 75% of the world's known total of reef building corals have been identified here. On land new species of birds, butterflies and frogs were found too.

Located in the heart of the Coral Triangle, with the Halmahera Sea and Pacific Ocean lapping the northern edges and the Ceram Sea to the south, this is an incredibly diverse area and while many others regions promote high diversity, there is no doubt that West Papua has something of an edge.

Locations

For the first few years of its diving career, West Papua was a pure liveaboard destination. One small resort sat quietly awaiting recognition, but the few people that did venture this far went by boat. Now though, there are plenty of boats, the first resort has expanded and several others are being built. It is easy to see why. It's only one extra hop by internal flight to Raja Ampat yet that fantastic sense of splendid isolation remains. Some islands still don't have names and once you are away from Sorong, chances are you won't even see a fishing boat.

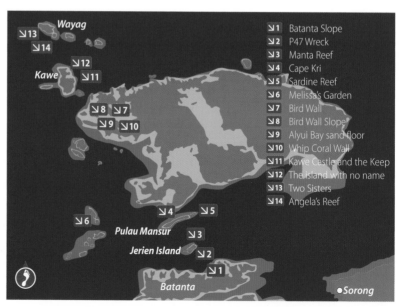

⬊1	Batanta Slope
⬊2	P47 Wreck
⬊3	Manta Reef
⬊4	Cape Kri
⬊5	Sardine Reef
⬊6	Melissa's Garden
⬊7	Bird Wall
⬊8	Bird Wall Slope
⬊9	Alyui Bay sand floor
⬊10	Whip Coral Wall
⬊11	Kawe Castle and the Keep
⬊12	The island with no name
⬊13	Two Sisters
⬊14	Angela's Reef

Destinations

Northern Raja Ampat

Liveaboards that cruise these isolated waters usually depart from Sorong on West Papua. The airport is just outside the city so you will be collected and taken to your waiting boat at the nearby jetty. Until very recently, most arrivals were actually at the amusing little airport on Jefman Island opposite the city. Its location comes with a dash of wartime history. Japanese aircraft used the airstrip on Jefman as a base to attack the American forces stationed in Biak to the east. After the war, the Dutch used it as a military airfield and eventually it became Sorong-Jefman Airport. This may seem to have little relevance to the majority of divers except to explain that whichever airport you arrive at, you are unlikely to see the city before being whisked off to your floating hotel. The region has developed as a distinctly liveaboard destination. However, all is not lost for land lovers as you will get to walk on many deserted beaches and possibly even visit a pearl farm. There are now also two ecologically sound resorts on tiny **Kri Island.** This speck of land lies to the northwest and in the heart of the Dampier Strait. Guests are collected from Sorong by boat. *Distance from airport: 15 mins*

Southern Raja Ampat

With the continuing development and exploration of this area, many liveaboards have now extended their routes to go further south from Sorong. Some even arrive from the far south after departing from the Nusa Tenggara islands. This means that the fourth king, Misool island, and the coastal areas opposite on West Papua (Triton Bay and Fak Fak) are all becoming by-words for adventurous, off-the-beaten-track diving. There is also another new resort in this area. Located on **Misool**, transfers from Sorong use the resort's fast boat and only go every 10 days or so. *Distance from airport: up to 5 hrs*

Places to stay and things to do at all these destinations are listed in Drying out on page 112

Sunset in Kawe; day trip around the islands; local mother and baby; breakfast in Raja Ampat; pearl farm, swimming at Wayag

Dive log

Raja Ampat

The northern islands of the Raja Ampat group were the first to be explored by divers, simply because they can be easily reached from the airport. This is a remote area where tourism has only recently become a growth industry and transport options are still limited.

Once you are out on the water you will see just how unpopulated the area is. Most islands are limestone and there is little natural water. The people who live here tend to be seafaring and remain fairly close to Sorong. All this is good news for divers. The corals are pristine and the quantity of tropical fish is outstanding. Clouds of fish are so thick you can barely see through them. On some dives you can count 14 different corals in a patch just a metre square. Larger animals are less common: turtles and sharks are wary and stay away from noisy divers' bubbles, though there are several manta cleaning stations. The wrecks of two Second World War planes are found here and no doubt others will be discovered as more time is spent in the area. Conditions are generally easy with good visibility and consistent water temperatures. Strong currents are comparatively rare but they can pick up at short notice so it's sometimes necessary to slip into the lee of a site to avoid them.

▼1 Batanta Slope	
🌀 **Depth**	17 m
◐ **Visibility**	fair to good
🌊 **Currents**	none
⬤ **Dive type**	liveaboard

Often the first stop on liveaboard routes, Batanta Island has some decent muck diving sites and at night is targeted as being one of the few places you can see picturesque dragonets. Living amongst the rubble, these tiny fish are the closest relatives to the mandarinfish, although they are not quite so skittish nor as brightly coloured. The site also has a variety of shrimp, including coral banded shrimp and playful mantis shrimp, banded pipefish, lots of huge nudibranch and cuttlefish. On very rare occasions, the mimic octopus has been seen here too.

The picturesque dragonet, the only close relative of mandarinfish

P47 Wreck, Jerien Island

🧭	**Depth**	35 m
🌓	**Visibility**	good to stunning
〰	**Currents**	mild
🌐	**Dive type**	liveaboard

On 2 October, 1944 two American fighter squadrons, the 310 and 311, took off from their base at Noemfoor Island near the city of Biak. Their mission was to attack a Japanese fleet thought to be near Ambon Bay but, on arrival, they discovered that the reports had been misleading. After strafing a few enemy craft they decided to return to the closest base: 310 Squadron landed at Middleburg but 311 Squadron was caught in bad weather; they flew until they ran out of fuel and were forced to ditch near Jerien Island. All seven crew were rescued. There are now two plane wrecks sitting on the base of the reef; one belonged to flight leader, Steven O'Benner (P47D-21), the second was element leader Kenneth J Crepeau's (P47D-16) although no one is sure which is which. One plane is deeper and not easily accessible, while the other is upside down at 30 metres. It is virtually intact and covered in some light coral growth.

Manta Reef, Jerien Island

🧭	**Depth**	8m
🌓	**Visibility**	good to stunning
〰	**Currents**	medium to strong
🌐	**Dive type**	liveaboard

As the boat approaches this reef the crew watch for wing flaps and the race is on to see if there are mantas. As you drop into the water the smaller ones are flying right beneath the dive tender. The current here rips across the plateau, pulling divers away from the entry point but in the same direction as the mantas. There is little coral so the strategy is to find some dead rock and use a reef hook to stay still. Waiting for just a few minutes is usually enough for them to come back. Larger ones sit still, feeding in the current (no hooks required by them). You can creep closer but need to be cautious as these animals are still wary of visitors.

↘4	**Cape Kri**	
🧭	**Depth**	24 m
◐	**Visibility**	good
〰	**Currents**	can be strong
〰	**Dive type**	liveaboard

Kri island sits in the middle of the Dampier Strait so is swept by some strong currents. Cape Kri is no exception to this, the dive is calm in patches but as you drift along the reef to the tip, you can hit some incredible currents coming from all directions. It's easy enough to stay close to the reef and avoid them. The extremely pretty slope has masses of colourful corals, with the cover becoming more intense the further along you go. There are schooling fish, wrasse, butterflies and angelfish above the corals and even greater numbers of anemones with their commensal clownfish down on the reef. There are also moray eels and longnose hawkfish, glassy sweepers, leaffish and even a comet fish. Approach the point where the current starts picking up and you really had no choice but to hook on. At this end you will see plenty of jacks, barracudas, bumphead parrots, midnight snappers, batfish and masses more fish. This is the site where Australian scientist, Dr Gerald Allen, recorded 283 fish species on a single dive.

Wobbegong shark in hiding

⬂5 Sardine Reef

🕐	**Depth**	20 m
🌓	**Visibility**	fair
〰	**Currents**	can be strong
⬗	**Dive type**	day boat/liveaboard

Only a little way from Cape Kri, this ranks as one of the best coral reef dives we have ever done. A sloping wall with sandy patches and coral outcrops is covered in masses of corals: hard, soft, cup, tubastreas and all in rainbows of colour. And just to make it even more beautiful the amount of schooling fish is incredible and not just the variety but the quantity of everything imaginable. A dive like this seems to prove the point of just how diverse this marine environment is. But it's not just about schooling fish, at the bottom of the reef, is the tasselled wobbegong. He was under a ledge – you will know it is a he if the hugest claspers are sitting out to his side. A little further along is the epaulette shark.

⬂6 Melissa's Garden

🕐	**Depth**	25 m
🌓	**Visibility**	fair
〰	**Currents**	can be strong
⬗	**Dive type**	day boat/liveaboard

Melissa's is in the Fam group of islands, due east of Kri. The flat, oval shaped reef is topped by three small rock islands, with bases that have been shaped by wave action creating bizarre mushroom-like formations. The entire reef is coated in hard coral outcrops with small soft corals, masses of crinoids and fish – although fish in the singular is an understatement when it comes to describing the substantial numbers of schooling fish hanging about. It takes at least three dives to see this reef as each section displays different features. The sandy bottomed edges are smothered in garden eels and rocky areas are home to an octopus or two. The currents can be quite strong around the bases of the small islands that rise up from the reef but tuck

in on the leeside to watch the masses of anthias, sergeant majors, damsels and butterflyfish. Several teenage stage batfish hover nearby while the adults are out in the current. Peak under a hard coral head to find a couple of juveniles still displaying their orange rims. Swimming further along the reef you encounter a lot of big snapper and sweetlips, two whitetip sharks, a turtle and one huge barracuda that is being tailed by a school of small

ones. There are plenty of smaller animals too, including imperial shrimp, mushroom coral pipefish and a juvenile rock mover wrasse. This is also a good site for the spotting a wobbegong. They are so hard to see when settled right on the top of some coral, their textured skins blending into the scenery, but they are easy enough to spot if they are moving. More tuna swim by out in the blue and banded seasnakes seem to appear around every outcrop.

Raja Ampat epaulette shark; dancing with the fish inside Melissa's Garden

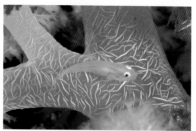

From inside Alyui Bay: allied cowrie; the Denise pygmy seahorse; soft coral goby and a toadfish

↘7 Bird Wall	
Depth	30 m
Visibility	good
Currents	mild - strong
Dive type	day boat

Inside Alyui Bay on the western side of Waigeo, are a cluster of dives that line either side of the bay. This quite narrow waterway has dramatic walls towering overhead and equally dramatic walls below the waterline. Bird Wall is one of the more popular sections. The dramatic sheer surfaces are coated in lots of tiny crusting corals, sponges and tunicates. The fan corals are quite small but many are home to pygmy seahorses, which are very often in clusters of three or four. Other fans are covered in a mass of transparent skeleton shrimp and on the next will be an allied cowrie. Tiny cracks in the reef are home to flame fire shells with their electric currents while orang-utan crabs are hiding inside bubble corals and whip coral have gobies and shrimp running up and down their stems.

☺ There's nothing like barefoot on a Misool beach...

Our dive itinerary took us south from Sorong and through the Misool islands, in the southern part of Raja Ampat. This a beautiful area with limestone rock islands, caves and outrageous diving. We spent five wonderful days diving on outstanding reefs covered in giant seafans chock-a-block full of pygmy seahorses. We saw three different types in total and they seemed to be in every fan. There were colourful soft corals and so many fish! Schools of surgeonfish, giant sweetlips of many varieties, barramundi, several varieties of fusiliers, on most dives. Not to mention trevally of all kinds, barracuda, and my favourite dogtooth tuna. Clownfish, well, there was the Ocellaris or fake clown, spinecheek clowns and dusky clowns everywhere. One day we were surprised by a school of Mobula mantas, always a delight.

We tried a new dive site and a blue-ringed octopus was found in 15 feet of water! Gusti, one of the dive guides, found a different species of pygmy seahorse on red fan, a lovely bright red and white variety. Mantis shrimps make for a great fun dive and I always think of my old friend Larry Smith who invented Mantas shrimp 'tamers'. One of our guys even got a shrimp to come out of his hole and do an acrobatic flip just like Larry taught us to do! With a good light you can find the lovely purple/pink squat lobsters on the colossal barrel sponges as well as all sorts of creatures hiding in caves. On a dive in a channel, we found some wild and very large bright yellow nudibranchs called Notodoris minor, quite a sight to see.

Misool Fiabacet was a very lovely island with my favourite orang-utan crabs on bubble coral and some just sitting on ledges. There is another dive site here called 'Black Rock' but we renamed it 'Like a Dream'. When that feeling of euphoria does not leave, when you never want to come up, then you know that this is why we come all this way and keeps us coming back for more. A layered canvas of pastel fans, that went on forever. Hundreds of fish of all different varieties. Sweetlips getting cleaned all over the place, beautiful shallows full of life, a living aquarium, definitely like a dream! One night in Misool, the crew had a beach party for us with a delicious sunset. There is nothing like barefoot on a remote beach in the middle of exquisite rock lime stone islands, yummy.

Cindi LaRaia, President, Dive Discovery, San Francisco

⬂8 Bird Wall slope

🕐 **Depth**	30 m
◑ **Visibility**	good
〰 **Currents**	mild-strong
⬯ **Dive type**	day boat

At the base of Bird Wall a large slope drops downwards from 25 metres or so. The flat seabed is a little rubbly with little coral, but it is the place to start hunting for Colman's shrimp and all the creatures that have commensal relationships with the toxic fire urchin. There are lots of urchins, mostly the paler coloured ones. Several have commensal cardinalfish, one a squat lobster but look long enough and a handsome Colman shrimp couple will be spotted. This dive is usually done more than once, which is a very good thing as you need time at depth to examine all the fire urchins to find one with a zebra crab. There are also lots of other small creatures here, like lionfish, a toadfish and plenty of nudibranchs. At night there are gobies hiding on soft corals, crabs on other soft coral, pygmy seahorses on a yellow fan, the solar powered nudibranch and some unusual tiny shells on the gorgonians.

⬂9 Alyui Bay sand floor

🕐 **Depth**	25 m
◑ **Visibility**	fair to good
〰 **Currents**	slight
⬯ **Dive type**	shore

A distinct change from elsewhere in the bay, this dive has a flat sandy floor with almost nothing on it except some patches of seagrass. But what a great place for lots of critters! There are tiny cuttlefish, lots of shrimp in all sorts of varieties, upside-down jellyfish including some that sit on the back of crabs, several porcelain crabs, seagrass pipehorses and bluespotted rays. A large group of urchins are completely smothered in cardinalfish, which seems quite unusual while another urchin has a needle shrimp in it. Blue starfish have squat lobsters sitting on their arms.

⬂10 Whip Coral Wall

🕐 **Depth**	10 m
◑ **Visibility**	fair to good
〰 **Currents**	slight
⬯ **Dive type**	shore

Dropping into the water on the tip of a tiny island inside the bay, you head in one direction or another. The choice is yours as the current splits here. Both directions are quite beautiful with, one way, masses of yellow soft corals and lots of schooling fish: mackerel, fusiliers, batfish, rainbow runners, sweetlips and midnight snappers.

In the crevices on the wall are orang-utan crabs, nudibranchs, soft coral gobies and even the marbled dragonet. Heading the other way on a second dive, the corals are just as beautiful but with more fans and black corals. There is a also deep rubbly gulley, which is bereft in comparison, yet attracts cuttlefish and mantis shrimp hide in the rubble. At the end of the gulley, the wall continues with more corals and more dramatic topography. Another ridge divides the wall, the current picks up at this point and attracts more schooling fish, which swoop along the ridge.

Indonesia Dive Log West Papua: Raja Ampat

Kawe Castle and the Keep

Depth	31 m	
Visibility	fair to good	
Currents	none	
Dive Type	liveaboard	

Kawe Island sits right on the Equator and much is made of the fact that you can moor in the southern hemisphere and dive in the north. The area is noted for its dramatic underwater sea mounts and this dive is the pinnacle of that. Pun intended.

Approaching this circular, straight-sided seamount you are met by forbidding walls that rise above like castle walls topped with battlements. A gouge cuts through the outcrop and is filled with midnight snappers and surgeonfish. At its mouth, a bright pink fan houses a whole family of pygmy seahorses. Descending to the base, a complete circuit reveals a small cave. This dungeon has a tiny exit higher up the wall. Schooling batfish patrol outside like sentries while masses of small fish cower in black coral bushes. The sheer walls are tempered by corals and crinoids, marbled dragonets, nudis and flatworms. Another sharp knife cut in the wall is packed full of red soldierfish and a lone barramundi cod.

A saddle leads to a satellite pinnacle off to the northwest side. Swimming across this drawbridge takes you up to about 15 metres where there is less soft coral but more and larger black coral bushes. Out in the blue, Napoleon wrasse hover beside titan triggerfish and schools of snapper.

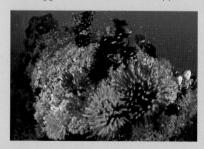

66 99 This truly amazing site had not been named when we dived it, but after three dives we felt it named itself. The overwhelming impression was of just one thing... a medieval castle complete with battlements and a keep.

⬂12 The island with no name

🕐	**Depth**	32 m
◑	**Visibility**	good
🌊	**Currents**	mild
🌊	**Dive type**	liveaboard

Just a few feet from the Equator this very beautiful island has, rather surprisingly, no name. The dive site starts on a steep wall and at its base there is a deep cave to explore. At the rear are flame fire shells that reveal an electric current running through their tentacles. Back out on the wall a tiny fan houses the Denise pygmy seahorse. The wall itself is smooth sided with many sponges, crusting algae and tiny corals. It flattens to a ridge beneath the limestone cliff where the rocky topography is fairly barren. Amongst the boulders are some unusual creatures like Paguritta hermit crabs and blue ringed octopus. This dive can be done at night, when the wall comes alive with nocturnal crustaceans and nudibranchs. Psychedelic bobtail squid nestle on the wall beside decorator crabs. It's easy to enter the cave accidentally so be careful! Back on the top, cuttlefish feed in the shallower waters.

⬂13 Two Sisters, Wayag

🕐	**Depth**	26 m
◑	**Visibility**	fair to good
🌊	**Currents**	none
🌊	**Dive type**	liveaboard

In the far north of Raja Ampat, Wayag has some of the most spectacular scenery in the region. The bay on the island's west is full of tiny, emerald topped, limestone islands that create a maze of turquoise waterways. It is a very beautiful area and a smooth mooring. The Two Sisters dive sites are twin pinnacle rocks situated outside the mouth of the bay. The underwater views are not as spectacular as the land scenery but these are very pleasant dives. Little Sister has a display of big gorgonians and some black coral bushes while Big Sister is better for looking for small creatures. There are great nudibranch finds including the *Notodoris minor*, *Chromodoris kuniei* and quite a variety of flabellina species.

⬂14 Angela's Reef, Wayag

🕐	**Depth**	20 m
◑	**Visibility**	fair to good
🌊	**Currents**	none
🌊	**Dive type**	liveaboard

Mostly dived at night, this pretty reef is dotted with patchy coral outcrops that emerge from the most beautiful, coarse white sand. There is some good critter life with many animals wandering over the sandy seabed looking for their evening meal. Lots of red pleurobranchs have emerged from their daytime hidey-holes, snake eels poke their noses up from the sand and have shrimp sitting on their nostrils. Dwarf scorpionfish are wandering past a variety of shells. Pink allied cowries are seen on the corals while crocodilefish, flatheads and slipper lobsters hide below. The divemasters are good at finding enormous nudibranchs that have huge imperial shrimps on them.

Indonesia Dive Log West Papua: Raja Ampat

Creatures of the night: a slipper lobster and the bobtail squid

Spice Islands

Steeped in history and riches from centuries past, the once famous Spice Islands are barely acknowledged by modern travellers. But divers, as is often the way, are blazing a trail into a region full of the most incredible coral reefs.

Sitting inside the Coral Triangle, the Banda Sea could be described as 'sealocked'. This body of water is completely enclosed by several other seas: to the west lies the small Flores Sea, southwest is the Timor, the Arafura Sea is to the southeast, and the Molucca Sea to the north. Together with the Banda Sea, these create a bridge between the Pacific and Indian Oceans.

At nearly 1,000 kilometres across, the Banda Sea covers around 20% of Indonesia's east-west dimension yet there is very little land inside this broad area. A ring of small islands encapsulates the sea but only a few of these are accessible. Buru, Ambon, Seram and a handful of smaller islands sit at the top of this ring while the Banda group sits in open water a little way to the southwest. Other islands spread westwards from Seram and around the ring eventually joining Timor and Nusa Tenggara in the far south.

Many more tiny islands and atolls are dotted throughout the Banda Sea and these, along with a substantial number of submerged reefs, are still unexplored. You can only wonder at what else might be out there.

Parts of the Banda Sea are very deep, falling to around 7,300 metres. The seabed here is the meeting point of three tectonic plates, which are responsible for occasional earthquakes. Several still-active volcanoes influence conditions too, but despite that, diving in these waters tends to be fairly straightforward. In the monsoon seasons, it can get a bit rough when crossing open waters. The calmest time for being on a liveaboard is between October and April while in other months, land-based diving is a better option.

Locations

With such huge expanses of open sea to explore, there is no doubt that the best way to see the Spice Islands is from a liveaboard which can cover almost the entire region in under a fortnight. There is just one vessel constantly plying the area, Archipelago Adventurer, but several others pass through the region mostly combining it with parts of West Papua or on transit trips from Nusa Tenggara in the far south. Land based operations are still limited but improving and one of these even has a satellite operation on Banda Neira, using the lone, but pleasant hotel located there.

Destinations

Ambon

Location of the regions' principal airport, Ambon island is also home to the only city for quite some distance. Ambon is also the capital of the province and a busy town that has had a colourful and often unhappy past. Once this was a real diver's haunt too, but after a period of civil unrest from 1999-2002, tourism virtually collapsed. The area is peaceful now and both tourists and divers are returning in small numbers. There are hotels in the centre of town but although it is worth touring, more appropriate accommodation can be found in closer the airport in **Latuhalat** village where a small dive resort is now fully operational. In late 2009, this will be moving to **Laha** village which is just about walking distance from the airport. (Flights in and out are minimal so noise should not be an issue). The new resort has a special bonus: its house reef will be the once legendary Twilight Zone. *Distance from airport: 5-15 mins*

Banda

The real heart of the Spice Islands, Banda does have an airport which is said to get a flight weekly from Ambon. It only takes 30 minutes on a small aircraft but is notorious for not going, or going early, if the pilot has something better to do that day. Now there's a novelty. There is one hotel on **Banda Neira** and a few guesthouses. The town is incredibly interesting, packed with history and charm. However, the majority of tourists arrive via liveaboard. The trip from Ambon is 120 nautical miles but is mostly broken with stops en route to dive. *Distance from Ambon airport: around 13 hrs*

Lucipara Atoll

This furthest outpost of dive trips in the region is reached after a 17 hour sail from Banda or Ambon. The crossing can be rough as there is no land on the way, but it is worth it. There is nothing else in Lucipara except a scattering of minuscule islands and reefs that break the surface. *Distance from Ambon airport: around 17 hrs*

Places to stay and things to do at all these destinations are listed in Drying out on page 112

Gunung Api; rainbow over Banda, arriving on Banda Neira; Fort Belgica; colonial home; Bandanese children; Archipelago Adventurer

Ambon

The islands of Ambon, Buru and Seram were once vital spice growing regions and much fought over by foreign colonial powers. Now though, they are visited for their mountainous rainforest interiors and incredibly diverse coastal waters.

The most important historically, and the best known island in the group, is Ambon. This particulary wierdly-shaped land mass is almost divided into two halves, with Leitimor and Hitoe peninsulas barely joined by a narrow neck of land. The sea in between is known as Amboyna Bay and it is these waters that made the area famous as a superlative muck diving region. There are dive sites all the way along the edges of the bay, making it a magnet for divers, but other sites are equally impressive. The outer edges of the Ambon, the coast of Seram and, in fact, reefs off the many smaller islands are just as fantastic.

⬐1 Tanjung Lain, Pulau Tiga	
◈ **Depth**	30 m
◐ **Visibility**	stunning
≋ **Currents**	ripping
◔ **Dive type**	liveaboard

Pulau Tiga means three islands, and this small island group is found off the west coast of Ambon island about an hour and a half from town. The three little islands are very beautiful and renowned for their pretty reefs but, at times, are also subject to currents that mimic the spin cycle of your washing machine. Obviously these are tidal and the conditions can be much calmer than that, but you can also drop in while they are bearable then find the currents lift rapidly to well over three knots. All the same, this is an impressive area. Tanjung Lain is most notable for masses and masses of Indian Ocean triggerfish. As you enter, the water appears almost black with them as they flit about obliterating the sun. The wall slopes downwards and is covered in fabulous soft corals. At about 28 metres, there is small point where the currents are ferocious but you can shelter in a bowl-shaped depression along with a blacktip shark, a huge bumphead parrot and a Napoleon wrasse. It's reassuring to see these guys struggling a little too.

Nusa Tiga

Ambon

Pulau Haruku

Pulau Saparua

Nusa Laut

⬐1

Ambon ●

⬐2

⬐3

⬐5

⬐4

⬐6

⬐1	Tanjung Lain	⬐4	Tadjung Nusanive
⬐2	Pertamina Wreck	⬐5	Waimika
⬐3	Laha I, II & III	⬐6	Amet, Nusa Laut

◥2 Pertamina Wreck

⬢	**Depth**	36 m
◑	**Visibility**	fair to good
☰	**Currents**	none to slight
⬤	**Dive type**	liveaboard

In Ambon harbour, just in front of the Pertamina refinery, is the wreck of a cargo ship. Its history is not clear but it is said to be WWII era and possibly Dutch. The structure is in good condition with one end lying at about 15 metres and the deepest point is about 37 metres where there are lots of new soft corals and tubastrea corals. Metal frames and railings loom over the old deck and are smothered in corals, sponges and ascidians. The growth is quite lush which attracts schools of small fish. After a complete circuit of the hull, there is time to explore the

shallow sections where there are a reasonable number of critters including a range of nudibranchs but mostly the

flabellina types that feed on hydroids. An octopus is seen regularly as he slithers in and out of gaps in the deck.

Tanjung Lain on Pulau Tiga; the Pertamina wreck

ⓥ3 Laha I, II & III

🌀 **Depth**	up to 42 m
◑ **Visibility**	stunning
🌊 **Currents**	none to strong
🚢 **Dive type**	liveaboard

Also known as the Twighlight Zone, these are the dive sites that first made Ambon hit the diver radar. Many suggest that the critter life here rivals the more famous Lembeh Straits. Laha I lies right under a jetty and a load of fishing boats. It is a really a murky, muck dive but with masses going on. At eight metres a bommie is home to a frogfish but fin past and over a steep slope to an area of sponges and detritus – and eels, shrimp, crabs, even a saron shrimp and thorny seahorses. Back up to a rubble bed where a whole load of mandarinfish skittering about even in the daylight. By sunset, the mandarins have started mating, more frogfish, cuttlefish, crabs and even a shrimp we had never seen. Laha II is the stepper part of the area and the place to head to depth to find the rhinopias. These tend to lurk at around 40 metres but there are two very beautiful creatures so it's worth a quick trip down and you are likely to see fire urchins with their hitchhiking zebra crabs and Coleman shrimp in this area as well. At 20 metres there are more seahorses, puffers, tiny trunkfish, leaffish, mating dwarf cuttlefish and a miniature yellow mantis shrimp. Other easy spots are pipehorses, the inimicus, stonefish and dwarf lionfish. Laha III consists of another rubble patch there are ornate ghost pipefish, juvenile puffers, clown frogfish and a giant frogfish, lots of different morays and several mantis shrimps, even banded pipefish with their pink eggs clustered on their tummies.

No wonder Laha is famous, clockwise from top: pregnant banded pipefish; frogfish; mandarinfish; *Rhinopias eschmeyeri*; mating dwarf cuttlefish; a longnose shrimp; juvenile yellow boxfish; sponge crab, wings of a shortfin lionfish; longsnout seahorse

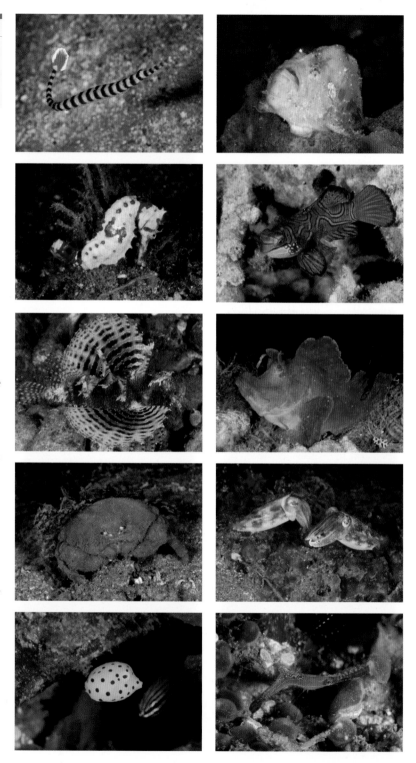

⊿4 Tadjung Nusanive

🕐	**Depth**	25 m
◑	**Visibility**	fair to good
🌊	**Currents**	can be strong
🌊	**Dive type**	liveaboard

Sailing south out of Amboina Bay brings a distinct change to the diving conditions. Rounding the point to open ocean means clearer water and better visibility but the currents can be strong. All the same, there is a fantastic dive right on point. The landscape is one of patchy outcrops and small walls leading to a sand and rubble seabed. There are small colourful corals so it is quite a contrast to the dives up near the town. There are a lot of animals too: clownfish and porcelain crabs are nestled in the folds of an anemone, an octopus hides in a cavern and imperial shrimp perch beneath a sea cucumber. There are a lot of shrimp too – inside crinoids, in bubble coral and tube anemone even the type that live on whip corals.

⊿5 Waimika

🕐	**Depth**	25 m
◑	**Visibility**	fair to good
🌊	**Currents**	none to mild
🌊	**Dive type**	liveaboard

Further along the southeastern edge of Ambon, the current is variable but lighter than on the point. This great dive is along a craggy wall coated in crusting corals, tunicates and sponges. The wall is quite steep and reveals a lot more small animals living in commensal relationships: orangutan crabs sit in the tentacles of a feeding hard coral, sangian crabs in the folds of a barrel sponge and porcelain crabs on anemones. Whip corals have both gobies and shrimp running along their surfaces while crinoids enclose squat lobsters and clingfish. Another unusual find is a large bivalve shell, similar to a flame fire shell, but with thicker tentacles. It is very unhappy at being disturbed by a torch beam, snapping open and shut constantly.

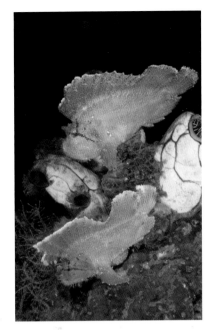

☺ The critter walk of fame

I have to say, the moment I broke the surface was a bit anticlimactic. My first impressions of Laha? Well it all seemed so grey, monotonous, so devoid of life, I couldn't grasp why people would rave so much about this site. Ambon's corals, schooling fish and reef, just five minutes' boat ride away, were so much more attractive and enticing. Contemplating this, I had descended to about eight metres when, out of the corner of my eye, I saw the yellow thorny seahorse. I hadn't seen one before, seen pygmies aplenty, but not the larger varieties and not up close so I was delighted. I looked at it a while, moved around, tapped the tank a couple of times and got the attention of another diver to show them that the dive wasn't just an exercise in patience. I went to move the leaf that was next to the seahorse, to get a better view, it was a cockatoo waspfish! Two quality critters in the same frame. A few fin kicks further, a stonefish was keeping a couple of frogfish company in the rim of a discarded tyre. I was bemused; you're just not supposed to see these things all at the same time!

Throughout the extended dive, the Maluku Divers guides pored over the unique habitat at hectic pace, throwing up rare and interesting finds, flamboyant cuttlefish – feeding no less – harlequin shrimps, various different octopi, an ugly little pegasus sea moth, brooding jawfish, multiple ghost pipefish, a solitary wonderpus. It was a critter walk of fame, just without the stars! No, stargazers don't count!

The highlight for me was the inimicus, or demon stinger, a pompous looking git, his expression suggested he'd had a pretty bad day! Laha is apparently still producing the goods, even improving; seven individual variations of rhinopias were seen in that same week, impressive by anyone's standards. Next time I see the rubble habitat of Laha, my heart will not be filled with apprehension, but with anticipation, for the exotic rarities I'll be about to discover!

Andrew Shorten, Owner, Maluku Divers

6 Amet, Nusa Laut

Depth	25 m
Visibility	excellent
Currents	slight
Dive type	liveaboard

Due east of Ambon, and a couple of hours' sail away, is the small island of Nusa Laut. The pretty but typical landscape on this island gives little indication of what lies below the waterline. After mooring off the small village of Amet, a ritual greeting with all the village elders takes place. They approach the liveaboard and come on board to check out the tourists. This may seems a little unconventional until you learn that this village has been diligently protecting their offshore reefs for many years. Some reefs in the region have been devastated by illegal fishing practices, but Amet's are absolutely pristine and full to bursting with fish. After the formalities have been completed, divers are finally allowed to enter the water – and discover it really was worth the wait.

An underwater promontory drops down to a sandy slope coated with whip corals. This is edged on either side by a flat sand bar. A gang of bumphead parrotfish hang near the edge of the sand bar and just beyond them are two gigantic schools of jacks. The number of fish is phenomenal. They seem unafraid of divers, continuing to move together and apart; huge waves swimming in perfect synchronicity, creating a spectacular marine ballet.

It's annoying to be out of bottom time, but returning to the shallows takes you back over the sandy area. There are bluespotted rays, a broad bed of garden eels, dancing razorfish and a spearchucker mantis shrimping who is peering out of his burrow.

This site is usually dived several times in a day and while it is tempting to revisit the jacks, there is so much more. The reef slopes are coated in good hard corals and if you pause above these, you will see more bumphead parrotfish and

possibly, a spotted eagle ray pass by. The shallow areas are marked by coral outcrops and gulleys which harbour some smaller creatures such as tomato clownfish and shrimp in an anemone, a juvenile pinate batfish and starfish in many colours. Under another small pinnacle, a cut-through is crammed full of feeding soft corals in myriad colours.

Banda

Famous for just one thing, the early spice trade, the Banda Islands are as lush and naturally rich today as they ever were. Back then, of course, it was all about nutmeg and the value of the reefs had not been recognised.

Five main islands, and a few small ones, are dominated by the towering presence of active Gunung Api. This mighty volcano influences the surrounding waters by supplying nutrients to the seas. This is a very rich area: species from virtually every group can be seen on the nigh-on perfect reefs. The 'king' or raja of Banda is well known for protecting his reefs from any marauding fishermen and has done so for quite some time. The result is fantastic diving in a healthy marine ecosystem with mostly easy conditions. The seas tend to be calm and currents are fairly mild when they do occur. Really strong currents are rare but those dives are often delayed until things settle.

↘1 Sandspit	
Depth	33 m
Visibility	stunning
Currents	none to slight
Dive type	liveaboard

Pulau Run is the infamous island that was traded between the Dutch, who got it and all the spices it supplied and British, who ended up with the island that later became known as Manhattan. Off the northern tip, the wall is mostly hard corals emerging from sandy slopes. The wall is interspersed with little caverns, crevices and overhangs. There are a few big animals out in the blue, including the briefest glimpse of an eagle ray, but the big stuff seems wary of divers – probably because they see so few. There is as much fish life here as you see in Ambon waters, but there seem to be many more fish that are nesting or with juveniles nearby. Rare, baby midnight snappers flit all over the reef as do adolescent ones. A cuttlefish hides warily under a fan at 32 metres, only to emerge, once the divers move off, and lay her eggs in a nearby staghorn. Up in the shallow areas are oriental sweetlips, batfish and lots of clownfish living in their anemones, including skunk clowns and Clarke's clowns that share premises.

↘2 Batu Udang	
Depth	32 m
Visibility	stunning
Currents	none to slight
Dive type	liveaboard

The next island east of Run, Pulau Ai is also surrounded by beautiful hard corals. Fin across the reef top and peer down over the wall edge to see ribbons of different species of fish all moving along the wall rim in tandem: tangs at the top, a line of rainbow runners, then snappers, then Indian Ocean triggers and so on. It's so perfect it's like an animated screen saver.

↘3 Batu Payang	
Depth	25 m
Visibility	stunning
Currents	none to slight
Dive type	liveaboard

Very similar to Batu Udang, this wall of hard corals is notable for an enormous section of organ pipe corals (Porites sp.) which is interspersed with large patches of clowns and anemones. The wall is covered in fans and soft corals so is very colourful and huge barrel sponges are topped by brightly toned crinoids.

↘1	Sandspit	↘4	Lava Flow	↘7	Selamo
↘2	Batu Udang	↘5	Mandarin City	↘8	Karang Hatta
↘3	Batu Payang	↘6	Batu Kapal	↘9	Pulau Soangi

🔽4 Lava Flow, Gunung Api

🕐	**Depth**	23 m
◑	**Visibility**	stunning
🌊	**Currents**	none to slight
🌑	**Dive type**	liveaboard

Gunung Api last erupted in 1998, spewing lava down its steep sides and into the sea. It devastated both the mountainside and the reef, leaving a sharp swathe of barren seabed. Two decades later, fast growing corals are rejuvenating: lettuce leaf and staghorn corals are prolific as are the fish: you see anthias, damsels and clownfish, including the spine-cheeked anemonefish, and even a few you don't recognise.

🔽5 Mandarin City

🕐	**Depth**	18 m
◑	**Visibility**	poor to fair
🌊	**Currents**	none to slight
🌑	**Dive type**	liveaboard

The most famous dive in the Banda islands is right under the jetty in Banda Harbour. This amazing muck dive can be brilliant in daylight but dusk is the time to see the mandarinfish. Described as 'mandarins on steroids', these little beauties are larger than any you will see in other places, even neighbouring Ambon. Entry is over a dark sand bottom with low visibility: currents running between Gunung Api and Banda Neira are not strong but fast enough to stir up the silty seabed. At depth you can search for, and will find, Colman's shrimp and squat lobsters on fire urchins. Back up the slope a little, and hiding in anything they can find, are banded pipefish, coral banded shrimp, snowflake morays, razorfish, octopus and juvenile butterflies. There is much more – this site is prolific.

Some of the creatures found in Banda Harbour, clockwise from top left: ornate ghost pipefish; juvenile many-spotted sweetlips; snowflake moray; mandarinfish; filefish; juvenile midnight snapper; whip coral crab; jewelled blenny

↘6 Batu Kapal

Depth	38 m	
Visibility	stunning	
Currents	none to slight	
Dive type	liveaboard	

The name of this site translates as Ship Rock and refers to a large pinnacle that looks like a ship's prow where it breaks the surface. There are several other pinnacles clustered around the main one so this site can be dived several times in different places. The walls surrounding the 'ship' are very beautiful, but the real highlight of this site is exploring the deeper areas. Off to the southeast, a seamound rises to 26 metres from the surrounding seabed at about 40 metres. Projecting from its base are the biggest fan corals you will ever see. These towering gorgonians can only be measured by comparing their height with the nearest divers who are simply overwhelmed by them. Barrel sponges try to compete in terms of size, but really don't have a hope. The fish life is prolific especially if the current lifts with large potato cod and barracuda visiting.

↘7 Selamo

Depth	18 m	
Visibility	good	
Currents	none to slight	
Dive type	liveaboard	

Tucked into a small bay on Banda Besar, but facing Banda Neira, Selamo is mostly dived at night as the shallow seabed makes it easy to explore the reef in the dark. As you enter the water, it's unusual to see it, but a honeycomb moray just might be out of his hidey-hole and searching the reef for dinner. They seem attracted to the torch beams and follow divers about in much the same way that lionfish often do on a night dive. Quite a lot of small fish, such as lionfish and scorpions are nestled in holes; parrotfish are doing the same but blowing their mucous bubbles for protection and tiny cuttlefish retreat into the tentacles of feeding corals attempting to remain unseen. This is one site where you may be lucky enough to see a Spanish Dancer which has a commensal Imperial shrimp living in its gills.

↘8 Karang Hatta

Depth	28 m	
Visibility	stunning	
Currents	none to slight	
Dive type	liveaboard	

Karang Hatta is on Banda's eastern limits. This really exciting dive takes place over a peninsula to the south of the island. The dive tender drops you into the water right over the point and right over some whitetip sharks. There are four or five that swoop away and back towards the divers and in and out of the schools of rainbow runners. A couple of barracuda infiltrate the gaggle of fish with triggers and snapper making it an all action moment. When it's time to move up and along the wall you find the typical scenery of huge sponges and lots of more fish. Up at the top of the reef are schools of bumphead parrots. There are about 15 that are at least a metre long. Returning to the site a second time, you find the sharks are still over the point and giving a repeat performance but this time you may notice more creatures along the wall, like a giant pufferfish tucked into a cavern and a few more barracudas, both chevron and great. The numbers of fish along the wall are overwhelming: there are mackerel, fusiliers, runners, snapper and triggerfish in the blue, while up in the shallows you can see the opposite with lots of small species including juvenile, bi-coloured parrotfish that can't have been more than five millimetres long.

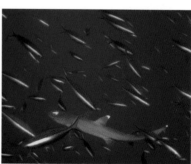

Batu Kapal fan dwarfing the diver; Imperial shrimp in the gills of a Spanish Dancer; whitetip shark chasing rainbow runners

⛴9	Pulau Soangi	
🧭	**Depth**	30 m
◐	**Visibility**	stunning
〰	**Currents**	none to slight
⬓	**Dive type**	liveaboard

This small island is usually dived when the liveaboard passes by on its way between Ambon and Banda. Soangi is an isolated, straight sided rock that emerges from the sea up in the middle of nowhere. Its steep sides are coated in trees and beneath the water you find the 'vegetation' continues as corals that are coating the walls. The sheer sides extend for some way before dropping off to slopes. There is also a ridge at depth that attracts pelagics. It is a very pretty site – all rainbows of colour and flitting fish. Like much of this region, there are huge sponges (it's quite amazing how big they are) interspersed with soft corals and fans. Pale blue finger sponges decorate the shallows where you find green and honeycomb morays and spotted soapfish. Sometimes the currents that surge around the island can create rougher than usual conditions.

Pufferfish in hiding, Karang Hatta

🌀 The Banda Buzz

What a place! These islands, viewed (by me at least) with only a tiny snippet of knowledge about their history, simply exude 'exotic'. A few of these islands are uninhabited and, from the deck of our beautiful, traditional, teak liveaboard schooner, would rise up out of each dawn as rugged, verdant, floating gardens promising richness of nature both above and below the water.

The underwater world is sparkling: pristine; rich with exotica of all kinds and offering a few special surprises. From the overloaded muck dive directly below the Banda Neira pier where the old Dutch-styled buildings (yes – cannons intact) still sit proudly looking over the water to the cruisey bommies in calm and prolific waters in various straits and passages around the islands – the reefs teem with all that you would expect in a place known for its infinite diversity.

This whole area seems to have been locked in time and the reaction of the marine life to the strange visitors from above-space reflected this. I have never had so many relaxed encounters with creatures normally difficult to engage. From morays of every species possible, which were far curiouser than normal and easy to hang around for photoshoots lasting minutes on end, to blue ribbon eels, mantis shrimp and various muck creatures living an obviously idyllic and laid-back existence in this rarely dived area, the show was awesome.

The highlight of the underwater scenery was, for me, the newly 'planted' coral garden perched on the 15 year old lava flow in the channel below Gunung Api. Just like a new garden bed full of flowery annuals in late spring and early summer, this patch was a palette of every pastel hue imaginable, and every shapely coral species ever seen. Cascades, sloping beds, walls, boulders, stands of fresh and healthy staghorn and all the fish you could want to see enjoying their playground. This is the only dive where I have ever seen the frantic and persistent mating 'dance' between two enormous (I mean enormous) dog-faced puffers. They circled each other at top speed around a coral 'racing' circuit spanning eight metres or so – but we never were able to witness the consummation of that pursuit as we eventually had to move on.

When the land beckoned, the exotica didn't disappoint. The 16th and 17th centuries hover over the old town of Banda Neira like a wraith. Buildings are a little crumbly and there's a wonderful museum-like air about the place, but the people are unspoiled and placid; the children shy but happy to be chatted to and given finger-hugging koalas to break the ice. The highlight as a 'tourist' was to visit and wander through the nutmeg plantation that was the birth of the spice trade in this area four centuries ago, still productive and being tended by an ancient master of the trade wielding the ubiquitous machete.

This is a special place. It is, uniquely, not a place to 'go diving'; it's a destination to absorb yourself in. You'll go away feeling privileged to have been granted passage into this world.

Sue Laing, Managing Director, the risk store, Sydney, Australia

Lucipara Atoll

Just five degrees south of the equator, this oceanic atoll is one of those places that is so completely unknown, even Indonesians look quizzically at any mention of it's name.

There are actually five archipelagic atolls linked together as the remote Lucipara group, each consisting of a scattering of tiny landmasses. A handful of reefs break the surface: the tips of underwater mountains, their steep and dramatic walls drop eventually to the seafloor at some 4,000 metres. Around the edges of the atolls are vertical walls with crystal clear visibility and, usually, mild currents.

With no substantial landmasses for some distance, Lucipara attracts many pelagic species of fish along with some bigger creatures. One of the most special are pods of pilot whales. Watch the horizon constantly as it is more likely than not that you will encounter them between dives as they surface for a couple of minutes, disappear for a few more, then reappear again a short distance away.

Lucipara Atoll

↘1 Pulau Maisel Barat
↘2 Pulau Maisel Tengal
↘3 Pulau Kadola
↘4 Pulau Bingkudu

↘1 Pulau Maisel Barat

🕐 **Depth**	30 m
◑ **Visibility**	stunning
🌊 **Currents**	none to slight
🌀 **Dive type**	liveaboard

Pulau Maisel lies in the northern section of Lucipara Atoll but this dive is on its southern side. A sloping wall drops down to 30 metres – and well beyond – and is coated in beds of hard corals. They are in great condition, but seem a little sparse in comparison to other parts of the atoll. Despite that, there are some large, brightly coloured fans at depth. The water is awash with schooling fish, so much so that you barely look at the wall: there are Indian Ocean triggers, huge tuna, lots of Spanish mackerel and batfish. When you do head up and look at the reef, you find lots of large morays, lionfish and scorpions. It's in this area that the pilot whales are seen as they pass through the channel between Maisel and Skaro Reef to the southwest.

↘2 Pulau Maisel Tengal

🕐 **Depth**	28 m
◑ **Visibility**	stunning
🌊 **Currents**	none to slight
🌀 **Dive type**	liveaboard

On the opposite, northern side of Maisel, this wall is a little steeper and also a lot prettier. The reef topography is marked by overhangs and small caverns which are covered in a mixture of corals, including more soft corals and large gorgonians in a variety of colours. There are as many fish with as many different species: swathes of rainbow runners and Indian Ocean triggers hover in the gin-clear water virtually blocking the view. There are masses of lionfish and more large morays, both green and honeycomb. There is good macro life sitting on the walls and the shallows too, but the focus is on all those fish in the blue.

↘3 Pulau Kadola

🕐 **Depth**	29 m
◑ **Visibility**	stunning
🌊 **Currents**	none to slight
🌀 **Dive type**	liveaboard

There are three islands in the Pulau Penyu atoll, northwest of Lucipara. Kadola, Mai and Bingkudu are miniscule specks of land ringed by circular reefs that drop to steep walls. The underwater landscape is very similar to the southern islands but still has huge numbers of fans and enormous sponges. In fact, this area is well known for the size of the sponges that are larger than the divers that pass by. Some fish shelter rabbit and lionfish. Young blacktip sharks pass by the wall in the distance.

↘4 Pulau Bingkudu

🕐 **Depth**	33 m
◑ **Visibility**	stunning
🌊 **Currents**	none to slight
🌀 **Dive type**	liveaboard

To the north of Kadola, the reefs off Bingkudu are, in reality, an extension of the same system. All the way around these islands are the most unbelievable numbers of fish: there are Spanish mackerel, jacks, snapper, rainbow runners, fusiliers and triggerfish. Schools of tuna pass by swiftly – the big animals don't come close to diver bubbles – and have members that are up to two metres long. A turtle zips past quickly too and appears to be even larger than the tuna.

Drying out

Facilities are limited in these far flung corners, but the good news is that what is there – be it hotels, dive centres or liveaboards – is of a very good calibre.

West Papua
Liveaboards
Archipelago Adventurer II, T+62 (0)361 282369, archipelago-fleet.com. Top class vessel with British-American management. Classy, extra spacious cabins, with large picture windows, smart ensuites and desks for all the photography and computer kit. Highly knowledgeable guides and a variety of regional routes.

Kararu, T+62 (0)361 282 931, kararu.com. Company with a long-standing pedigree in the region, with a great crew, food and management. Now with a new boat which, by all accounts is spacious and very comfortable.

Other options
Becoming Indonesia's most popular route after Komodo means there has been an influx of vessels into these waters but not all are here all year round. Operations range from budget to luxury and ones that cost more will be of a higher quality. Ensure you ask enough questions to get the right facilities for you (see page 8). Check out:

Bidadari, kmbidadari-cruises.com
Pindito, pindito.com
Seven Seas, thesevenseas.net
Also watch out for Dive-damai.com, due to launch in September 2009.

Diving and sleeping
$$$-$$ **Kri Eco Resort and Sorido Bay**, iriandiving.com. Both are on Kri Island near Sorong and owned by the same company
$$$ **Misool Eco Resort**, misoolecoresort.com. In the south of the region 4½ hours from Sorong by boat.

The Spice Islands
Liveaboards
Archipelago Adventurer II, T+62 (0)361 282369, archipelago-fleet.com. The first company to schedule routes frequently in this region and pioneers in both Banda and Ambon. Details as left.

Diving and sleeping
$$$ **Maluku Divers**, divingmaluku.com. Currently the only land based dive resort in Ambon, Maluku divers are in Latuhalat Village right on the waterfront. This resort has various room standards and a dive centre on site. However, they will be moving to Laha Village in late 2009 with a new full service resort being built in a traditional Mollucan style just 5 minutes from the airport and right on the Laha dive sites for shore diving.

For land based diving in **Banda**, contact Maluku Divers (above) who have a satellite operation there with a variety of accommodation options.

The Spice Islands
Several hundred years ago these were the most important islands on the planet, the source of a commodity that, per ounce, was worth more than gold: nutmeg. The fabled Spice Islands were so vital to16th and 17th century trade they sparked many battles between Europe's great seafaring powers.

In ancient times, the area was known to Chinese and Arab traders, who kept the source of these spices a well guarded secret. Explorers set off from Europe attempting to locate the islands. Many colonial powers fought each other, and local kingdoms Ternate and Tidore, for control of this highly lucrative trade. The Portuguese were the first colonists, taking hold until 1609 when they were driven out by the Dutch. There were brief periods of British rule but the islands remained under the thumb of the Dutch East India Company until Indonesian independence in 1945.

Ambon
The Dutch brought Christianity to this area: Ambon and the surrounding islands have both Christians and Muslims communities. Centuries later, the two factions could no longer tolerate each other and in January 1999, a fight between a Christian bus driver and a Muslim youth instigated two years of civil unrest. Parts of the city were destroyed and with interference from various sectarian groups, the violence continued until late 2002. Aside from occasional outbursts, the city is now finally peaceful.

It is said that Ambon is still partially segregated along religious lines. However, since the peace accord, there has been increasing interaction. Certainly driving around Ambon is safe enough and curious for tourists in that for every church you see a larger mosque is being built nearby, only to be dwarfed by an even larger, more ostentatious church. And so on.

There is much to see in the city, with lively market areas around the harbour; churches, forts, and buildings from the colonial period; memorials and cemeteries dedicated to those who fought in the Second World War. Dive operators will plan a short trip around the city highlights on request.

Martha Christina Tiahahu Memorial
This female freedom fighter is regarded as national heroine, having fought beside her father against the Dutch. He was executed on Nusa Laut and she was banished to Java, but starved herself to death on board the ship taking her.

Victoria Fort Built by the Portuguese in 1575, the huge walls facing the bay are still preserved while parts of the interior now lay in ruins.

Siwalima Museum On top of the hill above the city is this charmimg but old-fashioned museum which aims to preserve all aspects of local heritage.

Sleeping	$$$ US$150+ double room per night	$$ US$75-150	$ under US$75
Eating	$$$ US$40+ 2-course meal, excluding drinks	$$ US$20-40	$ under US$20

Banda

The Portuguese were first to take possession of Banda in the early 1500s. The British arrived in 1603 but soon after the Dutch took hold of Banda Neira. To establish their stake, the British built trading posts on Ai and Run islands, and by paying higher prices, undermined Dutch aims for monopoly. Tensions increased until, in 1615, the Dutch invaded Ai forcing the British to retreat to Run, but who that same night, launched a surprise counter-attack on Ai retaking the island and killing 200 Dutchmen.

A year later, a stronger Dutch force attacked Ai again. After a month-long siege the defenders ran out of ammunition and were slaughtered. At the same time, the Dutch forced a trading agreement on the Bandanese, holding them at gunpoint. Later they claimed the treaty had been violated, so slaughtered locals and enslaved many more. It is said this incident turned the Dutch presence purely as traders into the first overt colonial rule in Indonesia. European control of Banda was contested up until 1667 when the British traded the small island of Run for another small island – later known as Manhattan –giving the Dutch full control of the Banda archipelago.

Nutmeg Plantations This valuable trading commodity still brings Banda its main source of wealth because, despite many

efforts, nutmeg trees only really successfully grow here. Tours with a master horticulturist are quite something, as he picks the nuts off the trees and peels them apart, explaining the riches inside this seemingly innocuous plant. There are also cloves and cinnamon.

Banda Neira Town This fascinating place is an absolute must-see. Walking tours of the town start in front of the Maulana Hotel where there is a collection of swivel guns and other memorabilia. From here, the walk leads away from the waterfront through streets lined with wooden Dutch colonial houses. They are in various states of disrepair, but recently, more have being renovated. The small town **museum** is in one, with some curious artefacts from the Dutch era. A little further along is a newly renovated Dutch **church**. Built in 1852, gravestones line the floor. The now deserted **palace** of Governor J.P. Coen can be seen and in its garden is a bronze statue of King Willem III. However, the most overwhelming sight is **Fort Belgica**, which still hovers ominously over the town. This pentagonal structure has far reaching views. Although strategically placed, it was eventually seized for Britain by Captain Christopher Cole in 1810.

Banda Neira, clockwise from top: nutmegs straight from a tree; old plantation house, Dutch swivel guns; meeting the locals; the museum; Dutch colonial church; Fort Belgica.

Indonesia Drying out West Papua and the Spice Islands

Kalimantan

Indonesia's least known province is also home to one of her richest and most biodiverse marine environments. Stretching for over 160 kilometres along the coast opposite the Berau River delta is the Derawan Island chain.

A few years ago, the area was submitted to the World Heritage Organisation for consideration as a site of special interest. Marine surveys have been conducted by various bodies, including the Nature Conservancy, which conclude that this area has the world's second highest level of hard coral diversity after the Raja Ampat Islands. There are more than 460 different species of coral as well as over 870 species of fish. The environment is unique in that fresh water from the Berau River flows into the Sulawesi Sea, its broad river delta leading across a shallow sandbar to an extensive collection of patch and fringing reefs and, further from the coast, atolls.

There is very little land offshore. Of 31 islands only Derawan and Maratua have local villages on them, one and four respectively, while Derawan, Sangalaki and Maratua have resorts. Sangalaki is the largest Indonesian nesting site for green turtles; uninhabited Samama is a protected bird sanctuary, and Kakaban contains the world's largest and most diverse jellyfish lake, with four unique stingless species.

Unfortunately, this highly unique set of environments is threatened by the overly industrialized use of the Berau River and by overfishing near the islands. However, new 'zonal use' projects should protect against these issues while still allowing local communities to continue with their traditional livelihoods.

Conditions allow year-round diving in the area with traditional rainy and dry seasons only as predictable as anywhere else on the planet these days. Temperatures are typically tropical. However, the water temperatures are consistently higher than you would expect, often reaching over 28°C and rarely much below it. Even thermoclines are extremely unusual. Visibility is lower than you might expect due to river run off. The further offshore you go, the better it gets.

Locations
As these islands are less than easy to reach it has taken quite a while for resorts to establish themselves. However, the newer research studies have encouraged more divers to go and there are now five small resorts across now three islands. The region – and dive sites – still remains uncrowded but all things being equal, that is unlikely to last. A few liveaboards are starting to schedule seasonal routes that cover all the islands in the group.

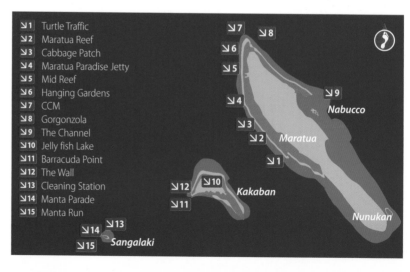

↘1	Turtle Traffic
↘2	Maratua Reef
↘3	Cabbage Patch
↘4	Maratua Paradise Jetty
↘5	Mid Reef
↘6	Hanging Gardens
↘7	CCM
↘8	Gorgonzola
↘9	The Channel
↘10	Jelly fish Lake
↘11	Barracuda Point
↘12	The Wall
↘13	Cleaning Station
↘14	Manta Parade
↘15	Manta Run

Nabucco

Maratua

Kakaban

Nunukan

Sangalaki

Destinations

Maratua

This, the most distant landfall from the coast, is also the largest island in the entire group. There are four villages sitting around a narrow strip of land, which defines a partially submerged atoll. Divers are unlikely to see much of the villages as the resorts here are somewhat isolated from local communities. Maratua Paradise sits closest to one, **Bohe Bukut**, on the western side of the atoll. Around to the northeast, a second resort sits on miniscule but picturesque **Nabucco** island, while to the southeast, another resort has recently been built on **Nunuken** island. These are still located within Maratua's confines and tend to dive the eastern side while Maratua Paradise dives on the west. The atoll is known for thresher sharks and the pelagic fish action at the Channel dive site.   *Distance from Berau airport: 3-4 hours, from Balikpapan airport 6-7 hours.*

Other options

All resorts take day trips to other islands although the choice can be limited simply due to travelling time. For example, Maratua resorts do not visit Derawan as it is just too far for a single day trip.

Derawan Closest to the Berau River mouth, Derawan resort was one of the first in the area and is best known for its macro dive sites. There is a village on the island that is said to have other facilities including a couple of guest houses.

Kakaban Sitting part way between Sangalaki and Derawan, this island has insufficient land to support people. It does have some of the most dramatic wall diving around its edges though and is the location of the jellyfish lake.

Samama Although larger than Sangalaki, Samama has no village and no resort, but is regarded as having excellent macro dive sites.

Sangalaki Far smaller than Maratua, there is just one tiny resort and no village on the island. It was an early contender in this area though and is undergoing renovation. The island is best known for manta ray populations and being a turtle nesting site.

Places to stay and things to do at all these destinations are listed in Drying out on page 125

Nabucco Island Resort; local children; Maratua Paradise Resort; sailing to Sangalaki; resort restaurant

Maratua

The largest, and only substantial, landmass on these offshore reefs, Maratua island is a bizarre upside down horseshoe shape that encapsulates a shallow sandy lagoon. Dotted about the peripheries of the northern part of the horseshoe are some smaller coral islands but, as you head south, the ring of land sinks slowly beneath the waterline, continuing as a loop of submerged reefs.

Across Maratua are four villages. Many of the local people are now involved in working at the three resorts on the atoll but the area was traditionally occupied by fishermen. This is no surprise once you have seen the reefs as they are teeming with schooling fish. The diving here is principally drift diving and currents can be strong at times.

↘1 Turtle Traffic	
🜨 Depth	22 m
◐ Visibility	fair
≋ Currents	intermittent
⬓ Dive type	day boat

Heading south from the Maratua Paradise resort, this site is just about the furthest away on this side of the atoll and can only be dived when the tides are just right. It's a site that really is all about turtles, which are present in uncountable numbers. The reef has a shallow flat top of hard corals – it's not the most pristine reef in the area – that drops to a sloping wall with sinuous winding topography. Beyond the outside curves there is a little current, but duck into one of the cut-backs and it drops away completely. The wall is marked by several bowl-shaped depressions, which are full huge green turtles. Sometimes there are seven or eight sitting together and, when divers come along, they take off rather lazily, swim for a little then come back to the same spot. A few are sitting on rubble patches waiting for a cleaner wrasse to do its duty, while others are looking for something to munch on. Apart from the oversized green turtles, there are quite a lot of hawksbills. These seem to be younger and are far more lively, nipping out to sea, up to the surface and back down again.

Harlequin snapper and blue chromis sheltering around a table coral

Maratua Reef

🕐	**Depth**	28 m
◑	**Visibility**	fair
〰	**Currents**	intermittent
🌊	**Dive type**	day boat

Just moments south of the resort, this wall has lots of cracks and crevices and again is covered mostly in hard corals. Lots of blue chromis flutter over table corals while harlequin sweetlips nestled beneath. There are big fans, soft corals and some huge sponges. This section of reef is in good condition: there are fewer fish but plenty of starfish, tiny flat worms and several large pufferfish.

Cabbage Patch

🕐	**Depth**	17 m
◑	**Visibility**	poor
〰	**Currents**	intermittent
🌊	**Dive type**	day boat

This shallow section at the top and inside the reef drop-off is mostly dived if the weather is not cooperating or at night. The visibility can be low as the surf stirs up the sandy patches. There are a lot of cabbage corals in mixed condition and a lot of algae too, but the surprise is that there is some really good critter life. You are likely to encounter a small cuttlefish, followed by crab-eye gobies, upside down jellyfish, plenty of pyjama nudibranchs, a *Glossidoris* species and a large puffer on the sand.

Crab-eye goby at Cabbage Patch

⊠4 Maratua Paradise Jetty

⊙ **Depth**	6 m	
⊙ **Visibility**	fair	
⊗ **Currents**	slight	
⊝ **Dive type**	day boat	

⊠5 Mid Reef

⊙ **Depth**	40 m	
⊙ **Visibility**	fair to good	
⊗ **Currents**	none to ripping	
⊝ **Dive type**	day boat	

The lagoon beneath the jetty is subject to an extreme tidal drop. At times you can look down from the boardwalk and see only blazing white sand, at other times, as the sea returns, there are baby batfish and small turtles. The seabed appears quite barren but is far from it – at night the lagoon is alive with critters. Near the reef edge, the corals have been damaged by surf and turned to rubble: mandarinfish live here. Patrolling across the sand, you are accompanied by lionfish who have learnt to hunt by following divers torch beams. These also highlight the spearchucker mantis and snake eels. Beneath the resort pylons, there are stonefish, schools of scrawled filefish, razorfish and catfish. curiously, much of the life is in shades of white, matching the sandy floor. No wonder you get the impression that this lagoon is barren.

The dive sites heading north from the resort are have a slightly different profile from those to the south: the walls become more vertical although they still wind in an out at times. This dive is touted as the one where you will see thresher sharks and, as most divers will recognise, that sort of statement from the divemasters is not to be taken too seriously. Regardless, on entry they head straight down past the wall to a very deep, level shelf at around 38 metres. The water is a little cooler and the currents quite a bit stronger so it's time to hook onto a rock and wait. Imagine the surprise when a few minutes later a thresher shark appears! These magnificent, five metre long, torpedo-shaped creatures are fantastically beautiful, their long, elegant tail sweeping in a magnificent arc away from their body. These sharks are wary though and although you are likely to see them more than once, they don't come close to the divers, especially if there are a few hooked on and blowing bubbles. Sometimes they ascend for curious look, but quickly descend again to a second shelf at about 50 metres, by which time you need to ascend anyway. At the bottom of the wall there are lots of sponges, fans and some colourful soft corals, but the shallows are mostly hard corals and not in the very best condition. The currents seem to attract a lot of bumphead parrots and solitary batfish, and there are many turtles resting in the cracks and crevices, their shells blending in with the surrounding terrain. In contrast to the big stuff, the guides know the locations of some impressive, macro creatures including a yellow pygmy seahorse, some orang-utan crabs and some very unusual nudibranchs.

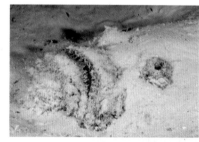

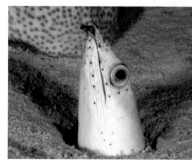

Under the jetty at night: leaffish, stone fish, snake eel and mantis shrimp.

Thresher shark (top) and Mid Reef

◢6 Hanging Gardens

⏱	**Depth**	32 m
◑	**Visibility**	very good
≋	**Currents**	none to slight
◐	**Dive type**	day boat

Entry over the edge of another section of the wall, but this section is coated in huge numbers of very large black coral bushes, all quivering and glittering in their various shades of gold, silver and bronze. At depth you can see silvery bushes that look like they might measure up to ten metres across. The shallower ones on the wall are interspersed with sponges and fan corals, a couple of which are known homes for the Denise pygmy seahorse. The wall is home to moray eels, tiny nudibranchs, anemones and gobies. Near the end you come across an area where some of the cutbacks have been bombed but strangely, the surrounding points are thick with schooling fish – butterflies, angels, fusiliers and moorish idols. Also saw half a dozen fantastic, tiny turtles and one really huge specimen swimming past in the blue.

◢7 CCM

⏱	**Depth**	34 m
◑	**Visibility**	very good
≋	**Currents**	none to slight
◐	**Dive type**	day boat

Almost at the very northern tip of the atoll, this segment of the reef is steeper and the visibility is about the best in the area. At the beginning of the dive the wall wiggles in and out as usual, but a little way along it straightens into a massive vertical cove where there are some – for 'some' read masses, literally hundreds – of batfish in a school. They are so prolific that you can't see the wall behind them, but unfortunately they are also spooked by the arrival of divers and quickly split up into much smaller groups, moving off in several directions. A large gang of jacks emerges from behind the original pack as they disperse, following on the tails of the batfish that head down to deeper waters. The rest of the dive continues alon the wall and reveals starry puffers, a lobster and anemones at the top of the reef there.

◴ Time and tides

One of the most interesting things about diving in Kalimantan (and something divers are rarely warned about) is the incredible tidal drop that occurs around these islands – and it's all because they sit on the top of open ocean atolls.

One minute you can see a lovely, white sand beach covered by glistening clear water then before you know it, the water has disappeared and left a barren patch of sand. It's just like this around Maratua: the water bungalows sit about three metres above the lagoon so it is easy to monitor the drop by watching the how close the sea comes to your doorstep.

Tides are, of course, created by the moon as it orbits the Earth. Both exert a gravitational effect on each other as they pull in opposing directions to create a balance. Down on terra firma, this isn't felt but is indicated by tides. Water likes to be level so when the moon pulls one way, the sea follows it. Bearing in mind that 'atoll' means a ring-shaped reef enclosing or nearly enclosing a shallow lagoon, any dive destination that is atoll based will demonstrate extremes of currents like it does at Maratua. Here, the lagoon fills up through a narrow channel, and empties again the same way. The force of the sea rushing in and out causes the extremes of current which are felt all the way around these islands but most obviously at the Channel dive site.

Elsewhere, currents on a dive site fall more in line with oceanic current movements rather than localized conditions like these.

The tiniest pygmy seahorse at Hanging Gardens; scorpionfish on CCM

Indonesia Dive log Kalimantan: Maratua

↘8 Gorgonzola

Depth	32 m
Visibility	very good
Currents	none to slight
Dive type	day boat

Located just around the top point of the Maratua atoll, Gorgonzola's wall is a little steeper than those further south, probably because the top v-shape of the island is hit by splitting currents. The landscape nearby consists of small rocky cliffs covered in trees that run right down to the waterline. This is unlike the flatter, west side of the atoll. On Gorgonzola, the hard coral slopes away directly from beneath the cliff line and looking down, the vertical view is interrupted by lots of gorgonian fans: all sizes, all shapes and all colours. One of the very smallest ones is another known haunt for the pygmy seahorse while longnose hawkfish try to remain unseen on some of the bigger fans.

Sangian crabs (top) and longnose hawkfish (right) are common residents on Gorgonzola

☺ Just what I'd been missing

Having not been on a 'proper' diving trip for nearly six years I was really excited to be going to Maratua. My 'new' dive buddy (in life also) has a lot less dives than I do and hadn't quite been bitten the bug yet but I was hopeful to change all this.

I enjoyed every single dive I did even though sometimes the strong currents made them challenging – particularly for my buddy. The highlights for me were a dusk dive on the jetty and the turtles we saw on every dive. (I am convinced that all the turtles were on holiday in Maratua). However, the most exhilarating dive had to be The Channel. We had been there only two days previously and had a good but non-conclusive dive in the hunt for the famous schooling barracudas. Was this second day going to be any different? We arrived at the site after the trip around to the other side of the island. We prepared to enter the water (no air in BCD) jumped in and went straight down. The visibility was good and the current was moderate. We finned along the wall looking out into the blue to see a large Napoleon Wrasse. Our guide, Andreas, took my buddy's camera and swam out to get a good shot.

We arrived at the front edge of the hollow where the channel through the reef starts and hooked in carefully. The current was suddenly so fast that our bubbles went down our backs. We looked into the blue in the hope of sharks and barracuda, but alas none today. We then moved (no need to fin) across the edge of the hollow, and just as we had been promised there were the barracudas in all their glory. Two enormous schools were swimming and dancing in the sea above us. They joined together then apart, making that typical barracuda circle very neatly for the photographers among us. We then moved up the reef to above the hollow and hooked on to watch the performance for a little longer and were graced with a large school of jacks swimming through the aquarium of barracuda's. But the time had come to leave them, so back onto the boat. It was an exhilarating and fabulous dive, just what I had been missing.

Carole Bellars, Group Financial Controller, London

9 The Channel

Depth	29 m
Visibility	very good
Currents	ripping
Dive Type	day boat

The most famous dive in this region, the Channel's reputation for barracudas is well earned, although you may need to dive it several times to be sure you are there when the currents are just right. The dive is a straightforward one: entry along the wall, past a sheer and beautiful drop with views into the most gorgeous deep blue water. There isn't much life extending from the wall, the currents ensure that corals and sponges grow flat to the surface.

As you approach the channel – a huge, flat and lifeless depression cutting through the wall – the currents move up a beat. If the barracudas are in residence, you will see them on one side or another. If not you can dive along the far side of the wall where the corals and fish are more prolific. However, the real reason for being here is the schooling barracudas: hundreds of blackfin barracudas form a massive conglomerate. These are tail-gated by a smaller school of yellowtail barracudas and from a shelf at about 15 metres, you can watch a school of jacks join them. The current remains strong the entire time as water gushes out from the lagoon, through the channel to the sea.

66 99 **If the currents aren't running at rip-your-mask-off levels, the barracudas sulkily disappear, it's simply no fun for them.**

Kakaban

Directly opposite Maratua, Kakaban is a geographic oddity that formed more than 10,000 years ago: movement deep in the earths crust forced land upwards, resulting in a lake of trapped seawater.

Approaching by boat you are faced with steep limestone cliffs covered in dense trees. These reach down to the water's edge giving an overall impression of an impenetrable wall of jungle. This barrier hides one of the most famed marine lakes in the world.

⏷10 Jellyfish Lake

🜨 **Depth**	5 m
◑ **Visibility**	poor to fair
🌀 **Currents**	none
🛥 **Dive type**	day boat

It only takes 10 minutes to walk from the jetty to the lake over a steep boardwalk path through the jungle. The interior of Kakaban opens to a swathe of mirror calm water fringed by mangroves. The lake is slightly above sea level and contains thousands of non-stinging jellyfish. These lost their natural defenses because there are no predators in the lake. Snorkelling with these saucer-sized, pulsating creatures is quite an experience although visibility is usually low: with a maximum depth of 17 metres, the water is affected by the algae covered bottom. In the shallows you can see many gobies, anemones and tunicates. Completely landlocked, the trapped saltwater is now topped up only by rain.

⏷11 Barracuda Point

🜨 **Depth**	33 m
◑ **Visibility**	fair to good
🌀 **Currents**	strong
🛥 **Dive type**	liveaboard

The walls around Kakaban drop to about 180 metres and currents that swirl around the island can be strong. Entry is straight over a bowl shaped depression in the reef with a drop down to 40 metres. You are meant to hang on the edge and wait for barracudas, but the current can move so fast, it is impossible to hook on and keep your mask in place! As the current pushes you along you pass beneath a school of barracudas (who are not struggling) until you round the corner onto the wall. This is the most magnificent reef with huge fans at depth. The site is well known for purple dart gobies but also for passing manta rays. The top tow metres of the reef has gorgeous coral gardens and dancing fish.

⏷12 The Wall

🜨 **Depth**	30 m
◑ **Visibility**	fair to good
🌀 **Currents**	none
🛥 **Dive type**	liveaboard

Returning to the wall but entering on the far side, you can see just how consistently impressive Kakaban's drop-offs are. Again topped by a pristine bed of hard corals where you can find clownfish and leaffish. The wall is covered in masses of fans and sponges. In fact, you can count nine or ten types of sponge all in one small space. There are many small caverns to investigate and inside are huge pufferfish and tiny gobies darting about. You need to watch out to the blue to as schools of oriental bonito pass by reflecting extensive waves of silver light. These are unusual for this area as are the lovely, yellow masked rabbitfish who dart about the reef in pairs, refusing to be photographed.

Life in the deep
Stealth predators

It's the dead of night: inky black skies are peppered with tiny glowing stars and, except for the splashing of our fellow divers, it's completely silent. We settle on the sand, turn on our torches and notice a small, fleeting movement at the edge of our vision. Rotating the beams, we see a lionfish hovering just beyond our pool of light. We move the torches a little and he follows. And snaps. We try it again, and again he trails behind the beam then snaps – clever boy! He's using our lights to stalk the tiny fish that are sitting just over the sea-bed and has managed to get himself a rather tasty dinner.

Mostly at night, it seems that fish are somewhat disoriented, even temporarily blinded by torch lights, and startled into stillness like a deer caught in car headlights. But not lionfish: they've learnt to take advantage of divers, sneaking up to swallow smaller, bewildered fish whole.

Lionfish are part of the *Scorpaenidae* family. Their closest relatives are scorpionfish and stonefish. The family is a relatively large one, including at least a dozen different varieties of lionfish. Their body shape is compressed and marked by ridges and spines. They grow to as much as 40 centimetres long, but spreading their pectoral fins can make them look much larger. They are also incredibly beautiful, yet have something of a split personality. Despite being so elegant and graceful, they harbour a mean and nasty secret. Lionfish are able to float fearlessly around the reef because they are one of the most venomous residents there. Their long, slender spines have small toxin glands embedded at the base. If the spine is pressed, it triggers a release of venom which is then delivered into whatever pressed on it.

The good news is that lionfish actually produce the weakest poison in their family. Scorpionfish have shorter spines, larger venom glands and a more potent sting, but it is the stonefish with even shorter, stronger spines, that have the largest venom glands. As they are so hard to spot, they are the ones most likely to be cause damage to humans. However, common to all is the effect of the neurotoxin, or nerve poison, that paralyses the victims muscles. For a small marine creature that will mean death. For a human, the consequences are usually less drastic, but can still be extremely painful. Like all marine fish, lionfish only attack when they are harassed. Mostly, their long feathery fins and bristling spines are used as camouflage. Nestled down amongst corals or seagrass they can be incredibly hard to spot and it's usually only when you disturb one that you realise they are there. Like all predators, lionfish instinctively know when to give up the chase if it seems likely to use more energy than it is worth, which also explains the clever adaptation to working in tandem with divers and their torch beams.

Lionfish are adaptable in other ways, too. As warm water creatures they live in the Indo-pacific (not the Atlantic and definitely not in the cooler climate off New York). Yet, in recent years, they have been seen many times in North Carolina and as far north as New York's Long Island. It is believed lionfish have become established along the US east coast because partially empty container ships leave Asian waters after sucking in huge quantities of seawater – along with all its residents – as ballast. This water gets pumped out again whenever and wherever more cargo is taken on board, the fish unceremoniously dumped somewhere off America.

↘1 Zebra ↘2 Spotfin ↘3 Shortfin ↘4 Twin spot ↘5 Common lionfish striking

Sangalaki

Small circular Sangalaki takes under half an hour to circumnavigate by foot, but the reefs that fringe its shores cover a far wider area. Extending from the beach, these slope gently for some distance and rarely drop much beyond 20 metres.

Although there are some shallow, coral clad walls, most sites are sandy bottomed reefs with garden-like outcrops of coral bommies where fish cluster. It's all rather pretty but the island became famous for just one thing, the manta rays that congregate here. It is said that you can see them on almost daily basis, but there are no guarantees! Over six dives on two different days we didn't see a single one. Disappointing but another reminder that the ocean is not a zoo.

⛴13 Cleaning Station

🕐 Depth	19 m	
🌓 Visibility	fair	
🌊 Currents	mild to medium	
🌀 Dive type	day boat	

Sangalaki's mantas are most often seen at the sites that lie off the northern coast. Shallow reefs lead to a sandy seabed that is dotted with small corals and lots of little fish. The dive starts over one large bommie that is undercut by several caverns where clusters of batfish are sheltering. There are many puffers: blue-spotted, porcupine and map types. Despite watching constantly for the elusive mantas as you drift over the pretty reef gardens, the biggest creature seen – and certainly impressive enough– is a huge thorny stingray that whizzes past divers at speed.

⛴15 Manta Run

🕐 Depth	21 m	
🌓 Visibility	fair	
🌊 Currents	mild to medium	
🌀 Dive type	day boat	

Once again, the mantas remain elusive so it's time to concentrate on the reef. Some of this is very sadly damaged by the Crown of Thorns starfish but in between the corals are interesting animals like mantis shrimp, the funeral jorunna nudibranch and blue ribbon eels. Queen triggerfish are actively building nests. Batfish are prolific all the way around Sangalaki, as are blue and yellow fusiliers and barramundi cod; even the fluttering juveniles are seen frequently. Drifting at eight or nine metres areas of quite good coral hide lobsters.

> ❝ ❞ I brief all our divers that mantas are an exceptional addition to any dive, but shouldn't be the sole focus. If we see them, that's superb, but if not, there is still so much other life to see. In reality, we have found there is no real pattern to the mantas appearances throughout the year. They are always there, but sometimes deep and single and sometimes shallow at the surface.
>
> They generally feed on microscopic plankton, and when there is plankton on the surface – especially on a hot sunny day and with a cold current – they can be seen feeding right at the top or just a few metres below. When feeding we have seen groups of 5-25 and one time in November, at least 100! We never guarantee manta sightings, but 95% of all divers who stay on Sangalaki for more than five days have encountered these majestic creatures!
>
> *Jeremy Stein, owner, Sangalaki Dive Lodge*

⛴14 Manta Parade

🕐 Depth	13 m	
🌓 Visibility	fair	
🌊 Currents	mild to medium	
🌀 Dive type	day boat	

The topography on this site is similar but the current is a little stronger. With still no sign of the mantas it's good to see a plethora of other ray species including a black-blotched stingray and quite a few bluespotted rays. An adult leopard shark followed by a turtle and many angelfish.

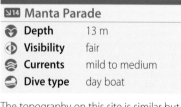

Black-blotched (top) and thorny stingrays (right)

Drying out

With such a small collection of resorts choosing one is not too difficult. Each island has its unique marine features, but Maratua probably has the broadest range of dive sites which is no doubt why it has the most resorts.

$$ **Maratua Paradise Resort**, T+60 882 4833, borneo.org. The largest resort in the entire region has enormous but slightly rustic wooden bungalows spanning both the lagoon and the beach. The rooms are detached, charming and face into some stunning sunsets. Delightful staff and dive crew, excellent meals and very spacious dive centre with a well-planned kitting up area and a camera room. Unlimited shore diving under the jetty.

$$ **Nabucco Island Resort**, T+62 (0)542 593635, nabuccoislandresort.com. On the eastern side of Maratua Atoll this resort has been built on top of a tiny limestone island making good use of a very small space. Well-furnished rooms are semi-detached and sit in a lush, tropical garden setting. Classy communal facilties, but no shore diving. Also the owners of Nabucco's Nunukan Island Resort, 30 mins south.

Other options
Derawan Dive Resort, divederawan.com
Sangalaki Dive Lodge, sangalaki.net

Balikpapan
Le Grandeur Hotel, T+62 (0)542 420155 legrandeurhotels.com. Smart, 3-star hotel in the city but on the coast. Facilities include pool, bar, restaurants and wireless internet, so great for a stopover.

Maratua Paradise (top) and Le Grandeur Hotel

Balikpapan

Kalimantan's major international airport is a busy and efficient entry point with many internal flights leaving for all over the region. Because of that most divers pass straight through en route to their dive destination. However, should you fancy a night or two in this bustling city, there are good facilities with several smart hotels and many shopping centres. It is more of a business destination, servicing the timber, mining and petroleum industries, than a tourist one though, so there are few things to see, the major exception being the **Samboja Orang-utan Sanctuary**, which is an hour by car from town. You can stay here overnight, or visit for a day, but it is difficult to make reservations in advance and even harder to get in on arrival (sambojalodge.com). Other than that, it's a city tour, which will include the handicrafts market, a Japanese cemetery from World War II and the crocodile farm at Teritip.

Berau

While Balikpapan caters for businesses, Berau's focus is highly industrial. The city is more correctly known as Tanjung Redeb and is divided by the Berau River. The centre is a colourful, typically Indonesian cluster of buildings, mosques and shops. Chances are you will only drive through

before boarding a transfer boat on the river. The long journey down to the delta then across to the islands is interesting enough in itself: you pass massive depots and barges that service the coal and timber industries, small villages, mangrove rimmed islands and finally, traditional fishermen's platforms built of bamboo.

Sleeping	$$$ US$150+ double room per night	$$ US$75-150	$ under US$75
Eating	$$$ US$40+ 2-course meal, excluding drinks	$$ US$20-40	$ under US$20

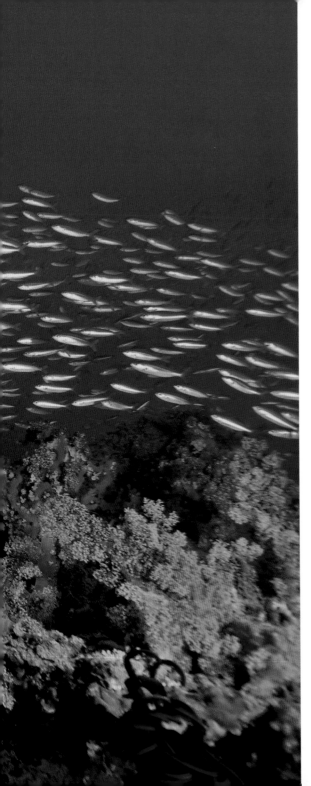

Malaysia

Narrowstripe fusiliers, *Pterocaesio tessellata*, swimming en masse

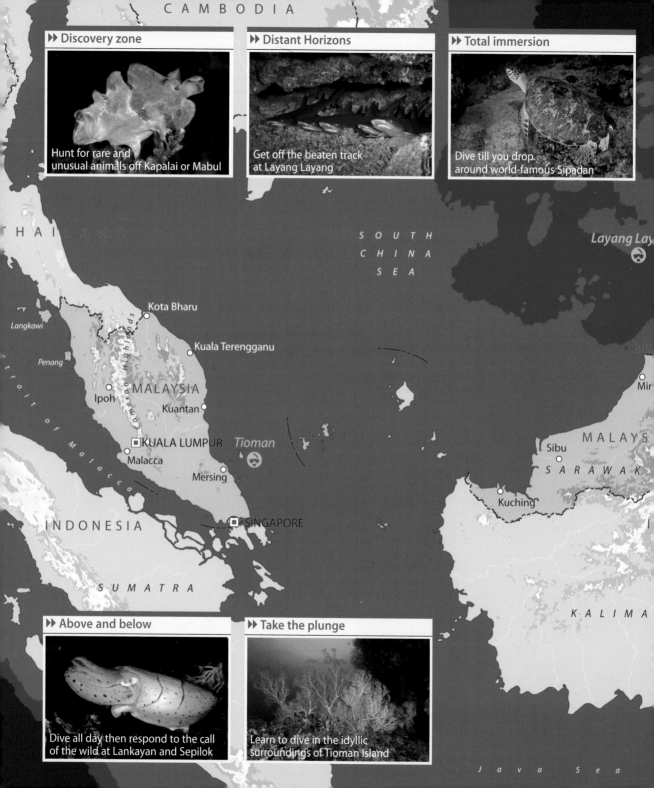

CAMBODIA

Discovery zone

Hunt for rare and
unusual animals off Kapalai or Mabul

Distant Horizons

Get off the beaten track
at Layang Layang

Total immersion

Dive till you drop
around world-famous Sipadan

THAILAND

Langkawi

Penang

Kota Bharu

Kuala Terengganu

Cameron Highlands

MALAYSIA

Ipoh

Kuantan

KUALA LUMPUR

Tioman

Malacca

Mersing

INDONESIA

SINGAPORE

SUMATRA

SOUTH
CHINA
SEA

Layang Lay

Mir

MALAYS

Sibu

SARAWAK

Kuching

KALIMA

BR

Straits of Malacca

Above and below

Dive all day then respond to the call
of the wild at Lankayan and Sepilok

Take the plunge

Learn to dive in the idyllic
surroundings of Tioman Island

Java Sea

Malaysia's dive profile is something of a double-edged sword. Divided by the South China Sea, one part of the country creates the western edge of the Coral Triangle so is a rich and lush destination with extremely high biodiversity rankings, while the other part is, like neighbouring Thailand, something of an outsider.

Both regions sit in Southeast Asian waters, but Borneo's position is what makes it the most favoured destination. Descend into the waters around Sabah to find a theatrical mix of pelagic predators living in tandem with rare and unusual creatures that are rarely bigger than your hand.

Across the sea, the small islands and reefs off the mainland are totally different but charming destinations in their own right, and well worth exploring in the right season. In fact, all of Malaysia's islands are worth discovering. Often as pretty as a picture postcard, these magical islands are, for many, a chance to escape from reality.

Drying out days become another voyage of discovery as Malaysia once again demonstrates its split personality. This is the most multicultural of any Asian country, with Malay, Chinese and Indian influences combining to create a unique experience.

Introduction

Malaysia

Essentials

Getting there

Reaching mainland Malaysia and capital Kuala Lumpur is easy, but as the country's best diving is actually on the island of Borneo, that is where most divers head. The obvious airline choice is Malaysian Airlines (malaysiaairlines.com), as they have frequent worldwide flights that land in KL. They are also the principal carrier for internal flights with connections to the Borneo states of Sabah and Sarawak as well as routes across the mainland.

There are other carriers flying to KL, Qantas, Qatar and Delta among them, plus Singapore Airlines have frequent flights to Borneo, with routes from Singapore to Kota Kinabalu, the capital of Sabah, Kuching (Sarawak) and even Brunei. Some of these may be run by their subsidiary Silk Air. In addition there is the ever-burgeoning, AirAsia (airasia.com). This low cost carrier, which started in Malaysia, now has flights across the region and as far as Australia.

Whoever you arrive with, you will need to transfer to either the Malaysian network or AirAsia for your internal flights. If you are going to Borneo, connections are straightforward and mostly same day.

Things are far more complicated if you are staying on the Peninsula and heading to one of the islands that lie off the eastern mainland coast. These are surprisingly difficult to reach and transfers are never included. If you do decide to head this way, you will need to fly into KL and then on to a coastal airport: internal Malaysian Airlines flights leave from the international terminal but if you are on AirAsia you will need to transfer from KL's international airport to the Low Cost Carrier Terminal. It's a 20-minute drive away so ensure you leave enough time between flights. Another option is Berjaya Air's seasonal charters to Redang and Tioman from Subang airport on the other side of the city. Getting there can take an hour or more and there are no direct public transport links. These flights are run by the Berjaya Hotel group, who also fly from Singapore's Selatar airport to both places. You can use these flights even if you are staying elsewhere but you may find it difficult to book (berjayaresorts.com).

Visas are generally not required to enter Malaysia. A visitor pass will be stamped into your passport on arrival but note that this can take quite some time.

Getting around

Sightseeing on the mainland is easy enough: taxis are metered and drivers are helpful; bus networks vary from classy air-con to local and lively; small ferries connect islands to shore. On Borneo, as most resorts are on islands, exploring the countryside would involve a transfer back to the coast so it would make more sense to arrange a tour. See page 163 for ideas.

Malaysia	
Location	2°30'N, 122°30'E
Neighbours	Brunei, Indonesia, Philippines, Singapore, Thailand
Population	25,274,132
Land area in km²	328,550
Coastline in km	9,323
Territorial sea in km²	152,367

Transfers

Once you arrive on Borneo, all major dive operators and hotels will collect you from the closest airport. Unfortunately, the same cannot be said of the islands off the east coast of the Peninsula. Getting to those is best described as challenging and this, along with the seasonal nature of the diving, is why they are less than popular with long-distance travellers. In reality, even the locals complain about the time and number of transport changes it can take to get from the cities to the islands.

For destinations in Sabah on Borneo, fly to Kota Kinabalu:

Kota Kinabalu The small capital city of Sabah is an ideal stopover. Hotels are close to the airport and include courtesy transfers.

Layang Layang The resort charters a small aircraft every couple of days. This private flight departs from Kota Kinabalu airport and is booked along with your package. It leaves early in the morning and takes about an hour so you will need to stay in KK overnight.

Lankayan You could drive this route but it's easier to get a Malaysian Airlines hopper flight from KK. In 45 minutes you will land at Sandakan where the resort will meet you for a speedboat ride to the island (45 minutes) or the short land transfer to their sister resort at Sepilok, for the orang-utan sanctuary.

Mabul and Kapalai All resorts clustered in the Sipadan area collect their clients from Tawau airport after a 50-minute flight from KK or a non-stop three-hour flight from either Kuala Lumpur or Singapore. This is followed by an hour's drive to Semporna then a trip by boat to the relevant island or hotel in less than hour.

For destinations off Peninsular Malaysia, head to Kuala Lumpur:

Kuala Lumpur Reaching the city centre takes over an hour from the international airport. Best described as a thriving metropolis, it may be worth a stopover, but if you just want a night's rest there are hotels near the airport with courtesy transfers.

East coast islands Connections to these islands are convoluted and time consuming – travel from KL to Tioman or Singapore to Perhentian can take as long as getting from London to KL. The best option is to choose one of the islands that has a small airport – Tioman or Redang only – or take a liveaboard that departs from Singapore, although there is only one of these.

From Kuala Lumpur, fly to the coast or, if you have plenty of time, take a bus to the closest coastal town as advised by your resort. Once there you will then need to take a taxi to the port and a small ferry across to the island. And then, finally, there may be a short land transfer to your resort. Buses depart from Kuala Lumpur and Singapore. All routes take a minimum of eight hours on the bus plus up to an hour for the boat crossing to Redang and nearly two hours for Tioman.

 Tourist information → the official government website can be found at tourism.gov.my. This site has links to various regional sites. For Sabah go to sabahtourism.com.

Fact file

International flights	AirAsia, Delta, Malaysian Airlines, Qatar, Qantas, Singapore Airlines, Silk Air
Departure tax	Included in your flight price
Entry	Visa not required for EU, USA and Commonwealth citizens
Internal flights	AirAsia, Malaysian Airlines
Ground transport	Buses, ferries and taxis
Money	US$1 = 3.5 ringgit (MYR)
Language	Bahasa Malaysia, English is widely spoken
Electricity	240v/plus type B
Time zone	GMT +8
Religion	Muslim, Buddhist, Hindu, Christian
Phone	Country code +60; IDD code 00; Police 999

Malaysia Essentials

Language

The national language of Malaysia is Bahasa which is spoken by 50% of the country's inhabitants. However, with large groups of other language speakers, English is also used widely. Despite the similarity in name, Bahasa Indonesia and Bahasa Malaysia are not exactly the same.

good morning (till 1200)	*selamat pagi*
good afternoon (1200-1400)	
	selamat tengah hari
good afternoon (1400-1900)	
	selamat petang
good evening	*selamat malam*
welcome	*selamat datang*
goodbye (if you are leaving)	*selamat jalan*
and if you are staying	*selamat tinggal*
yes	*ya*
no	*tidak*
please	*sila*
thank you	*terima kasih*
sorry!	*ma'af*
how much is...	*berapa harga ini...*
you're welcome	*sama-sama*
good	*bagus*
great dive!	*menyelam yang bagus!*
one beer/water	*satu bir/air*

Local laws and customs

Malaysia is Asia's melting pot. About half the country consists of indigenous Malay people, a third are Chinese, 10% are Indian and the rest are a curious melange of backgrounds. As such, cultural norms are an interesting and occasionally odd mix. On the mainland, some areas are strongly Muslim, which is the predominant religion. Be sure to dress conservatively if you are away from your resort. Although religious rules are not too stringent here, and many women wear western dress, take note of what locals are wearing and try to fit in. The Borneo states are far more Chinese influenced, and mostly Buddhist, with quite a large population of Filipinos working in dive-related areas.

Always be polite and friendly, and smiling works wonders. Bear in mind that people tend to dislike and avoid touching other people. Handshakes are tentative, and even touching a child is regarded as unacceptable. Likewise, pointing at people is thought be extremely rude as is using your index finger to get attention – it's what prostitutes do!

Safety

Generally, crimes against tourists are rare in Malaysia. Be sensible in big cities, leaving valuables like cash and passports in your hotel safe. Don't leave flashy dive or camera bags unattended, and no one should accept drinks from strangers. Of course, once you reach your island-based dive resort, these concerns become almost irrelevant as there's hardly anywhere to go.

Be aware that Malaysia probably has Asia's strictest laws on drug possession, which is punished by a jail sentence and whipping, while trafficking or possessing large amounts of any drug carries a mandatory death sentence.

It's been a few years since terrorism hit Malaysia's shores. After the Sipadan kidnappings back in 2000, the government stationed armed forces on all offshore islands. These places are now about as safe as you can get and the soldiers who watch over you are all utterly charming. However, many governmental advisories still recommend caution. Before planning a trip, take advice from those on the ground (your dive centre or hotel) and bear in mind that government websites naturally err on the side of caution.

🍴 Feeding frenzy

Malaysia and the eating out experience is something not to be missed. The three principal ethnic groups supply three fantastic cuisines: Indian, Chinese and Malay. Choosing between them is something of a quandary as each has been influenced by the others. An Indian meal here will have overtones of Malay spices, Chinese will have hints of India. Regardless, the food can be exquisite, not necessarily to cordon bleu standards, but always fresh and unfailingly spicy. Rice and noodles are the staples, but meats vary along with religions: beef is common in the Malay diet while pork is more common in Chinese meals (obviously the Muslim communities will not eat that). You may come across mutton (which can mean goat meat). Everyone eats chicken or seafood and fish is widespread. You can have fish curry every night for a week and it will never be the same twice. The European influence can be seen in the proliferation of bakeries but you may not recognize some of the local delicacies. However, it must be said that curry donuts are one of life's great inventions.

There are of course, downsides to all this: one is that if you have the opportunity to eat out in local restaurants you will do so as often as you can – take note of the restaurant name; and another is that if you are in a resort with meals included, you won't be able to eat out anywhere near as often as you would like.

Health

Apart from the usual hot sun and stinging bug warnings, Malaysia has few health issues for visitors, though note that you need to be careful with drinking water. All offshore islands are reliant on watermakers (often reverse osmosis) or importing water by tanker. You will probably be supplied with drinking water in your room. Should anything out of the ordinary occur, it is good to know that doctors and chemists are well trained, many in the UK, as there are close links between UK and Malay universities.

Costs

When it comes to costs, standards and value for money, there is little to worry about with Malaysia. On Borneo, the island resorts tend to be charming but fairly simple, with just enough creature comforts to keep people happy. The one downside is that there is little choice. The only island with more than one accommodation option is Mabul where your choice lies between a little classier or a little simpler. Daily rates reflect the various standards. Meals and diving are usually included in accommodation rates so your only extras will be souvenirs and drinks, which are not too heavily marked up – a beer is around US$3, a bottle of water about US$1.50.

For resorts on Tioman and other islands on the Peninsula, there is a greater choice of hotel classes. The majority are simple and a little rustic but if you want first class you can have that, too. Should you choose to stop over in Kuala Lumpur or Kota Kinabalu, again there are plenty of hotels in all categories.

Tipping is not expected anywhere – bigger hotels and restaurants will include a service charge on their bills. Most resorts have a staff fund box in reception or a small box in the resort's mini-van so you can leave something. What you leave is entirely up to you and should reflect the level of service you were given. For guides, drivers and divemasters, see page 11.

Dive brief

Diving

Malaysia is a geographically widespread country. There are 11 'mainland' states that sit between Thailand and Singapore plus another two states, and a federal territory, on the island of Borneo. When it comes to top class diving, Borneo is the place to head. Her two states, Sabah and Sarawak, and the Federal Territory of Labuan, are washed by the South China, Sulu and Celebes Seas. Being surrounded by open ocean currents makes for an incredibly diverse set of marine environments.

Sabah – which translates as the 'Land below the Wind' – is ringed by a mass of marine reserves, idyllic islands and 75% of the country's reefs. The diving here is superlative and your only problem will be choosing between resorts. Sarawak, on the other hand, has very little organized diving while the island territory of Labuan, which was once targeted for its interesting wrecks, has dropped off the dive radar – dive centres have disappeared and these wrecks are now only visited from Brunei, itself with only minimal dive facilities.

Peninsular Malaysia, which sits between the South China Sea and the Straits of Malacca, has plenty of diving but is often bypassed in favour of spectacular Sabah. The west coast is not regarded as much of a dive destination to those in the know. A history of heavy shipping, trade and industry has taken its toll on the marine environment. Over on the east coast, it's a different story. A string of picturesque islands lines the coast but because they are hard to reach, they are favoured mostly by Asian divers who live close by. Diving here is regarded as a 'stopover' or weekend training destination. However, if you have a few days to spare it can be worth a detour.

Malaysian diving is highly seasonal but restrictions vary. Dive centres on the Gulf Coast islands shut down between November and April as does Layang Layang north of Sabah. Other areas can be dived most of the year but visibility can be poor at times. All diving is principally land-based. There is one liveaboard based in Sabah, and one that sails up the mainland coast, but it is based in Singapore.

Snorkelling

If you are travelling with a non-diver who loves to snorkel, there will be suitable coastal strips and shallow lagoons but these can also be limited by weather conditions. Kapalai's lagoon is fantastic as is the reef just off the beach near Sipadan's old jetty.

66 99 We first dived off the Malay Peninsula many years ago and were disappointed. It seemed the only option was to head to Sabah on Borneo and there we soon found that every dive was utterly superior. But recently we returned to Tioman and what a revelation... OK, it's not quite as good but there is so much more there than we remembered or ever expected to find.

Dive data

Seasons	May to September, mostly good countrywide, October to April, restricted in some areas	
Visibility	5 metres inshore to 40 metres and over in open water	
Temperatures	Air 22-32°C; water 26-31°C	
Wet suit	3 mm full body suit	
Training	Courses are not common – ask in advance	
Nitrox	At some resorts on Mabul	
Deco chambers	Kuantan, Labuan, Singapore	

Diversity
reef area
3,600 km²

CORALS	7568
FISH SPECIES	1229
ENDEMIC FISH SPECIES	4
FISH UNDER THREAT	49
PROTECTED REEFS/MARINE PARKS	44

All diversity figures are approximate

Diversity

Malaysia is a widespread country so both its land and marine biodiversity is influenced by many factors, not least that there are coastlines bordering the Andaman, South China, Sulu and Sulawesi seas. The majority of the country sits outside the Coral Triangle, with just a short section of Sabah's east coast stretching along its border. It's really only the cluster of islands around Sipadan that fall inside this region and because of that, and the deeper seas nearby, they display the most impressive reef diversity. This side of Borneo also faces the Wallace Line (see page 54) which defines the different types of Asian fauna and flora and explains much of Borneo's incredible rainforest species.

Heading west around the top of Sabah, reef structures are a bit less impressive as the flatter, coastal sea plateau extends out towards the offshore islands. Corals are less prolific although few divers would ever really notice the differences in the quantity and types of marines species. Layang Layang, however, is a bit of an anomaly as it sits isolated in deep open water.

Between Borneo and the mainland is the shallow Gulf of Thailand. The coastline that faces into the Gulf has virtually no coral reef because it is edged by low-lying mangroves. However, the islands that sit a short distance into the Gulf are rimmed by small but diverse reefs. This shallow body of water restricts coral growth but there is still a lot to see in these waters.

Making the big decision

If you are travelling a long way to dive Malaysia it's a good idea to see more than one area. Sabah has several first-class options. Each island resort has its unique features so choosing where to go should be based on what you want to see. Do you want to swim with pelagics or spend your time with your nose down a hole hunting for weird and wonderful species? Travel between resorts is easy, making it possible to do a multi-centre trip. Dives off the Peninsula's east coast are lovely but they lack the variety of Sabah. They are well worth a quick stop but wouldn't keep many people entertained for more than a few days. The only other thing to consider is the time of year. A couple of these resorts are seasonal so choose your time carefully.

Bottom time

Sabah

Layang
Layang ▸▸ p138 Malaysia's South China Sea resort, nicknamed the Jewel of the Borneo Banks. This isolated atoll has Malaysia's most impressive open water diving. Outstanding visibility means you could never miss the hordes of pelagics.
The resort is closed from September to February

Lankayan ▸▸ p143 The only resort in the Sulu Sea, this lush green island is a nature lover's retreat. Walk in the mini jungle or in stand ankle-deep in water with baby blacktips around your toes. In the water it's heads down for a marine treasure hunt but remember to look up occasionally.
Dive all year, whalesharks from February to April

Sipadan ▸▸ p148 A legend amongst legends, this tiny island has a huge reputation. Sitting away from the shallower coastal reefs, its perimeter walls drop to unimaginable depths in the Sulawesi Sea. You can no longer stay on the island but visit from nearby Mabul and Kapalai.
All year, but unsettled weather in January to March

Kapalai ▸▸ p152 Edging the shallow Litigan Reefs, the jetty dives rank right up near the very top of the 'best muck diving in the world' list.
All year, but unsettled weather in January to March

Mabul ▸▸ p160 Just moments by boat from Kapalai, Mabul's diving is another marine treasure hunt with a few surprises to keep you on your toes.
All year, but unsettled weather in January to March

Peninsular Malaysia

Tioman ▸▸ p166 This island is a marine park. Surrounding waters are shallow and well suited to the beginners who flock here to train. However, there is lively and more challenging diving way offshore .
All year but June to September is slightly wetter

Sabah

This northern section of the rainforest island of Borneo has to be one of the world's most coveted dive destinations. And the reason why is simple. A couple of decades ago, that most famous of pioneers, Jacques Cousteau, dived around Sipadan and later produced a documentary about the island's turtles.

Of course, the dive industry had already discovered Sipadan but this new found, international fame attracted ever more people to the island to see what it was all about. The attention was justified: the island is actually the tip of an underwater mountain located in exceptionally deep water. The base is said to be at around 700 metres and is divided from the continental shelf by an even deeper channel. This, along with the shallow shelving Litigan Reefs to the north, has ensured that the ecology and diversity of the island will always be unique.

What is perhaps more interesting to the average diver is that almost all of Sabah's dive destinations have something special or unusual to see. This is due to the variety of reef systems and their locations around the top rim of Borneo. The island sits right in the middle of an incredible number of seas each of which has its own ocean current system, swirling around the coastline and influencing the marine ecosystem.

The most influential current is the Indonesian Throughflow (page 54) which transports water from the Pacific to Indian Oceans. It follows the equator, moving east to west. hits the Philippines and is broken into several smaller currents. Some of these run down the western side of Sabah; the other most important section runs between Sulawesi and Borneo.

Locations

Some people may be disappointed to find that they can't take a liveaboard all the way around Sabah and see several areas at once. The diving here is very much focused on the tiny islands dotted around the coastlines and then on the shores and coasts of each.

Most diving is day boat, yet there is very little travelling involved: 15 minutes in this direction from the jetty, 10 minutes in that. In fact, some of Sabah's very best diving is under the resorts' jetties. It is worth trying to do more than one of these destinations though, especially if you have travelled a long way to reach Sabah – fortunately, organizing a twin-centre is easy. Connections between any two resorts can be done within a day.

Destinations

Sabah

Layang Layang is just one of many islands in the Spratly Group at the southern end of the South China Seas. The Spratlys have long been fought over. For decades, China, the Philippines, Vietnam and Taiwan have laid claim to the isolated and mostly uninhabited islands nearest their territorial waters. As Layang Layang sits closest to Borneo, a Royal Malaysian Navy outpost was built there to ensure that Malaysia's interest over the Spratlys was not lost in the melee. And as it's surrounded by incredible coral reefs, creating a dive resort at the same time must have seemed an obvious choice. Layang Layang, or Swallow's Reef, is a submerged oval with just one tiny, barren island. This was expanded to create an airstrip which hangs above the outer edge of the reef. Beside that runs a narrow piece of land bordering a delightful, turquoise lagoon. At the far end is a small nature and bird preserve, but that's it. *Distance from airport: about 3 mins*

In the Sulu Seas and off the coastal town of Sandakan, **Lankayan** is not dissimilar in that once you are there, there is nowhere else to go. However, Lankayan is lush where Layang is dry. The island is ringed by a shining white beach and covered in a labyrinth of unruly green jungle. It can be circumnavigated on foot easily in under an hour, providing the tide is out. It's all so lovely it's almost a cliché – too cute for words or even a postcard but not too pretty for the dive resort that nestles at one end. Clusters of bungalows hide under the pandanus and coconut palms. *Distance from airport: 1½ hrs*

Places to stay and things to do at these destinations are listed in Drying out on page 147

Further around to the east coast, the town of Semporna is the gateway to Borneo's most famous destination, **Sipadan**. However, accommodation on Sipadan was closed in 2004 and most hotels moved their operations to nearby **Mabul**. This is a comparatively large island, covering 20 hectares, with a variety of resorts all the way around its shores and even one offshore in a converted oil rig. Strange but true. There's also a small village that can be visited although the focus is mostly resort based. **Kapalai** is the only other option in this area. There's no land here, just a miniscule sandbar with eco-friendly, wooden water village bungalows perched over its gorgeous lagoon. You can walk on the sandbar at low tide, but again, there is nothing else. *Distance from airport: minimum 2 hrs*

Places to stay and things to do at these destinations are listed in Drying out on page 163

Lankayan island, Layang Layang Resort; orchid from the gardens at Sepilok; Seplilok; Sipadan-Kapalai

Layang Layang

Fly an hour northwest from Kota Kinabalu into the South China Sea to find yourself hovering over a series of miniscule land masses known as the Spratly Islands. Sitting at the southern end of the group is Layang Layang.

This tiny land mass sits on the edge of an incredible lagoon, its outer walls constructed of pristine hard corals. These drop away from the outer edge to unfathomable depths and offer a haven to masses of pelagic life. While the corals and reef life alone are worth a visit, most come for the curious hammerhead phenomenon: every Easter, large schools swarm into Layang then head off again a few weeks later. At other times turtles, reef sharks and schooling pelagic fish are common. The resort is also a bird sanctuary where rare brown boobies nest. Conditions here are variable. The atoll is very exposed: winds can whip the sea into a frenzy and the dive boats struggle to exit the channel to the outer reef. Currents can be strong and surface conditions rough. Late in the year, when the winds really pick up, the resort closes for a few months. However, in season, when conditions are good, they are very, very good – and visibility can seem limitless.

⬛1 Wrasse Strip	
🔻 **Depth**	35 m
◐ **Visibility**	fair to stunning
🌀 **Currents**	medium to strong
⬤ **Dive type**	day boat

On the northern side of the atoll but at its westernmost end, Layang's dive sites tend to be sloping reefs rather than a rapid drop down to a sharp wall. This makes for excellent multi-level diving. Most of the time there is a current on Wrasse Strip, but it's a manageable one, although on a 'good' day, the current will even carry you along to the Valley so you get to do two sites at once. However, this dive is best when the current is less strong and you have time to admire the shallower parts of the reef. The gentle slope is covered in a variety of hard corals and crusting sponges. Its fairly pretty terrain inhabited by soldier and triggerfish and all sorts of wrasse. Many cluster under table corals where you can also spot reef fish such as boxfish, angels and butterflies. Just past 20 metres the slope drops into a sloping wall where there is a bed of waving gorgonians, whip corals and some lush soft coral growth.

Layang-Layang Resort
MALAYSIA

⬛1	Wrasse Strip	⬛5	The Tunnel
⬛2	The Valley	⬛6	Wreck Point
⬛3	Sharks Cave	⬛7	Dogtooth Lair
⬛4	D-Wall	⬛8	The Lagoon

Layang Layang

⊻2 The Valley

Depth	35 m
Visibility	stunning
Currents	medium to strong
Dive type	day boat

At first glance, this site looks like nothing much, just a flat slope with small crusting corals, sponges and some fish. But descend to 30 metres and the action starts: lots of small whitetip sharks and handfuls of large grey reefs appear out in the blue; there are dogtooth tuna and several giant trevally. These swoop to and fro in the current that pushes against the western tip of the lagoon. A cluster of blackfin barracuda joins the throng then, as you start to ascend, another huge ball of barracuda appears overhead. Back up in shallower waters there is a 'valley' scooped out of the reef where you can find large turtles resting, many juvenile whitetips under some bommies and a gigantic ball of schooling jacks. Napoleon wrasse, batfish and more turtles arrive and if you focus your attention on the reef you can also see smaller animals like parrotfish, puffers and razorfish.

⊻3 Sharks Cave

Depth	31 m
Visibility	stunning
Currents	medium to strong
Dive type	day boat

Dropping down this nearly vertical wall, you will encounter two different sandy shelves. Depending on the currents, and the direction you approach from, you will probably drop to the deeper shelf first. It sits at about 35 metres where an overhang creates a small cave. The divemasters are at pains to point out in their briefings that there are no sharks in it despite the name. The cave rim has nice soft corals though and there are often large grouper tucked into a recess at the end. Just as you start to leave the cave, and very rarely, a small whitetip shark may come past to have a look. Heading back up the wall, you pass a lot of small fish living on or around the corals and sponges, while off the wall the schooling fish are prolific, with large groups of butterflyfish. When you hit 25 metres you should find the second cave which is a little larger than the first and is more likely to have sharks in it.

⊻4 D-Wall

Depth	27 m
Visibility	stunning
Currents	can be strong
Dive type	day boat

This can be one of Layang's more difficult sites and if the wind is from the wrong direction, divemasters will avoid it. The site is at the eastern end of the atoll, and there can be quite a lot of swell getting out to the site (at least the boats are fast). Entry is over a sandy patch that leads down to the steepest wall in the atoll. Drifting along in a moderate current, you are likely to be joined by a hawksbill turtle, quickly followed by another and then a juvenile. There is little time to stop and admire the barrel sponges, fans and decent soft coral growth, nor look for the frogfish that you have been briefed will be there. However, this is no time for disappointment as yet another big turtle comes along, followed by some juveniles. A whitetip passes below and there are three dog tooth tuna following them. This is also the site where hammerheads are seen but only during the early months in the season.

Masked pufferfish avoiding the camera; a juvenile whitetip line-up at The Valley

A diving recipe

Dive, eat, sleep in hammock under trees. Dive, eat, chat, dive, eat, sleep. Repeat until your time and money has expired.

Layang Layang is a relaxed and friendly place, the staff are easy to deal with and know their sites and the critters well. The diving is superb and although it was the end of the season there was still the odd hammerhead cruising about. It was unusual NOT to see turtles on each dive and I was starting to feel a little blasé about seeing whitetips (if that's possible...)

Each dive brought a feeling of awe. The water clarity and colour, the size, abundance and variety of fish life or even the scale of the reef walls and drop-offs were all difficult to comprehend.

"Wow!" is about the most adequate way to sum up the whole experience.

*Estelle Zauner,
Chiropractor and
Dive Instructor,
Newcastle, UK*

5	The Tunnel	
Depth	27 m
Visibility	fair to great
Currents	mild to strong
Dive type	day boat

Sitting just outside the exit channel from the lagoon, this dive has interesting, multi-level terrain covered in lots of healthy hard corals. The best part of the dive is in the shallower sections before the reef drops to a wall. There are several gullies in the reef, one of which is a distinct tunnel shape. Along its sides are masses of reef fish including several kinds of butterflies, arc-eye hawkfish, coral trout, wrasse and fusiliers. On the sloping parts of the reef large turtles lumber past, stopping briefly to gnaw at a sponge and smile for the camera. This site is equally good at night – if the current is low – when morays emerge from their hidey-holes and crustaceans come out to feed.

Picasso trigger; Layang corals; arc-eye hawkfish

↘6 Wreck Point

🕐	**Depth**	23 m
◑	**Visibility**	fair to good
🌊	**Currents**	slight
🛥	**Dive type**	day boat

There really isn't much of a wreck on this site: once there was said to be an old freighter lodged on the reef but all that remains now are a few bits of metal that you are likely to fin over without even seeing them. However, this dive is one of the prettier coral gardens around the atoll rim. There are sandy patches with a few outcrops scattered across them. The small channels between lead down through nice swim-throughs then on to a small wall. Visibility can be low as the currents are just strong enough to stir up the sand although this is one of the more protected sites. Looking for the marine life in this section is more about the smaller animals. Although you will see at least one turtle, look out for bright tomato clownfish in their bubble-shaped anemones, reindeer wrasse juveniles, majestic angelfish and also a lot of other angels of various types.

↘7 Dogtooth Lair

🕐	**Depth**	25 m
◑	**Visibility**	fair to good
🌊	**Currents**	mild to strong
🛥	**Dive type**	day boat

Lying behind the resort, this site gets mixed currents. From the surface you can admire a racing pod of dolphins playing in the waves while below, your dive profile becomes a zigzag pattern along the wall and slope. The dive site is named after the pack of enormous tuna that often lurks here but it is equally likely to have schools of jacks and turtles – although every dive on Layang has turtles. You would have to be asleep to miss them. Rumour has it that this is also another prime site for the schools of hammerheads that appear in huge gangs around Easter when the resort is at its busiest. At other times whitetips park at the cleaner stations for a spruce up as do honeycomb groupers. Looking down in the flat reef areas, there are lots of nudibranchs along with robust ghost pipefish and banded coral shrimp hiding under small corals.

↘8 The Lagoon

🕐	**Depth**	10 m
◑	**Visibility**	poor
🌊	**Currents**	none to slight
🛥	**Dive type**	day boat

If you are interested in fish nurseries, then it's worth diving right in front of the resort. You can start from the boat jetty or walk a little way past the swimming pool and slowly fin back. The visibility is never outstanding but there are loads of critters. On the sandy sea bed are masses of dragonets, upside-down jellyfish, gobies with their commensal shrimp partners, twintail and headshield slugs and pipefish. Holes in the sand reveal the spearing mantis shrimp surrounded by sail fin gobies. Small corals are ringed by tiny white triggerfish, baby lionfish, juvenile butterflies, damsels and sweetlips plus the outrageously coloured Picasso triggerfish. Look out for the unusual anemone with pink tips that protects tiny clownfish. Should you visit Layang towards the end of the year it is likely you will dive inside the lagoon quite often.

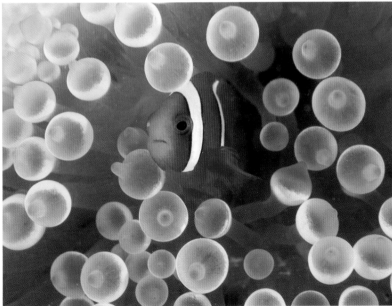

Big-eye trevally, aka, jacks; juvenile Clarke's anemonefish – this is the orange variation

Malaysia Dive log Sabah: Layang Layang

Life in the deep
Hey dude – let's talk turtle

As divers, we all know just how wonderful an encounter with a turtle can be. They are surely the only reptiles to be regarded with such affection, even cropping up frequently in popular culture: think Disney's Crush and his son Squirt who coined that "Hey dude" phrase; or Teenage Mutant Ninja Turtles and the 1960s rock group. The turtle represents Mother Earth for many indigenous people – for native Americans, it even created 'turtle island', more commonly known as North America. In Aboriginal Dreamtime, the symbol of a nesting turtle laying its eggs represents the difficult road of motherhood, while in India, turtle carvings are found at temples so people can deposit their hurt and anger with them before entering.

Turtle is a generic term for the group of reptiles that includes tortoises and terrapins. There are about 300 species in total but only seven are marine turtles. These are very similar to look at with a body that is shielded by a special bony shell developed from their ribs. All turtles have beak-like jaws instead of teeth; are air-breathing and surface regularly to refill their lungs, and as they drink sea water, cry salty tears to get rid of excess salt. Female turtles lay eggs only on dry, sandy beaches but they do not care for their brood, they simply lay and run. The hatchlings emerge at night after an incubation of around two months, and once in the sea hatchlings 'disappear' until they grow to dinner-plate sized juveniles.

Sadly, all marine turtles are endangered but the good news is the lay-and-run process makes it relatively easy to help even the most endangered populations. Conservation projects collect eggs and protect them or simply watch over nests for both animal and human predators, ensuring as many youngsters as possible return to the sea. Numbers in parts of Asia have increased so it's not difficult to find a turtle underwater: green and hawksbills are incredibly common as breeding projects continue to ensure their survival. However, telling the difference between them is less easy:

Green These animals have an oval carapace that is black-brown or green-yellow with a feathered scale pattern. Their heads are small and blunt, they grow to 1.5 metres long and live in tropical and subtropical waters. Strict vegetarians, breeding females are found mostly in Australia and Indonesia. This species is heavily exploited for turtle soup.
Hawksbill Their carapace is thin, flexible and highly coloured with a mottled pattern. Look for a narrow pointed beak reminiscent of a hawk. They grow to less than a metre and are found in many seas. Breeding females are found principally in Australia. They eat invertebrates and sponges and are in serious decline due to the trade in tortoiseshell.

Other turtles you may see in your dive travels will be **Loggerheads** which are under a metre long with a rusty carapace and a similar, but less defined, pattern to green turtles. These are most commonly seen in the Mediterranean. **Leatherbacks** are the largest at 180 centimetres. Their carapace is leathery (not hard) and they live in open water and coastal habitats of the Pacific, Atlantic and Central and South America. The **Olive Ridley** and **Kemp's Ridley** are the smallest marine turtles at 70 centimetres. Olives lives on isolated tropical beaches from Australia to Africa and South America while the Kemp's are only found on a couple of beaches in Mexico and Texas. **Flatback** turtles are a metre long but known only in tropical Australasia – Australia, Papua New Guinea and Indonesia.

↘1 Green turtle ↘2 Hawksbill ↘3 Just hatched turtles growing in a holding tank
↘4 Young turtle awaiting release ↘5 Release into the open ocean

Lankayan

Just an hour or so by boat into the Sulu Sea, Lankayan is surrounded by a set of flat plateaux that gradually shelve and drop off into a healthy reef system. There are no great walls here but gentle slopes covered, primarily, in hard corals.

In 2000, the island was declared a Marine Conservation Area after a survey confirmed high biodiversity and little coral bleaching. Conditions are easy, really strong currents only occurring every now and then, and the water's surface is smooth. Visibility is variable and is often quite poor due to shallow reef structures, proximity to the mainland and high levels of plankton. Diving here is all about looking for the animals that thrive in these nutrient-rich conditions. And there are plenty, but note that this is principally a destination for small and unusual animals like the almost invisible tozeuma shrimp or rare rhinopias. There are also several wrecks to explore. Whitetip and nurse sharks are seen, and a very special treat is walking with blacktip sharks. The shallows here are a nursery for them. You can stand in ankle-deep water and have 50-centimetre long babies swim around your toes!

Lankayan is a nesting site for both green and hawksbill turtles. The beach is patrolled at night to protect female turtles as they lay. After they return to the sea, eggs are collected and placed in a small hatchery for incubation. The last of the bigger creatures to visit is the whaleshark. The resort announces its passing migration but you can never guarantee them being there for any long term planning.

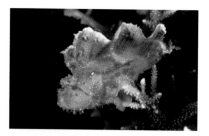

⇘9 House Reef and Jetty Wreck	
🕐 **Depth**	16 m
◑ **Visibility**	fair
🌀 **Currents**	slight to medium
🌊 **Dive type**	shore

Although there are many dives in the waters near to Lankayan, this site is the one that gets done more often than any other: partly, that is because it can be done whenever you want, day or night; and partly because there are several sections to the dive and you can do as much or as little as you fancy. Entry is right under the pier where a rope on the seabed leads down eventually to the wreck of a small fishing boat. First of all, you could spend quite some time just hanging around the pylons and struts that form the jetty itself. Each surface is being coated by small corals, sponges and algaes forming miniature reefs. However, it's best to head down and keep these shallows for off-gassing later. Following the rope, there is lots of activity on the way to the wreck: a discarded tyre is full of catfish that come racing out if you shine a torch on them; and a bit further on clusters of trunkfish and cardinalfish shelter inside a group of tyres, their treads smothered with hingebeak and cleaner shrimps. When you reach the wreck there are puffers and a lot of lionfish. Decorator crabs and spider crabs shroud the slowly

⇘9	House Reef	
⇘10	Lankayan Wreck	
⇘11	Froggie Fort	
⇘12	Moray Reef	
⇘13	Mosquito Wreck	
⇘14	Twin City	
⇘15	Jawfish Lair	
⇘16	Mel's Rock	

rotting timbers which are covered in small corals, sponges and little shells, including some minute cowries. A school of jacks hovers over the mast. On the way back up, another rope diverts divers back via two pyramids made of timber. These artificial reefs attract nudibranchs and batfish and many others. On the sand are an incredible number of cowries, blue-spotted rays and the odd decorator crab with an upside-down jellyfish sitting on its back. Needlefish hover over the many anemones occupied by both skunk and Clarke's clownfish and there is one very unusual saddleback anemonefish family.

Leaf scorpionfish on staghorn branches; striped catfish hiding inside a tyre

⬂10 Lankayan Wreck

🕐 **Depth**	25 m
◑ **Visibility**	poor to good
🌊 **Currents**	mild
⬳ **Dive type**	day boat

Lying upright in 30 metres are the remains of this illegal fishing trawler. It was sunk on purpose after being caught poaching in the Sulu Sea in 1998. The boat is only about 30 metres long and in reasonable condition, though the timbers are quickly rotting down as it sits on the seabed. The decaying structure is being colonized by a lot of different marine species. The exterior is already coated in enormous oyster clams, sponges and tiny soft corals. Check out the compartments in the hold where the fishermen used to hide their catch for lionfish, while groupers and coral trout patrol the hull and schools of ever-present jacks hang above. Macro life is unusual – there are several black coral bushes and one with yellow tentacles is used as a disguise by tozeuma shrimp and squat lobsters. Brown and white striped pipefish crawl over the remains of the deck.

⬂11 Froggie Fort

🕐 **Depth**	22 m
◑ **Visibility**	poor to good
🌊 **Currents**	mild to strong
⬳ **Dive type**	day boat

Consisting of a sloping oval-shaped reef, this dive proves to be something of a surprise. Around its base, emerging from the sand, are rows of short, pastel-toned gorgonians. And beneath these is where you often find the star of the dive – a rare *Rhinopias frondosa* or weedy scorpionfish. This outrageously patterned and highly decorated fish is only about the size of a hand and is also flat like its relative, the leaf scorpionfish, but is distinguished by beautiful markings and fronds on its skin. They are hard to spot so stay close to your guide who should know where they are hanging about. Up at the top of the mound, where the hard corals are in particularly good condition, is a broad bed of staghorn coral. Several white leaffish reside among the branches, adults sitting beside their young. Despite the name, there aren't always frogfish.

⬂12 Moray Reef

🕐 **Depth**	28 m
◑ **Visibility**	fair
🌊 **Currents**	none
⬳ **Dive type**	day boat

A short boat ride north of the island is this long flat mound which rises from 28 to 14 metres. It's worth starting the dive by swimming over the more barren sandy areas just beyond the reef as, at depth, there are some monster-sized nudibranchs crawling about and you may spot flounders and a few shells. On the reef itself there are lots of hard corals and quite a few burgundy red sponges which seem to be decorated with matching dark red crabs. There are a surprising number of small schooling fish around and as the visibility here is better than at some sites you can watch them skimming over the reef top. Balls of catfish and bluespotted rays take refuge beneath the bases of the staghorn corals while above them there are lots of cardinalfish, quite a few batfish and a couple of cuttlefish.

Rhinopias frondosa on Froggie Fort; the Lankayan wreck

🕐	**Depth**	21 m
◑	**Visibility**	fair to good
🌀	**Currents**	slight
⬱	**Dive type**	day boat

This wreck of a small Japanese boat from the Second World War is sitting right on the edge of the reef on its side. The hull is in good shape but the rest of the timbers are slowly rotting away. This has created a base for good colonization of small corals and sponges and a lot of very large lionfish which flit about the wreck. It's possible to continue this dive on the reef slope beside it where you can see Sangean crabs on a sponge. Going up the reef, the first section is in pretty poor condition, with lots of algae and dead coral, but in the shallows it suddenly turns into a good coral garden with enormous elephants ear corals and huge plate corals. Look beneath these for both crocodilefish and young nurse sharks lurking in the shadows.

Giant cuttlefish; Lankayan's baby blacktips

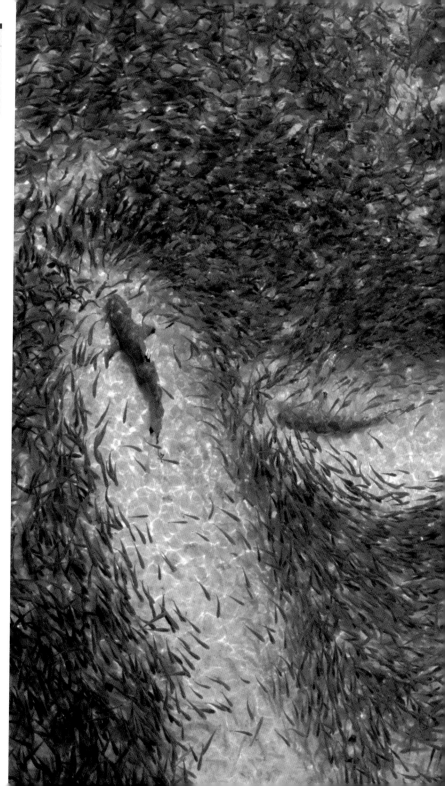

N14 Twin City

Depth	23 m
Visibility	poor to fair
Currents	none
Dive type	day boat

It's a shame that the visibility can be poor here as there is so much to see. The site consists of a small sea mound separated from a bigger one by a sandy gully. This measures about two metres wide and as you fin over it you will see a nudibranch every few feet – some are mating. On the mounds there are loads of little shrimp on the black corals and more shrimp on the bubble corals. There are plenty of fish too, but they can be harder to see in the gloom. If you poke about under the corals, you may spot the tail of a coral cat shark or a small whitetip, but like its tiny relative, it is hiding under more coral. Up at the top of the bigger mound there are friendly cuttlefish and blue-spotted rays.

N15 Jawfish Lair

Depth	22 m
Visibility	poor to fair
Currents	mild
Dive type	day boat

True to its name, this site is renowned for its resident giant jawfish. The divemasters delight in showing off their pets and tempt them out of their burrows with scraps of fish. The jawfish will come right out and, despite having a huge head, are actually much smaller than that smiling, tennis ball-sized face would have you think. These chaps grow to 25 centimetres or so long, unlike a standard jawfish which rarely tops 10 centimetres. The remainder of the dive involves investigating the extensive variety of corals looking for pipefish, frogfish and orang-utan crabs, all of which are regularly found here. You may even spot a baby nurse shark taking refuge under a table coral.

N16 Mel's Rock

Depth	20 m
Visibility	poor to fair
Currents	slight to mild
Dive type	day boat

Mel's is a round sea mound characterized by several large bommies sitting on its top. These are swarmed by schools of fish but if the visibility is low they appear as ghostly shadows in the blue. The main attraction then becomes searching for the small critters that live amongst the soft corals and algaes. There are several types of flabellina nudibranch and the highly decorated *Chromodoris kunei* nudibranch. Orang-utan crabs reside in soft corals plus juvenile sweetlips and blennies. Bigger creatures include cuttlefish, which blend in perfectly with the background, and blue-spotted stingrays under small table corals. There are even translucent shrimps hanging on the black coral bushes.

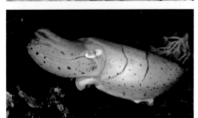

Crab-eye gobies; cuttlefish; nurse shark; the enormous giant jawfish

Drying out

There are several dive operators and many hotel options in Kota Kinabalu, with a variety of price ranges, but once you head for the islands, there is only ever one choice.

Kota Kinabalu

$$$ **Sutera Harbour Resort**, T+60 (0)88 318888, suteraharbour.com. A convenient and pleasant complex with several hotels, a spa, golf course, sports facilities, many restaurants and free airport transfers. The resort also owns the North Borneo Railway and can arrange a variety of day trips.

Diving

City based diving is rarely a first choice but if you have a couple of days to spare in Kota Kinabalu, you could visit the nearby islands and marine park (see page 162).

For dive operators check out:
Borneo Dream – borneodream.com
Down Below – downbelow.co.uk

Layang Layang

$$ **Layang Layang Island Resort**, T+60 (0)3 2162 2877, layanglayang.com. On an isolated island in the Spratly Group, this resort's rooms are built in 'longhouses' and feel rather like a comfy, old-fashioned American motel. All rooms have balconies and good views towards the sea. Weekly packs for roughly US$1400 include all meals and diving.

Lankayan

$$ **Lankayan Island Resort**, T+60 (0)89 765200, lankayan-island.com. Again just one resort on this picture-postcard perfect island (image right). Simple, comfortable rooms are dotted amongst the trees and face the sea. Laid-back island atmosphere.

Weekly packages from US$1200 include all meals, transfers and diving.

Sandakan

$ **Sepilok Nature Resort**, T+60 (0)89 765200, sepilok.com. Delightful wooden chalets overlook a tropical garden rimmed lake. This very peaceful resort also has a collection of 150 different Asian orchid species and a fabulous restaurant plus it's just a few minutes' walk from the orang-utan sanctuary entrance.

Kota Kinabalu

Because getting to Borneo means going through Sabah's capital, you may as well take a day to see this pleasant, small city and her surrounds. The **KK Heritage Walk** is a guided two-hour walk around the city's landmarks including Australia Place, one of the oldest parts of town, then on to various museums, monuments and memorials. Contact the Tourism Board; about RM100 per person. Those who have the inclination to climb mountains will be sorely tempted to take a slightly longer break and scale **Mount Kinabalu**. Trips take two days so if time is short, visit Malaysia's first World Heritage Site, **Kinabalu Park**, and experience just a little of the incredible range of plant, animal, insect and bird life. **Poring Hot Springs** are nearby and day trips that cover both will be around US$60. A slightly more relaxed day can be had by taking the North Borneo Railway journey through the countryside to the agricultural region of Papar. The restored 100 year-old train chugs past mangrove swamps, villages and markets. Return trip about US$70.

Sandakan

Sepilok Orang-utan Sanctuary

Founded in 1964 to rehabilitate orphan orang-utans, the sanctuary consists of 43 sq km of protected land at the edge of Kabili Sepilok Forest Reserve. With up to 80 captive or abandoned orang-utans living in the reserve at any time, the aim is to help them readjust to life in the wild. Public access is strictly managed. At feeding times, the animals come down to feeding platforms so are easy to see and some older, permanent residents will approach visitors. There is a boardwalk trail through the forest where you can see snakes and local plants. There is also a Sumatran rhino breeding programme in progress., coconut trees and shrubs, some of which are specific to this region.

Turtle Island Marine Park Not far from Lankayan is this set of three islands where turtles come to nest. Now a marine park, there are no established diving facilities here and accommodation is very limited, but it's a good day out for non-divers.

	Sleeping	$$$ US$150+ double room per night		$$ US$75-150	$ under US$75
	Eating	$$$ US$40+ 2-course meal, excluding drinks		$$ US$20-40	$ under US$20

Malaysia Drying out Sabah: Layang Layang and Lankayan

Sipadan

A legend for divers the world over, Sipadan is one of those dive destinations that everyone knows about and everyone wants to see. This deep green, circular island, rimmed by bleached white sand and encapsulated by a perfect blue sea, is now shut but, fortunately, only in terms of accommodation.

In 2004, a move was made to turn the island into a World Heritage Site. Concerns were voiced by environmentalists that the effects of continually increasing diver numbers would irreparably damage the reefs. It was also felt that people staying on the island were affecting the already fragile ecosystem. Sipadan is a small island but with about a dozen dive sites and the damage was obvious. After much to-do, including a court case in Kuala Lumpur, all resort operators were asked to leave and a programme to rehabilitate the island commenced. This included the removal of all buildings except those used by the Parks Service and a beach clean-up which, it is hoped, will aid turtle nesting.

Divers now stay at the nearby resorts on Mabul and Kapalai which schedule dives to Sipadan. Numbers are restricted and it should be noted that while some people report easy access, there are just as many stories of permits being refused. Time will tell how much this helps with the regeneration of the reef system and whether World Heritage status will be granted. Sadly though, the arguments surrounding these plans continue with ever more concerns regarding diver numbers, incidences of illegal fishing and the lack of on-the-ground protection. The arguments become particularly steamy whenever an incident gets out into the public arena. One such issue was when a barge carrying building materials hit the reef just beyond the old pier causing – it is said – substantial damage. Yet tales of how bad this damage really was vary depending on who you speak to. (The authors have been advised by reliable sources that it does not affect the diving as the damage occurred in an unremarkable area where divers are unlikely to visit.)

Regardless of all this, if you are looking for big stuff, then Sipadan is a must. Turtles are everywhere, so prolific and inquisitive that they will follow you around. Sharks are easy to spot and there are phenomenal numbers of barracudas. There are also plenty of smaller animals to hunt for in the shallows when conditions allow. Currents are variable and most dives are done as drifts. Although they are not always that strong, the currents can quickly turn fierce resulting in a complete about-face halfway through a dive.

↘1 South Point	
Depth	25 m
Visibility	fair to stunning
Currents	mild to strong
Dive type	day boat

The furthest site from the island's jetty, South Point is not at all dissimilar to her neighbouring dives. In fact, nearly all the sites here have a similar profile. The island is rimmed by a steep wall that is said to eventually drop to over 700 metres. It is topped by a sloping plateau where the corals can be colourful depending on whether the currents have encouraged them out to feed. However, where this site stands out is that it seems to be a haven for all the island's turtles. Although some people report diving here and not seeing a single one, usually there are so many that you can hardly move past them. They are incredibly inquisitive and not at all afraid of divers. One can be feeding on a coral outcrop (attracting masked and imperial angels or butterflyfish who scavenge for their scraps), then see a diver, and decide that is far more interesting. They will desert their meal and swim over to join them. The top of the reef is a little scrappy but you may spot a shark or school of bumphead parrots.

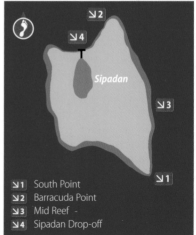

↘1 South Point
↘2 Barracuda Point
↘3 Mid Reef -
↘4 Sipadan Drop-off

2 Barracuda Point

Depth	28 m
Visibility	good to stunning
Currents	mild to ripping
Dive type	day boat

Perhaps Sipadan's most famous dive, this submerged point sits to the east of the boat jetty. The wall is sheer and the crusting corals and sponges make it incredibly colourful. As you descend to 30 metres there is a full quota of schooling small fish – butterflies, tangs and surgeons – but most outstanding is the enormous number and sizes of black coral bushes. Every one seems to have a longnose hawkfish in it, or be swarmed by lionfish, and interspersed with gigantic fans in many colours.

Turtles swim along with divers to keep them company, sometimes one will have a batfish hovering beneath his belly. At the top of the reef the corals are less impressive but gangs of whitetip sharks rest peacefully on the sand. Grey reef sharks approach from behind, heading for the school of jacks that are just around the bend. Large turtles visit cleaning stations while Napoleon wrasse and giant tuna pass by in the blue. Although the dive starts along the wall and drifts towards them, the infamous barracuda school is usually spotted from the surface. There are hundreds in the ball, maybe thousands, sitting right on the top of the reef. They move slowly in perfect synchronicity, sliding apart for a few moments only to reconfigure swiftly into a perfect spiral – simply breathtaking.

❝❞ To find a world of beauty, separated from the ordinary, that is the siren song of diving. Occasionally, the experience far exceeds the dream. This was one of those moments. Floating in the middle of the universe, never wanting to leave.

Bruce Brownstein, Venice, California

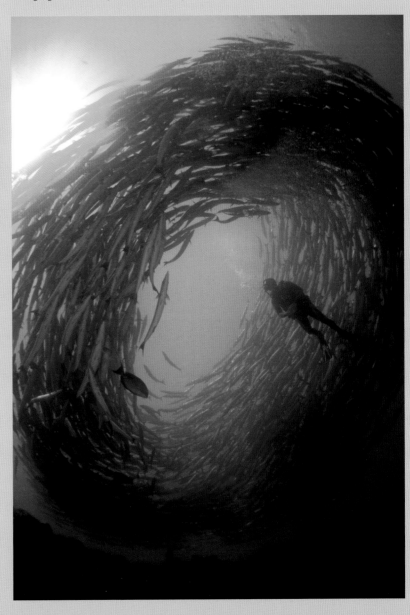

Malaysia Dive log Sabah: Barracuda Point

⚙ Secret Sipadan

There are around a dozen Sipadan dive sites and, given the tiny footprint of the island, you might be forgiven for thinking that they are more or less the same. In truth there is really quite a variety and the lesser-visited sites could be headliners in any less spectacular destination. It surprises me that these others are so often ignored so every time I head this way, I do my best to see at least one of these quieter sites.

The usual Sipadan profile is of a wall or slope that flattens out in a section before plummeting into the abyss. By contrast, one of my favourite 'secret' dives is Turtle Patch which is best dived as a gentle drift along the shallows. It's really a pleasant change from the norm. Although numerous elsewhere, great numbers of turtles frequent this area to rest on the sandy floor and feed on the sponges. Healthy acropora corals also abound and seem to be thriving since the removal of the resorts from the island.

The unimaginatively named Coral Garden is another dive where I like to restrict my depth to less than 10 metres. A lot of underwater photographer buddies do this too, as finning over Sipadan's shelf means you can take in the diversity of coral growth and marvel at all the vividly coloured basslets and anthias that swarm the shallows. Every now and then I find myself peering over the edge into deeper water to look for the marauding hordes of bumphead parrotfish or turtles quietly nestling on a ledge. Hanging Gardens is similar and features terraces of *Dendronephthya alcyonarians* soft corals in various pastel colours of lemon, lavender and rose overflowing to the next terrace below.

I always enjoy seeing the healthy numbers of whitetip sharks in Sipadan, but on some sites there can be too many other attention-seeking marine creatures to allow time to appreciate them. At Whitetip Avenue they take more of a leading role. Cruising with the normally gentle current is great for inspecting all the sponges and gorgonians that have taken root in the ledges and fissures of this section of the wall. There is also so much fish life I have to remind myself to keep an eye out to the open sea where there can be a lot of whitetips, grey reef sharks and the occasional meaty pelagic. So while the big names of Sipadan undoubtedly deserve their glory there is much reward to be had in exploring this gem of an island as a whole.

Gavin Macaulay is a director of Dive-The-World.com, Kota Kinabalu

⊻3	Mid Reef	
🕐 **Depth**	16 m
◐ **Visibility**	fair to good
🌊 **Currents**	slight to strong
⬭ **Dive type**	day boat

On the wall that runs between Barracuda and South Points is a dive that can be difficult at times. You can enter while the water is dead calm then, within a few moments, run into currents moving at an unimaginable speed. Sudden chilly thermoclines, down- and up-draughts can all turn the site into a roller-coaster ride and be a lot of fun for all that but watch your buoyancy! Then again, it can also be completely still. There are masses of turtles here as well, some resting on little ledges on the wall, others heading off to investigate other sections of reef. The wall itself has many fans and black corals decorating the steeper surfaces while, up on the plateau, the hard corals harbour lots of interesting small animals that you can hunt around for when the currents are being cooperative.

Sipadan sharks and coral scenes

◤ Sipadan Drop-Off	
🕐 Depth	35 m
◐ Visibility	fair to good
🌀 Currents	slight to strong
🌊 Dive type	shore

What made Sipadan so popular was the jetty drop-off. You could simply wander off the beach and onto the amazing wall. It was known as the best house reef in the world for many a year. Within a 10 metre or so fin you can slip over the lip of the reef and find schools of batfish or jacks right there to greet you. You descend past small crevices and overhangs all painted with brightly coloured coral and every tropical fish imaginable. It is likely that you will see at least a shark or two, and a dozen or so turtles. At night, the shallows are alive with crabs and shrimp, the sandy beach area has shells and gobies and beneath the jetty are many urchins, starfish and schools of catfish. To the east of the jetty, at around 18 metres, is the entrance to Turtle Cave, a series of interconnecting caverns. It is fairly dangerous inside, full of the remains of drowned turtles: it is thought they go in at night and get lost as there is no light to guide them back out. Beware – the same could happen to divers who enter without both a torch and a divemaster.

Blue-spotted ray; yellow-mask angelfish

66 99 One turtle was so nosy he deserted his meal to check out the camera, then promptly bit the flash! Perhaps the bright orange strobe looked like a sponge.

Kapalai

Just a short motor from Sipadan and Mabul, this idyllic destination was long overshadowed by the more famous members of the group. Sitting right on the edge of the Litigan Reefs, it may be the smallest of the three islands but it is now getting the attention it deserves as one of Southeast Asia's best macro destinations.

Although charted on older maps, there is only a sand bar remaining from what was once a small island. At low tide you can walk along the beach that emerges, spotting shells and tiny critters caught in puddles. This flat topography is similar underwater, yet visibility here is reasonable as the reef mounds are washed daily by the tides. Corals tend to be low lying to the contours of the landscape but they're all pretty healthy and a haven for masses of weird and wacky critters. The resort itself is a water village – eco-friendly wooden bungalows perch on stilts over an aquarium-like lagoon. This is a delightful place, relaxed and friendly. Diving here is year-round and suitable for everyone as currents are easily avoided.

⑤ Recep 1	
🕐 Depth	26 m
◑ Visibility	poor to good
≋ Currents	slight to strong
⬭ Dive type	day boat

This is a classic Kapalai critter dive. From the moment you hit the undulating seabed until you are nearly out of air, you will see curious critter after curious critter: drop down over the small wall into a gully with a sandy bottom. Spot a blue ribbon eel then a white leaffish. The gully leads to a flat hard plateau where there are robust ghost pipefish, ornate ghost pipefish and many whip corals. On them are tiny stripy shrimp, then clear bodied shrimp on the next whip with minute cowries sitting beside them. There are masses of nudibranchs including the *Chromodoris bullocki* and some really impressive little ones that look like bunnies. More leaffish, more ribbon eels, very tame mantis shrimp and an octopus, and at the top of the little wall are orang-utan crabs and turtles. The current across the plateau here can be really strong so when that happens it's best to stay up at the top levels and look for baby cuttlefish hiding in soft coral.

Malaysia Dive log Sabah: Kapalai

⑥ Sweetlips Table	
🕐 Depth	17 m
◑ Visibility	fair to good
≋ Currents	slight
⬭ Dive type	day boat

This dive consists of a series of shelving mounds with small corals and sponges and only around a five metre difference between the bottom and the top. There is less current on this site as it's a little closer to shore and more protected. It's just as much fun though with lots of nudibranchs, the spearchucker and thumbcracker mantis shrimps, porcelain crabs, and catfish in a ball. There are small turtles and tiny sharks hiding under hard corals. Unusually, you can see free swimming blue ribbon eels, which duck quickly back into their holes. These tend to be in clusters so a blue male might be beside a yellow one, the female. The divemasters are great spotters and find tiny cockatoo waspfish. Of course, there are always sweetlips here, usually hiding under a table coral. It's common to spot juvenile sweetlips doing their manic, fluttering dance. If you travel across the gully at the eastern end, you will arrive at Mantis Ground.

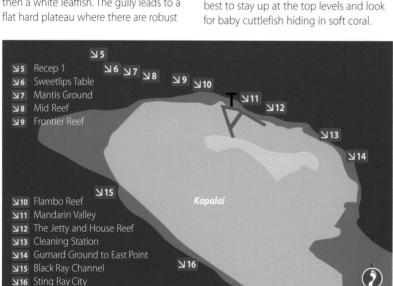

⑤	Recep 1
⑥	Sweetlips Table
⑦	Mantis Ground
⑧	Mid Reef
⑨	Frontier Reef
⑩	Flambo Reef
⑪	Mandarin Valley
⑫	The Jetty and House Reef
⑬	Cleaning Station
⑭	Gurnard Ground to East Point
⑮	Black Ray Channel
⑯	Sting Ray City

Kapalai

The spearing mantis shrimp in its burrow

⊠7 Mantis Ground

🕓	**Depth**	18 m
◑	**Visibility**	poor to fair
≋	**Currents**	slight to medium
⬮	**Dive type**	day boat

This is one of the divemasters' favourite dive sites – a high-voltage critter hunt with masses of animals that hide in burrows and holes in the seabed. There are really big octopus that hang on top of the rocks, doing their best to mimic the hard texture, while beneath the rocks playful mantis shrimp run in and out of their burrows. Just inches away are several enormous spearing mantis in orange or beige. Jawfish dart in and out of their holes to feed. Leopard cucumbers are worth peering at as there are some very large swimming crabs clinging on to their skin. Very pretty pink leaffish sit motionless in the hard coral branches and blue ribbon eels appear from their holes. That most impressive of nudibranchs, the solar powered version, appears in pairs. White eyed morays peer out of their holes too and there are also lots of fish, including a school of 20 or so batfish.

⊠8 Mid Reef

🕓	**Depth**	21 m
◑	**Visibility**	fair to good
≋	**Currents**	slight to medium
⬮	**Dive type**	day boat

This site is beside Mantis Ground and could be combined with it, but not if you take the time to look for all the animals. Again, there is a pair of solar powered nudibranchs and you have to wonder if they have travelled between the two sites while you are off-gassing. The whip corals are rich with tiny animals like the highly camouflaged *Xenocarcinus conicus* crab and tiny 'bumble bee' shrimp, all jostling for prime position on the narrow surface. There are many small gobies and jawfish on the seafloor, plus this site has some bigger animals including a gang of turtles. Some healthy fan corals house spider crabs, longnose and pixie hawkfish. One patch of finger sponges has the tiniest of pink frogfish. (A year after doing this dive, we returned and he was still in exactly the same place. The divemasters monitored him for the whole year and watched him grow into an adult.)

⊠9 Frontier Reef

🕓	**Depth**	26 m
◑	**Visibility**	fair to good
≋	**Currents**	slight
⬮	**Dive type**	day boat

This continuation of the reef mounds in front of the resort comes closest to 'shore' at this point. Heading directly out from the jetty but just a few minutes' boat ride away, you can drop over this section where there is quite a lot of rubble and bits of junk that create small patches of artificial reefs. At the furthest point, a small area of coral houses a few critters and some curious batfish while snappers swim past in a hurry. However, on this site it's worth spending more time swimming slowly over the debris checking what has started to colonize it. There are a lot of lionfish, many scorpionfish in different hues and batfish hovering around. Different types of morays have tucked themselves into the crevices along with banded coral and hingebeak shrimp. You can swim all the way back to the jetty from this site, passing the tiny wreck.

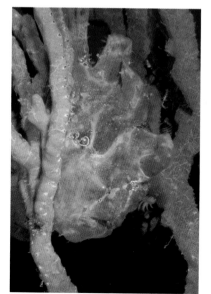
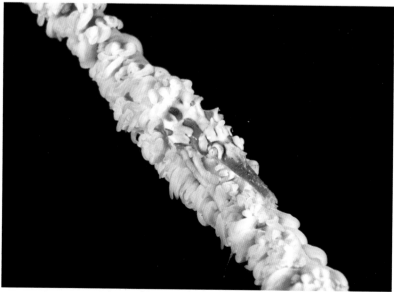

Giant frogfish, pretty in matching pink sponges; this tiny spider crab, with no common name, is *Xenocarcinus conicus*

↘10 Flambo Reef

🕐	**Depth**	12 m
◑	**Visibility**	fair to good
🌊	**Currents**	none
🌅	**Dive type**	day boat

Another of the gentle reef mounds sitting at the front of the resort with the usual undulating topography. Descending to the base of the mound, you find lots more of the little critters you see on the nearby sites but here you can also move off to a flatter area where some small coral and rock outcroppings protrude from the seabed. These are mobbed by sweepers and many of these bommies are cleaning stations. There's a lot of activity especially in the morning and if you peer around the sweepers you may find a resident leaffish. There are blue ribbon eels but the star of this dive is often a minute black frogfish with orange freckles and white webs between his toes! Elsewhere, there are shrimp inside sponges, several juvenile emperor angelfish, colourful nudibranchs and quite a few black flatworms that have a neon-pink rim around their body.

↘11 Mandarin Valley

🕐	**Depth**	7 m
◑	**Visibility**	fair to good
🌊	**Currents**	none
🌅	**Dive type**	shore

This dive is part of the house reef and jetty area, but it is regarded as a special dive as the focus is 100% on the single square metre where a mandarinfish colony lives. It's easy enough to find the spot as the surrounds are barren, caused by so many divers sitting around and peering at these incredible tiny fish. All mandarinfish dives are done at dusk and divers descend just before and wait. It takes a few minutes for the fish to come out and then there are suddenly a couple of dozen skittering around the rubble. There are many mid-sized ones (the females) but only a few full size ones (males) plus loads of juveniles. The babes are a slightly different colour, paler and with spots rather than the full, multi-coloured squiggle pattern. After about 10 minutes some mandarins will rise up to mate, the process going on for about half an hour.

↘12 The Jetty and House Reef

🕐	**Depth**	25 m
◑	**Visibility**	fair to good
🌊	**Currents**	slight
🌅	**Dive type**	shore

Kapalai's dive jetty extends out at a right angle over a small drop-off. The area under and around it is perhaps the most popular dive here – although dive in the single tense is misleading. You can stay under the jetty in the lagoon, drop down and turn left, or right, or head straight out and down to the wreck. At dusk you can do Mandarin Valley then move on. There are simply too many options that have been known to make many a diver miss the daily boat dives, although you can also start one of the boat dives along the reef edge and swim back. One popular option is to head down to the wreck then back to the wall. This old wooden fishing boat has very little on it in terms of its original purpose, but there are some interesting creatures hiding around the rotting hull including huge frogfish decorated with splotches and hairy bits.

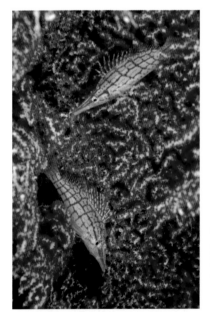

Longnose hawkfish nestled in a fan coral; the flamboyant cuttlefish being flamboyant

Beneath the hull, where it sits upright on the sand, there are lots of morays all neatly lined up in a row. The seabed nearby reveals gobies and the spearing mantis shrimp.

Swimming back up towards the jetty, you come to the base of the small wall. The corals are a mixture of hard and soft, none particularly big or prolific but it's still a substantial and healthy system. Sponges, tunicates and hydroids sit between the corals so there are plenty of hiding spaces for the critters that live here. On your first dive, the divemasters will point out all the known residents, which will include ornate ghost pipefish hiding inside whip corals and banded pipefish in a small cavern. The females are often pregnant and you can spot the swathe of pink eggs right across the tummy.

It doesn't matter whether you turn left or right at the jetty steps as the profile is much the same. Across this upper section of reef you can see various pipefish and morays, squat lobsters in crinoids, lots of decorator crabs, slipper lobsters and plenty of shrimp. Some of the more exotic creatures seen regularly are the flamboyant cuttlefish and the incredible blue-ringed octopus. These are spotted at dusk and often near to Mandarin Valley.

Directly under the jetty (perfect for a night dive) are crocodile fish and peacock flounders while the fans growing on the pylons are full of pink and white striped squat lobsters. There are tiny crabs on the sponges, sleeping parrotfish in their mucous bubbles, juvenile batfish and even baby nurse sharks on a fly by!

Too numerous to count, the residents of Kapalai's jetty include, clockwise from top left: ornate ghost pipefish using soft corals as camouflage; the *Reticulidia halgerda* nudibranch; giant frogfish – this one has been caught yawning to catch some prey; imperial shrimp beneath a sea cucumber; a pinate batfish at teenager stage; a moray eel; pregnant banded pipefish; the male blue ribbon eel

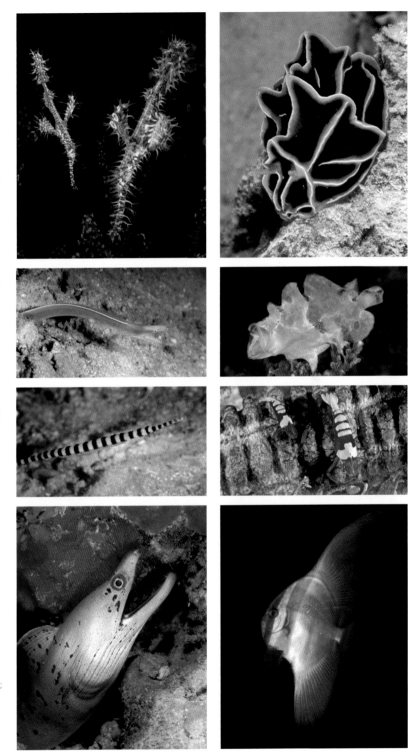

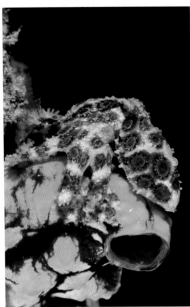

⌧13 Cleaning Station

🕐	**Depth**	16 m
◑	**Visibility**	fair to good
🌊	**Currents**	none
🚢	**Dive type**	day boat

This is an extension of the house reef running off the eastern side of the jetty. The dive boats shuttle divers about 300 metres along the reef then leaves them to make their way slowly back. The profile is still a small wall, dropping down to the seabed which can be as shallow as 14 metres. The best plan is to hover at about 12 metres so you can watch the sand and the wall at the same time. There is masses of marine life: nosy turtles swim past, shy cuttlefish stand away from the divers and batfish join in for the swim to see where the divers are going. On the sand there are crocodilefish, lots of crab-eye gobies, peacock razorfish and several marbled dragonets. You may spot a pillar-box red frogfish trying to hide on a brown sponge, then a little further along there will be a matching juvenile. Inside an anemone are skunk clownfish and 'popcorn' shrimp. This is a bit of a long swim but there is so much to see along the way: jawfish with eggs, octopus, shrimps with their commensal gobies, and if you arrive back at the jetty near dusk you may see the mandarinfish or one of the blue-ringed octopus that are always here.

⌧14 Gurnard Ground to East Point

🕐	**Depth**	14 m
◑	**Visibility**	fair to good
🌊	**Currents**	none
🚢	**Dive type**	day boat

If you head to the far corner of the house reef and then fin to the east rather than back to the jetty, you come to two more sites that can be dived together. The topography is similar but these sites are slightly more exposed so can get a bit of current and visibility will drop. As always there are impressive nudibranchs on the reef wall, including very large olive-black hued nembrothas without any distinctive markings along with their more common green-with-red-spots relatives. Large barramundi and stonefish hide under a small bommie covered in sweepers, which in turn disguises the juvenile scorpionfish you can see here. Sometimes.

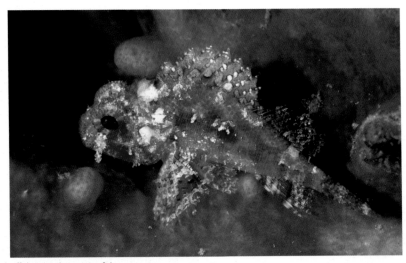

The dangerous but beautiful blue-ringed octopus; leaffish; juvenile scorpionfish

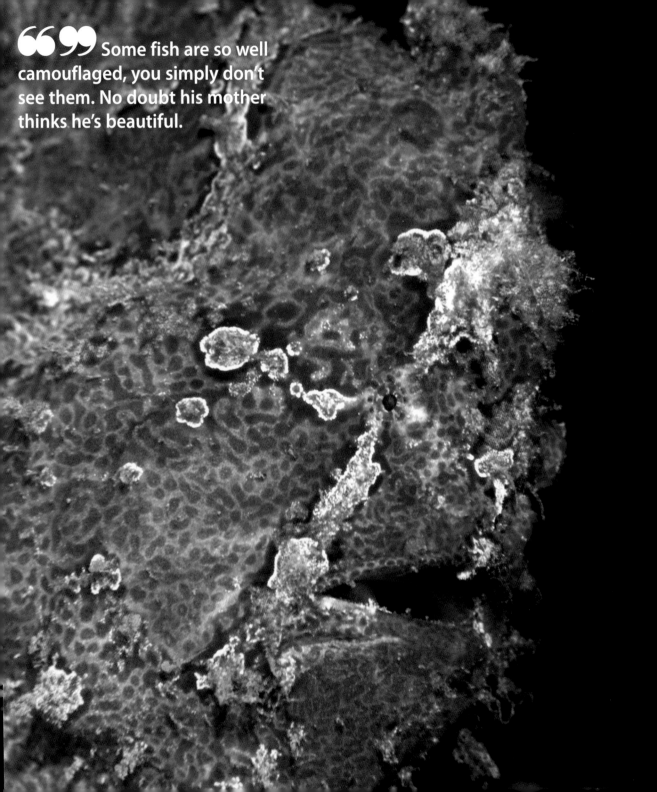

“ ” Some fish are so well camouflaged, you simply don't see them. No doubt his mother thinks he's beautiful.

Life in the deep
Marine voyeurs

It isn't quite what a diver might intend – to sit and watch others indulge in that which should really be kept private, but it's precisely what you need to do if you want to see one of the marine realm's most breathtakingly beautiful creatures. Every night, just after sunset, you can slide beneath the jetty at Kapalai and attend a peep show of a very special nature: droves of tiny mandarinfish creating babies.

There are many famous muck-diving sites where you can hope to see these intensely pretty little fish but this is one where an encounter is almost guaranteed – almost, because shyness is an integral part of their nature. Mandarinfish keep very much to themselves, living in stable colonies amongst the cracks and crevices in coral rubble. There's plenty of hiding space and food is easy to come by. But even if you know all that, spotting these members of the dragonet family is still pretty difficult. Until you put a light on them, they are just grey flitting shadows and only their Latin name, *Synchiropus splendidus*, hints at their extravagant skin colouring. As adults they are rarely more than five centimetres long and when they do come out to play, they are only in the open for the time it takes the sun's fading rays to give way to complete darkness.

Once it does, the colony of mandarins emerge from their lairs to start their evening courtship ritual. The tiny fish dash around, greeting their friends and pecking at the tiny crustaceans they feed on. In the gloom you will glimpse two little shadows approaching each other, a larger male and a smaller female. Most of the time, she will back away but if she fancies her suitor, the pair will rise upwards through the water until they are about 50 centimetres above the reef.

However, the girls are picky – not just any male will do. Several fish will be happily feeding when a larger male makes his first approach. Sometimes a pair rise upwards only a few inches but the suitor is rejected with a quick kiss and the female returns to her dinner. Occasionally, two males appear to fight over a favoured lady, a younger, less experienced male trying to muscle in on the action. But each female knows when the man of her dreams has arrived, and accepting his proposition, the pair swim up through the water with the lady resting on her lover's pelvic fin.

After a few seconds, and at the height of their swim, they pause for a brief moment, then disappear at the speed of light. This pause is the vital moment. If you focus on the lovers you may spot a puff of white. It lingers behind them in the dark even as they dart back down to safety. The cloud of white is mingled eggs and sperm. Mandarinfish are the smallest of all marine species to spawn into open water. Like other spawners, they produce millions of eggs, but their parental duties are over once they're deposited into the water. The eggs drop down into the cracks of the coral and are left to grow into larvae. Not only do divers become willing voyeurs, but you get to witness the birth of a new generation of these exotic reef dwellers.

1 The male mandarinfish hunts in the rubble, looking for a suitable – and willing – female, sees one he fancies and **2** rises upwards, fins extended to display his prowess. **3** He then drops back to the seafloor and approaches his intended. **4** If she decides he might just do, she rises up into the water column with him and **5** they then simultaneously release both eggs and sperm. In this last image, the white puff between their bodies, is the egg mass.

◈15 Black Ray Channel

◉	**Depth**	17 m
◐	**Visibility**	fair to good
◈	**Currents**	none
◔	**Dive type**	day boat

The dives on the outer, or southern, side of Kapalai are in less good condition which is a little surprising as they are closer to the deep waters outside the Litigan Reefs. You would expect upwellings to encourage coral growth here but most are small and growing low to the topography. There are some creatures of note though. This site doesn't live up to its name but does have a lot of orang-utan crabs. On one small bommie there are five leaffish, a cuttlefish and a big scorpionfish. Black coral bushes have tiny shells sitting in them and many small skeleton shrimp.

◈16 Stingray City

◉	**Depth**	16 m
◐	**Visibility**	fair to good
◈	**Currents**	none
◔	**Dive type**	day boat

A small rocky wall gives way to a sandy gully about 50 metres wide and followed by a raised mound. In the gully there are plenty of the promised blue-spotted rays, several anemones, all with shrimp in them but no clownfish which seems odd, and even a large crocodilefish (below). As you fin towards the mound you are likely to encounter a huge turtle on the sand. The mound is covered in small hard corals and sponges. There's not a huge amount of fish life although there are quite a lot of nudibranchs crawling around.

◈ Conservation

The survey team back-rolled into the water and descended with slates, pencils, rulers and cameras, equipped to record data from one of the permanent monitoring sites. Twice a year for the last 10 years, indicator species of fish and invertebrates have been counted to provide a snapshot of the health of the reefs in the Tun Sakaran Marine Park. As I focused on my task, a deafening explosion was heard, shattering the tranquillity of the shallow reef and breaking my concentration. When we surfaced, there was no sign of any other boats nearby and the Sabah Parks rangers on our boat had seen and heard nothing.

That afternoon we conducted an exploration dive on the same reef area and, by chance, this was the exact site where the fish bombing had occurred in the morning. The destruction was fresh with corals shattered by the explosion. The majority of fish had been taken by the bombers but a few lay motionless on the sea bed, evidence of the force of the explosives.

Tragically, fish bombing is occurring on a regular basis in many parts of Southeast Asia. Yet, there is still hope! In the Tun Sakaran Marine Park, Malaysia's newest Marine Protected Area, the Semporna Islands Project is working to stamp out this destructive activity with the cooperation of the local community which depends on the reefs for its livelihood.

For me, conservation is about people living in harmony with their surroundings and I became involved in the Semporna Islands Project to play an active role in the protection of the reefs and islands here. SIP is working to empower local people and involve them directly in the protection and preservation of their Park. A Community Ranger Scheme is also being set up, and through education and awareness campaigns it is hoped that the reefs will recover and the exceptionally high biodiversity found in the Park will be safeguarded for the benefit of both visitors and local people.

Although it breaks my heart to see the effects of the destructive fishing practices, such as bombing, on the reefs in the Park, every dive gives me renewed hope. In between counting sea urchins and recording rubble instead of coral, are hiding some rare and remarkable marine creatures. A plethora of nudibranchs and flatworms, mantis shrimp, moray eels and lobsters, means that it is always worth looking closely at what seems at first to be a barren reef.

Helen Brunt,
Sabah Coordinator,
Semporna Islands Project

Mabul

Perhaps a little closer to Semporna on the mainland but an equally short ride from Sipadan, Mabul is the largest island in this group. Also on the edge of the Litigan Reefs, it was for a very long time home only to the sea gypsies of the Bajau tribe.

They still occupy a small, rickety water village but now compete for space with several dive resorts of varying standards. Offshore, there is even a hotel housed in a converted oil rig. It is frankly one of the ugliest things you will ever see, until you get beneath it and discover it's also one of the best muck dives you will ever do. Or in fact, several dives, because like much of this area, dive sites can be done in several different directions.

Well known as a macro destination to die for, Mabul rarely disappoints although, like Kapalai, there is evidence of past reef bombing. Conditions are easy enough although there are occasional currents and these may divert a chosen dive to another day. Dives tend to be shore dives and focus on the ones closest to the resorts as each has a stunning house reef. If you are staying at Kapalai, the most visited sites are those under the Oil Rig and a couple of the shallow ones near to it.

↘17 Paradise 1 & 2	
🕐 Depth	21 m
◐ Visibility	fair to good
🌊 Currents	none to strong
🚤 Dive type	day boat

In front of the Sipadan Water Village the beach leads to a flat bottom of sand and seagrasses. This is Paradise 1, a cracking dive where divemasters lead you from one weird animal to the next with hardly a moment to admire each. There are flying gurnards, fingered dragonets, dwarf lionfish, snake eels, inimicus (or devilfish), filefish and longsnout pipefish. Even weirder fish such as hairy decorated filefish, a wacky long-legged crab and juvenile stonefish are just millimetres long. Tiny mantis shrimp peek out of their burrows and flounder try to disguise themselves. Small octopus hide beneath coconut shells and even smaller blue-ringed octopus sneak into old beer bottles. Palm fronds get caught on buoy lines and are used by squid to lay their eggs. Sometimes there are upwards of 20 females laying. A little further along to the west is Paradise 2, which has slightly fewer 'muck' critters but more free swimmers like batfish and young wrasse, clownfish in their host anemones and, at dusk, you may spot mandarinfish.

↘18 Coral Reef Garden	
🕐 Depth	16 m
◐ Visibility	fair
🌊 Currents	slight
🚤 Dive type	day boat

Not such a well known dive, this site starts a little way back from the Water Village but you swim towards and finish the dive in front of it. At the beginning the sea bed seems barren with only a few piles of old junk – coconut trunks, bricks and tyres that have been colonized a little. The visibility is lower on this patch as it is very sandy and even the slightest currents stir the sand up into the water. As you swim along, you might encounter a female cuttlefish laying her eggs in the old roots of a coconut trunk while a little further, there are some patchy outcrops of coral an another cuttlefish, perhaps the male. Buried in the sand beneath is a stonefish and the enormous spearing mantis shrimp is hiding right beside the tail of the stonefish, his eyes poking out of his burrow and somehow mimicking his neighbour's wary stare. There are plenty of shrimps and crabs on anemones and bubble corals, a juvenile cuttlefish, whip coral gobies and even some gorgeous, pure white, mushroom coral pipefish.

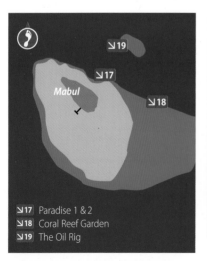

↘17 Paradise 1 & 2
↘18 Coral Reef Garden
↘19 The Oil Rig

Creatures from Paradise (the dive) include filefish and seahorses

19 The Oil Rig

🌀 **Depth**	18 m
🕐 **Visibility**	poor to good
🌊 **Currents**	slight to medium
🌊 **Dive type**	day boat

The massive and incredibly ugly oil derrick parked just off Mabul's shores is, rather surprisingly, an exercise in nature's power over man. Humanity does its best to mess up the landscape but nature has its own cunning ways of turning that around. The pylons supporting the rig are quite eerie, reminiscent of a wreck dive, and swarmed by jacks and snappers. The seabed below is studded with man-made detritus, yet the creatures don't seem so bothered and have started their own, personal recycling programmes: ropes have been colonized by iridescent sponges that shelter tiny gobies; piles of building detritus have stonefish squatters; and a giant moray

called Elvis lives under an old cage. There are crocodilefish and flying gurnards carpeting the sand, ornate ghost pipefish in fans and lime green frogfish hang out in old car tyres. A pile of metal sheets and pipes has yet more frogfish in varying colours, scorpionfish and morays are everywhere; and there are mantis shrimp and jawfish, cardinals and nesting sergeant majors. The list could go on.

A secondary dive is often done to the northern side of the rig. Outside the pylons where there is more light reaching down to the reef – plus less damage and detritus from when the rig was positioned here – you can investigate the small patches of reef. These are all quite pretty with lots of soft corals and fans that are equally well colonized. This is an area where the divemasters find it a challenge to ensure you see one of their frogfish

pets. There are both miniature painted frogfish that are still in their black-spotted juvenile stage and tiny clown frogfish. There were masses of other things there too: some large nudibranchs mating, lots of *Chromodoris bullocki* including juveniles that are only a few millimetres long. Groups of ornate ghost pipefish are found frequently but they aren't always living where you expect them to be – like inside crinoids or on fans – but are sometimes hovering around flat elephant ear sponges, making them appear to be easy fodder for their predators.

The oil rig pylons are constantly mobbed by schools of fish; tiny cuttlefish sheltering in a sponge while a giant frogfish pretends to be one.

Temperatures rising **Borneo**

Sabah's dive destinations are well established and so well regarded that few people stray from such well-trodden paths. But that's not to say that there aren't many more tempting places to visit. For those who like a little more adventure try the wrecks near Labuan, accessed from Brunei, or Miri in Sarawak further to the south. Or even just try some city based diving – it's only minutes from Kota Kinabalu to the closest marine park.

Tunku Abdul Rahman Marine Park The closest dive sites to the big city are in this marine park. Named after the first Malaysian Prime Minister, the protected area covers five small, forested islands, the most popular and largest being Pulau Gaya. There is a small resort located there, but the majority of divers who visit are day trippers. It's a good place to do a course or a day's check-out diving as it takes less than half an hour to reach the reefs. The islands are ringed by mangroves which form a sanctuary for a variety of birds and insects, plus a nursery for marine creatures. However, this also means that visibility isn't as good as elsewhere. The best time is from March to October.

Pulau Tiga Just two hours offshore to the southwest of Kota Kinabalu, Tiga became well known because the TV programme *Survivor* was filmed there. This lightweight reality entertainment show suddenly had the island renamed Survivor Island. As such it attracts a certain sort of visitor. There is a lone resort and dive centre so you can tread the same paths and swim the same reefs as those who put themselves through the process of trying to be famous. There are two more islands in the park: Kalmpunian Besar is a small sand cay and Kalampunian Damit, or Snake Island, is a breeding ground for seasnakes. Again, diving is between May and September.

Labuan Federal Territory This small island, 8 km off the west coast of Sabah and a short hop from the Sultanate of Brunei, is an intriguing wreck diving destination. The island has a deep-water harbour and has always been a busy commercial centre. Now it's a duty free port with waterside markets, hotels, nightclubs, and excellent restaurants. The marine park consists of three small islands with pretty beaches ringed by some shallow reefs suitable for

snorkelling. However, the real draw is the cluster of accessible wrecks. A couple (the American and Australian wrecks) are from the Second World War while the Blue Water and Cement wrecks are more recent. This last is suitable for beginners, but the others require more advanced diving experience. Fish and coral growth on all the structures is said to be reasonable, which is a good thing as the local reefs suffer from sediments and low visibility. The best dive season is between May and September.

Mataking As soon as Sipadan was threatened with closure, new resorts started to emerge nearby. Mataking is the latest and building quite a reputation. The reefs here are shallow and gentle but in the past there has been some damage. However the resort is working hard to regenerate the reef by introducing a well regarded 'reef ball' project. These artificial reefs give baby corals a foundation to latch onto and help attract fish species by giving them protection. Meanwhile, there is a proliferation of small, colourful creatures plus rays, turtles and so on. The island itself is quite large and ringed by a stretch of white sandy beach. There's even an outdoor spa set under the mangrove trees. Just

watch out for the coconut crabs which come to visit at night. Diving is year round and the island seems perfect for everyone, even non-diving chums.

Miri, Sarawak With so much amazing diving in Sabah, you could be forgiven for thinking that neighbouring Sarawak would have dive potential too. There is some potential but sadly it is nowhere near the quality of that to the north. The reason for this is two-fold: several rivers along this coastline drop substantial amounts of sediment into the shallow coastal waters and these waters are particularly shallow – the coastal plain extends a long way and is often only 15 metres deep. There are only handful of dive operations here with nowhere near the facilities and infrastructure that Sabah has. However, Miri, just over the border from Brunei, is the exception to all this as just offshore there are a dozen or more decent reefs, a couple of small wrecks and you can even dive around the pylons of oil rigs. The dive quality seems to be quite like that of Peninsular Malaysia. The best dive season is between March and August.

Drying out

Sipadan no longer has accommodation so for dedicated divers there is just a lone and lovely resort on Kapalai, while Mabul has a greater selection of resorts. These are of varying standards, from budget to top-notch, and rates. All resorts have an on-site dive centre plus restaurants and other leisure facilities.

Kapalai

$$ **Sipadan Kapalai Resort**, T+60 (0)89 765200, sipadan-kapalai.com. This water village resort is absolutely delightful – rooms are spacious and bug free (image right). No air-con, just sea-breeze cooled. The resort has expanded and been upgraded since Sipadan was closed but remains spacious. The divemasters are master critter spotters. Weekly packs cost around US$1200 and include all meals,

transfers and unlimited diving. Sipadan trips are subject to permits.

Mabul

$$$-$$ **Sipadan-Mabul Resort & Mabul Water Bungalows**, T+60 (0)88 230006, sipadan-mabul.com.my. Long established operator with two resorts, the original with basic accommodation and a second, better, set of water bungalows. Weekly packages, from around US$1200-1800 including all meals, transfers and diving. Sipadan trips are subject to permits.

Liveaboards

MV Celebes Explorer, T+60 (0)88 224918, borneo.org. The only liveaboard operating in this region. Cruises depart from Semporna jetty for 3 day, 4 day or weekly itineraries around the Litigan Reefs.

Malaysia Drying out Sabah: Kapalai and Mabul

Sabah's rainforests

This one Malaysian state is regarded by many as having some of the world's most important flora and fauna species. Over half of the state, about 5,000 square kilometres, has been set aside to create rainforest reserves and wildlife parks to ensure the protection of the interior and the many unique plants and animals that live there.

Driving from Tawau to Semporna en route to the offshore islands, you may find this hard to believe: you pass palm oil plantation after palm oil plantation and wonder what the coastal lowlands must have once been like. To see the real Sabah, you will need to head far inland. Although there are over 200 mammals living in these forests you will be lucky to see many as they retreat further inland at the faintest hint of disturbance. There are

escorted tours running to and through all these reserves. Most are walking tours and you can stay overnight. The best time to visit is during the fruiting and flowering season which is from March until October.

Danum Valley Conservation Area Within striking distance of the Sipadan area and home to Asian elephants. (These are said to have such incredible hearing they can hear people from many miles away.) The Sumatran rhinoceros, which is endangered, sun bears and clouded leopards are known to inhabit the area too, but are rarely seen. Visitors do see birds like the hornbill species.

Tabin Wildlife Reserve On the eastern side of the state, this protected forest area of 120,500 hectres has populations of the three largest mammals in Sabah: the Borneo Pygmy Elephant, Sumateran

Rhinoceros and Tembadau (a species of Asian wild cattle).

Kinabatangan Wildlife Sanctuary This reserve is nearer to Sandakan and sits on a river floodplain. The wildlife species here include proboscis and leaf monkeys and crab-eating macaques. By the river there are mud-skipper fish and many estuarine crocodiles. The bird watching is regarded as spectacular with several types of hornbill, kingfishers and the endangered Sunda ground cuckoos.

Sleeping $$$ US$150+ double room per night $$ US$75-150 $ under US$75
Eating $$$ US$40+ 2-course meal, excluding drinks $$ US$20-40 $ under US$20

Peninsular Malaysia

Malaysia's mainland is a hot destination for Asian residents. Both qualified and trainee divers head to the islands off the east coast to relax, do a little diving or continue with courses they have started at home.

In the summer months, April to October, the conditions here are perfect for that, with gentle currents, shallow reefs and warm waters combining to make an ideal long weekend. You would think this would also make it an ideal stopover or add-on for long-haul divers too, but sadly this area is less appropriate for two reasons. One is that it simply takes too long to get here. The majority of visitors to all these islands tend to be long-term travellers who are trekking up and down the coast and can reach the islands without having to worry about time constraints.

The other reason is that the diving here is subject to the seasons and the vagaries of currents that run through the South China Seas. Malaysia's east coast sits directly below the edge of the Gulf of Thailand. This very shallow sea averages less than 60 metres deep and, with twice daily tides, is susceptible to heavy sedimentation and river run-off. From November to February, the northeast monsoon brings rain so the water is cool and visibility is minimal. During these same months, the South China Sea Current comes from the north and pushes this murkier water down from the Gulf to Malaysia. You just can't dive here then: it's too windy and the visibility can drop to below five metres. In the summer months though, the wind and current patterns reverse bringing clearer waters up from Indonesia. It's never crystal clear but can get up to 30 metres at times. Diving is said to be available from April to October but in reality, if it's stormy and few people are about, dive centres cancel their trips. Even when the weather is lovely, visibility can still be limited. Yet many of these islands are so picturesque that if you're in the region and you're just as happy to absorb the atmosphere, you may enjoy what diving there is. Conditions may have restricted reef diversity and coral numbers but many good creatures are sighted – whalesharks cruise the coast and turtles are frequent visitors. Schooling fish are prolific and if you can get a little way offshore the dives can be as spectacular as many more famous areas. However, the focus is always on smaller creatures as seeing them isn't dependent on clear water.

Locations
If you have the time to explore more than one of these pretty islands, those mentioned opposite are regarded as having the best diving and facilities.

Destinations

Tioman Island

As lovely as you might remember if you have seen Hollywood 1950s classic *South Pacific*, which was filmed here, Tioman's high central ridge of jungle-clad mountains drops sharply on the island's western side to a series of small villages that sit in sheltered coves. These are picturesque and face west, catching spectacular sunsets. The most popular stops are those with a jetty, meaning ferries from Mersing on the mainland can drop passengers close to their bungalows. **Salang** on the northern tip, **Ayer Batang**, Tekek and **Genting**, as you head south, are the busiest with a selection of accommodation and dive centres. It can get rather lively as these areas attract a lot of long-term travellers. Other 'villages' are likely to be a lone resort at the upper end of the scale. These are quieter but the focus is on the resort complex.   *Distance from airport: minimum 8 hrs*

Other options

Perhentian Islands Inside the Terengganu Marine Park, the two Perhentian islands are tiny, pretty and very 'Robinson Crusoe'. Resorts and bungalows tend to be small and simple, but there is a good variety. Dive sites are around rocky outcrops with cracks and crevices to investigate. There's plenty of coral growth and all the typical fish species – angels, butterflies, jacks and so on.

Redang Island Just below Perhentian and also part of the marine park, Redang is quite a well developed island with a tiny airport and some top-end hotels. This was Malaysia's first marine park and has the best visibility as there are deeper drop-offs. Dive sites circle outcrops which have sandy terrain on the eastern side and rocky on the west.

Lang Tengah Touted as one of the nation's best-kept secrets, this undeveloped little island has pristine beaches and an unspoiled tropical jungle interior. Diving is, like its neighbours, gentle and easygoing. There are only a few small resorts here and it's all fairly simple and laid-back.

Tenggol Island Further south, this island is touted as having some of the best diving on the Peninsula. It's a bit further offshore and has better visibility. The west of the island is a steep-sided wall that descends down to 30 metres where interesting boulders can be found. Again, there are only a few small bungalow complexes here.

Places to stay and things to do at these destinations are listed in Drying out on page 169

Mersing; Bahara Rock; sunset of the Malaysia coast; Tioman island; Chebeh; MV Black Manta at Jack Rock

Malaysia Peninsular Malaysia

Tioman

Approaching Tioman by boat you are faced with a classic Asian island vista if ever there was one. Its hilly central spine reaches so far into the sky that most days the top is shrouded in puffy white clouds while the tiny coves and beaches at its base are bathed in warm sunshine.

The island is a designated marine park and for a long time was pretty much regarded as only a learn-to-dive destination. The sheltered bays made it ideal for novices to take a course or brush up on skills learned elsewhere.

However, while the coastal bays are calm and easy, there are some very exciting and challenging dive sites a little way offshore. Although the visibility is never crystal clear, these are well worth seeing. The underwater landscape of enormous granite rocks is reminiscent of parts of the Similan Islands way over in the Andaman Sea. Huge boulders have tumbled together creating interesting swim-throughs coated in soft corals and attracting a wealth of marine creatures. Plus there are a couple of small wrecks that lurk in the shallows.

↘1	**Pulau Chebeh**	
🧭	**Depth**	23 m
🌓	**Visibility**	fair
💨	**Currents**	slight to medium
⚓	**Dive type**	day boat

The most northerly site from Tioman, this offshore dive is surprisingly pretty. The topography of the island above water is one of huge granite boulders so there is a strange sense of déjà vu – well, if you have ever been to the Similans. The look is much the same below the waterline, with more gigantic boulders and rocky areas that create nice swim-throughs. There is a bit of current here but it's not too strong to be a nuisance and no doubt encourages the growth of all the small fan corals, which are in a variety of pastel colours. Some areas have masses of small silvery fish like sweepers and sardines. There are batfish chasing each other about, probably males competing, then you come across several more throughout the dive. Overhead there are some pelagic species: four big barracuda, a small turtle and later a large tuna. The Similans angelfish lives here, there are cowries, and bluespotted rays seem to be nestled under every crevice.

Leopard shark

www.whitemanta.com

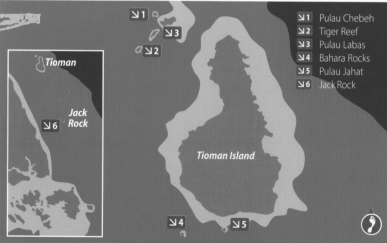

↘1	Pulau Chebeh
↘2	Tiger Reef
↘3	Pulau Labas
↘4	Bahara Rocks
↘5	Pulau Jahat
↘6	Jack Rock

Tioman

Jack Rock

↘6

↘1 ↘3 ↘2

Tioman Island

↘4 ↘5

⚓2 Tiger Reef

🕙	**Depth**	22 m
◑	**Visibility**	fair
🌊	**Currents**	none to strong
🌊	**Dive type**	liveaboard

Not dissimilar to Chebeh, Tiger Reef has more pinnacle-shaped boulders to swim around. Entry is over the one with the mooring buoy at about five metres, then you drop to 12, swim through a crevice between two sections and make your way around all the pinnacles to see what is about. There are needlenose barracuda in a massive swarm, snappers nearby, more Similans sweetlips and, again, several bluespotted rays. At the base of the dive in a sandy bowl, you might encounter a small bumphead parrotfish – small being comparative as you soon find a male (probably) and three females. The 'male' was the biggest we've ever seen, about a metre and a half long. The stunning nudibranchs pale in comparison.

⚓3 Pulau Labas

🕙	**Depth**	13 m
◑	**Visibility**	good
🌊	**Currents**	slight
🌊	**Dive type**	liveaboard

Because there are two distinct sides to this site, it is often used for night dives. On the inner side of a cluster of rocks is a sheltered moon-shaped reef. There are crevices and tunnels between the rocks and in daylight you can swim though and out to the other side. That gets strong currents though, so isn't part of the night dive. Instead, divers can spend time in the shallow waters investigating the area around the rocks and under the hard corals. There are sleeping bumphead parrots as well as smaller parrots in their bubbles, plus a huge number of other sleeping fish tucked into nooks and crannies. Tiny crabs cling to fans while hermit crabs are skittering across the coral rubble trying to avoid all the urchins on

the surface. There are also some very unusual nudibranchs and flatworms that would remain invisible if it wasn't for a torch beam.

▶4 Bahara Rocks

Depth	13 m	
Visibility	fair	
Currents	none	
Dive type	liveaboard	

Back down off the south of Tioman, this site is located under a lighthouse, which is perched on a pinnacle that just breaks the surface There can be quite a bit of surge around its base. The reef is shaped like an amphitheatre running away from the central rock. Extensive beds of staghorn and elephant ear corals lead away to a patch of rubble where the coral has been devastated, then the reef drops down to a broad area of soft coral bushes and whips that form a pink and mauve forest: it is a very, very pretty sight. To the side is a series of outcrops with several overhangs being mobbed by millions of glassy sweepers. The life seems less interesting here – there are the usual nudibranchs, pincushion stars and white eyed morays – but that's probably only because you don't see far beyond the ethereal waves of colour in the water.

▶5 Pulau Jahat

Depth	20 m	
Visibility	fair	
Currents	slight to medium	
Dive type	liveaboard	

Translating as Naughty Island, the story goes that it was so named as fishermen of old used to lose their nets on the rocks. This island is made up of granite boulders and underwater the giant rocks give way to a flat sea bed covered in a mix of sand and rubble. The corals are not quite so prolific but it is still pretty. Visibility runs at about a dozen metres, which is regarded as standard here, but it's no problem to spot the marine life as there is so much including lots of bluespotted rays, from one that is is just a few inches across the disc to quite a large adult. There are lots of nudibranchs, masses of clownfish on anemones, a few small fish like bass and damsels, and lots of whip gobies – lots of whip corals in fact. The dive goes from the south end of the island to the north, the north having a bit more current and some of the rocks have better hard coral cover.

▶6 Jack Rock

Depth	20m	
Visibility	poor to fair	
Currents	none to ripping	
Dive type	liveaboard	

This lonely pinnacle is in the middle of nowhere, halfway back to Singapore. It drops from two metres above the surface to 22 metres at the flat seafloor. The visibility is renown for being awful, and currents strong, so when you drop in on one side, and find the visibility is up to 10 metres, you are relieved. The first part of the dive is on the clear side of the rock and takes you down to the base which is covered in hard, soft and whip corals. A couple of crevices are known baby shark haunts – you can just see their tails. There are unusual nudibranchs and large starry puffers. A bit of the dive is then spent around on the murky side then, as you come back up to about five metres on the clear side you come into the current and one of the most amazing moments in diving – there are swarms of small silvery fish, but the excitement isn't due to their presence but because of the speed they are moving, both around the pinnacle and the divers. It's impossible to describe.

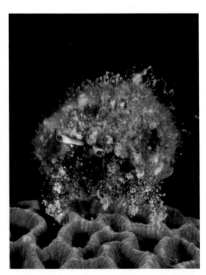

Reef scenes and creatures from around Tioman Island

Drying out

❝ ❞ Hotels abound on Tioman and there is no doubt you can get anything – any style, any budget – your heart desires. However, as authors, we cannot give personal recommendations as it's been too many years since we stayed there. We returned recently, but on a liveaboard that sailed from Singapore and can't recommend that enough. The hotels below have a good reputation.

$$$-$$ Japamala Resort T+60 (0)9 419 7777, japamalaresorts.com. On the southwest corner Tioman, this small, boutique hotel bills itself as jungle luxury living. Check for their seasonal promotions which are very good value.

$$-$ Minang Cove Resort, T+60 (0)7 799 7372, minangcove.com.my. Also on the south of Tioman and set in a lovely cove. The reef just offshore is said to be great for snorkelling. Run by a British-Malay couple with an onsite dive centre.

Liveaboards

White Manta Diving T +65 9677 8894 whitemanta.com. This highly professional Singaporean company has 2 vessels, *White* and *Black Manta*. From November to May, they sail and dive Thai waters, but from June to October, they cover north and east of Singapore. Trips vary from 2-4 days to Tioman, Pulau Aur and Kuantan in Malaysia plus some wrecks and islands in nearby Indonesian waters. *Black Manta* is very comfortable and the food is fabulous.

Tioman

Most people come to Tioman to relax, swim and dive. There isn't much else to do and chances are you won't move far from the village you are staying in as each is independent of the next with no roads connecting them. Nightlife is minimal although there are restaurants and bars. (To this day we daydream of Tioman fish curry!) The main day out is to walk across the island from Tekek to Juara on the east coast. It's a long haul uphill and takes about four hours through the jungle. Take plenty of water and catch a ferry back.

Peninsular Malaysia

Kuala Lumpur Malaysia is a nation built on its cross-cultural differences and nowhere is this reflected more than in the capital. If you're up for a few days of city lifestyle, KL is as lively as any, and perhaps for many divers, too lively. You can admire architecture that ranges from aging colonial mansions to state-of-the-art skyscrapers. Go to the 88-storey Petronas Twin Towers for the heart-stopping view from the sky bridge or explore the early art-deco building that houses the central arts and crafts market. Food, shopping and entertainment are all equally influenced by the cultural differences in the country.

Melaka This historic city and port could be worth a diversion from KL as it's only 2½ hours away. A prosperous trading post in the 16th century, the Portuguese, Dutch and British all colonized here. There are many cultural remnants, from the Dutch Town Hall to the Portuguese port, British built churches to ancient Chinese temples. Plus there are museums, markets and gardens to explore.

Cameron Highlands Located 1,500 m above sea level, the highlands are famous for their pleasant weather, tea plantations and cool temperatures. The main town is Tanah Rata. From there, you can also take extensive hill walks, past waterfalls and forests ending at one of the tea houses. Some tours stop at the Batu Caves on the way, with its sacred Hindu temple. This is 227 steps uphill.

East Coast Made up of three states, the east coast is punctuated with several small cities and large towns. Although each is charming enough, there is little to hold diver tourists here for more than a day although places like Mersing will give you a feel for a rustic Malay sea port and Kota Bharu is an introduction to more traditional Malay culture. Each town has a mosque, a temple, a market. Some of the bigger ones will have a small museum although tourists are charged far more to enter than locals.

 Sleeping $$$ US$150+ double room per night $$ US$75-150 $ under US$75

 Eating $$$ US$40+ 2-course meal, excluding drinks $$ US$20-40 $ under US$20

Philippines

Circular batfish and Bluestreaked fusiliers mob the wreck of the *Alma Jane* in Puerto Galera's Sabang Bay.

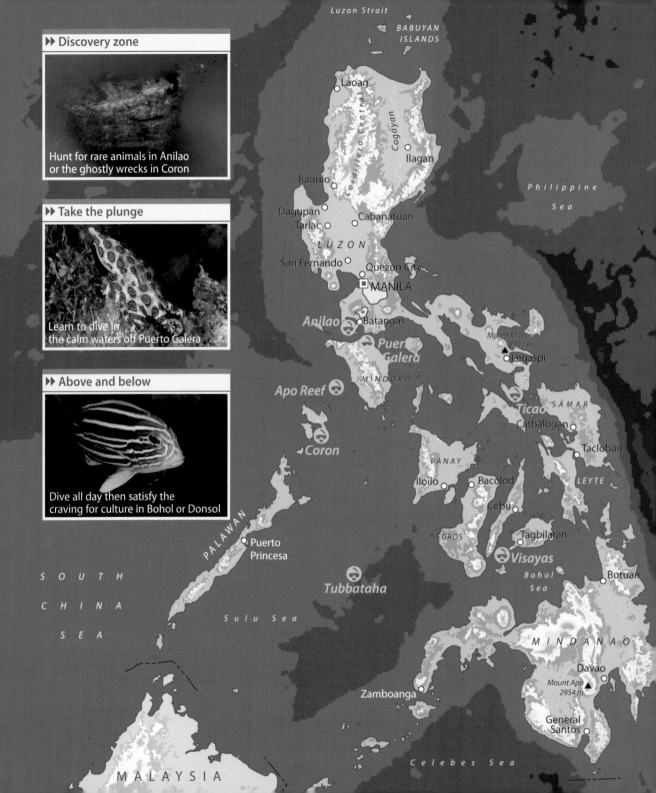

▶▶ Discovery zone

Hunt for rare animals in Anilao or the ghostly wrecks in Coron

▶▶ Take the plunge

Learn to dive in the calm waters off Puerto Galera

▶▶ Above and below

Dive all day then satisfy the craving for culture in Bohol or Donsol

Luzon Strait

BABUYAN ISLANDS

Laoag

Cagayan

Ilagan

Philippine Sea

Baguio

Dagupan

Tarlac

Cabanatuan

Cordillera Central

L U Z O N

San Fernando

Quezon City

MANILA

Anilao

Batangas

▲ Mount Mayon 2421 m

Legaspi

Puerto Galera

S A M A R

MINDORO

Apo Reef

Ticao

Catbalogan

Tacloban

PANAY

LEYTE

Coron

Iloilo

Bacolod

Cebu

NEGROS

Tagbilaran

Visayas

Butuan

PALAWAN

Puerto Princesa

Bohol Sea

S O U T H

C H I N A

S E A

Tubbataha

Sulu Sea

M I N D A N A O

Davao

Mount Apo 2954 m ▲

Zamboanga

General Santos

C e l e b e s   S e a

MALAYSIA

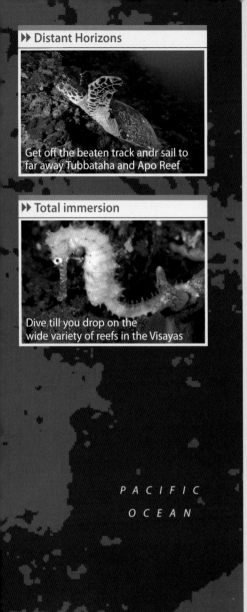

▶▶ Distant Horizons

Get off the beaten track andr sail to far away Tubbataha and Apo Reef

▶▶ Total immersion

Dive till you drop on the wide variety of reefs in the Visayas

PACIFIC OCEAN

0   100   200 km

0   50   100 miles

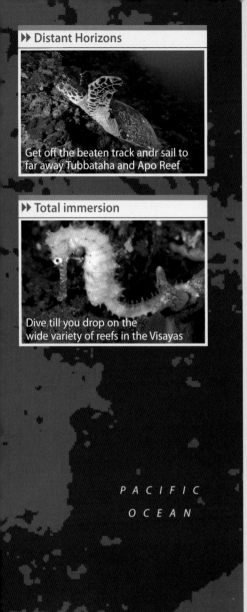

The islands of the Philippines are surrounded by the second largest expanse of water inside the Coral Triangle, forming its northern apex. The rich marine biodiversity here has only recently been acknowledged. The country may be just a short hop away from more popular routes for well-heeled divers but it should come as no surprise that the numbers of coral and fish species rank as high as anywhere else – even competing with neighbouring Indonesia.

The variety of diving can be outstanding. Sandwiched between the Pacific and the South China Seas, the reefs are tantalizing: thick with tropical fish and colourful gardens of coral. In some areas there is a wealth of unusual small marine animals, while in others there are swarms of pelagics or the chance to explore a fleet of Second World War wrecks.

Considered something of an enigma, above the waves outlying island destinations retain a charming sense of the past. Idyllic sea views are interrupted only by rows of brightly painted *bancas* – traditional timber and bamboo outriggers – that are lined up, awaiting the next day's quota of divers. It would be hard to beat the romance of sitting at night under a coconut palm on a snow-white Filipino beach, cool sand between your toes and wondering what the next day will bring.

Essentials

Getting there

Philippine Airlines once had an extensive network that went right around the world. Now though, their longhaul flights are principally from America or Australia. Other flights are likely to be a code share with another airline. Most frequent is probably Singapore Airlines but there are flights with Qatar (qatarairways.com), Northwest, Asiana and many others. All these deposit travellers in Manila on a regular basis while Silk Air (silkair.com) and Qatar have flights to Cebu City located in the central Visayas region. For those already in Asia, low cost carrier Jetstar (jetstar.com) flies to Manila. Air Asia (airasia.com) and Tiger Airways (tigerairways.com) fly to Clark Airport but this is three hours drive north of Manila. Philippine Airlines (philippineairlines.com) and Cebu Pacific (cebupacific.com) both have good regional and internal networks.

Visas are not required for entry for most nationalities, but there are variable and sometimes hefty departure taxes. For internal flights the cost can be 30 pesos or 200 pesos (US$5) while international is US$18 depending on exchange rate.

Getting around

Apart from those mentioned above, there are several other internal airlines in the country: Air Philippines (airphils.com), South East Asian Air (flyseair.com) and Asian Spirit (asianspirit.com) can get you almost anywhere although some internal trips, especially in the Visayas, can be just as easily achieved by fast catamarans. Note that their schedules change frequently.

One of the peculiarities of Filipino dive travel is that few hotels and operators automatically offer airport transfers. This is because they often involve both a drive and a small hop on a ferry. However, if you request transfers, they will be arranged for you or you will be given instructions on independent travel (see opposite). Taxis are metered; drivers are especially helpful, ensuring you reach the first available ferry as sometimes an extra one will have been added or, in low season, stopped.

For day-trips, and in the cities, there are buses and taxis but always try to use air-con versions of both. There are also jeepneys, a legacy of when American forces were stationed here during the Second World war. These customized vehicles are colourful and cheap but not exactly a comfortable ride. On the islands, there are tricycles (a three-wheeled motorbike with a two-seater sidecar) and the ubiquitous and ever charming *bancas* – wooden outrigger boats that use huge bamboo poles as stabilizers. Self-drive car hire is rarely available, so for day-trips and tours, speak to your dive operator who will arrange a car and driver for you.

Philippines	
Location	13°00'N, 122°00'E
Neighbours	Indonesia, Borneo, Hong Kong, Palau, Vietnam
Population	96,061,680
Land area in km²	298,170
Coastline in km	33,900
Territorial sea in km²	679,774

Transfers

Depending on your arrival time, it may be possible to transfer straight to your chosen dive destination. However, if you are not being collected it is worth an overnight stop before starting fresh the next day. If you are taking an internal flight, Philippine Airlines depart from the newer, more comfortable, Ninoy Aquino Airport. Smaller, low-cost airlines leave from the old terminal, which can only be described as chaotic. Amusingly so, but chaotic all the same.

One piece of good news regarding internal flights is that excess baggage rates are low. At 50 pesos per kilo you can afford not to worry about a few kilos over but you will be charged, no matter how much you sweet-talk the check-in agent. Curiously, hand luggage does not always seem to get weighed.

For the destinations in the north and west fly first to Manila:
Manila As there is little reason to stay in the city, book a hotel near the airport that includes courtesy transfers (see page 187) and avoid the busy downtown area, which is prone to traffic jams.
Anilao The drive from Manila takes up to three hours. Transfers are not included as most guests are locals and they drive there. Ask your resort to organize a private car or mini-van for you.
Puerto Galera Road transfers from Manila to Batangas port take 2½ hours, followed by an hour by ferry. A few resorts have set times for a shuttle to and from downtown Manila while others will book a private transfer at a premium.
Donsol and Ticao Island Take an internal flight from Manila to Legaspi where you will be met by your dive operator. By road to Donsol is one hour plus an additional 1½ hours to Ticao by boat.
Coron Take an internal flight from Manila to Busuanga. Your operator will collect you by car for the drive to the harbour (for liveaboards) or onwards by boat to your resort in 20 minutes.
Tubbataha Flights from Manila land at Puerto Princessa where you will be met by your liveaboard operator.

For destinations in the Visayas, fly to Manila then take an internal flight (this usually requires an overnight stop) or fly to Cebu and transfer as follows:
Bohol For Panglao and Cabilao, transfers involve a 20-minute taxi ride from the airport to the port then the next available fast ferry to Tagbilaran on Bohol (oceanjet.net, 1½ hours) where your resort will meet you. To Alona it's 40 minutes by road; Cabilao is an hour by road and boat. This is all less of a hassle than it sounds.
Negros Oriental for Dumaguete Arrangements as above to the port followed by a boat to Dumaguete. Ensure you get one of the fast boats (oceanjet.net) as these are very comfortable. From Cebu, the trip takes three hours; Bohol to Dumaguete is just 1½ hours. Resorts meet guests at the dock.

Tourist information → the WOWPhilippines official websites can be found at wowphilippines.co.uk and .com.us, .com.sg, com.hk, .com.ca and philippinetourism.com.au.

Fact file

International flights	Cebu Pacific, Philippine Airlines, Qatar, Qantas, Singapore Airlines, Silk Air, United Airlines
Departure tax	US$18
Entry	EU, USA and Commonwealth – valid passport for stays up to 21 days
Internal flights	Asian Spirit, Cebu Pacific, South East Asian Air,
Ground transport	Jeepney buses, ferries and taxis
Money	US$1 = 47 pesos (PHP)
Language	English and Tagalog plus regional dialects
Electricity	220v/plus types A and C
Time zone	GMT +8
Religion	Roman Catholic
Phone	Country code +63; IDD code 00; Police 166

Manila's old domestic terminal; the ubiquitous jeepney

Philippines Essentials

Language

Despite centuries of Spanish domination, English is actually the language of the Philippines and is spoken by pretty much the entire nation. The national language, Filipino is a derivative of Tagalog, the most widely spoken indigenous language. If you ask any divemaster or hotel staff what they speak, they look at you quizzically then usually come up with Tagalog but automatically revert to speaking English. The great joy of this is that most Filipinos are very chatty and have a great sense of humour, easily understanding their guests' jokes and comments. Here are a few Tagalog words you are likely to hear:

hello	kumusta
goodbye	paalam
welcome	mabuhay
yes	o-o
no	hindi
I don't know	di ko alam
please	paki
thank you	salamat po
sorry!	paumanhin po!
how much is...	magkano...
good	mabait
great dive!	tamang sisid!
one beer/water	isa pa pong beer/tubig

Filipino food stall with local specialities

Local laws and customs

This is a deeply religious land although it's easy to forget that as you stand beneath the Manila city skyline which is obliterated by posters depicting American movies, pop stars and mobile phone companies. The Philippines were a Spanish colony for 350 years and 85% of the country is Catholic. The country was sold to America in 1898 for US$20 million and it remained a US possession for 50 years. The American influence appears to be dominant but deep down the Filipino nature is devout.

Outside Manila or Cebu, life is more relaxed with fewer Western influences. There are no specific courtesies or dress codes to be observed but be respectful and always bear in mind that despite the laid-back demeanour of most Filipinos, at least one member of their family is likely to be a priest or otherwise involved with the church. They love to talk about this and will entertain you with great stories of the divemaster's brother, the Priest's birthday party or some curious historical tale: for example the late 1700s cathedral that dominates the Legaspi skyline was evidently built entirely by women.

Safety

When it comes to safety, geography is all important. All government advisories warn against travel to Mindanao and the Sulu Archipelago (Basilan, Tawi-Tawi and Jolo). These islands in the far south are the base for the extremist Muslim Abu Sayyaf group so should be avoided. The dive regions covered in this guide are some distance from southern Mindanao and have been unaffected by these problems. However, there have been some isolated terrorist actions in the country, including a few incidents in downtown Manila. Before wandering off from your hotel get some local advice. Having said that, there is no reason to stay downtown but if you do, the risk is probably no worse than any major city: don't carry valuables around especially after dark, don't leave a bag unattended and don't move away from well lit and well populated areas.

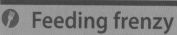 **Feeding frenzy**

Not exactly renowned for its culinary masterpieces, the Philippines is still an interesting place to eat out. Residents are great ones for parties and banquets but the style of food is relative to location. Rice is the staple of any meal and pork and fish the most popular forms of protein. The dish you will see most is 'adobo' which consists of pork or chicken braised in garlic, soy sauce and vinegar and cooked until almost dry. For those who love spicy food, the Bicol region (the southern tip of Luzon) is the place to go. The most famous dish is Bicol Express: minced pork spiced with the hottest available chillis. Halo-halo is such a popular dessert it is almost a national institution: a glass is filled with shaved ice, milk and sugar and a selection of coconut, sweet purple yam, caramel custard, jackfruit, tapioca or red beans. However, fruits like mango and pineapple are an easy option and always delicious.

Once you are on the islands or in a resort, it is extremely unlikely that you will find anything to trouble you; even petty crime is minimal as it really doesn't sit well with the people's religious nature. What also doesn't sit well is any form of drug use and the penalties are severe.

Health

Healthcare facilities depend on where you are. Manila has plenty, the islands have fewer and of varying standards. However, health risks are generally low. AIDs is spreading, as is the sex trade, so be wary. There are insect-borne diseases but these tend to be in remote, hilly regions rather than on the coast. Malaria is virtually unheard of in the Visayas but is a problem in Palawan.

Drinking water can be an issue. It is rarely supplied in resorts although some better hotels will supply purified (distilled) tap water. Check before drinking anything that might be in your room. Buying bottled mineral water can be expensive, see below. Some areas still have brackish tap water so you will know straight away not to drink it.

Costs

Travelling and diving in the Philippines is easily affordable and can be very good value. Accommodation options vary both by cost and quality. There are very few resorts that rank over four star – most tend to be in the two to three star range, yet, in some places it's easy to find tiny cottages with room rates so low it's hard to believe it. Naturally, these are simple and facilities are often extremely basic. In more popular areas, standards are much higher with a greater variety of hotel styles and price brackets. Very large complexes are fairly rare as land is at a premium and there simply isn't enough passing tourism to justify that type of resort. Most dive-specific resorts will be mid-range. Whatever you book, remember that quality is reflected in the room rates so compare carefully.

The cost of food and drink can also be aligned to location. At a simple beach bar, a local beer may be just under US$1 compared with an average of US$2, while in smarter resorts the cost will creep up to as much as US$4. Bottled mineral water is much the same: the supermarket price can quadruple in a restaurant. Meal prices are still reasonable especially if you can get your divemaster to take you to his favourite haunt.

When it comes to tipping, you will find that most dive resorts and smaller hotels will simply leave a tips box on the reception desk. It's completely up to you if you leave something but rounding up the bill seems to be the done thing. High-end establishments may add a service charge of 10% and some show a government tax of 12%. In better restaurants tipping is the norm, at around 5-10%; in small ones, round up the bill. For drivers, guides and divemasters, see page 11.

Philippines Essentials

Sablayan museum reef display; Donsol cemetery; arriving in Coron at dawn

Dive brief

Diving

Can you imagine a country with 7,107 (or so) individual islands all ringed with coral reefs? That must be something like 70,000 dive sites to choose from. What a concept.

The Philippines are located within the Pacific's Ring of Fire and, perhaps more significantly, the country marks the upper tip of the Coral Triangle. This imaginary boundary also encompasses the Solomons, Papua New Guinea, Indonesia and parts of nearby Borneo. Within this small space there are more marine species than elsewhere on the planet – more varieties of coral, more fish and more critters. The Filipino islands have their fair share of this wealth. There are luxurious coral reefs, awesome walls, mysterious wrecks and countless fish-laden marine reserves.

This is also a dive destination that once suffered from a reputation for fish bombing and environmental damage to the reefs. However, you will be surprised at the number of small exclusion bays that are patrolled by local villagers. The people have learnt the value of creating protected nursery grounds, if only to be able to fish beyond the no-go zones. There are a huge number of marine reserves across the country including two UNESCO Biosphere Reserves and two World Heritage Sites,

while several other reefs are now under consideration for similar status.

In most areas, dive conditions are fairly easy-going. The islands are naturally tidal and currents can be strong at times especially on the open atolls. Dive centres sensibly divert to protected sites when necessary. Visibility is generally good; murkier in the shallows and in lagoons like Coron yet crystal clear in the open ocean waters around Tubbataha and Apo Reef.

Snorkelling

For the non-diver who likes to join in the fun, the Philippines is a feast. Small reefs run right up to the beach, shallow drop-offs are protected and currents are fairly predictable. The water is warm and usually clear enough for surface huggers to still get a good peak below the water line. Options are plenty and the only thing to watch out for is kicking the coral or putting your feet on something sharp or stinging.

Discovery

A few dive regions in the Philippines are particularly seasonal with diving restricted to just a few short months each year. Go out of season and you are likely to lose your diving more often than not. The effect of this is that large sections of these

66 99 The first time we visited the Philippines, we would sit content at the end of each day and wonder why we had never considered this destination before. The diving was so good, we went back within a year just to see if it really was as good as we first thought. It wasn't – it was better. Another trip later, even better, yet we still know we need to go again.

Dive data

Seasons		June to October, rainy; November to February, cool and dry; March to May, hot and dry; typhoon risk in May
Visibility		10–40 metres
Temperatures		Air 23°–32°C; water 25°–30°C
Wet suit		3 mm shorty or full body suit
Training		Courses available in most resorts, standards vary
Nitrox		Not easily available
Deco chambers		Manila, Batangas and Cebu

Diversity
reef area
25,060 km²

HARD CORALS	577
FISH SPECIES	2942
ENDEMIC FISH SPECIES	79
FISH UNDER THREAT	70
PROTECTED REEFS/MARINE PARKS	52

All diversity figures are approximate

seas have still not been fully explored. Likewise, diving from a liveaboard is less common here than in other Asian countries so adventures into unknown waters are rare.

Diversity

With the Philippines sitting squarely inside the Sulu-Sulawesi Sea, inside the Coral Triangle and inside the Ring of Fire, there can be absolutely no doubt that these reefs are incredibly rich. One recently published, long-term academic study even suggests that this may actually be the world's most biodiverse marine environment. It points specifically to the Visayas and the waters near Verde Island opposite Puerto Galera. On the other hand there are many other published research studies that have recorded higher diversity in Indonesian waters than neighbouring countries. One school of thought explains this away as simply being because Indonesia is a larger country.

For divers though, this sort of comparison is less relevant than knowing that there are few places in the world where you will see such a variety of marine life. The downside is that the sea is also a huge economic provider for the country so it's good to know that well respected conservation groups are committed to developing sustainable marine projects across the country.

Making the big decision

No matter where you go, the Philippines is a friendly, welcoming country with plenty to offer the travelling diver – not least a well established dive industry across a wide range of destinations. There are only a few liveaboards so to get a broader view of the country it's best to choose two slightly different destinations and build a two-centre holiday: a week of wrecks and one of macro say, or a liveaboard to an isolated atoll followed by week at a more lively island resort. There are a variety of dive types in each area so if you simply want to kick back and relax in just one place, that will work too.

Bottom time

Luzon

Anilao ▶▶ p182   Local divers have done their best to keep this fantastic destination to themselves. Superior muck dives nudge colourful reefs just a short drive to Manila.
An all year destination, best November to May

Ticao and Donsol ▶▶ p184   Still a developing dive region: unexplored reefs remain unexplored due to weather restrictions and the focus on the star attraction: whalesharks migrate here in the winter months.
Dive all year, whalesharks from February to April

Mindoro

Puerto Galera ▶▶ p190   Bright and lively, well developed and well explored, this is a resort region with something for everyone from its famous macro sites to some small wrecks and up-tempo drift dives.
All year, but rainy from June to August

Apo Reef ▶▶ p197   Visited almost exclusively by liveaboard, this enormous open water reef system is unfailingly impressive even though it is only now recovering from over fishing.
All year, but rainy from June to September

Palawan

Tubbataha ▶▶ p202   This World Heritage Site in the middle of the Sulu Sea is as isolated as you can get with virtually no land in any direction. The best in the Philippines for (almost) guaranteed big animals.
Very short season from February to May

Coron ▶▶ p206   One of the dive world's most interesting wreck destinations with many Second World War era ships sitting on the seabed. The small reefs are attractive too, despite year-round low visibility.
All year but the best time is October to May

Visayas

Panglao ▶▶ p216   More delicious white-sand-edged, coral-ringed islands than you can possibly imagine. And all with a huge variety of dive sites – reefs, walls, steep drops, shallow bays and caverns.
All year but June to September is slightly wetter

Dumaguete ▶▶ p221   Doing its best to rival some of the world's best-known critter havens, the coastal bays are full to bursting with unusual animals. However, Apo Island, one of the country's best open water dive sites, is close enough to vary the pace.
All year but June to September is slightly wetter

Luzon

Looking at some maps, Luzon, the Philippines' third largest landmass, hardly seems to rank being named. Yet this northern island is the location of capital, Manila and several vital seaports so is the country's most important economic zone.

The island is volcanic with a mountainous interior while the coastline is a long and tortuous affair broken by many small coral-infested bays as well as large freighter- and cargo-boat infested ones. The Luzon island landmass actually divides two of Asia's most important seas. On the east, it abuts the Philippine Sea and the Pacific Ocean. The all-important North Equatorial current moves across the Pacific and hits eastern Luzon and the Visayas broadside before becoming two separate currents: the north-flowing branch heads to Taiwan and Japan while the Mindanao current flows south. The west side of Luzon faces towards the South China Seas and Vietnam in the far distance. Winds funnel up and down this long corridor and change direction bi-annually.

It's the combination of these winds and currents that affects the various marine ecosystems. There are no substantial reef systems in the north of Luzon and reefs in the central areas were badly damaged by the violent and devastating eruption of Mount Pinatubo in 1991. Subic Bay, just south of Pinatubo, had been a Spanish, then Japanese and finally a US naval base. The wreck dives here were popular until Pinatubo took her toll, covering both the wrecks and coral life with a layer of ash, smothering both. Of course, this damage was insignificant compared to the loss of life, but diving here is really only for hardened wreckies as thick layers of ash make for very poor visibility.

But all is not lost for diving Luzon – in the south there are two dive regions, one on each side of the island. Anilao, on the Calumpan Peninsula has fabulous muck and reef diving, while on the south-eastern Bicol Peninsula, diving is still a growing business as people hear about the manta and whaleshark populations.

Locations

Diving in Luzon is always land based and most sites are close to the shore. It's unlikely that either of these dive areas would keep a hardened diver happy for an extended period – a week is about right – so it may be best to combine one of these destinations with another in a different part of the country.

↘1	Dead Palm
↘2	Mainit Point
↘3	Secret Bay

Mabini
Anilao
Bagalangit
Maricaban

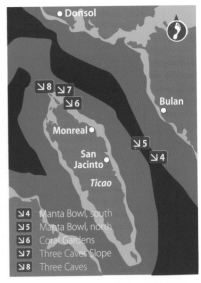

Donsol
Bulan
Monreal
San Jacinto
Ticao

↘4	Manta Bowl, south
↘5	Manta Bowl, north
↘6	Coral Gardens
↘7	Three Caves Slope
↘8	Three Caves

Destinations

Anilao

From Manila to Anilao is only around 125 kilometres but this coastal area is light years away from the hustle and bustle of the capital. After diverting away from the busy six-lane highway that eventually ends at the port of Batangas, a narrow road winds through small towns and semi-rural landscapes to finally reach the seaside town of Anilao. This is a tiny affair, sitting on a two-road junction. A narrow, bumpy road leads south along the Calumpan Peninsula, winding it's way over steep hills that drop sharply to the sea below.

It's no surprise that this dramatic environment attracts so many Manila residents especially on weekends. (Go midweek and have the whole place to yourself.) There are masses of small hotels perched precariously on hillside terraces. These are mostly dive resorts and there are said to be around 70 in the area, plus some have other sports or spa facilities. A few small villages are dotted along this road: shops and restaurants are minimal, and would be difficult to reach without a car, but its not really necessary to have one as the resorts are fully equipped. *Distance from airport: 2½-3 hrs*

Donsol and Ticao Island

Dive tourism is still developing in the Bicol region at the southeastern end of Luzon, and what diving is there is highly seasonal. Consequently, there are only a handful of hotel options. These are in a tiny area just outside Donsol town and a lone bay on the island of Ticao opposite. The two main resorts in **Donsol** are both located just past the river mouth and near the government-run whaleshark interaction office. It is possible to stay here and do daytrips across to Ticao. The resorts both have onsite restaurants and there is one café on the beach about halfway between them. There are a few shops back in Donsol town about 20 minutes away and good facilities (hotels, shops and banks) in Legaspi (one hour). Across the Ticao Pass, **Ticao** has just one dive-orientated resort located on the north coast in pretty and peaceful Taclogan Bay. There is an onsite dive operation and restaurant. The closest facilities are in the small town of San Jacinto which you are unlikely to see but you can walk to the village homes on either side of the resort for a taste of local life. *Distance from airport: 1½-3 hrs*

Places to stay and things to do at all these destinations are listed in Drying out on page 187

Ticao; Our Lady of the Gate, Legaspi; children in a village; San Miguel; Crystal Blue Resort; Mt Mayon

Dive log

Anilao

About 10 kilometres long and jutting into the waters of the Verde Island Passage, the Calumpan Peninsula's steep hills and craggy shores continue down below the surface to a series of stepped terraces. These harbour a surprising amount of macro life. Directly opposite Anilao are Maricaban island and the Sombrero, a flat-topped pinnacle ringed by surf, which makes it look like a classic Mexican hat.

The diving here is quite special, although for some, that may be a surprise. Years back the reefs gained a reputation for being wrecked by poor fishing practices but years of education by environmental and conservation groups has ensured that the area has been allowed to rejuvenate. Dives close to shore are rife with soft corals; offshore and opposite, open water dives are alive with pelagic fish while the tip of the peninsula has amazing muck dives that cluster around hot water sea vents. In bad weather, offshore island sites are hard to reach, but the protected bays are usually accessible all year round.

↘1 Dead Palm	
🜨 **Depth**	25 m
💧 **Visibility**	poor to good
🌊 **Currents**	slight to medium
🌀 **Dive type**	day boat

One of the many dive sites that parallels the rocky shoreline, this series of slopes and terraces drops down to 35 metres or so. The divemasters stop at 25 metres as a golden fan has a family of the *Barbiganti* pygmy seahorses on it – including some pregnant males. Moving north along the reef, the seascape is one of small outcrops and huge barrel sponges punctuated by a few large pink fans. Almost every surface is decorated with multi-coloured crinoids. Octopus nudibranchs, morays and blue spotted rays are all prowling around.

↘2 Mainit Point	
🜨 **Depth**	27 m
💧 **Visibility**	fair to good
🌊 **Currents**	slight to strong
🌀 **Dive type**	day boat

Cazador Point is the most southern on the peninsula and, just offshore, some volcanic boulders break the surface and mark this dive. To the east, there is a little damage but the closer to the boulders the better it gets. There, the reef is outstanding, coated in black coral bushes and hard corals with masses of crinoids adding colour. At the western end there are anthias, fusiliers and butterflies; anemones and clowns; a small school of needlenose barracuda and a gang of batfish. And then there are all the blue ribbon eels, morays and rays.

Anilao's Mainit Point is at the edge of Secret Bay: muck dives and reef dives are just minutes apart

☷ Secret Bay, east and west

⊗	**Depth**	28 m
◐	**Visibility**	fair to good
☰	**Currents**	slight
⬯	**Dive type**	shore/day boat

The dark sand bay beside Mainit Point was once deserted until a large hotel complex was built and its secret status was no more! The sandy beach leads to a bed of rounded pebbles, then to a long, slowly descending slope. It's hard to describe this as a muck dive as there is very little muck. The seabed is quite barren but the critter life is superlative. On the western side a flat scrappy bed of sponges and algaes provides camouflage for the smallest, whitest frogfish you will ever see. At under an inch long as adults they are virtually invisible. Common seahorses have only been seen once or twice but there are fire urchins, squat lobsters, jawfish, mantis shrimp and many juvenile fish that are hard to identify.

Diving towards the eastern side of the bay you pass many of the creatures met on earlier dives, like the aggressive panda clown and peacock flounders in the shallows. However, on this side, down at about 25 metres, the seafloor flattens out into an enormous jacuzzi. Streams of bubbles percolate from the seafloor, hot water vents revealing the volcanic activity in this region. There is less animal life just here – too warm perhaps – but heading back up the slope there are dwarf lionfish, scorpionfish and incredibly beautiful, unusual nudibranchs. Other species include dragonets, lots of commensal shrimp and goby partnerships, sea snakes, tiny octopus, cowries, squid and masses of mantis shrimps.

The residents of Secret Bay on the Calumpan Peninsula include, clockwise: *Cuthona kanga*, a nudibranch from the Aeolid sub order (named for Aeolus, Greek god of the wind); seahorse; hingebeak shrimp; squid; mantis shrimp; white frogfish (this one is an adult and the size of a thumbnail); Orange and Black Dragonet (that is it's proper name); crinoid shrimp

Philippines Dive log Luzon: Anilao

Ticao and San Miguel

The Ticao Pass neatly divides the landmass of south Luzon from Ticao and Burias islands. Waters flowing through this channel are fed by the San Bernadino Straight, itself fed by the North Equatorial Current as it crosses the Pacific Ocean. These conditions conspire to make this the most plankton-rich area in the Philippines so it's no wonder that two of the ocean's largest filter feeders are attracted to the area.

The diving here is relatively new and really best described as undiscovered. At present there are just a handful of well-known and regularly dived sites. Sailing along the beautiful shorelines of Ticao, you look down at the ocean with its shadowy glimpses of reefs below and you just know there is so much more to discover. The most frequently dived site, the one that attracts divers from around the world, is Manta Bowl yet San Miguel Island – divided from Ticao by a tiny channel – is probably just as rewarding.

Philippines Dive log Luzon: Ticao and San Miguel

◪4 Manta Bowl, south

🌀	**Depth**	22 m
👁	**Visibility**	fair to good
🌊	**Currents**	slight to strong
🛶	**Dive type**	shore

There are two distinct entry points for this dive which is described as an inverted bowl on the seabed. Sitting in the middle of the Ticao Pass, divers see only the sloping seabed as they move across it in the ever present currents, hoping to see a manta ray pass by. The current is often at rip-your-mask-off speeds and it can be quite hard to move about. The terrain is actually quite pretty with flat areas broken by outcrops of hard coral. These sit along raised ridges running parallel to each other and with the current. To stop and look at the marine life you really need a reef hook, and when the current does slacken there is actually a little time to spot some very good macro animals including very unusual nudibranchs and sea urchins. Even when the mantas aren't about (which by all accounts is a bit of a hit-and-miss affair) you can see plenty of pelagic life like whitetip sharks and schools of small tuna that are 100-strong. These move past in formation avoiding huge, mating trevallies.

◪5 Manta Bowl, north

🌀	**Depth**	27 m
👁	**Visibility**	fair to good
🌊	**Currents**	slight to strong
🛶	**Dive type**	shore/day boat

The other dive in the famed Manta Bowl drops a little deeper. The down currents tend to push you to depth so you need to watch your gauges as there is no slope or reef top for a safety stop. From this side of the channel, which lies nearest to Ticao island, divers are warned that the corals are less than pristine but in places they are not too bad. The boats drop divers in ahead of the site to drift back over the bowl, moving from one possible manta feeding station to another. Again, if they are away, there is some nice macro life with quite a lot of anemones and their commensal clownfish adding colour to the rubbly seabed.

Colourful coral outcrops and banded seasnakes in Manta Bowl

⛉6 Coral Gardens

🕐	**Depth**	25 m
◑	**Visibility**	fair to good
〰	**Currents**	slight to strong
⌒	**Dive type**	shore/day boat

San Miguel island lies off the northern end of Ticao and is actually two craggy, green hills divided by a bright white sandspit. There's a tiny fishing village on this beach – and many children who are unbelievably delighted with visits from divers. Sailing into the bay is a visual feast as is the view underwater. There are dives on both sides of the bay with reef formations butting right up under the rocky cliffs. The terrain at Coral Gardens is covered in broad beds of soft corals, which are in perfect condition. These are so extensive it's a delight to see. Forests of whip corals rise vertically from the slope, then a little further along, small hard coral outcrops display hundreds of multi-coloured crinoids. Inside there are crinoid shrimp and clingfish. Olive green tubastrea trees break up the gentle vista. An unusual find is the bicolour goatfish seen on this reef in groups of tiny juveniles. Of course, there are the usual reef creatures: gobies, angels, catfish, clownfish in their anemones, butterflyfish and many nudibranchs.

⛉7 Three Caves Slope

🕐	**Depth**	45 m
◑	**Visibility**	good
〰	**Currents**	mild to strong
⌒	**Dive type**	day boat

Leaving from the small fishing village but heading in the opposite direction from Coral Gardens, you see many small caves in the cliffs walls. These are infested with birds' nests, the kind that get harvested. The caves of this dive are an extension of the landside geography, but divers, especially those with cameras, often don't reach them. As soon as you drop in on the downwards-leading slope, you spot critter after critter. It's all very exciting: stop to photograph a nudibranch laying eggs and you realize a mantis shrimp is watching you do it. Move to a ball of crazy dancing catfish, then spy the moray hovering beside them. There are tube worms and starfish and many brightly coloured fire urchins. Look inside them for hitchhikers and you are likely to spot at least one kind.

❝❞ Mike, our fabulous divemaster, spotted a Coleman's shrimp pair without knowing what they were. I screamed in excitement and scared the poor guy so much he nearly hit the surface.

⛉8 Three Caves

🕐	**Depth**	27 m
◑	**Visibility**	good
〰	**Currents**	mild to strong
⌒	**Dive type**	day boat

After the slope, it's time to move along to the caves. Entering a little further away from the bay, you drop over an absolutely sheer wall that turns at a perfect right angle. The surfaces are quite impressive as they are coated in cup corals and other small corals. Next you descend to a shelf that leads into a small cave that becomes a short swim-through. Passing a juvenile batfish inside, you fin along to a much bigger cave. Inside it is quite dark and there's not a huge amount of life, just some unusual rock formations that mimic stalactites and are covered in feathery white hydroids. However, the rubbly cave floor reveals dwarf scorpionfish. Back out in the open water larger fish appear: sweetlips, midnight snappers and some angels. Dropping further towards the third cave there are large and pristine fans but you have to be careful with depth. Gassing off in the shallows passes quickly as you pass over the thick cover of soft corals looking for crabs, shells and lots of nudibranchs, many with their egg rings.

Philippines Dive log Luzon: Ticao and San Miguel

Male and female Coleman's shrimp – the female is the larger; juvenile sweetlips

Donsol

In past years, Donsol was simply unheard of in the diving community. This small village existed peacefully enough with local fishermen hunting for what they saw as traditional food sources. However, the mouth of the Donsol River attracts one of the planet's largest aggregations of whalesharks. These gentle giants migrate here every year to feed on the rich source of plankton.

Unfortunately, the whaleshark population was diminishing until the World Wildlife Fund got involved. Working with the local government, who declared the area a marine sanctuary and outlawed killing the whalesharks, the tide was turned. A new government-run interaction programme was established and is now a vital part of the community despite the short season.

Whaleshark sightings start as early as November and can last till as late as June, but local guides recommend the best time to visit is between February and May – earlier or later and you run the risk of bad weather as typhoons run up the Ticao Pass. As soon as it rains, these massive creatures head down in the water column. It's not that they disappear, you just can't see them due to the poor visibility. Sunlight brings them back to the surface to feed. For January to May 2008, 106 whalesharks were seen, 37 of these were new animals.

Mike and Alan at the Whaleshark Interaction centre: both are divers and guides. You can only snorkel with the whalesharks here: the image below was taken while diving in Thailand.

❝❞ All the way from London and not a single whaleshark. It was enough to make you weep into your beer. And it wasn't that we spent hours on the water and just missed them... no, a typhoon blew in and completely wiped out the time we had there.

⊙ Fish Tales

It is said that the best times to join a whaleshark tour are during the months of February to May so my friends and I decided to travel to Donsol on a clear April morning. As we arrived at the town's tourism office early that day, I noticed that the place had an undeniable calmness to it. The sun was shining brightly, the sky was the shade of radiant baby blue, and the undulating tiny waves of the water were a mix of dark blue and seaweed green. The whole area gave off a sense of tranquility – you could never imagine the abundance of giants lurking in its placid waters.

After a brief orientation, a marine park ranger escorted us to the beach where a line of boats were waiting. No sooner had we left the shore eager to interact with these creatures when one of our spotters saw one in the distance. At his signal, my friends and I quickly grabbed our masks, snorkels and fins, jumped into the water, and followed our guide.

The two spotters told us the whaleshark was swimming straight towards us, but the water was murky and made visibility underwater a little difficult. That was probably due to the large quantities of plankton present. Even so, I remained floating in the water waiting patiently to see a glimpse of the animal when all of a sudden an enormous fish appeared only a few feet in front of me! At the sight of its shark-like physique and its gaping mouth,

huge enough to swallow me whole, my initial reaction to the encounter was that of stunned fear, which left me completely motionless for a few seconds. After recovering from the initial shock, I realized I was directly in its path! And seeing that it had no intention of slowing down, I hurriedly swam to the side and allowed it to glide right by me. As the whole length contentedly moved past, I could clearly see the white spots that distinguish this fish from all the rest.

Shortly after getting back on the boat, our spotters directed us to another whaleshark. Our guide suggested we try to swim alongside it. I attempted to keep up with the group, but it proved to be too strenuous for me. Luckily, our guide saw me struggling and reached for my hand, helping me to swim faster. I was able to stay and interact with it for a minute until I got too tired. Amazingly, just as it was about to disappear in the distance, another one emerged out of nowhere!

Swimming with whalesharks is an experience every nature enthusiast dreams of having. On that particular April morning, I was lucky and got to swim with 12 different whalesharks. And even though I only spent a few seconds with each of them, those moments of awe and wonder are forever embedded in my memory.

Nana Enerio, business graduate, Manila

Drying out

Beach style hotels and dive operations are limitless in Anilao but definitely limited in the Bicol region. However, it is regarded as a growth area with a high-focus on tourism. There are many reports of new hotels being built so it is worth checking for developments with a Philippines Tourism office.

Manila

$$ **Heritage Hotel Manila**, T+63 (0)2 854 8888, millenniumhotels.com. Only eight minutes from the airport, this first-class hotel is perfect for quick stopovers. Transfers are included.

Anilao

$$ **Crystal Blue Resort**, T+63 (0)921 299 9155, crystalblueresort.com.ph. Charming small hotel near the southern end of the peninsular. Extremely well run with helpful staff, great food and beautifully decorated rooms. Balconies have superb ocean views. Dive packs are exceptional value and include all meals. Diving services are operated by **Adventure Bound,** see below. The friendly Filipino guides are very good spotters.

Ticao

$ **Ticao Island Resort**, T+63 (0)918 910 2185, ticaoislandresort.com. The only dive resort on Ticao, nice location with individual *nipa* (thatched) bungalows. Rooms are simple but comfortable with hot water and air-con. There is an onsite dive operation plus **Adventure Bound** (below) also work here.

Donsol

$ **Woodland Resort**, T+63 (0)920 863 0191.
$ **Vitton Beach Resort**, T+63 (0)927 912 6313. Located near the government run whaleshark interaction office. Both resorts have the same owner. Rooms are very basic – Vitton is a little newer and Woodland has nice gardens.

Legaspi

$ **Neuhaus Inn**, T+63 (0)528 204103. Walking distance from the airport (if you don't have dive kit) this motel-style inn is spotless and perfect for early flights. No restaurant but a meal delivery service that is good value and prompt.

Diving

Adventure Bound, T+63 (0)2 840 5523, adventurebound.com.ph. This Filipino company has diverse operations in many fields. They supply dive services as listed above plus organize travel to several other regions in the Philippines. Offices are based in Donsol town, so will arrange diving and hotel packages on request.

Anilao

This area is really all about watersports, with diving, snorkelling and kayaking facilities all along the coast. For those who like to trek, there is some very scenic countryside. The resorts can arrange island hopping and snorkelling trips for non-divers. Lake Taal, which is actually about halfway between Manila and Anilao, may be worth a diversion. In the centre the crater lake is a volcanic island, with another lake inside that.

Bicol

To reach Donsol or Ticao you fly into Legaspi city in Bicol. The area has both historical and natural attractions.
Legaspi A thriving and bustling small city, this is a good place for shopping, restaurants and local markets.
Mount Mayon The most active volcano in the country, the cone overshadows Legaspi and much of the surrounding region. It is 2,460 metres high and last erupted in 2006.

The visitors' centre about halfway up has impressive views back to the black sand, coastal beaches.
Cagsawa Ruins In 1814, one of Mayon's eruptions (there have been 47 in total) poured lava down it's steep sides and onto the village of Cagsawa. Over 1,000 people took refuge in the church but it was completely engulfed. Now just the belfry remains along with a few walls.
Our Lady of the Gate As you drive away from the airport you will see this imposing baroque church hovering over the Legaspi landscape. It's worth a diversion as the ornate exterior façade is regarded as extremely symbolic. The church was built in 1773, supposedly by Franciscan Monks, but locals maintain that it was actually built completely by women.
Donsol River Tour the river by boat at night to admire a unique mangrove eco-system lit by millions of fireflies – which are actually light emitting beetles.

 Sleeping $$$ US$150+ double room per night $$ US$75-150 $ under US$75
Eating $$$ US$40+ 2-course meal, excluding drinks $$ US$20-40 $ under US$20

Mindoro

One of the Philippines' larger islands, Mindoro is divided from Luzon's Calumpan Peninsula and Batangas City by the Verde Island Passage. Some say this narrow body of water is the most bio-diverse on the planet. You could be forgiven for blindly agreeing as you cross to Puerto Galera accompanied by a pod of pilot whales and another of frolicking dolphins.

Mindoro is a derivative of *Mina de Oro*, and so named by the Spanish after they found gold on the island. Their galleons also spawned Puerto Galera, meaning port of the galleons. These transported gold, silks and spices to and from the Americas. The Spanish realized that the bay was an ideal location as the deep natural harbour gave safe haven from storms with easy passage through the extensive coral reefs. Now, the island is principally agricultural yet it is also one of the most lively dive-tourism areas in the country.

These waters were first declared a marine reserve way back in the mid-1930s; in 1973, they became a UNESCO Man and Biosphere Reserve. A recently published study by the International Union for Conservation of Nature indicates that these waters may even be far richer than anyone imagined with pointers to them having the highest marine biodiversity in Asia. However, the same study also states that these waters are under threat as the Verde Island Passage is one of the busiest shipping lanes in the country. Extremes of weather also conspire to cause damage to some of the shallow reefs, although from a diver's point of view this may not seem particularly obvious. Many faster growing soft corals are recolonizing the area.

Drop onto any dive site around the Puerto Galera promontory and it's soon clear that diversity here is high regardless. Verde Island to the north also has several well regarded dive sites with clear waters and strong currents attract large numbers of pelagic fish. Weather and tides mean you have to pick your day to dive it though as crossing the channel in rough seas is rather uncomfortable.

This intensive focus on one tiny part of Mindoro may leave people wondering about reefs around the rest of the island. You would expect there to be a selection of diving destinations further afield but surprisingly there isn't, only Apo Reef on the far western side. This has recently become a fully protected National Park and is now under submission to UNESCO as a World Heritage Site.

Locations

Choosing which part of Puerto Galera to stay in is simply about how busy or quiet you like things, while those who want to see Apo really need to get on a boat.

Destinations

Puerto Galera

This very busy and popular resort area runs along a minuscule stretch of Mindoro's north coast. The town of Puerto Galera is set slightly inland, behind a bay enclosed by San Antonio and Boquete islands and a promontory that leads towards Sabang. The convoluted coastline twists and turns creating many small coves. It seems that each one has a cluster of hotels sitting on its white sand beach. The most popular are Sabang and Big and Small LaLaguna beaches. **Sabang** is very lively and fairly crowded, but has the most extensive range of good holiday facilities with shops, bars, restaurants and nightlife. (It should be noted that the style of nightlife here won't appeal to everyone.) Access to town is simple too, but most importantly, the best dive sites are within a short distance. To the west, **Big** and **Small LaLaguna** beaches are a little less populated than Sabang but you can walk around the coast to reach the shops and nightlife there. Land in these three main bays is at a premium as they are backed by steep hills. Hence most hotels sit on narrow strips with their rooms clambering up the hillside – the views can be great specially at sunset. The bays are continually busy with boats, including those nipping about with divers, so they are not somewhere for relaxing on the beach and swimming. There are several other smaller bays, with just a lone resort, but these tend to cater for a specific nationality. An option for those who prefer more of a traditional beach holiday, is to head to **White Beach**. It's about 40 minutes by boat west from Sabang. Sunbathing, swimming and lounging about are favoured activities but it can get busy here, too. It's also some distance from the principal dive sites.   *Distance from airport: minimum 3½ hrs*

Apo Reef

This isolated reef system is another of those liveaboard-only destinations with most divers visiting in that way. Several liveaboard itineraries that start in Coron divert to include Apo; there are also occasional trips that start from Puerto Galera or even Anilao. Itineraries change frequently and are seasonal so you could consider staying on Pandan Island, a tiny dive resort off the west of Mindoro. From here, you can reach Apo in a very long day-trip.   *Travel from either Puerto Galera or Coron is an overnight sail*

Places to stay and things to do at all these destinations are listed in Drying out on page 199

Apo National Park; Ferry from Batangas; fish market; sunset at Apo Reef; Sabang, Puerto Galera

Philippines Mindoro

Puerto Galera

This small area at the top of Oriental (east) Mindoro gets the lion's share of dive tourism, no doubt due to it's location. It's only 150 kilometres from Manila and easy to get here. The dive industry grew rapidly through the enthusiasm of local people coming down for long weekends.

Those early dive pioneers would hardly recognize it now. The main beaches are about as bustling as you can get and the coastal landscape, where it has access to the shoreline, is packed full. Despite the fact that development continues at quite a pace, the promontory remains highly picturesque: the shoreline twists and turns; cliffs drop to partly submerged boulders and gentler hills drop to tiny bays with small communities in them.

This remains a captivating landscape yet the prime attraction is that along almost every inch of this coast is a potential dive site. Hillsides extend to coral-clad reef slopes, sandy bays drop to the seafloor and reveal a broad spectrum of curious critters. Local dive operators tend to focus on promoting the incredible macro life – and you can't blame them for that as it is incredible – yet this area has much more to offer such as deep water reefs dotted

with small caves and a surprising number of wrecks. Even the protected bay that sits behind San Antonio and Boquete islands has some interesting muck diving.

Generally, conditions around Puerto Galera are fairly easy. Dive sites are all in close proximity to each other and on days when there is a little current, you may end up doing two at once. Strong currents do occur on tidal changes but they are rarely a problem as the operators will choose sites that avoid them.

Where currents can be really strong though is on Verde Island, a 40-minute ride by speed boat into the middle of the channel. The dives there are renown for currents – one site is even called the Washing Machine for obvious reasons – so are only suitable for confident divers and are only reachable when the weather conditions are right.

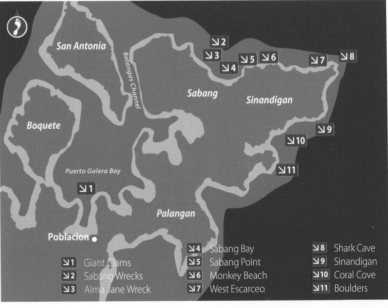

⊾1	Giant Clams	⊾4 Sabang Bay	⊾8 Shark Cave
⊾2	Sabang Wrecks	⊾5 Sabang Point	⊾9 Sinandigan
⊾3	Alma Jane Wreck	⊾6 Monkey Beach	⊾10 Coral Cove
		⊾7 West Escarceo	⊾11 Boulders

◥1 Giant Clams

🜄	**Depth**	17 m
◐	**Visibility**	poor to fair
🜨	**Currents**	none to strong
🜮	**Dive type**	day boat

This very unusual dive sits inside Puerto Galera Bay exactly at the point where the currents from the Manila and Batangas channels converge. The location is scenic but conditions are highly variable. One day there will be enough current to turn this into a drift dive – the visibility will drop way down as the movement stirs up silty sections of the seabed. On other days, the water is still and the visibility clear, which reveals the dive's most famous residents, seahorses. The site is called Giant Clams because you enter in the shallows beside a cluster of them. They vary from about the size of a football to way over a metre. From here you descend down a gentle slope to a level sand patch where algaes, seagrasses, soft corals and small sponges support a wealth of macro animals. There are minute frogfish, crinoids stuffed full of commensal residents (squat lobsters, tiny fish and shrimp), the Pegasus seamoth, razorfish, morays and quite a few unusual nudibranchs. And of course, there's the seahorses who wander from sponge to stick to soft coral. Apart from the life on the seabed, there are a few coral outcrops. One distinctive patch has huge barrel sponges, which are growing sideways around some table corals. There is an enormous number of fish living here too, including cardinals and anthias inside the coral branches and butterflyfish above.

◥2 Sabang Wrecks

🜄	**Depth**	20 m
◐	**Visibility**	fair to good
🜨	**Currents**	slight
🜮	**Dive type**	day boat

On the outer edge of Sabang Bay is this three-wreck dive. Scattered across the seabed at around 20 metres, you can wander from a 12-metre steel-hulled yacht to either of two old wooden boats. One was a passenger boat, the other a fishing boat, thought to be Vietnamese in origin. The vessel structures are less interesting than the life that has colonized them. There are plenty of batfish, which tend to follow divers from one to the other of the wooden boats, and many damsels, wrasse and surgeonfish hanging around them. There are a lot of juveniles, including sweetlips, using the structures as a nursery ground. It's easy enough to spot the lionfish and morays but there are also some well camouflaged scorpionfish. The best camouflaged creatures though are the giant frogfish, which are a challenge to find but they are always there.

Reticulated dascyllus (damselfish); squat lobster living in a crinoid at Giant Clams; the pink blob is a giant frogfish on one of the Sabang wrecks

⬛3 Alma Jane Wreck

🕐	**Depth**	31 m
◑	**Visibility**	fair to good
〰	**Currents**	slight
🛥	**Dive type**	day boat

On the outer edge of Sabang Bay, three minutes from shore, this old cargo boat was sunk to make an artificial reef. The *MV Alma Jane Express* was scuttled in March 2003 and settled upright at 30 metres. She was a 60-ton, 35-metre-long steel-hulled cargo ship built in Japan in 1966. Little remains to indicate her past working life but the boat has become a special dive as it attracts a huge number of pelagic fish. Dropping down to the rudder you meet the first school of curious batfish then, as you ascend, another, larger group hover around the metal framework at deck level. There are schools of fusiliers, snappers, golden rabbitfish, lionfish and a solitary flutemouth that follows divers around.

⬛4 Sabang Bay

🕐	**Depth**	19 m
◑	**Visibility**	fair to good
〰	**Currents**	slight
🛥	**Dive type**	day boat

A little to the east of the wrecks is possibly the bay's most popular dive. There is very little in the way of topography, just one large log, and a few bottles and tins, but a broad patch of seagrass is home to some amazing macro life. There are tubeworms covered in shrimps, occasional anemones and quite a few clowns, all with even more shrimp. Striped puffers sitting about on the sand and ornate ghost pipefish families sit in a crinoid. As you move back up the slope there is a another patch where horned seastars decorate the seabed. In this area are huge flying gurnards, hermit crabs and incredibly gorgeous pegasus seamoths, which appear in couples, chasing each other around the sand.

⬛5 Sabang Point

🕐	**Depth**	19 m
◑	**Visibility**	fair to good
〰	**Currents**	slight
🛥	**Dive type**	day boat

The dive on the point is just past the eastern end of the bay where the currents tend to swirl. This supplies nutrients to the reef so the corals here are some of the best in the area. A slope drops down to a small wall where you first encounter a huge yellow fan before heading past many crinoid-covered outcrops to an enormous flat hard coral. Everything is big here: all the way along the wall and down to about 25 metres are more fans and whip corals, some barrel sponges the size of humans and equally large elephant's ear sponges. Naturally, all of these attract a good range of colourful fish including filefish, parrots and, every now and then, a turtle will be seen.

The *Alma Jane's* resident batfish

⛟ 6	**Monkey Beach**	
⛟	**Depth**	32 m
◔	**Visibility**	good
⛭	**Currents**	slight
⛟	**Dive type**	day boat

Falling to 20 metres, this slope makes an easy dive, except when the currents are running – you can pick up quite a lot of speed here. If you drop in the middle of the bay, you will find a wreck at 18 metres, tilted to the side. Said to be an old fishing vessel, the hull is coated with small soft corals and sponges. Back up the slope there are frogfish and jawfish living in the sandy patches. Mantis shrimp are all over the place, ducking and diving away from their nosy human visitors.

⛟ 7	**West Escarceo**	
⛟	**Depth**	20 m
◔	**Visibility**	fair to good
⛭	**Currents**	none
⛟	**Dive type**	day boat

At the western tip under the lighthouse, this dive can get strong currents but is mostly done in a slack tide. The reef is a series of rubble terraces with small drops and a few coral outcrops. It is barren in patches due to typhoon damage a few years back, but it is starting to regenerate and, for small animals, can be a great dive. Look for orang-utan and porcelain crabs in the anemones, scorpionfish and some unusual nudibranchs. There are a lot of mantis shrimp skittering about too.

🌐 Love story

I'd been to the Philippines on business many times, however, each trip was just a brief stopover in Manila, three or four days max. I was based in Hong Kong and came to Puerto Galera by mistake. The best mistake of my life!

I stayed for two weeks. I was astounded. Not just by the diving, but the whole set up. The town, the people, the atmosphere. And the diving... wow. I vowed to return. My next visit was for a long weekend as I was looking for a place to do my IDC. Having looked up and down the beach, I settled on the operation at Atlantis – there really was no other choice for me. As a newly qualified instructor, I decided to extend my career break and stay for six months. Aside from teaching and leading dives, I found myself unable to stop talking to people about how much I loved this place. About two weeks before I was due to leave, whilst pulling the anchor in for the first dive of the day, I looked out to the ocean and thought, "this IS my office"! It was a done deal, here I am, and here I'll stay.

But the story wouldn't be complete without a bit of romance would it now? About six months after arriving, I met a wonderful woman, Rose, and having been together for about three years we tied the knot in June 2008…

Paul O'Toole, Sales and Marketing, Atlantis Dive Resorts, Puerto Galera and Dumaguete

Enormous fans line Sabang Point; Cryptic wrasse, porcelain crabs and nudibranchs on West Escarceo

Life in the deep
Butterflies in the sea

No matter where you dive, how grey the habitat, high the sea or low the visibility, it seems that if you look closely enough, you'll spot a small, gaudy creature brightening up the vista. Nudibranchs are often referred to as sea butterflies – iridescent colours, bizarre patterns, variable shapes and erratic sizes will liven up almost any dive. If it wasn't for the fact that most are a bit on the small size, they would probably be the main attraction.

Part of the mollusc phylum, nudibranchs are a sea slug and pretty closely related to the slimy garden version. Up the front they have an oral cavity and tentacles, just behind on their backs, are the rhinophores or sensors and further along are their gills. Often these features are hard to spot as nearly all nudis are wildly dressed. Some have outrageous colours, others bright patterns and others adapt to their environment by mimicking a soft coral or hydroids. These can be the hardest to spot. The important thing about all those weird patterns and colours though, is that they signal to other animals that nudibranchs are highly toxic. They are preyed upon by a few other animals: crabs, seastars and fish will nibble on them although mostly at the planktonic stage.

Their life cycles are short, usually lasting just a month or two. These animals are hermaphrodites but nudibranchs do not self-fertilize. Two lone males will meet up on the reef, slither around each other for a few moments, then, laying head to tail, will extend a special tube from their side. They exchange sperm sacs then crawl away, turn female and start to lay a lacy egg ribbon. If you see one, chances are the parent will be close by. And if that ribbon was yellow, for example, chances are the parent was too. Eventually the ribbon will disconnect from the reef and hundreds of tiny larvae, each encased in a shell will float off. As soon as they make contact with an appropriate food supply, they metamorphose into a juvenile. This behaviour is fairly consistent, although a few rare species, like Bennett's Hypselodoris, actually hatch crawling juveniles.

Spanish dancers and sea hares are closely related to the nudibranch group, as are flatworms. All have similar lifestyles, although flatworms and Spanish dancers both do that marvellous flamenco dance if you are lucky enough to spot them on the move.

⬂1 **Ceratosoma trilobatum** The central wings that protrude from the 10cm long body of this nudi are its defence mechanism. A predator will attack these first but be in for a shock as they store glands containing defensive secretions.

⬂2 **Flabellinidae species** The garish cerata or lobes that decorate the thin tapering bodies of this nudibranch group transmit a warning to other animals. These small nudis eat stinging hydroids, then store the stinging cells in sacs at the end of their cerata.

⬂3 **Phyllodesmium longicirrum** Nicknamed the solar powered nudi, this relatively large animal (12 cm) has finger like cerata on its back. These store microscopic algae which photosynthesize, creating a source of energy for their host.

⬂4 **Nembrotha cristata** part of a group of three Nembrothas (kubaryana, cristata and guttata) this 6-cm-long creature is easily spotted on tropical reefs. It is less easy to pick the differences, defines by the amount of red as well as green on margins and gills.

⬂5 **Halgerda malesso** Mostly found in or near the sponges which are their food source, this 7-cm-long Halgerda is in the process of laying a delicate egg ring.

⬂6 **Hypselodoris bullockii** This beautifully coloured nudibranch comes in a variety of tones and hues from palest beige to apricot to mauve. Insufficient research has been done to confirm whether the different colours are in fact different species.

↘8 Shark Cave

⬥	**Depth**	28 m
◑	**Visibility**	poor to fair
≋	**Currents**	none
⬯	**Dive type**	day boat

One of Puerto Galera's deepest dives, this is located well away from the coast. There is no sloping reef so it's not possible to do a multilevel dive. Instead you drop into the blue then down to what seems like a

↘9 Sinandigan (aka Nudi) Wall

⬥	**Depth**	21 m
◑	**Visibility**	fair to good
≋	**Currents**	slight to strong
⬯	**Dive type**	day boat

This stretch of reef is quite funny. Despite being a wall dive, the focus moves to the slope between two sections of the wall that is full to bursting with nudibranchs.

↘10 Coral Cove

⬥	**Depth**	23 m
◑	**Visibility**	fair to good
≋	**Currents**	slight to strong
⬯	**Dive type**	day boat

The terrain on this protected dive site is quite similar to West Escarceo. From about six metres, the gentle drop has a few small shelves and overhangs. Weird critters live

flat plateau but is actually a series of long terraces. Beneath these are some very deep cave-like fissures that are known to have sharks inside. Small whitetips pace to and fro under the protective ledges before disappearing into the dark recesses. Out on the plateau the level surfaces are surprisingly pretty as they are carpeted in masses of tiny pink soft corals. A few large fans punctuate the level areas while on the seabed you can spot seagrass ghost pipefish and balls of catfish.

And not just a few different species, but countless different ones, including some that you are unlikely to have seen before. The dive starts at the smallest of fan corals which has half a dozen pygmy seahorses on it. Then as you move towards the slope you can hardly fin a metre before spotting a nudi and another and another. There are also magnificently patterned flatworms, orang-utan crabs, snowflake morays and masses of small fish.

around the small coral outcrops: jawfish pop their heads up from their burrows, as do adult and juvenile blue ribbon eels, while mantis shrimp run in and out of theirs. One of the more exciting finds is an incredibly cute, resident black clown frogfish, and the local divemasters are good at spotting more nudibranchs. There are also a lot of fire urchins and you can see the tiny white snail that lives on them as a parasite.

Puerto Galera marine life varies from top level predators to impossible-to-spot creatures like the pygmy seahorse and bubble coral shrimp

11 Boulders

🌀	**Depth**	26 m
◐	**Visibility**	fair to good
〰	**Currents**	slight
⚓	**Dive type**	day boat

Sitting on the dive boat beneath an almost vertical, sharp and craggy cliff face you are faced with a series of large boulders that break the surface. Rolling backwards into the water between them, you find some of the most interesting terrain around this coast. The boulders seem to have tumbled down from the cliff, falling close together and forming swim-throughs that create a winding path down to the level base of the site. Despite wanting to stop to explore the caves and tunnels for all the marine life that lives inside them, the divemaster signals to head down to the base that flattens suddenly. A rubbly area is coated in crusting sponges, hydroids and algaes and punctuated with finger sponges and crinoids. It's the spot to go searching for the resident thorny seahorses – and it's no problem to find them. They are always there, along with peacock razorfish, the usual range of clownfish in anemones, nudibranchs, adult blue-ribbon eels and young cuttlefish. More of a surprise as you move back up to the boulders is when the divemaster you are with goes crazy. You know he has found something but he's too excited to tell you he's just found a stunning, and rather unimpressed, blue-ringed octopus. This sort of thing doesn't happen all that often, but when it does...

" " **Suddenly Goto, our divemaster, went ballistic, performing a wild victory dance underwater. We watched amused until he slowed enough to show us what he had found.**

Apo Reef

Isolated and lonely, Apo Reef is the largest coral reef in the Philippines and one of the country's most significant reef systems. The surrounding National Park consists of three small islands and two separate submerged coral reefs, divided by a channel. These jointly cover around 34 square kilometres.

↘1   The Lighthouse
↘2   Shark Ridge
↘3   Apo Point

Lying 33 kilometres west of the town of Sablayan on Mindoro, the reef and its surrounding waters now have suitable recognition – and protection – as the Apo Reef Natural Park project. However, this wasn't always so and over past decades it has had a chequered history. Apo was first officially declared a marine park by President Marcos and a special 'Tourism Zone and Marine Reserve' by the local government. For many years it attracted divers but destructive fishing practices discouraged marine tourism. When divers stopped coming altogether, the situation worsened. However, interest never completely waned and conservation bodies, working in conjunction with local government, culminated in submitting the project to UNESCO for consideration as a World Heritage Site. Fishing within the reef was banned by the government in 2007 and Apo Island is now open to help generate funds for its protection. This also helps provide an alternative source of income for fishermen in the area.

      There are several environments inside the park's boundaries and the buffer zone. These include coral reefs, seagrass beds and a shallow lagoon ringed by mangrove forests, which acts as a spawning ground and nursery for marine species as well as a sanctuary for birds.

↘1   The Lighthouse

🕐 **Depth**	40 m
◐ **Visibility**	fair to good
🌀 **Currents**	mild to strong
🌊 **Dive type**	liveaboard

This dramatic wall drops down to great depths – and with such good visibility it would be easy to hit the seabed at 50 or more metres without realizing. At around 40 metres you have to force yourself to quickly admire the beautiful fan corals and barrel sponges before coming back up to a more suitable depth on the wall. This is plastered in a variety of hard and soft corals and is very colourful. Sea cucumbers climb the vertical surfaces past giant lobsters while huge quantities of schooling fish flit past. Up on the flat shallow reef top the corals are more patchy but there are masses more fish and creatures like octopus are common. Patient divers may even see them as they start mating under a coral.

↘2   Shark Ridge

🕐 **Depth**	40 m
◐ **Visibility**	fair to good
🌀 **Currents**	mild to strong
🌊 **Dive type**	liveaboard

Possibly Apo's most famous dive, this is simply a sharp vertical wall that drops from a plateau at 12–15 metres way down to the bottom of the wall at 50 metres. The dive plan is to head to about 40 to look for the sharks but it's a hit-and-miss affair. There are very large whitetips that swoop in and out past divers and a glimpse of a blacktip or grey reef might occur. The wall itself has fans and some nice coral. Early morning fish life (this dive is mostly done at dawn) up on the plateau is fascinating, with all the schooling fish getting an early morning clean: rainbow runners, fusiliers, snappers, surgeons and sweetlips. It is interesting to watch the runners come down in gangs to cleaning stations. You can also see more whitetips, plus turtles, napoleon wrasse and cuttlefish here.

Fan corals on Shark Ridge; Apo's Lighthouse Wall

⛴ Apo Point	
🕐 **Depth**	40 m
🌓 **Visibility**	fair to excellent
🌀 **Currents**	slight
🌊 **Dive type**	liveaboard

The water over the sandy shallows of Apo Island is incredibly warm but with very low visibility so descending feels a bit like swimming through milk. Yet the further you drop, the clearer and cooler it gets. There are incredible numbers of fish – large schools of Indian Ocean triggers, pyramid butterflyfish, rainbow runners, snappers and damsels. Although the

scools of fish are prolific, looking down at this part of the reef, it's a bit disappointing to see signs of past destructive fishing, which has led to an outbreak of the Crown of Thorns starfish. All the same, it is great to admire the power of nature as there are also a lot of wide areas showing healthy coral regeneration. A curious note is that divemasters look for, or try to buy from local fishermen, as many giant triton snails as possible. These are one of the few known natural predators for the Crown of Thorns and are said to attack and eat them if placed in close proximity.

Like much of Apo, you can do this dive in two directions. Returning to the entry

point at another time of day is a good idea as sections of the wall are significantly different. Heading the opposite way from the fist dive, and before descending over the wall, you encounter an area of whip corals that line a ridge at about 25 metres. There are so many silhouetted against the dark blue water that the impression is of a graphic painting. Lots of small turtles populate this area and will settle down between the whips for a while to eat before swimming off. They don't seem at all wary of divers. Back up on the shallow reef top several giant cuttlefish hang near protective hard corals. They seem to be in pairs.

Diving the Big Blue: scenes from Apo Point

Drying out

Puerto Galera's many resorts are all about nationality – many target a specific group so you may have language problems if you don't fit that profile – and location: beach or village. Apo Reef is limited to liveaboards and a lone island resort.

Puerto Galera
Dive Resorts
$$ **Atlantis Dive Resorts**, T+63 (0)43 287 3066, atlantishotel.com. A resort that truly focuses on its diver guests. In the middle of Sabang Beach bay, the hotel is built on terraces in a fun style with white-washed, curved walls (image right). Rooms vary in size and shape but are all well decorated and with internet access. Classy in-house restaurant; well thought out dive facilities and a camera and computer room. Dive courses available. Packages with all meals and unlimited diving are fantastic value.

Other options
$$$ **Buri Resort and Spa**, buri-resort.com. Boutique resort in a quiet location just inside Puerto Galera Bay. Diving pick-up service supplied by Asia Divers.

$$ **Marco Vincent**, marcovincent.com. Well-regarded medium size resort just off White Beach. Dive centre with fast boats for easy access and a shuttle from Manila.

$$ **Oceana**, oceanadive.com. Newly renovated resort on Dulangan Beach about half an hour from Puerto Galera.

Apo Reef
Liveaboards
Expedition Fleet, T+63 (0)2 890 6778 expeditionfleet.com. The only consistent dive liveaboard operator in the Philippines with a variety of boats and itineraries. Four-night Apo Reef itinerary or a week-long trips also includes Coron. Boats are simple but comfortable with excellent dedicated dive facilities. Itineraries change by season.

Hans Christian Andersen, T+45 (0)86 182488, hcaexplorer.com. This 20-cabin Danish owned and operated vessel runs 7-day cruises from Puerto Galera to Coron, including Apo Reef. With minimal diving facilities on board, it's best suited to divers with families or occasional divers. However, the cruise is a great way to explore this region. Also seasonal trips to the Visayas.

Other options
$ **Pandan Island Resort**, T+63 (0)919 305 7821, pandan.com. The closest, in fact only, resort near Apo Reef. On-site dive centre.

Puerto Galera

Poblacion The town of Puerto Galera was originally a fishing village but is now a busy small town. Sitting on Muelle Bay, it has a selection of services including banks, restaurants shops and a public market. Beside the Catholic Church is the Excavation Museum, which has a large number of ancient Chinese artefacts and pottery found in the area plus a display of underwater photographs.

Tamaraw and Aninuan Falls If you fancy a change from seawater to fresh, there are waterfalls at Tamaraw, near the village of Villaflor (14 kilometres from Puerto Galera). They have a natural swimming pool at their base. Aninuan Falls are about 45 minutes' walk from White Beach. It's uphill all the way through a dense tropical forest.

Mangyan Village Home to Mindoro's once coastal nomads, these tribes have tried to avoid outside influences in order to protect their own culture. You can visit the village on the bank of Big Tabinay River, but it's best if you have a guide. Nearby, on Small Tabinay River are gold-digging sites.

Apo

Apo Island Of the three spits of land in the Apo Reef Natural Park, only this one is used for tourism. You can picnic then walk to the lake in the centre which is ringed by mangroves and used by many seabirds. The beach is delightful and there are good snorkelling spots.

Sablayan The closest town to Apo, this coastal centre sits on a long river estuary lined by colourful fishing boats. There is a small museum with a display on the Mangyan tribes plus historical finds and a very cute coral reef room. There is also a large, covered town market, some small shops and restaurants.

Pandan Island This lovely, private eco-styled resort is just 20-30 minutes from Sablayan and is really the only hotel of note in this area. They have a small turtle sanctuary and there is good snorkelling because of that. The diving here is reasonable and there is access to Apo.

 Sleeping $$$ US$150+ double room per night $$ US$75-150 $ under US$75
Eating $$$ US$40+ 2-course meal, excluding drinks $$ US$20-40 $ under US$20

Palawan

The island province of Palawan is just about as far west as you can go and still remain inside Philippine waters. It is an area famed for its outstanding natural landscapes as much as its incredible underwater realm.

Curiously, this diverse area is one of the most frequently targeted in the country as it is home to both the unique Tubbataha National Marine Park and the historical Second World War wrecks in Coron Bay.

It's only an hour or so by plane from either Manila or Cebu to Palawan, a dive destination in its own right. However, most divers travel straight through and out into the Sulu Sea to the Tubbataha Reefs. These were designated a World Heritage Site in 1993. The National Park was expanded more recently to include the smaller Jessie Beazley Reef. Tubbataha's North and South Reefs and are separated by an eight kilometre wide channel. Both are landless, except for one tiny sand cay on each, used by birds and turtles as nesting sites.

Naturally, all this makes the park a liveaboard-only destination and one that is very much subject to the weather. Most of the year, the Sulu Sea is rough and windy so diving on these reefs is limited to just a three or four month period.

Coron, on the other hand, is a year round destination. Island upon island mark the 1,400 or so square kilometres of the Calamian Island group. The scenery is spectacular and the seas surprisingly calm. To the east is the Sulu Sea, to the west the South China Sea, so you would expect this location to be subject to pretty strong currents as sea moves around the islands, passing between the two bodies of water. Instead the channels and bays are mostly mirror calm and currents below the surface are minimal.

Locations

These two dive areas may be in the same political region but they are a long way apart. You can reach Palawan by flying from Manila and Cebu, and Busuanga (for Coron) from Manila. You can even fly between Coron and Palawan which would create an ideal two-centre holiday as the flight takes just an hour or so. You can also do both areas individually by liveaboard but sadly not together because the sailing distance between them is too great. Another good option is to join a Coron-bound liveaboard that starts further afield, for example from Puerto Galera or Anilao. That way you will pass by Apo Reef in both directions and stop there at least once.

Destinations

Tubbataha

Possibly one of the most open and isolated regions you will ever visit, you can go to Tubbataha only when the seasons are right. Between March and May, being out in the Sulu Sea is all about being encompassed in one huge expanse of bright blue skies over deep blue seas. When the weather is perfect, so are the conditions. When storms blow in, unless you are on a large, stable boat you may wish you hadn't bothered. Trips run as late as June but, with the continuing change in global weather patterns, this later period now seems subject to occasional typhoons. There are stories of boats leaving Puerto Princessa on Palawan, only to have to return a few hours later when the weather changes. There are no land-based options in the marine park, the only human residents being the armed rangers from the Philippines Department of National Defence who attempt to guard the atolls 24/7. *Distance from Palawan: around 9 hrs*

Coron

The Calamian Islands lie to the north of Palawan but fall within the same regional group. The main island is Busuanga, with Coron Island sitting off its southwest tip. Culion Island is opposite and there are countless more small ones in the channel between and all the way around Busuanga. This very picturesque vista has many twists and turns and enough hiding spots for any fleet of boats, let alone those which served the Japanese Imperial Navy. Many people dive this area from a liveaboard but for those who prefer land-based there are plenty of options with a fair selection of small resorts. Some could best be described as way too rustic but a few are delightful with professional dive centres attached. You can stay on land in or near **Coron Town** if you like a busier environment with easy access to shops, restaurants and so on. Other options are to head to one of the dive resorts on **Sangat**, **Decanituan** or **Uson,** all of which are smaller, quieter islands but only a few minutes by boat from Coron's town jetty. These resorts have good access to a variety of wreck and reef dives inside the bay. There are also two resorts on **Dimakya Island** which is on the northern side of Busuanga. These are larger and more formal affairs. *Distance from airport: 1-1½ hrs*

Places to stay and things to do at all these destinations are listed in Drying out on page 213

Cruising past Sangat; Dimakya; Culion by night and day; Philippines liveaboard; Black Island

Philippines Palawan

Dive log

Tubbataha

Steep-sided walls rim oval reefs with visibility to die for. Enormous drops are coated in impressive gorgonians and sponges. In the open water, reef sharks, barracuda and tuna all cruise by at a lazy pace. Turtles ponder over reef tops and rays flit by frequently. This is Tubbataha, a huge open space in the middle of the Sulu Sea and the Philippines' most impressive World Heritage Site.

Three reefs make up this marine park: Jessie Beazley is a small oval-shaped reef a couple of hours short of the main park. North Reef (or atoll) is a rectangular platform about 16 kilometres long and 4.5 kilometres wide. South Reef is smaller, triangular shaped and less than two kilometres wide. Both atolls enclose shallow, sandy lagoons.

Tubbataha can only be dived in the late spring due to potentially rough sea crossings at other times. Currents are variable and most dives are drifts. Tenders follow diver bubbles in case of a change of direction but arrive early on a spring morning, and you are likely to be greeted with a glassy surface and nothing but sunshine. While this is not the prettiest of reef systems – reef tops have been damaged by past illegal fishing and coral growth is inhibited by natural weather conditions – this is definitely the place for big guys.

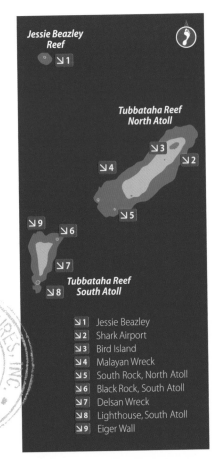

Jessie Beazley Reef
↘1

Tubbataha Reef North Atoll
↘3
↘4 ↘2
↘5
↘9 ↘6
↘7
Tubbataha Reef South Atoll
↘8

↘1	Jessie Beazley
↘2	Shark Airport
↘3	Bird Island
↘4	Malayan Wreck
↘5	South Rock, North Atoll
↘6	Black Rock, South Atoll
↘7	Delsan Wreck
↘8	Lighthouse, South Atoll
↘9	Eiger Wall

↘1 Jessie Beazley

Depth	32 m	
Visibility	good to great	
Currents	slight to strong	
Dive type	liveaboard	

Jessie Beazley is a regular stopover for liveaboards. Dives are done along the walls according to the tides and currents. The reef to the north is in good condition with a shallow top level rising to five metres and the deepest vertical wall dropping to a sandy bed at about 60 metres. The walls are covered in fans and branching corals with plenty of hawkfish. However, the main action is off in the blue where there are plenty of pelagic species including barracuda and tuna, several shark species (but only whitetips come in close) and quite a lot of schooling fish. Heading southwards on the reef, the dive feels fairly similar but has the bonus of a slightly better upper level. There are big stands of *porites* coral here housing lots of small colourful fish plus pufferfish and lobsters. At night in the shallower sections there are saron shrimp peeking out from the coral, decorator crabs, tiny squat lobsters and seahares.

N2 Shark Airport

Depth	35 m
Visibility	stunning
Currents	can be strong
Dive type	liveaboard

One of the north's gentler dives, a long slope drops away from the reef rim before turning into the wall. There are overhangs, caves and crevices that drop into no man's land. The visibility is amazing so you can see a long way down. The wall is decorated with sea fans and some soft corals while pelagic fish pass by. Jacks, rainbow runners and the ever-present whitetips hover on the tails of snappers. Heading back up, the sloping section pans out into a long strip of sand – the 'airport' – surrounded by coral heads. For some reason, this ledge is almost always covered in whitetip sharks which rest here in neat squadrons. This is a great site for a night dive too, with many hermit crabs and shells, although the sharks will have taken off by dusk.

N3 Bird Island

Depth	7 m
Visibility	fair
Currents	slight
Dive type	liveaboard

Situated on the north face of North Atoll, this tiny, sandy island is a seabird refuge and the shallow lagoon that surrounds it is a refuge for young turtles. You see so many as you move across on the dive tender that you lose count. The lagoon is under eight metres deeps but on the outer edge a wall that drops to 30 metres plus. The wall's dive profile is much like the others here so it makes a change to drop into the shallow waters in the late afternoon to see what you can find in the seagrass beds, which hide small creatures like crabs, flounders and starfish while a small ray or two might flit past.

Little and large: hermit crabs and whitetip reef shark on Shark Airport

N4 Malayan Wreck

Depth	32 m
Visibility	stunning
Currents	can be strong
Dive type	liveaboard

Inside the lagoon on the southwestern edge of the atoll is an exposed rusting wreck, known as the *Malayan*. It gives its name to the site but you don't dive on it. Outside on the reef edge, a gentle slope drops way down into the sea. As the topography is comparatively gentle there are many ledges worth exploring. Moray eels and lobsters are easy to spot and you might even encounter a nurse shark lurking in one. You will definitely see reef sharks along with plenty of turtles, although there are sharks and turtles everywhere in Tubbataha. It becomes a standing joke back on board as divers compete over the numbers seen but they are often wary of divers and rarely swim close. The top level of the reef consists of a garden of mixed corals punctuated by sandy patches with typical fish life plus a few giant clams, sea cucumbers and pufferfish.

⬃5 South Rock, North Atoll

Depth	28 m
Visibility	fair to good
Currents	slight to strong
Dive type	shore

On the southwest corner of the north atoll, this shallow reef ledge sits between 10 and 20 metres before dropping to a deeper wall. This makes it a double value dive as you can do the slope at night and when the currents are calm but if the currents are up a bit, it's worth dropping over the wall to see all the pelagic action. There can be so many jacks and snappers in dense schools that at times you ignore the fans and barrel sponges on the wall behind. The slope is also quite impressive with a variety of corals and reef fish – angelfish, unicorns and fusiliers, lionfish and scorpions. There are sightings of leopard sharks here but you are more likely to see the ever-present whitetips. At night, there are large sea cucumbers with their hitchhiking imperial shrimp and crabs and some of the biggest lobster you will ever see.

⬃6 Black Rock, South Atoll

Depth	38 m
Visibility	stunning
Currents	slight to strong
Dive type	liveaboard

The geography of the south atoll is a little gentler than the sharp walls of the north and this sloping reef is a good example of the dives here. It eventually drops well beyond where you should be – you have to watch your depth when the visibility is so clear. The wall has a substantial number of gorgonians and impressive barrel sponges swarmed by schools of reef fish. Rainbow runners are interspersed with an occasional tuna or barracuda while on the wall there are squirrel and soldierfish, lionfish and morays. Eagle rays have been seen here but most exciting, on the right day, are the mantas. They are not a regular attraction but when they do arrive there are often several of them. It is most likely that you will get to snorkel with them rather than dive as they hang around for hours at a time, lazily flapping about.

⬃7 Delsan Wreck

Depth	38 m
Visibility	stunning
Currents	slight to strong
Dive type	liveaboard

Heading to the southeast corner of the South Atoll, you encounter what remains of the *Delsan*. This vessel is said to have been a log carrier but now sits exposed on top of the reef. The dive site is not all that different to Black Rock but it does have a far larger area of shallow reef top which is in pretty good condition. There are a lot of small, colourful reef fish that flit about the leather corals, whip corals and sponges. These include anemones with clownfish plus several types of damselfish, blue chromis and anthias. Hawkfish perch on the top of corals and scorpionfish on sponges. Surprisingly here, the bigger pelagic animals have come up to the shallow water and you can see the turtles, sharks and even a small school of jacks that are normally further down in the water column.

Manta ray visiting Black Rock; golden fan corals on Eiger Wall

↘8 Lighthouse, South Atoll

⬙	**Depth**	29 m
◉	**Visibility**	stunning
≋	**Currents**	mild to strong
⬯	**Dive type**	liveaboard

There are several dives within sight of the Lighthouse, which all spread away from the southern point on a sloping gradient. The reef's surface is covered in a swathe of small leather corals, whips and sponges which attract starfish, anemones and clownfish and the ever-present damsels and anthias. Closer in to shore are some seagrass beds where rays sometimes feed – you can see both grey rays and blue-spotted rays hovering about – and also more turtles, many of which are quite young and only the size of dinner plates.

↘9 Eiger Wall

⬙	**Depth**	38 m
◉	**Visibility**	stunning
≋	**Currents**	mild to strong
⬯	**Dive type**	liveaboard

Sitting between the north and south atolls, this site is subject to strong currents. Entry is over a flat top, then a very steep vertical wall drops to over 50 metres. Swimming down you pass humungous gorgonians and as you reach the 30 metre mark you can see a lot of soft corals below. A cavern at 38 metres reveals an upper surface just dripping in small white soft coral, like an upside-down snowstorm. Back up the wall you pass a few more sharks, blacktips this time, before arriving on the top plateau to be greeted by a school of jacks silhouetted against the sun.

Harlequin sweetlips, turtles and jacks: all common residents on the Tubbataha reefs

Philippines Dive log Palawan: Tubbataha

Coron

Despite its proliferation of coral reefs, Coron Bay became famous due to the shipwrecks that litter the seabed. The remains of the Japanese fleet lying there are seen as second only to those in Micronesia's Truk Lagoon.

To date around a dozen wrecks have been located, and although they are principally supply boats rather than warships, their historical value is boundless. For divers, they are particularly attractive as they are so much easier to dive than Truk: this lagoon is much shallower. Even better, Coron is usually one of the calmest dive destinations you will encounter. To a certain extent, that is to its detriment as the visibility is never very clear, probably only ever reaching 15 metres. The water is thick with plankton, which corals feed on, growing swiftly and turning the wrecks into lush artificial reefs. Inside them, it is pretty murky and requires careful buoyancy.

This marine ecosystem is affected by the huge number of pearl farms that hover over and around so many of the wrecks. These too, take advantage of the plankton for the pearls to flourish. Divemasters say that before the increase in the number of farms the sea was much clearer, adding that the pearls are there to feed on the plankton, which they eat, digest and return to the ocean as more plankton. A bit simplistic perhaps, but the result is a slightly gloomy dive. All things considered, gloom on wrecks seems appropriate and certainly doesn't affect the enjoyment of the dive. However, Coron isn't just wrecks: small reefs here are in good condition too.

◤1 Siete Pecados, Coron Town	
🕐 **Depth**	22 m
◐ **Visibility**	poor to fair
≋ **Currents**	none
⬯ **Dive type**	liveaboard

Often used as a check-out dive, the 'seven sins' are just to the east of Coron Town's lighthouse. Being so close to town, the visibility here can be pretty poor which is a great shame. This shallow wall has many hard coral outcrops. At its base, where it flattens to the seabed, are large, healthy soft corals, sponges and fans. Back on the wall there are some interesting tunicates that live in clusters on the end of stalks and look as much like a bunch of tulips as they possibly can. There are filefish in a variety of colours including lime and grey. These hang about under the table corals. There are also a surprising number of starfish species in different colours. This long reef system is quite extensive and can be dived in several places as submerged islands are connected by small saddles. A small conservation programme running here monitors fish numbers which are on the increase.

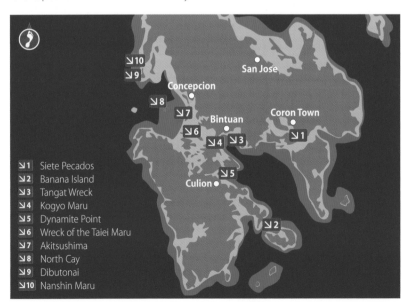

◤1	Siete Pecados
◤2	Banana Island
◤3	Tangat Wreck
◤4	Kogyo Maru
◤5	Dynamite Point
◤6	Wreck of the Taiei Maru
◤7	Akitsushima
◤8	North Cay
◤9	Dibutonai
◤10	Nanshin Maru

San Jose
Concepcion
Coron Town
Bintuan
Culion

Bunch of flowers! The *Nephtheis fascicularis* tunicates and strapweed filefish on Siete Pecados

N2 Banana Island

🏵	**Depth**	26m
◑	**Visibility**	fair to good
🌊	**Currents**	none
🛟	**Dive type**	liveaboard

Known more correctly as Dicalabuan, this island is a cluster of delicious white-sand beaches linked by sand spits. Definitely a Robinson Crusoe moment. Descending on the reef, the first things you see on the wall are huge bushes of black coral with swarms of razorfish hanging off the top. The reef is a bit scraggy in patches, and with some algae, but this seems to have attracted a lot of less frequently seen creatures. There are tiny blue flatworms, plenty of clownfish, upside down jellyfish and a lot of damsels: you might even see a damsel spit out it's fry. The luminous Springer's Demoiselle (right) lives here.

N3 Tangat Wreck

🏵	**Depth**	32 m
◑	**Visibility**	fair
🌊	**Currents**	none
🛟	**Dive type**	liveaboard

The actual name of this Japanese freighter is much debated: perhaps the *Morazon Maru* or even the *Mamiya Maru*. It sits a short distance from Tangat Island so is usually called the Tangat wreck. The vessel is fairly shallow but lies right beside of one the pearl farms. The security guys are rather wary and hang about while divers are underwater. The hull is 140 metres long and at the stern you can see and old gun turret. Down behind that is the rudder where juvenile batfish are always hovering, then heading up the side you can swim in and out of the holds. These are empty and safe to explore. Up on the deck, the wreck has a good cover of corals, mostly black coral bushes, and a lot of small fish. At one end, a huge barrel sponge seems to attract lionfish that perch on the rim and, while swimming across to the mooring line, you can often see huge jacks.

Lionfish on the *Kogyo Maru*

○ History in the making

The wrecks that litter the Coron seabed are not what most divers expect. These are not battleships or vessels of war, but the remains of a Japanese naval supply fleet. In the late summer of 1944, the Japanese were attempting to supply and reinforce troops that were fighting in the Philippines. In September, the US Third Fleet sent Task Force 38 on a series of naval air strikes against Japanese forces right across the country. They made heavy air strikes against ships moored in Manila Bay that resulted in the sinking of 15 vessels. The Japanese swiftly moved their remaining ships to anchorages that they thought would be out of range of US naval aircraft and land-based bombers.

One of these destinations was Coron Bay where a fleet of around 24 ships arrived on 23 September, anchoring in the coves between Busuanga, Culion and Coron islands. At 0500 the next day, a US Navy strike force of 96 fighter escorts and 24 dive bombers took off to raid Coron. This was a long distance carrier based air strike and would allow the aircraft only a brief time over the Japanese fleet. It isn't known how the Americans found the fleet but photos taken from the air show few signs of camouflage on the ships below. It seems the Japanese felt they were safe in these remote bays. At 0900 the strike force reached Coron and, after a 15-minute attack, left behind the burning and sinking ships.

⊻4 Kogyo Maru

🕐	**Depth**	32m
◑	**Visibility**	fair
🌊	**Currents**	none
🌅	**Dive type**	liveaboard

This Japanese freighter is 158 metres long and was carrying construction materials supposedly for building an airfield. She is now lying on her side with some of those still inside the holds. After dropping down the mooring line, which is tied to the central bridge, it's best to fin downwards past the mast before entering the nearest open hold. Inside are rolls of fencing or some other diamond-shaped, webbed material. (They are heavily coated in silt so it's hard to see precisely what the material is.) The next hold along has some bags of cement and an almost intact bulldozer inside. It's a little easier to pick out shapes here. Next, you can swim through parts of the engine room before heading back up to the mast area where the black corals are very lush and there are lots of fish. The top level is actually the side of the hull (now facing up) and is covered in a huge amount of lettuce leaf and leather corals.

⊻5 Dynamite Point, Culion

🕐	**Depth**	20 m
◑	**Visibility**	fair to good
🌊	**Currents**	none
🌅	**Dive type**	liveaboard

A short distance from the town on Culion island , this reef sits in a channel between several other small islands. Like most of the inshore reefs, the visibility here can be disappointing – five metres – especially as this is an incredibly lush reef. Entering over a shallow sloping wall, the water has that strange green hue caused by a mix of plankton and silt. It improves a little as you fin along the wall and there is no doubt that the conditions are feeding the hard and soft corals. They are very impressive with large fans, wide table corals, whips and some black coral bushes. In between, elephants ear and huge barrel sponges rise up from the seabed. The fish life is less obvious, probably because you are too busy admiring the seascape, but there are small filefish, chromis, bass, damsels and some jellyfish that must measure a metre from the top of their dome to the end of their tentacles.

66 99 Dynamite point? well, maybe it was bombed once, but now this reef is full to bursting with corals, fish and rainbows of colour.

Diving on the *Kogyo Maru;* giant jellyfish and iridescent reef colours on Dynamite Point

6 Wreck of the Taiei Maru

⊙	**Depth**	28 m
◐	**Visibility**	fair
≋	**Currents**	none
⌒	**Dive type**	liveaboard

The *Taiei Maru* (also called the *Okikawa Maru*) was an oil tanker which, at 180 metres long, is one of the larger wrecks in Coron. She sits upright on the seabed with a slight list to the port side. As she is comparatively shallow she is also one of the most rewarding to dive. The mooring buoy is hooked on at about 10 metres and the deck is at 15-ish so there is plenty of time to look around.

After descending, it's a good idea to head straight down to the rudder, which measures about eight metres from top to bottom. Swarming around this are masses of pelagic fish: schools of batfish, yellow snappers and some sweetlips. The seafloor reveals lots of smaller animals, including some unusual nudibranchs. Some of the divemasters then take an unusual turn – you can swim through the narrow propeller shaft behind the rudder and emerge about 30 metres later in the engine room. This is a very tight passage with a lot of silt so once you are inside you must go forward. Most people will find it easier and just as much fun to head back up to near the deck, from where you can penetrate some of the holds, which are open and well lit. You soon find the engine room going this way. Most of its machinery is still intact. After that you can swim through to more

of the holds although they are mostly empty. Back up on deck, there are lots of clownfish in their anemone hosts that jostle with the thick coral growth on the metal struts and flat surfaces. There's a winch there too. Heading towards the

bow, you will see that this section of the boat sits a little away from the main part of the wreck: it broke off either when bombed or as she went down. This is another good area to swim inside a little way as, again, it is fairly open and well lit.

" Amiable groups of young batfish nestle around the remains of the *Akitsushima*, completely unaware of her antagonistic past.

↘7 Akitsushima

🌀	**Depth**	38 m
◑	**Visibility**	fair to good
🌊	**Currents**	none
🌀	**Dive type**	liveaboard

The only warship sunk in Coron Bay, the *Akitsushima* was a seaplane tender 118 metres long and 16 metres wide. Now lying on her side, at the stern there was a crane, which was used to lower the planes down into the water. However, when the ship was hit the stern broke away and the crane is now a short distance away on the seabed. The visibility can be murky and seems to gets worse the further down you go. There is a lot of black coral, especially on the two masts jutting horizontally out over the seabed. Beneath these you can find a school of young, teenager stage, batfish. Swimming inside you can explore the holds, which originally covered three levels, but time will be against you. On the deck are two circular gun placements. These can be seen at the bow and midships, sitting between the two masts.

↘8 North Cay

🌀	**Depth**	10 m
◑	**Visibility**	fair to good
🌊	**Currents**	none
🌀	**Dive type**	liveaboard

This white-sand island is an ideal location for night dives. Entry off the beach leads to a completely deserted seabed with just a few blades of seagrass. The dive is done along the tiny wall with its patchy corals and outcrops as there is more life there. It is a good place for spotting pufferfish and crocodile fish; then, as the light drops, you start to see hermit crabs, oysters, quite a lot of sleeping fish, cuttlefish and baby lionfish. About halfway along the wall there is a patch of branching hard corals that provide shelter for seahorses. They mostly stay a long way back inside the coral although they are moving about.

◉ Getting wrecked

Insufficient historical research has been done on the ships that have been found in Coron Bay: some have been misnamed and some that are known to have gone down here have never been found. There are several more diveable wrecks including:

Olympia Maru This army cargo ship laden with 1,250 tons of rice and supply materials, dropped anchor west of Tangat. Forty dive bombers attacked, eventually scoring direct hits to the engine room and exploding the fuel tank on the port side. The origin and name of this vessel has not been verified but she is 180 metres long and sits at a depth of 25 metres.

Irako As a Navy provision ship, the *Irako* was carrying reconnaissance planes. She tried to hide between Tangat and Lusong Islands but a direct hit to the midship section set the bridge alight and the vessel began to sink by the bow. The wreck is 147 metres long and sits at 43 metres.

Kyokuzan Maru Because the hull, cargo holds and engine room of this vessel are still intact – plus the lifeboat davits have been swung out – it is believed that the crew scuttled this army cargo ship, then abandoned it off the north coast of Busuanga. She is 136 metres long and sits at 41 metres.

The Gunboats There are two gunboats or submarine hunters, both suitable for shallow dives or snorkelling. One is at Lusong Island, is 35 metres long and the stern breaks the surface at low tide. The other, at Tangat Island, rests on the coral reef on the east side. She is 43 metres long, lying at 19 metres.

Skeleton wreck All that remains of this steel-hulled fishing boat are the keel and ribs – hence the name. Little else is known except that she was beached. The skeleton is now within easy snorkelling distance from shore. The bow is at just five metres deep and the deepest point is 22 metres at the stern.

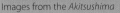
Images from the *Akitsushima*

⌑9 Dibutonai Reef

🕐	**Depth**	15 m
◐	**Visibility**	fair to good
≋	**Currents**	none
⏤	**Dive type**	liveaboard

There are many delightful bays sitting off even more delightful islands around the edges of Busuanga and Coron. Dibutonai lies off the western side of the group. The fringing reef is a classic shallow one where you would never get much deeper than 15 metres without a shovel. The sandy bottom has seagrass beds – with large balls of stripy catfish – and there are anemone and clownfish combinations dotted about. The water in these shallows is very warm, possibly stopping the corals from becoming really prolific. However, there are plenty of fish and many more interesting small animals like nudibranchs and flatworms. Juvenile pinnate batfish seem common too.

⌑10 Nanshin Maru, Black Beach

🕐	**Depth**	35 m
◐	**Visibility**	fair to good
≋	**Currents**	none
⏤	**Dive type**	liveaboard

Of all the wrecks here, this is the one with the least clear history. Some sources name her *Nanshin Maru* (but there were dozens of Japanese vessels using this name), while locals say she is not a Japanese ship at all but a fishing vessel that is only about 20 years old. They tell of it coming aground on the island, and when the salvage company came to pull it offshore, it sank. Either way, the wreck now sits near the bottom of a steep slope. The visibility as you descend is much better than the rest of the area as this is on the outer, western side of Busuanga. Passing over a seabed of pure white sand with blades of seagrass, keep an eye out for tiny cuttlefish. The wreck itself is quite pretty with lots of

corals and whip sponges and the usual school of batfish. You can finish the dive on the reef nearby, it's not in brilliant condition but there are plenty of fish including juvenile many-spotted sweetlips.

Seahorses live in the corals at Dibutonai; looking down onto the hull of the *Nanshin Maru*

Drying out

Palawan options are at two extremes of the scale, with lots of choice in Coron and almost none in Tubbataha. For liveaboards in both areas, research for new schedules and if you find any new vessels plying these routes, try to get recommendations before booking.

Tubbataha
Liveaboards
Expedition Fleet, T+63(0) 2 890 6778 expeditionfleet.com. The only consistent dive liveaboard operator in the Philippines with a variety of boats. Vessels are large and stable, cabins are very simple but comfortable. Tubbataha itineraries change by season and include direct routes or transition trips that sail via Apo Reef.

Other options
Strangely in such a big, seabound country there are few reputable liveaboards. Some small wooden vessels sail to Tubbataha in season, but bearing in mind the conditions involved in the overnight crossing, these may not be a good option. **M/Y Oceana Maria**, previously located in Palau, and **M/Y Vasco** may be worth enquiring about: adventurebound.com.ph. Also watch out for Philippines Siren, launching in 2009: worldwidediveandsail.com

Coron
Liveaboards
Expedition Fleet, T+63 (0)2 890 6778 expeditionfleet.com. Review as above. Week long Coron cruises include Apo Reef.
Hans Christian Andersen, T+45 (0)86 182 488, hcaexplorer.com. This 20 cabin large, Danish owned and operated vessel runs seven days cruises from Puerto Galera to Coron. There are only minimal diving facilities on board so it is best suited to occasional divers or divers with families.

Other options
Coron Bay is a fairly compact one so it is not absolutely necessary to dive here from a liveaboard. All land-based resorts are able to access most wreck and reef dives in a day trip. However, liveaboards that cruise Coron often include Apo Reef, so it may be worth considering that first. The following resorts are well regarded and are all based on small offshore islands:

$$ **Sangat Island Reserve**, T+63 (0)920 954 4328, sangat.com.ph.
$$ **Dive Link, Uson Island**, T+63 (0)918 926 1546, divelink.com.ph.
$$ **Discovery Divers, Decanituan Island**, T+63 (0)920 901 2414, ddivers.com.

Sangat Island's resort is on that sliver of beach

Coron

Arrive in Coron Bay by boat and you will never forget the breathtaking vistas of towering, sharp volcanic walls dotted with small green trees clinging on for dear life. Inside the channel, the walls give way to soft and gentle hills then it all drops into the deep blue sea.

Busuanga Island The largest island in the group and location of Coron Town, this island attracts those who like to get out into the great outdoors. There are river mountain and jungle walks, hot springs and horse riding at Makinit and even a wildlife park at Calauit.

Calauit Island Off the northwest tip of Busuanga, this animal sanctuary covers 3,700 hectares and has both endemic and African animals: giraffes, zebras and gazelles live alongside Calamian deer and Palawan peacocks.

Coron Town The town is quite small and easy to explore on foot. You could stick to the town market, souvenir or pottery shops or trek the 720 steps up Mount Tapyas for a 360° scenic view.

Kayangan and Barracuda Lakes Twenty minutes by boat from Coron Town, Coron Island's fringing reefs and mangroves disguise entrances to the island's hidden lakes. There are seven in total, of which Cayangan and Barracuda are most visited. The lakes are landlocked but are 70% fresh water and 30% salt water indicating hidden channels leading in from the sea. You can dive and snorkel in Barracuda. At the base of the lake are fantastic rock formations described as a naturally-built cathedral. Access for divers requires a difficult uphill walk with your kit.

Culion Island The most renown town in this region, Culion is famous for once being a leper colony. Established in 1906, the community grew when families followed their afflicted relatives there. It was said to be the safest place in the country during the Second World War as the Japanese would not set foot on the island for fear of getting ill. Its status is memorialised in a huge Caduceus (the international symbol of medicine) carved into the hillside. You can visit the hospital (although patient numbers are now minimal) with its museum plus the 17th century Spanish church and fort.

Island Hopping It's impossible to list all the very beautiful islands in this region. The scenery is every visitors image of the ultimate castaway idyll. Calambuyan, North Cay and Dibotonai islands are picture postcard perfect. Talampulan Island is occupied by local fisherman. The shore line is lined with colourful *bancas* (fishing boats) and well-preserved bamboo huts.

🛏 **Sleeping**	$$$ US$150+ double room per night	$$ US$75-150	$ under US$75
🍴 **Eating**	$$$ US$40+ 2-course meal, excluding drinks	$$ US$20-40	$ under US$20

Visayas

Half-way down the Philippine map is the Visayas, the central region of tiny islands, deservedly famous for their powdery white beaches and relaxed lifestyle. Once the preserve of long-term travellers who tried to keep it quiet, the islands' reputation finally leaked out.

Now, though, this is one the most visited dive regions in the country as conditions here are somewhat more consistent than in other areas. The Visayan Islands – and there are countless numbers of them – divide the archipelago neatly across its centre. The region is completely enclosed by seas, from the mighty Pacific to the tiniest of internal seas: the Sibuyan Sea lies to the northwest, the Samar is northeast, the Camotes Sea to the southeast and the Bohol Sea to the southwest. Each of these small bodies of water is connected to the larger ones around them.

Naturally, the Pacific Ocean has the biggest influence on the marine realm as it delivers the North Equatorial Current to both the Visayas' eastern seaboard and Luzon island. It splits there and its forces are diverted both north and south. On the western side of the region, the Sulu Sea and Palawan island create a barrier to the South China Sea. What makes the Visayas special for divers is that there is a mixture of marine species from both east and west. The species brought in by bigger ocean currents seep in at the edges then move southwest across the Bohol Sea to the Sulu Sea. This connects to the South China Sea through the Mindoro and Balabac Straits creating a 'melting-pot' of marine species.

The most popular dive areas tend to be in the very heart of the Visayas group. The islands that radiate out from Cebu are partly enclosed in all directions. No matter which way you head, there is a bigger landmass behind or beside each affording additional protection to the islands, bays and coves so the reefs flourish.

Locations

Choosing between one utterly lovely island and another can be a thankless task, so it's good to know that they are all fine destinations. For an initial trip to the region, it's worth considering an island that has easy access to other areas. For example, from Bohol you can dive Panglao, Cabilao and Balicasag. There are so many wonderful dive areas in the Visayas that it's amazing that there are no liveaboards (at least not at the time of writing). Some appear but then just as quickly disappear. However, diving is supported by lots of high-quality, often European-run, dive centres and local conditions are fairly easy going.

Destinations

Bohol

Southeast of Cebu island, location of the Philippines' second international airport, is ever popular Bohol, renown for its natural attractions, interesting history, sandy beaches and offshore islands ringed by coral reefs. **Panglao** island is the most popular. It's just a hop away from Tagbilaran city and, as it's connected to Bohol by a causeway, can only just be described as an island. **Alona Beach** was the first to be developed and is now a lively place with many beach-front hotels of varying standards. There are dive shops in the resorts as well as independent dive shops all vying for trade. There are also plenty of bars and restaurants so the once calm ambience has gone up a notch or two. As the island has developed, accommodation options have spread further from this central area too, so if you want peace and quiet head to nearby Doljo or Bolod beaches. Just off the northwest coast of Bohol is Sandigan Island, again connected to Bohol by a causeway, but another hop further offshore from that is **Cabilao.** Like Panglao, this once sleepy little place has expanded since it became more popular with dive tourists. There are still only three resorts sitting away from the small villages. Cabilao is reached by boat. The last island option for this area is **Balicasag**. It's about 40 minutes or so by boat from the tip of Panglao and, as it's a marine sanctuary, has just one resort and a small village on the island. *Distance from airport: minimum 3 hrs*

Negros Oriental

Running parallel with long, thin Cebu island, Negros is a draw for divers who travel to her southern tip and **Dumaguete.** The city is the island's most important, but to the south of that the coastline is riddled with tiny, darksand bays that have fantastic muck diving. The landscape is fairly rural, even so close to the busy town and port, but several resorts have occupied the bays. It's a peaceful area, with the closest facilities in town. From there you can reach **Apo Island** (not to be confused with Apo Reef near Mindoro) which is the country's most successful marine sanctuary and a burgeoning ecotourism destination. Facilities are minimal though so most divers visit by day trip from the Dumaguete resorts. *Distance from airport: minimum 4 hrs*

Places to stay and things to do at all these destinations are listed in Drying out on page 227

The Chocolate Hills; Sumilon; jeepney on Cebu; sunset on Alona; banca boat boy

Philippines Visayas

Panglao, Bohol

Just a quick hop from Cebu to Bohol and you'll find a destination loved by anyone who has ever been out this way. Panglao has become more sophisticated, especially around Alona Beach but it still manages to retain that 'no news-no shoes' feel.

There are several dive centres, many charming small hotels and masses of stunning dive sites, all within minutes of shore. Just off the perfect white beach are caves to swim through, deep walls smothered in coral and enormous elephant ear sponges that hide matching football-sized frogfish.

⊾1 Alona Beach Sanctuary

🕙 **Depth**	12 m
◑ **Visibility**	good to great
🌊 **Currents**	slight to medium
🌀 **Dive type**	day boat

Pristine Alona Beach is very shallow, so much so that at low tide boats struggle to cross it. To protect the reef from damage a section is buoyed off and the area below is now a sanctuary. At high tide the reef is at 10 metres and at its edge, the drop-off descends to about 20 metres. The wall is cut with vertical crevices and there is a broad array of hard corals and fans, tunicates and small sponges. It's colourful with plenty of fish to admire both day and night. In fact, the reef top is one of the best night dives in the area and slow inspection of the many small outcrops will reveal a myriad of weird critters. There are parrot and cardinalfish, flatworms, shells, nudibranchs, frogfish, tiny cuttlefish, more tiny cuttlefish nabbing cardinalfish and lionfish preying on whatever they can.

⊾2 Crystal Sanctuary

🕙 **Depth**	22 m
◑ **Visibility**	good to great
🌊 **Currents**	slight to medium
🌀 **Dive type**	day boat

Starting below the small hill that marks the eastern end of Alona Beach (with Crystal Hotel above) this dive starts at about 10 metres and leads down a fairly steep slope down to 26 metres. It's quite a pretty area, not at all dissimilar to the wall in the middle of the beach near the mini-sanctuary. There are more fish flitting around some hard coral outcrops though, possibly because there is slightly more current here. Unicorn and batfish are the most common larger species, although you may catch a quick glimpse of some jacks or barracuda. However it's the smaller creatures that are most prolific. There are plenty of nudibranchs, sea cucumbers and starfish on the sand plus clownfish in their anemone hosts, mantis shrimp and morays.

⊾1	Alona Beach Sanctuary
⊾2	Crystal Sanctuary
⊾3	Kalipayan
⊾4	Arco Point
⊾5	Snake Island
⊾6	Pamilican Island
⊾7	Doljo
⊾8	Pungtud
⊾9	Black Forest
⊾10	Divers Dream
⊾11	Cathedral Wall

Tagbilaran

Panglao

Balicasag

Pamilacan

⌧3 Kalipayan

🕐 **Depth**	20 m
◑ **Visibility**	fair to good
≋ **Currents**	slight
⬯ **Dive type**	day boat

An extension of the house reef at the end of Alona Beach, Kalipayan is an easy dive and can be a good spot for snorkelling as the wall starts at about three metres. The conditions are normally calm and the visibility is good, so even surface huggers can see down to the base at about 20 metres. At this depth there are some nice fans and soft corals. Coming up the wall you see a lot of coral groupers and a juvenile batfish or two. Like the rest of this inner reef, the best life is the small stuff and it can be impressive at night when the crabs, shrimp and shells all come out of their hiding places; you can see as many as five on a single dive.

⌧4 Arco Point

🕐 **Depth**	28 m
◑ **Visibility**	good to great
≋ **Currents**	slight to medium
⬯ **Dive type**	day boat

Heading east from the beach, is this small, submerged point. In the top of the reef, sitting right in the beautiful white sand, is a blue hole about two metres wide. This descends through the reef and emerges on the wall at about 20 metres. The tunnel is lined with soft corals and whips, lots of small morays and fish. After exiting you swim to the base of a completely vertical wall where there is one of the largest purple fan corals you will ever see. A patch of tubastrea is a known haunt for frogfish. The wall winds in and out, lined with plenty of corals, then it's back up to the sandy flat reef for a safety stop. You can go critter hunting over the sand where there are motionless pipefish, ribbon eels, pufferfish and many sand dwellers: look for the *inimicus* or devilfish.

⌧5 Snake Island

🕐 **Depth**	23 m
◑ **Visibility**	good to great
≋ **Currents**	medium to ripping
⬯ **Dive type**	day boat

South and a little east of Alona, this site is also known as Cervera Shoal. The dive takes place over a submerged island plateau that drops from 12 to 40 metres and is subject to strong currents at times. In the past the plateau was dynamited but the flat surfaces are regenerating and, for some unknown reason, the reef attracts a lot of sea snakes. You would have to be unlucky to miss them as they are fairly prolific. As you drift with current across the site you will also see garden eels poking up from the sand, pufferfish and sometimes a cuttlefish.

⌧6 Pamilican Island

🕐 **Depth**	35 m
◑ **Visibility**	good to great
≋ **Currents**	medium to ripping
⬯ **Dive type**	day boat

A few minutes east of Snake Island, Pamilican is a real one – with land and a lighthouse. It was also attractive to illegal fishermen, but the reef is now protected by local people. Translated literally, Pamilican means 'the resting place of the mantas' and it is said that large numbers can be seen there. More likely is a drift dive across a sloping reef that drops to a wall punctuated by a few small caves. There are large fans at depth. The corals back at the top of the reef are colourful – whips and olive green tubastrea are decorated by bright crinoids.

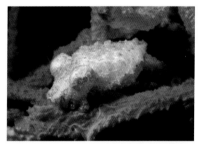

Snake eels and juvenile cuttlefish in the Alona sanctuary; soft corals and crinoids at Pamilican

↘7	Doljo	
🕐	**Depth**	32 m
◐	**Visibility**	good to great
〰	**Currents**	slight to strong
⌷	**Dive type**	day boat

Just around the northwestern point of Panglao the topography changes to deep, sloping wall formations. The drop-off is coated in fans interspersed with enormous elephant's ear sponges. As the current here can be strong at times these are used by several types of fish as a perch. They sit inside and watch the passing show, and if that show includes lunch, so much the better. You can hop from a pink sponge with a pink scorpionfish to a grey sponge with a matching frogfish. The divemasters like to play games with divers, waving vaguely at an area to see if you can spot the well-camouflaged creatures. There are also long, trailing finger sponges that are equally good hiding spots for small black frogfish and several schools of young batfish, which are often just the size of your hand.

↘8	Pungtud	
🕐	**Depth**	24 m
◐	**Visibility**	good
〰	**Currents**	slight to medium
⌷	**Dive type**	day boat

Bordering the submerged wall on the western tip of Panglao, this dive can be swept by currents. As you descend over the first section of wall, it blazes with brightly coloured feeding soft corals. There are snapper and mackerel off in the blue and large puffers sit closer in. As you round the bend, the current drops away and you have more time to investigate the wall's residents. You can find interesting small creatures like orang-utan crabs and bright nudibranchs. Up on the reef flat are ever more curious critters: snake eels, twintailed slugs and spinning balls of catfish. Banded seasnakes are surprisingly common; you can see several swimming up and down the wall to feed. Ornate ghost pipefish are another special find but you will have to poke your nose into all the crinoids to see them.

Balicasag

Just 40 minutes southwest of Bohol is one of the region's best known marine sanctuaries. Balicasag Island is under the jurisdiction of the Philippine Navy whose aim is to preserve the pristine reefs that circle the island.

Surrounded by a pure white, sandy beach, the island is fringed by a narrow reef shelf that drops suddenly to substantial depths. There is an amazing spread of coral species from branching hard corals in the shallows to the delicate fronds of black corals in deeper water.

↘9	Black Forest	
🕐	**Depth**	33 m
◐	**Visibility**	good to stunning
〰	**Currents**	slight to strong
⌷	**Dive type**	day boat

The island's principal dive, Black Forest, is a swathe of incredibly prolific black corals that shimmer in tones of gold and silver whenever the current is running enough for them to extend their tentacles to feed. Black corals are in the scientific order *Antipathiaria* and tend to be found in deep waters. However, the ones here grow right up to 30 metres. It is thought that these black corals have adapted to the shallower depth as they are living in the shadow of the island. Cool water upwellings supply deep water nutrients so the corals are fooled into thinking they are deeper than they are. There are many animals hiding around the branches – giant frogfish and flutemouths are regular finds. Meanwhile, out in the blue are balls of jacks, batfish and moorish idols. A big school of barracuda passes by; then, as you ascend, you find ledges and patches of sloping sand. Looking down you will spot many nudibranchs, pipefish and some tiny scorpionfish.

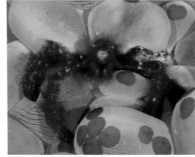

Pungtud wall in rainbow tones; yellow damselfish and orang-utan crabs hide in the corals on Doljo

N10 Divers Dream

Depth	22 m
Visibility	good to stunning
Currents	slight to strong
Dive type	day boat

Also known as Divers Heaven, this starts with a typical gentle slope that is covered in an array of hard corals before dropping swiftly to around 35 metres. This part of the wall is sharper than around the other sides of the island and is interspersed with cracks and caverns to investigate. There are some fan corals and more black corals, but the focus tends to be out in the blue where there are often passing schools of jacks and barracuda as well as surgeonfish, fusiliers and snappers.

N11 Cathedral Wall

Depth	27 m
Visibility	good to stunning
Currents	slight to strong
Dive type	day boat

With a similar profile to Divers Dream, you could be forgiven for thinking that the dive at Cathedral Wall is the very same.

However, it's on a different stretch of coast and because it's done at a different time of day there are bound to be other animals passing by. Look off the wall for schools of butterflyfish and moorish idols, then spend some time investigating the wall as there are many small creatures hiding there. Fans often have longnose hawkfish while coral banded shrimp and pipefish lurk inside tiny overhanging caves.

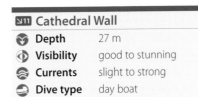

Scorpionfish nestled into a sponge at Cathedral Wall; Balicasag's Black Forest; ornate ghost pipefish in a crinoid at Pungtud

Cabilao

It takes about two hours to sail up to Cabilao from Panglao but as a day-long dive trip, it's worth it. Or stay here; the island is as lovely as any in the area.

Like Alona, these reefs have shallow, flat tops that drop away to walls but one of Cabilao's features are extensive areas of good hard corals. Another is that from December to April, there is the possibility of seeing migrating hammerhead sharks although sightings are rarely reported these days. Not that it matters, as the marine life here is both prolific and varied.

↘12 The Lighthouse

Depth	30 m
Visibility	good to stunning
Currents	slight to strong
Dive type	day boat

This dive is noted for exceptional visibility, but this comes along with some fierce currents. It's these that were said to bring the hammerheads to this site. The top of the reef slopes quickly down to a wall that is interspersed with cracks and crevices. These are full of corals, sponges and tunicates. In the shallows a seagrass bed has creatures like catfish, tiny caverns full of banded pipefish, stone, scorpion and leaffish. If you were staying here, obviously it would be a great night dive.

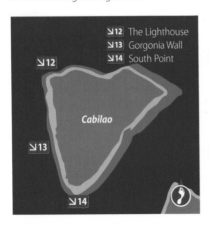

↘13 Gorgonia Wall

Depth	34 m
Visibility	fair to good
Currents	slight to strong
Dive type	day boat

A classic multi-level dive, this reef runs along the shoreline and beach in front of La Estrella resort. The dive attracts some current at certain times of day: you can stay at five metres or so to stay out of it, or drop all the way to the base of the wall which is actually at 60 metres. Stopping at a more sensible depth, around 30, you can see a shelf a fair way below that is completely coated in black coral bushes and huge fans. It all appears to be in extremely good condition, then as you ascend back to a lesser depth you swim past small caverns full of fish. As you come up to around 10 metres, the scenery changes again to patchy coral outcrops. These act as home to banded pipefish and balls of catfish, then, finally, at the top are some seagrass beds where frogfish and seahorses are sometimes seen. The variety of marine life here is staggering.

↘14 South Point

Depth	22 m
Visibility	fair to good
Currents	slight to strong
Dive type	day boat

Heading to Cabilao's southern tip, the landscape changes to a sharp and craggy coast. Beneath this is probably the most spectacular hard coral growth you will encounter in the Visayas, as good as almost any part of the region. The wall drops for some way but the best corals are actually growing between about five and twelve metres. They are all in pristine condition and in the afternoon, when this dive is usually done, they are bathed in rays of sunlight. At the top, the table corals have spread to extreme widths which allows them to catch more light. Dancing in and out of the branches are countless numbers of anthias, chromis and damsels. They drop out of site as you approach, reappearing as you pass by. Off in the blue you may spy some jacks as they chase the endless schools of minute baitfish that are chasing even smaller plankton.

Seasnakes are common in the Visayas, and can be seen at Apo (left); Cabilao corals

Dumaguete, Negros

The coastal reefs of eastern Negros were once regarded as overfished. Then a sanctuary was established, the local fishing communities learned about the value of the dive dollar and the area is now riddled with projects for sustainable fishing.

This is probably one of the best macro locations you will ever find. Think of a critter, mention it to the divemaster and off you go to see it. And just in case you might (unbelievably) get bored with all that, a short sail away is the country's most successful marine sanctuary, Apo Island. An experiment in marine rejuvenation, this splendid island is home to turtles, schooling pelagics and pristine hard corals.

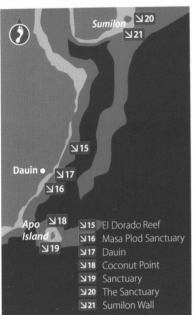

Sumilon	⬊20
	⬊21
⬊15	
Dauin ● ⬊17	
⬊16	
Apo ⬊18	
Island ⬊19	

⬊15 El Dorado Reef

🕐 **Depth**	16 m
◐ **Visibility**	fair to good
🌊 **Currents**	slight to strong
🌀 **Dive type**	shore

Right in front of El Dorado resort is this amazing beach dive. Wander out from the restaurant then fin down over the dark-sand slope, descending to about 20 metres then around a circular bed of staghorn corals, past some coral bommies and back up to the seagrass bed near the start. There is some rubbish about: a few tyres and logs that encourage animals to hide. It's a bit like a treasure hunt. At night, in a single dive you can see five or six different types of frogfish, crinoid shrimp, and a few leaffish. Shining your torch around, you may suddenly spotlight a barracuda, which is a bit of a shock in the dark! Then there are plenty of shells, flatworms, crabs, shrimps and blue-spotted rays moving around the sandy areas.

⬊16 Masa Plod Sanctuary

🕐 **Depth**	22 m
◐ **Visibility**	fair to good
🌊 **Currents**	none
🌀 **Dive type**	day boat

One of the first sanctuaries in the area, this one is roped off so that no fishing can take place, not even with a hook and line. Consequently fish life within the invisible boundaries is prolific. The reef falls gently down to about 25 metres and is covered in patches of hard coral. It's one of those reefs where the lower you go, the more you will see as so many creatures are taking refuge under the corals. There are huge groupers and even larger, but juvenile whitetips, plenty of triggerfish and some sweetlips. On the sandy edges are mantis shrimp and catfish. Under little crevices are pipefish and balls of catfish. Young batfish hide too, they are still quite skittish as are blue-spotted stingrays. Looking out from the reef, you may even spot some passing tuna.

The 'spearchucker' mantis shrimp has an adapted claw that spears prey; juvenile whitetip at Masa Plod

17 Dauin

🌀 **Depth**	30 m
🕐 **Visibility**	fair to good
🌊 **Currents**	slight
🌀 **Dive type**	shore/day boat

For anyone interested in small and cryptic marine dwellers this small bay is simply heaven. Dauin has become an institution in the dive world. For those who would give their right arm (or more likely their camera) for a glimpse of an ornate ghost pipefish, flamboyant cuttlefish or even the mimic octopus, this one bay ranks right up there with the best known muck diving regions.

Although the site is really one bay, there are several dives within its confines. Some divers will rush around the amphitheatre-shaped landscape and back up to the shallows, but most will divide the bay into sections and go back time and time again. The bay now has a plethora of dive names that describe its various sections. On either side, there are small reefs that are principally hard corals. A wide stretch of dark sand reaches between them. One shallow section is covered in seagrass, another – much deeper – is coated in finger sponges. But beyond that, the terrain is essentially featureless and the only landmarks are man-made.

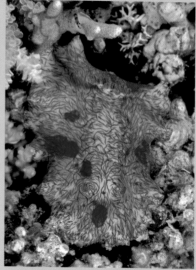

The Slope As you head south and down across the crest of the slope, there are a few rotting logs surrounded by balling catfish, old tyres with dwarf lionfish inside and flying gurnards on the seafloor. A little further in a hollow, a black crinoid houses a few ornate ghost pipefish. As you fin past you may see snake eel noses poking from the sand. But look carefully! This is where the mimic octopus is seen. He resides close to the snake eels and, in fact, usually appears as one. The giveaway is when he extends a lone tentacle pretending to be a sea snake then suddenly transforms into a mantis shrimp! Quite a spectacle.

The Rubbish Pile This is not a completely fair nickname for the spot at the deepest point of the bay where a small area of rubble is decorated with fingers sponges. It's possible that the movement of water -

through the bay deposits additional detritus here. In between the sponges are sticks, tins, bottles and other bits of trash. This is the known home patch of several seahorses. They are permanent residents and you can often see a male with a tummy full of eggs. The spot is also good for morays, the amazing flamboyant cuttlefish and stonefish encounters.

Cars Now regarded as a separate dive, if you were to fin a little north of the rubbish patch, you would come across the wrecks of some old cars and a wooden *banca*, which are smothered in life. The cars are full to bursting with lionfish and batfish. There is even a rare, juvenile zebra batfish and flamboyant cuttlefish on occasion. Out on the sand are several anemones. Shrimp dance around them while tiny porcelain crabs nestle in the folds.

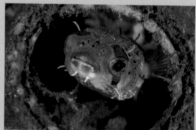

Top: barred blenny and red-splashed platydoris nudibranch; above: seahorse, mimic octopus and pufferfish in a tin

Dauin Sanctuaries Had you finned south of the rubbish patch, and up to 22 metres, you would encounter one of Dauin's protected zones. Spin along the deeper edge of the coral sanctuary where some small walls and overhangs are worth investigating. There are a lot of small fish here – butterflies, damsels and so on – but as you come to the shallow areas make sure you look below the small bommies to see if you can spot a baby whitetip shark. Likewise, if you had turned north from the seahorses, you would go past the cars and to the other edge of the bay. The corals here are home to some lovely fish. There are butterflies and rabbitfish, juvenile angels and triggers, mostly the small ones rather than the ones that chase your fins.

The Seagrass Back up at eight metres, there is a broad patch of sea grass in that makes a perfect, extended safety stop. You can spend a very long time here hunting for critters. There are more froggies and seahorses – different species to what you have seen elsewhere – blennies, gobies, cockatoo waspfish, fingered dragonets and the Pegasus seamoth.

Shortfin lionfish and clown frogfish, below; the rarely seen, juvenile zebra batfish, right

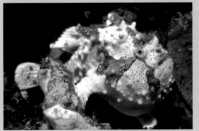

66 99 **You could spend your entire holiday on this one site. We almost did, but realised it would be daft to miss the rest of the area. We'd head off to see other sites but the call was too strong... we went back to Dauin at least once every day.**

Apo Island

In the channel between Negros and Siquijor islands, Apo is an open water dive region that contrasts sharply with the shallow waters on the nearby coast. This is big blue territory with all sorts of pelagic species.

This pretty island is only three kilometres across but its centre is quite high and topped with a lighthouse. The shoreline swaps between sheer, dark rock boulders and bright white beaches that lead down to the now protected reef. The island's highly successful marine sanctuary is run by the local villagers with great enthusiasm and as time goes on it becomes more and more of a model for well planned ecotourism. You can stay on the island at the small lodge. It has power only part-time and there's no running water. However, it is interesting to see how a sustainable marine project can work to the benefit of both the locals, whose lifestyle has improved, and the surrounding environment. These days many people regard this as one of the best big-fish dive sites in the Philippines.

ⓘ18 Coconut Point

Depth	28 m
Visibility	stunning
Currents	slight to ripping
Dive type	day boat

Coconut Point is the big-thrill experience. It catches some very strong currents, especially as you head out to the point, and as ever it's the currents that attract the fish. The dive commences over a flat reef with a good cover of hard corals. It then slopes out to a tongue with steep walls where jacks, snapper and rainbow runners patrol. There is a sandy cut that provides shelter for when the current is really ripping and from here you can watch turtles, groupers, Napoleon wrasse and whitetip sharks. Schools of big eye trevallies compete with Spanish mackerel, barracuda and midnight snappers. Clouds of anthias and fusiliers are always seen here and damsels dance around the hard coral. The sloping section of this site is a very good place to look for turtles – one friendly resident is very old and his shell is encrusted with barnacles – and sea snakes on the prowl.

ⓘ19 Sanctuary

Depth	20 m
Visibility	good to excellent
Currents	slight
Dive type	day boat

Diving inside the sanctuary is limited to a small number of people each day but if you manage to do this, it's well worth it to see the swathes of hard coral and the small fish that are attracted to this safe haven. There are always clouds of fusiliers, butterflies, angels, sweetlips and different species of surgeonfish. The two most interesting patches are the clam beds, where the sanctuary monitors growth and spread, and the area of clownfish and anemones. You could spend most of the dive playing with the nemos!

Pristine water clarity and marine life inside the Apo Island sanctuary

Sumilon

Once justifiably famous as the first marine reserve to be established in the Philippines, Sumilon Island Marine Sanctuary lies off southern Cebu.

Many years ago, directors at Dumaguete's Silliman University initiated a project to protect around 50 hectares of the island's fringing coral reef. The marine reserve was declared a no-fishing zone in 1974 but in 1984 the reserve was entered by force and the entire zone was devastated. Corals were destroyed and fish stocks wiped out.

The good news, though, is that the island now independently protects the reefs having learnt that the long-term effect of this sort of activity only results in a shortage of fish and seafood catch which was the island's main source of living. These dives can be reached from either Panglao or Dumaguete.

↘20 The Sanctuary

🕐	**Depth**	35 m
🔆	**Visibility**	fair to good
〰	**Currents**	none
🚤	**Dive type**	day boat

The reef flat leads to a drop that bottoms out at about 35 metres. However, the dive is most interesting near the top where part of the regeneration project is in plain sight. A raft of car tyres has been dropped over some old dynamite damage. As always, these seem to attract an incredible array of marine creatures. Moray eels wind their way into the inside curve of the tyre and if you poke your nose down you find coral banded and hingebeak shrimps living with them. Further down the slope there are decent soft corals and a variety of reef fish like hogfish that graze on the sand. Patches on the sandy seabed that are thick with garden eels and mushroom corals.

↘21 Sumilon Wall

🕐	**Depth**	25 m
🔆	**Visibility**	fair to good
〰	**Currents**	none
🚤	**Dive type**	day boat

Heading downwards on this steeper slope there are some cracks and crevices to investigate. The marine life is typical of the region: clownfish in their anemones and snapper and butterflyfish cruising the wall. There can be some current running here and when it lifts there is a good chance of seeing large schools of pelagic fish like tuna and jacks. The visibility is best from December to May when reef sharks and rays are seen. Back on the top of the reef many hard corals regenerating. The football-size colonies are decorated by small fish darting about – these include blue chromis, orange anthias and black and white striped damsels.

🌊 Take sanctuary

The Philippines once had a reputation for decimated reefs: stories of destructive fishing leaked out and divers stopped visiting. The good news, which spread far less quickly, was the establishment of several marine sanctuaries. Their aim was to protect the reefs and to re-educate those whose livelihoods depended on the sea. As far back as 1974 Dumaguete's Silliman University initiated the region's first marine sanctuary at Sumilon Island. Its success led to the creation of a second sanctuary on Apo Island.

The Apo villagers had traditionally subsisted on fishing and were struggling with a decline in their fish stocks. These were so low they were forced to travel further and further from the island. To counteract the lack of food and income they started using destructive fishing practices. The university team took some of these fishermen to see the sanctuary at Sumilon which by then was teeming with fish. They were able to see how the sanctuary could serve as a nursery to restock the surrounding area. It took three years of dialogue between the university and the fishermen, before a few island families agreed to establish and police a no-fishing zone. It extended along 450 metres of shoreline and 500 metres from shore. Fish sizes and numbers soon increased inside the sanctuary. The knock-on effect was more and bigger fish populating the reefs on the peripheries of the sanctuary. By 1985, the remaining islanders had seen the success of the sanctuary project and agreed to support it, making it legally binding through the local municipal government.

While the road may have been rocky as the disaster at Sumilon shows, by 1994 the Apo Island success led to the Philippine government establishing a national marine sanctuary programme with about 400 sanctuaries nationwide. There is another at Masa Plod near Dumaguete.

Destructive fishing practices include:
Dynamite fishing: started with explosives left over from the Second World War.
Japanese Muro-ami: fish are chased into nets by pounding on coral with rocks.
Cyanide: introduced for the aquarium trade.
Small-mesh nets: newly developed nylon nets.

Even the most enthusiastic diver will struggle to see more than a handful of the Philippine islands. The Visayas have their fair share: some are lively, some completely in tune with nature. Perhaps the most attractive – for divers anyway – after the ones in this chapter are Malapascua and Moalboal. Both have well-established diver-friendly infrastructures. First-hand reports are below.

Boracay The best known island in the region's northwest, this is a national marine preserve. It was also the original backpacker hang-out so is one of the most popular – and populated. There are said to be over 20 dive centres and many more hotels all packed into a total land area of 10 square kilometres. Opinions on the diving vary but this island has a stunning beach and is known for its restaurants, bars and nightlife. Fly from Manila to Caticlan Airport, then catch a boat from the harbour.

Siquijor Sitting opposite Dumaguete on Negros, and on the far side of Apo Island, Siquijor is less well known for diving than her near neighbours, but the island has had an interesting cultural past as it was 'discovered' by the Spanish in the 16th century. There are rainforests, mangroves and waterfalls, ancient churches, convents and caves. To get to Siquijor take a ferry from Cebu, Tagbilaran or Dumaguete.

Southern Leyte Sogod Bay is on the tip of southern Leyte and is enclosed by two fingers of land. Panaon island lies on one side, and Limasawa island on the other. This area is only just building a reputation as a dive region due to the whalesharks that pass through the bay. These are seasonal (from late November until May) but the reef diving is said to be very good in places. Fly to Cebu airport then catch a fast ferry to Maasin on Southern Leyte.

◑ Tales from the deep

Malapascua We visited this island in January, which was meant to be the dry season although it rained torrentially for the first week and made getting dry virtually impossible until the second week of the holiday. So why travel to the other side of the planet, to get up at 5am then sit on the seabed at 20 metres staring into the blue for an hour? We did begin to wonder after the fifth morning of diving Monad Shoal, seeing nothing except the odd nudibranch, when from the depths emerged a thresher shark. The torpedo-shaped shark with that amazingly long graceful tail circled for about a minute and then swam off. It then came back to treat us to another circuit. Some of the best diving was from the protected house reef where the highlights were flamboyant cuttlefish, frogfish and catfish. The dusk/night dive at Lighthouse Reef was fascinating as we watched tiny mandarinfish darting around like hummingbirds, flirting with each other and finally mating. We moved on and spotted three seahorses and a very cute baby bobtail squid. Occasionally we were startled by large bangs – we assumed by fisherman still using dynamite to catch fish. Overall the diving was relaxed, fish life diverse and people friendly although it lacked the big schools of fish we enjoyed in other places.

Clare Vincent-Silk and Spike Brown,
St Albans, England

To reach Malapascua, fly to Cebu airport; transfers are then 4½ hours by bus followed by 30 minutes by boat.

Moalboal After our first wonderful week on Alona Beach, we transferred to Moalboal, keen to experience the variety of diving the Visayas has to offer. Our resort, Magic Island was at the southern end of the Moalboal Peninsula by Pescador Island, which is one of the more popular dive sites. This was described as having unfriendly walls and that seemed spot on. The walls were much darker, with light just being absorbed and creating a curtain to what lies behind. It was a strong contrast to our previous colourful dives at Alona. However, getting closer revealed a variety of life from frogfish to pygmy seahorses. Another dive at Sanctuary became another favourite. We had never seen anything quite like it: a seafan forest. Large, pristine fans spread from 20 metres into the depths and along the reef as far as we could see.

Our last dive of the holiday was at Ravanala. From the *banca* we rolled into the blue and followed a large sloping reef with plenty of lionfish, anemones and scorpionfish. Looking closer revealed more macro life amongst the hard corals. Back up in the shallows, the reef showed all it's colours and as we ascended into the sun we took in the moment knowing it was the start of our journey back home. A few days after we left, we heard that some of the divers we had been diving with had a magnificent encounter with a whaleshark – how typical!

Mike and Samantha Muir,
Warwickshire, England.

To reach Moalboal, fly to Cebu airport; transfers are then 3 hours by car.

Drying out

Alona Beach on Panglao has the widest choice of accommodation options but bear in mind that not all resorts have a dive centre. Instead they will be affiliated to the one next door or down the road. However, resorts on other Panglao island beaches are likely to have their own dive centre. Likewise, the resorts on both Cabilao and Dumaguete will have full, on-site dive facilities.

Bohol

Dive Resorts

$$ The Ananyana, Panglao. T+63 (0)38 502 8101, ananyana.com. Top class dive resort with beautiful rooms overlooking Doljo Beach. Not the cheapest option, but sometimes you just have to indulge. On-site dive centre, spa and restaurant.

Other options

$ Alona Palm Beach Resort, T+63 (0)38 502 9141, alonapalmbeach.com. Modern accommodation, right on beach. Affiliated to nearby atlantisdivecenter.de

$ La Estrella, T+63 (0)38 505 4114, laestrella.ph. On Cabilao with a range of room standards; Cabilao Divers on-site
$ Sun Apartelle and Sun Divers, T+63 (0)38 502 9171 sun-divers.net. Self catering rooms set back from Alona Beach.

Dumaguete, Negros Oriental

Dive Resorts

$$ Atlantis Dive Resorts, T+63 (0)35 425 2327, atlantishotel.com. Sister resort to Atlantis in Puerto Galera with similar standards of service and facilities. Located on Lipayo Beach bay, 20 minutes south of Dumaguete. Rooms are nicely decorated. Dive courses available. Packages with meals and unlimited diving are fantastic value.

Other options

$$$-$$ Bahura Resort and Spa, Dauin, bahura.com. This new and modern resort is right on Dauin Beach. Smart rooms with a dive centre and spa on site.
$ El Dorado Beach Resort, Lipayo, Dauin. eldoradobeachresort.com. This resort has been recently renovated. Restaurant on the beach front and dive centre on site.

Bohol

Tagbilaran You could spend a lazy day touring some of the features of the town's old Spanish settlement. There are a few 17th- and 18th-century churches and some attractive tree-lined plazas, colonial houses and a small museum.

Loboc River Take a cruise along the jungle-rimmed river in a pumpboat passing local villages, or you could go hiking in the hills.

Chocolate Hills The most famous Bohol attraction is this weird landscape of 1200 grassy mounds that look like someone tipped up bags of sugar in rows. In the summer, the domes turn brown as the covering, grassy vegetation dries out, transforming the area into rows of 'chocolate' mounds.

Tarsier Foundation The province is also home to the world's smallest primate, the tarsier. This diminutive creature is endangered. You can see them at the Tarsier Research and Development Centre at Corella, 14 kilometres from Tagbilaran. There is a netted enclosure, where the tarsiers are fed, bred and monitored. Alternatively, take the tarsier trail through the forest and watch out for one.

Negros

Dumaguete This busy coastal city is home to Silliman University. The shops and markets are fun to visit and there is some colonial architecture including an 18th century bell tower. The botanical gardens, zoo and aviary are worth a visit.

Casaroro Waterfall An hour by car from Dumaguete, the Valencia Mountains harbour a small nature reserve nestling in the river valley. Hiking for an hour takes you to this waterfall which drops into a stunning natural swimming pool.

Twin Lakes Located in the mountainous area above San Jose, and inland from Dumaguete, Balinsasayao and Danao Twin Lakes are a haven of pristine flora and fauna. Kayakers who can rent a small *banca* and cross to the deserted side of the lake under a dark forest canopy.

Sleeping	$$$ US$150+ double room per night	$$ US$75-150	$ under US$75
Eating	$$$ US$40+ 2-course meal, excluding drinks	$$ US$20-40	$ under US$20

Thailand

Hunting on the reef at Phi Phi,
the lionfish, *Pterois volitans,* gets
an easy meal.

▶▶ Distant Horizons

Get off the beaten track
in the far away Mergui Archipelago

▶▶ Discovery zone

Hunt for rare pelagics and unusual
creatures at Richelieu Rock

Bilugyun
Islands

Nakhon Sawan

Mae Nam Pa Sak

Mae Nam Mun

Nakhon
Ratchasima

Mae Nam Ping

*Khao
Laem
Reservoir*

T H A I L A N D

Mae Khlong

Monthaburi

BANGKOK

Thon Buri

Chon Buri

C A M B O D I

*Bight
of
Bangkok*

Phet Buri

Chanthaburi

Ko Chang

Ko Kut

Prachuap
Khiri Khan

*G u l f   o f
T h a i l a n d*

Koh Tao

Mergui Archipelago

Kawthaung

Ranong

Koh Samui

Burma Banks

*A n d a m a n
S e a*

Koh Surin

Richelieu Rock

Surat
Thani

Koh Bon

Koh Tachai

Khao Lak

Similans

Krabi

Phuke t

Trang

Phi Phi

Songkhla

*I N D I A N
O C E A N*

Introduction

▶▶ **Total immersion**

Dive till you drop in the world-famous Similans marine park

▶▶ **Take the plunge**

Learn to dive in the novice heavens off Phi Phi and Koh Tao

▶▶ **Above and below**

Dive during the day then satisfy a thirst for nightlife in up-tempo Phuket

SOUTH
CHINA
SEA

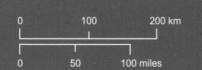

0   100   200 km

0   50   100 miles

Sitting right on the western edges of SoutheastAsia, Thailand could be regarded as the region's dive outsider. Geographically beyond the borders of the Coral Triangle, Thailand still reflects much of the marine beauty of her neighbours, but her principal dive sites are rather more influenced by the effects of the Indian Ocean rather than the Pacific.

From the smaller, peaceful reefs south off Phuket to the high drama of the Mergui Archipelago to the north, the variety of diving can be impressive. Even the murky waters around the islands in the Gulf of Thailand are lush enough to keep most divers smiling.

Thailand may not be as diverse as other parts of Asia – biodiversity rankings are lower by quite a way – but with more than its fair share of pelagic animals, you can forgive it almost anything. Especially as this is one of the most likely places you will get to dive with that revered gentle giant, the whaleshark.

When it's finally time to let the nitrogen leach out, days on land can be a treat. Thai culture is rich – think orange-clad monks and golden Buddhas – the nightlife is heady and the cuisine is outstanding. And the often contradictory elements of tradition and cutting-edge modernity are somehow held together by the charming people.

Essentials

Getting there

Thailand is one of Southeast Asia's easiest countries to travel to. There are several international airports but the best diving is based in the south so you will aways need an internal transfer to reach it. This means you have two main arrival options: either Bangkok or Singapore. International flights via Singapore are often nicer as the city makes a great stopover (see page 272) and as airports go, Changi is one of the best. Of course, if you have never been to Bangkok this equally fascinating, but far busier city, is well worth seeing.

Singapore Airlines' flight network is particularly good for dive trips starting in Phuket. Their regional subsidiary, Silk Air (silkair.com) and their low-cost carrier, Tiger Airways (tigerairways.com) have six or more daily flights to Phuket between them. If you're heading to Koh Samui you can still fly from Singapore using Bangkok Airways connections (bangkokair.com).

For travel via Bangkok, Thai Airways (thaiair.com) have plenty of connections to Samui, Phuket and also Krabi, just south of Phuket. And then there is a plethora of other options, such as low-cost carriers AirAsia and Nok Air (nokair.com) plus full service carriers like Japan Airlines and Cathay Pacific, although onward flights are mostly a codeshare with Thai. There are a few carriers that fly direct to Phuket (asiana.com) but these are mostly based in Asia. Jetstar (jetstar.com) flies direct from Sydney and Melbourne. All the airports are efficient and visas are required only if you intend to stay for longer than 30 days.

Getting around

If you hope to do any extensive land travel Thailand has a decent bus system, trains linking Bangkok with the south and ferries to all the islands. For days out, there are metered taxis, buses called songthaews (a covered pick-up truck with bench seats at the back) and the ubiquitous tuk-tuk. This motorized rickshaw is based on a motor-cycle with a bench seat behind the driver and a canopy overhead. Never get into a tuk-tuk without prearranging a price and you must bargain. However, you are more likely to see them in Bangkok, or as a tourist attraction elsewhere.

Self-drive car hire is available, and all major rental companies are in the country. There is no reason to avoid hiring a car as the roads in urban areas like Phuket are up to western standards but driving in busy centres is best described as challenging. The famous calm Thai nature takes a back seat when faced with a traffic jam.

For organized land tours, ask your dive centre for a recommendation. It's perfectly OK to wander off on your own. Although traditions are still evident, westernized standards prevail. Thai nature means you will always find someone willing to help. Nearly everyone speaks English or another European language.

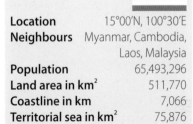

Thailand	
Location	15°00'N, 100°30'E
Neighbours	Myanmar, Cambodia, Laos, Malaysia
Population	65,493,296
Land area in km²	511,770
Coastline in km	7,066
Territorial sea in km²	75,876

Transfers

Transfers from your arrival airport are no problem – just ask your hotel or dive centre to pick up you and all that heavy luggage. Depending on the package you have booked, this may cost a small sum, or be free. Should you arrive at Phuket and your pre-booked transfer isn't in plain sight, simply ask anyone who looks like a driver for help. They will contact your booking service for you. People are friendly and happy to make a call. Transfers to offshore islands can be more expensive, ranging from about US$25 per person on a public ferry to US$75 by speedboat.

For destinations near Phuket:

Phuket Town It's unlikely you will be staying here as the town is away from all the beach areas, but if you do stop for a night, pre- or post- a liveaboard say, the airport bus runs to Phuket City Bus Terminal on Phang Nga Road. The trip takes an hour. Buses from this terminal also go to Krabi and take about two hours.

The beaches There are around 10 main beach areas on Phuket ranging from a 10-minute drive from the airport to an hour to Ao Chalong or Nai Harn, the furthest away.

Phi Phi Islands Hotels and resorts on Phi Phi are located in Tonsai Bay and Laem Tong. To reach either from Phuket Airport, go to the port in Phuket Town and take a speedboat or a ferry (one to two hours). The speedboats go to either beach but ferries stop at Tonsai Bay only so if you are staying at Laem Tong you will need to get a shuttle on a long-tail boat. Departures are twice daily.

For destinations near Krabi:

Krabi Town Like Phuket Town, this isn't a place many divers stop, but the trip from the airport is only 20 minutes and costs about US$15 by taxi. The jetty for trips across to Phi Phi is here, with ferries across four times daily.

The beaches Transfers from the airport are simple enough. Taxis and private shuttles take between 15 and 30 minutes; better hotels will collect their guests.

For destinations near Koh Samui

The beaches If you are flying to Samui to stay on one of her beaches, the airport is just a short hop from some of the most popular. Taxis take 10-30 minutes or your resort will collect if you request a pick-up in advance.

The Gulf Islands For the more diver-friendly islands that are a little way from Samui, you will need to catch a ferry from Maenam Pier. The trips takes up to two hours. Speedboats leave from Bophut or Nathon and take about an hour depending on your final destination.

 Tourist information → the official government website can be found at tourismthailand.org. This site has links to various regional sites and is in a variety of languages.

Fact file

International flights	AirAsia, Bangkok Airways, Singapore Airlines/Silk Air, Thai Airways
Departure tax	Included in your ticket
Entry	EU, US and Commonwealth – valid passport required for stays of up to 30 days
Internal flights	Bangkok Airways, Thai Airways
Ground transport	Good countrywide bus connections, trains and ferries to all islands
Money	US$1 = 35 Thai baht (THB)
Language	Thai but English is widely spoken
Electricity	220v, plug types A and C
Time zone	GMT +7
Religion	Principally Buddhist
Phone	Country code +66; IDD 001; Tourist Police 1699

Language

Thai is a tonal language – two words may look and be spelled the same way but will be pronounced differently and mean different things. That makes it hard enough for the average westerner to learn but to make matters worse, it has a different alphabet so you won't be able to read it anyway. Yet like most countries, the Thai people are honoured, and amused, if you try a few words. Here are a few basics to help you charm your divemaster or waiter.

hello, goodbye	*sa-wùt dee krúp (kâ)*
yes/no	*chái/mâi chái or: krúp (kâ)*
thank you	*kòrp-kOO/mâi ao*
no thank you	*kòrp-kOOn*
excuse me, sorry!	*kor-tôht krúp (kâ)*
how much is…	*tâo-rài…*
where's the…	*yòo têe-nai…*
great dive!	*Dam naam dee mak mak*

(Use *krúp* for males and *kâ* for females.)

Local laws and customs

Thai etiquette is based around courtesy and calmness. Thais are taught from an early age that it is important to maintain *jai yen* (cool heart). Consequently, public displays of anger are rare and generally do not achieve the desired effect. Keep a cool head at all times and you won't go wrong.

On the subject of heads, never touch a Thai there, not even an affectionate pat for a child. Never show the soles of your feet or use a foot to point. Feet are the lowest part of the body so it is considered an insult. The Thai royal family is much revered, so no criticism is allowed, not even in jest. Buddhist monks should be treated with equal courtesy. Women should never touch one; in fact, if one walks towards you, stand aside to avoid any embarrassment. If you visit a temple or are away from the beach, sensible, modest clothing is preferable. On the beach, well anything goes!

Safety

Thailand has been relatively stable and although personal safety hasn't been too much of an issue, there is occasional unrest. However, common sense should keep you safe. There is a continued threat of terrorist attacks in the provinces in the far southeast of the country, closer to the Malay border. This is not a dive region so it isn't really an issue unless you intend to also head across to the islands in the Malay Gulf. If you do, consider flying.

Women should be aware that they may get hassled a little so teaming up with a dive buddy could be a good idea. Petty crime can be more of a problem, especially in tourist areas. In places where nightclubs are upscale and uptempo, drink spiking does occur. There are also tales of travellers on internal buses or trains being handed a drink by a friendly local then waking up hours later having been relieved of their wallets.

Dive centres tend to be in well populated and traveller-friendly places. If you have made arrangements with a local operator they will collect you from the airport then deposit you safely at your accommodation or dive boat. Camera carriers should be aware that Pelican cases scream an invitation to a petty thief, as do laptop bags and mobile phones. Don't leave dive equipment unattended, especially not swanky dive bags with big logos plastered all over them. Note that penalties for possession of drugs are severe and can include the death penalty.

❶ Feeding frenzy

Thai cuisine has to be one of the world's most delicious with its unique blend of the four major taste sensations – hot, sweet, sour and salt. Although there are regional differences, Thai food is known for two things: its combination of fresh herbs and spices and the delightful presentation. Meals are a feast for the eyes as much as the mouth with dishes decorated by carrots carved into roses and cucumbers turned into swans or something equally fanciful. A Thai meal is mostly based on aromatic jasmine rice which is indigenous to Thailand. This is served with meat dishes that use extensive quantities of chillies, lime juice and lemon grass amongst many other spices. The salt factor is always added with Nam Pla, a thin sauce made by fermenting fish and salt. It smells awful but tastes fantastic.

One of the simpler Thai dishes is Pad Kaphrao, a dish of beef, pork or chicken stir-fried with Thai Holy basil, which has a stronger flavour than the herb used in other countries. Another favourite is Pad Thai, rice noodles with prawns or chicken, spices, chopped peanuts and egg. If you like spicy foods, try Tom Yam, a hot and sour soup with a mix of meats. Red curry, made with red chillies, and green curry, made with green chillies, are the two dishes you will see on every menu. These are soup-like meals and served with plenty of rice. Always ask for mild the first time round (or beware of the consequences) or go for a Massaman curry which is slightly more Indian in style.

Health

In tourism-focused areas, staying healthy is not an issue. Standards are high and there are decent medical facilities should you need help. Basics, like aspirin and insect repellent, are easy to get. Only drink bottled water and beware of too much sun and mosquitoes at dusk. There is very little risk of malaria in the southern coastal regions, and mosquitoes don't make it out to sea. However, dengue fever, which is also mosquito borne, is becoming more common in the wet season. Take the same precautions as you would for malaria (cover up and use a repellent) but there are no protective drugs available. Also be smart when it comes to extra-curricular activities. Thailand has an epidemic of HIV infection and AIDS and HIV is common amongst prostitutes of both sexes. For vaccinations required, see page 288.

Costs

Thailand is more expensive than it used to be and certainly a little pricier than her neighbours, but facilities here are often that bit classier. It's still good value for money although everyone's idea of value varies. You can get a decent two-course meal and a local beer or two while sitting under a coconut palm watching the sun set often for less than US$20. The excellent local brew, Singha, is around US$1.75 a bottle. One particularly good feature is that bottled water is almost always supplied in your room, usually a half litre per person per day. It's not a big issue in terms of cost but a nice touch.

Room rates can be whatever you need them to be. In the dive areas, US$40 will buy a comfortable but simple room, while a more upmarket hotel can cost anything up to US$100. Naturally some resorts are far more expensive, and rates are higher in Bangkok where it's worth paying for comfort. Tipping isn't the norm although in touristy areas it's becoming more common and good service should be rewarded. For drivers, guides and divemasters, see page 11.

Dive brief

Diving

Thailand's diving is defined – or perhaps confused – by its position between two seas. The western coastline faces the Indian Ocean and is heavily influenced by its deep water currents and contrasting monsoons. From May to October there are often driving, onshore winds pushing in from the southwest. This limits diving to more protected areas around Phuket. The Similans are out of bounds as it's simply too rough. By November, calm seas return when the monsoon swaps over to the northeast. Over in the Gulf, the wind patterns have the opposite seasonal effect so diving there is only really worthwhile in the midsummer months.

There are reef structures all the way along both coastlines but on the west these are far more extensive, particularly around the offshore islands. All the way from south of Phuket right up to Myanmar, there is fantastic diving. Colourful corals and sea fans are plentiful. There are huge granite boulders creating spectacular swim-throughs and swarms of colourful fish. Pinnacles rise from the deep and submerged reefs offer protection in more isolated regions.

In contrast, the Gulf and her islands are subject to their position in a very shallow sea. At less than 60 metres deep, and with twice daily tides, they are susceptible to heavy sedimentation and river run-off. These harsh conditions have restricted reef diversity and coral numbers. All the same, there is good diving to be had around a few of the southern islands, but the further north you go, heading towards Bangkok, the more likely it is that visibility will disappoint.

Snorkelling

Thailand is a mixed bag: currents are unpredictable and often strong, and wind conditions can change rapidly making for rough surface conditions. Many of the better dive sites visited by liveaboards are exposed and submerged pinnacles may be off-putting for all but the strongest swimmers. However, there is decent snorkelling in the coastal areas – the small bays around the Similan Islands have dazzlingly clear water, while the Phi Phi Islands are fairly protected. Some of the Gulf Islands are also good, especially as the seabed is shallow and gently shelving.

Diversity

With toes sitting in two completely unrelated seas, Thailand's marine diversity is even more disparate than neighbouring

> **"** When asked why we keep returning to Thailand, we can only quote all the special moments: dawn on the Burma Banks watching whales breach; the moment the light went out at Richelieu Rock as a whaleshark swam over us and when we met another in Mergui a day later; a perfect pink ghost pipefish on a perfect pink coral; the inky depths of a wreck at night. We have never been disappointed diving off Thailand's west coast.

Dive data

Seasons	November to May on the west coast, May to October on the east coast
Visibility	5 metres inshore to 'infinity' in the Andaman Sea
Temperatures	Air 30-34°C; water 27-30°C
Wet suit	3 mm full body suit. Take a rash vest for the fourth dive
Training	Courses available in Phuket, Krabi or the Gulf
Nitrox	Available on land. May be limited on liveaboards
Deco chambers	Pattaya, Bangkok, Phuket and Koh Samui

Diversity
reef area 4,000km²

HARD CORALS	428
FISH SPECIES	1415
ENDEMIC FISH SPECIES	17
FISH UNDER THREAT	53
PROTECTED REEFS/MARINE PARKS	16

All diversity figures are approximate

Malaysia. What's more, Thailand is the only Southeast Asian country not included in the Coral Triangle, so the variety and quantity of marine species are far lower than those in either the Philippines or Indonesia. Fish are the best example, with both of those countries having recorded numbers of around 3,000 species while Thailand has a mere 1,400, which is still far more than somewhere like Egypt with just 750 or 500 in the Galápagos.

Thailand's western coastline borders the Andaman Sea, which is part of the Indian Ocean and as such is subject to the more rigorous ocean currents there. These bring in clearer waters which in turn creates a greater interchange of species from further afield. The visibility is better and sunlight reaching down to the reefs ensures lush coral growth. In contrast, the Gulf of Thailand on the east faces the South China Seas. This is separated from the main ocean currents running past the land mass that is Vietnam and Cambodia. Reef structures are less impressive as the gulf is so shallow (with an average depth of 45 metres compared to over 800 in the Andaman) and currents moving from the north drag sediment from three enormous river mouths at the top of the gulf. This doesn't mean that there aren't good quality reefs or lots of fish. On one hand, the conditions bring additional nutrients and plankton to the waters while on the other coral growth is still limited by the conditions.

Making the big decision

Once you have decided to dive Thailand, choosing a specific destination may seem daunting. However, Thailand is highly seasonal, so your choice will be influenced by when you can go. If it's between November and May, then you're heading to the west of the country. If you are limited to May through October, the Gulf of Thailand will make for a better holiday, although not necessarily the best diving. If you're a qualified diver, then there is no better way to explore the wonders of the Andaman Sea than on a liveaboard.

Bottom time

Phuket gulf

Phuket, Krabi and Phi Phi ▶ p238	Three well developed holiday centres form an imaginary enclosure for some delightful day-trip diving. Easy access to surprisingly rich reefs that support a wealthy marine ecosystem plus the country's best wreck dive. *Diving all year but best from November to May*
Andaman Sea **Similans** ▶ p248	The ultimate Thai marine park with diving around picture-postcard perfect islands and equally impressive reefs. Head out on a liveaboard to explore both sides of these incredible reef systems.
Koh Bon and Koh Tachai ▶ p254	Now included in the Koh Similans Marine Park, these open water pinnacles a short sail to the north are the ones that attract the big stuff.
Richelieu Rock ▶ p256	The Surin Islands are a separate marine park but far less dived as they are mostly used as a way-station to Richelieu Rock. This legendary dive destination is the do-not-miss dive of the country and possibly of your life.
Mergui Archipelago ▶ p258	The waters of the Andaman sea just across the Myanmar border are still relatively unexplored. Isolated reefs and submerged pinnacles equal those in neighbouring Thailand. *Diving from November to May only*
Gulf of Thailand **Koh Samui and Koh Tao** ▶ p268	The reefs that surround the delightful Gulf Islands are subject to variable conditions but are still pleasant dives. A few local pinnacle dives are occasionally sensational. *Limited diving all year; best from May to November*

Thailand Dive brief

Phuket gulf

Just a one-hour flight from Bangkok, or 90 minutes from Singapore, is Thailand's best shore-based diving. The waters that lie between Phuket Island, Phang Nga Bay, the coastal town of Krabi and the Phi Phi Islands are dotted with small islands and rich coral reefs.

Although part of the Andaman Sea, this area acts more like a giant bay or gulf and would be one except for a narrow channel dividing Phuket from the mainland. Water flows in from the Andaman Sea but the seabed is far shallower and conditions are very different to those on the reefs west of Phuket and outside this gulf.

Dive sites are scattered right across this region but the far north near Phang Nga is affected by several river mouths. Further south, sites that lie between Phi Phi and the southern tip of Phuket are clearer as they are subject to stronger currents and tides. However, the visibility in this whole area is never crystal clear. At an average of 15 metres year round it's not too bad, but will seem low if you have been out to the Similans. Despite that, there is very good diving and much of the area holds marine park status. The corals at Shark Point are truly spectacular while Phi Phi is mobbed by an amazing amount of fish. There are some big animals – turtles and whitetip sharks – and a good deal of small creatures like lionfish, puffers and angels. And of course, this is Thailand's most inspiring scenery – *The Man with the Golden Gun* was filmed on Koh Tapu in Phang Nga Bay while *The Beach* made the Phi Phi Islands more famous than they were already.

Locations

With two airports and masses of facilities, both for divers and non-divers, this an ideal starting point for both nearby and more distant diving. As most of the local dive sites can be reached from any base, the best way to choose which of these three destinations to stay in is probably to consider how busy you like your nights to be: if you hate the sound of loud music avoid beaches like Phuket's Patong; if you're happiest on an island, go to Phi Phi; if you want something in between, try the beaches near Krabi.

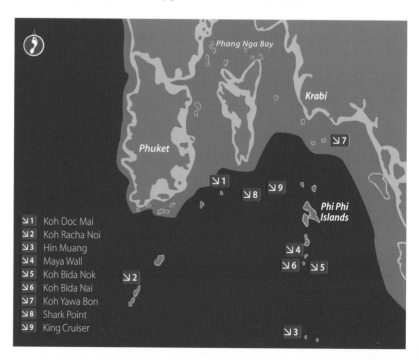

↘1　Koh Doc Mai
↘2　Koh Racha Noi
↘3　Hin Muang
↘4　Maya Wall
↘5　Koh Bida Nok
↘6　Koh Bida Nai
↘7　Koh Yawa Bon
↘8　Shark Point
↘9　King Cruiser

Destinations

Phuket

This island has it all, from loud and raucous to comparatively calm and quiet. Beaches encircle the island but the most popular are on the west coast. Near the airport are **Nai Yang** and **Nai Thon**, which have just a handful of top-class resorts between them, then moving south are **Bang Tao**, **Pansea** and **Kamala**, which become progressively busier as they approach **Patong**, Phuket's wildest resort area. The once pristine stretch of white sand, backed by a handful of small hotels and palm trees, is now a thriving town with shops, restaurants, bars and every type of hotel known to man. The nightlife is livelier and more sexually-driven than will suit some, with masses of girly bars, lady-boy bars and gay bars. It is all done – mostly – with enough humour and charm to be inoffensive but this is not the area to come to if you are looking for that castaway feel. Next south, **Karon** and **Kata** beaches are similar but quieter. There are bars but it rarely gets as rowdy. Just before Phuket's south tip are **Nai Harn** and **Rawai** beaches, then as you turn the point you reach **Chalong Bay**. These last three are far quieter and although there are some bars, nightlife mostly consists of watching the sun set with a cocktail followed by a decent meal. These are probably the most suitable for divers, too as they are close to Chalong Jetty where dive boats anchor. It is also the main departure point for liveaboards to the Similan Islands Marine Park and cruises further north. You can still take your pick of whatever resort style suits you best as almost every beach or resort has a dive centre that will make arrangements for you. *Distance from airport: 10-60 minutes*

Krabi

This compact and bustling town is bypassed by holidaymakers and divers alike for the beautiful beaches nearby. The main one is **Ao Nang**, a long stretch of white sand in a delightful crescent-shaped bay. There are plenty of hotels to suit a variety of budgets plus a good selection of restaurants, shops and bars. The feel is far less built up than many of the beaches over on Phuket. At the northern end, around a small headland, Ao Nang becomes **Nopparat Thara** beach, which is less developed. The sunsets on both are amazing, and the food superb. To the south is the favoured **Railay** area. Once purely a travellers' haunt, to get here you need to catch a boat. There are no roads on this small promontory just three beaches connected by footpaths: **Railay West, East** and on the outer edge, **Phra Nang**. Again, there are a variety of hotels from small backpacker-orientated guesthouses to top of the range. *Distance from airport: 20-60 minutes*

Phi Phi islands

The Phi Phi islands are certainly the ones that attract a crowd. Intensely beautiful with steep limestone cliffs dropping to gorgeous sweeps of sand, made famous by movie stars and then more famous by the devastating tsunami of Boxing Day 2004. The damage was terrible, but more on land than below the water. The islands are almost back to normal and as busy as ever. Phi Phi Lei is uninhabited while **Phi Phi Don** has no roads but plenty of resorts. It is almost two islands really, with two high, tree-clad hills connected by a sandspit. There is accommodation in **Tonsai Bay**, the 'village', or **Laem Tong** which is a little quieter as you can only reach it by boat. Both places have a good selection of bars and activities so are never completely quiet and are inundated by day trippers, including divers, on a daily basis. *Distance from airport: up to 3 ½ hours*

Places to stay and things to do at all these destinations are listed in Drying out on page 263

Phuket from the air; Chalong Bay; Phi Phi restaurant; Patong Beach; Koh Racha Noi

Phuket, Phi Phi islands and Krabi

No matter where you are staying, you will have access to the same dive sites. Some day trips are short, some are a few hours away, and you can even do an overnight trip to reduce the travelling to these varied dive sites.

Thousands of divers flock to Phuket to take advantage of the abundant facilities but dive sites just offshore tend to have reduced visibility, sometimes as low as five metres. The gentle coastal beaches are great for less experienced divers and trainees but the seabed may be stirred up by motorized watersports enthusiasts. Sail offshore for an hour or so and the difference can be surprising. Things are much the same in Krabi: originally a haunt of backpackers and long term travellers, beach dives are also a bit murky but there are small islands with pleasant reefs within striking distance. Another hour or so in a traditional longtail boat will drop you by untouched reefs, where the only other divers are the ones you arrived with. Phi Phi probably has the best dives within the closest distance of your resort, but you will still need to travel to reach the most impressive sites.

↘1 Koh Doc Mai (Flower Island)	
Depth	20 m
Visibility	fair
Currents	slight
Dive type	day boat

One of the closest dives to Phuket, the trip to this site takes about an hour from Ao Chalong. Flower Island is uninhabited and covered in thick jungle. The name is said to refer to the underwater flowers – or corals – rather than land ones. Visibility is about the lowest in this 'gulf', possibly because of the proximity to Phuket. The dive is along the wall that rings the island. You can fin

all the way around but are likely to run out of time. The corals are in decent condition and there are two small caves to explore. The first, at about 17 metres, has quite a small entry, maybe 10 metres across the mouth. It narrows down to a dark tunnel which is not for entering. A little further along a much wider-mouthed cave has lots of life around the walls and you can go inside to the back although you really need a torch. Outside on the wall and as you ascend, there are more colourful soft corals and small fans that protect white collar butterflies. Crevices are full of hingebeak shrimps and glossidoris nudibranchs.

SEA FUN DIVERS
PHUKET   THAILAND
E-mail : info@seafundivers.com

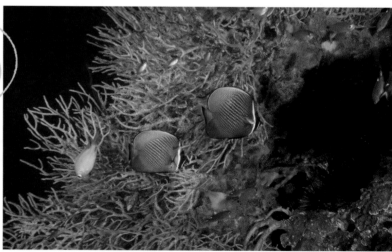

⊠2 Koh Racha Noi

⊘	**Depth**	24 m
◑	**Visibility**	fair to good
≋	**Currents**	slight to medium
⊜	**Dive type**	day boat

Racha Noi and her sister island Racha Yai (large rock and small rock) have some of the best year-round diving near Phuket with many small, protected bays to hide in if it's windy. At the top of Racha Yai these feel just like swimming pools. They drop gradually to the sandy seabed and the currents are mostly gentle. Nutrient-rich waters attract large schools of tropical fish which makes it perfect for novices. The reefs at Racha Noi on the other hand are a bit deeper so the currents can be stronger. There are many sites but two of the more popular are Maritta Rock and Camera Bay. The island scenery is lovely, rather like the Similan Islands but without the beautiful turquoise water. In fact, when you enter, you find it is quite green although the underwater terrain is still dramatic, and mimicking what you see above. There are many huge boulders with small corals growing on them and emerging from a sandy rubble bed. These dives turn out be great critter hunts. There are spearing mantis shrimps, many nudibranchs and even rarities like the pegasus sea moth. A little further on are ornate ghost pipefish in a crinoid, and if you inspect beneath the leather corals there are some unusual shells. The fish and coral life is quite good with some decent stands of hard coral and table corals where friendly octopus lurk. Both the long pipehorse and pufferfish hover over the sand. You are also likely to see the Crown of Thorns starfish, which is so beautiful but sadly does so much damage. To the south of this island, a couple of sites are known for attracting manta rays and reef sharks but operators avoid these sites on windy days.

Fans, shells and enormous granite boulders at Koh Racha Noi; soft corals and sponges in the Gulf

⊠3 Hin Muang (Purple Rock)

⊘	**Depth**	25 m
◑	**Visibility**	good to excellent
≋	**Currents**	mild
⊜	**Dive type**	day boat

If you ask a divemaster what you'll see, the likely response will be anemones and clownfish. And what an understatement that would be. This completely submerged reef is shaped a bit like a loaf of bread that someone has chopped across the middle and is aptly named. Purple hued anemones form enormous carpets, more than you will ever seen in one place. Then there's the purple and pink soft corals that drip down the gully and, if you look closely, you'll see that the whole place has purple toned fish: scorpionfish, lionfish and even octopus display indigo hues hoping to stay hidden. There are some bigger animals hanging around, too, but it's hard not to focus on all the tiny critters hidden in the folds, branches and crevices. The macro life is wonderful. The gully provides shelter from the currents and clownfish dart out curiously to check out the interlopers. Tiny caves are full of purple cleaner shrimp and, occasionally, you'll find rarer creatures hiding along with them. Ornate ghost pipefish – in shades of purple – are often seen by those who take the time to look. The furthest south of these sites, Hin Muang is in open water so the visibility tends to be much better.

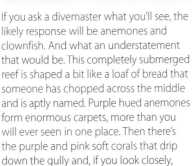

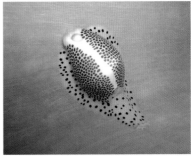

Thailand Dive log Phuket gulf: Phuket, Phi Phi islands and Krabi

■4 Maya Wall, Phi Phi Lei

⏱	**Depth**	20 m
◑	**Visibility**	fair to good
🌊	**Currents**	mild to strong
⛴	**Dive type**	day boat

Just beyond Maya Beach (think Leonardo DiCaprio), this dive is a continuation of Phi Phi's dramatic topside scenery. The wall of the island and a row of enormous granite boulders that sit a few metres away form a long enclosed channel. Swimming though you encounter several large turtles and a lot of fish. At the end of the channel the boulders become more sporadic, creating lots of nooks and crannies to investigate. The hard corals are interspersed with brightly hued fans, and there are a huge number of very impressive 'comb' corals that grow vertical branches. Towards the end a shallow cave has nudibranchs, clown triggerfish and the Similans angelfish.

■5 Koh Bida Nok

⏱	**Depth**	23 m
◑	**Visibility**	fair to good
🌊	**Currents**	slight
⛴	**Dive type**	day boat

About a kilometre or so south of Phi Phi Don are Bida Nai and Bida Nok islands. Both are steep-sided limestone pinnacles that erupt vertically from the ocean. Locals climb the walls to steal the birds' nests and there are ropes and ladders hanging along the sides. You can dive all around Bida Nok (meaning Inner Father) but the life is most prolific on the southeastern tip with its tongue-shaped promontory. Boulders are punctuated with bright fans and some very pretty corals. There are many schools of fish including snapper and triggerfish. After exploring this area, you can fin to the north which is a little shallower and into a hard coral garden with a mix of staghorn and table corals. There are anemones with their clownfish, lots of scorpionfish and, on the sand, even tiny stonefish.

■6 Koh Bida Nai

⏱	**Depth**	25 m
◑	**Visibility**	fair to good
🌊	**Currents**	mild to strong
⛴	**Dive type**	day boat

Outer Father is usually done as an early morning dive when the rising sun is just waking up all the fish. The visibility is good here at this time too, running to around 15-20 metres. Entry is over some hard coral bommies, followed by an extensive patch of pristine staghorn that leads down to a completely barren patch of sand with just the odd whip coral. This area is dramatic with the filtered sunlight casting striped shadows across the sand. Turning past this, there is an oval mound covered in large fans and many soft corals that attract the most astounding amount of feeding fish, from baitfish right up to jacks and tuna. All the predators chase after each other, causing ripples of silver and metallic grey though the deep blue sea – really a very impressive spectacle. On the mound an orange fan has formed a 3-D cross shape and a dozen lionfish nestle in the corners, swooping on and off to get a meal while pufferfish chase the runners about. All in all, a very impressive dive.

■7 Koh Yawa Bon

⏱	**Depth**	14 m
◑	**Visibility**	good
🌊	**Currents**	slight (can be strong)
⛴	**Dive type**	day boat

Just a short boat ride from Ao Nang beach, a cluster of seven small islands and a few rocky pinnacles are surrounded by a group of dive sites. The one at Yawa Bon is the most unique. The limestone formation of the island has been eroded over the years, leaving curious stalagtites and a tunnel running beneath. The dive starts at about six metres where you enter the tunnel on one side and swim into the darkness. It continues all the way through and can be exited about 50 metres away on the opposite side. It grows ever darker the further you go so you need a torch to see all the life: crabs, murex shells, young nurse sharks and spotted morays. The most exciting moment is ascending inside a cavern inside the pinnacle of limestone. The chamber has an air pocket at the top. It's very eerie as the only light is a soft glow from directly beneath. Because this dive can get strong currents, only advanced divers are taken here, although it's a great introduction to cave diving.

Healthy reefs and corals found around the Phi Phi Islands

⊠8 Shark Point (Hin Musang)	
⊗ **Depth**	16 m
◑ **Visibility**	fair
⊜ **Currents**	slight to strong
⊝ **Dive type**	shore

" " The soft corals on Shark Point are impressive enough to rival distant Fiji.

This site's Thai name translates as wild cat but there are no more of those here than the sharks of the English name. The story goes that sometime in the past, a dive company owner called this reef Shark Point just to get people to go there. It really should be called Soft Coral City or something similar. The dive starts near an exposed pinnacle top that has some surf and surge pushing across it. Below this is an extensive series of pinnacles, bommies and outcrops, all plastered with enough soft corals to wow even the most hardened diver. These are even impressive enough to rival distant Fiji, known as the soft-coral capital of the world.

Sadly, the visibility here can be awful, as low as five to seven metres which the divemasters describe as a good day. Regardless, the reefs are really beautiful with lots of barrel sponges ringed by ever more soft corals and fans. There are some good macro critters on the sand: stonefish and nudibranchs, dragonets and stingrays. A few bommies are colonized by whole gardens of anemones. They mostly house apricot coloured skunk clownfish while a nearby hard coral table has a dozen white-eyed morays running about its surface at speed, ducking in and out of crevices. Some say that seeing a leopard shark here is almost guaranteed but you would have to be lucky and swim right over one in these murky waters before you would spot it. The current on this dive can get quite lively, but it is easy to avoid that by tucking behind the bommies.

⑨ King Cruiser

🕐	**Depth**	31 m
◑	**Visibility**	fair
🌊	**Currents**	slight to medium
🌀	**Dive type**	shore

The *King Cruiser* passenger ferry was making its way across to Phi Phi when it found itself several kilometres off course. It ran into a pinnacle not far from Anemone Reef and sank slowly. There were about 500 people on board but fortunately there was no loss of life. All this happened in May 1997 and in just a decade the hull has become a rich artificial reef. The wreck is sitting almost upright on the seabed at 32 metres: it is 85 metres long and 25 metres wide. The ferry had a twin hull so the dive starts by descending to the rear where there are the most amazing numbers of

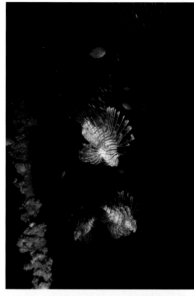

fish swirling between the two rudders. These small sardine-sized silver baitfish are being preyed on by gangs of aggressive lionfish. Swimming inside between the two hulls a little, you will see the giant barracudas that lurk here, no doubt equally well stuffed with the smaller fish. Ascending back upwards, the hull is well covered in newly developing crusting corals, sponges and a huge amount of oysters and barnacles. This wreck can't be penetrated, as the cabin sections are starting to collapse, but you can peer inwards though the old window holes and see the passageways that would have led to the cabins. There are masses of fish right across the rusting structure with schools of mackerel and jacks, fusiliers, surgeons and rabbitfish, while up on the top deck there are countless scorpions and plenty of tiny orange anthias.

Life in the deep
Wild horses

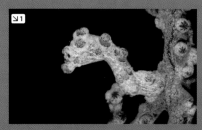

Of all the creatures in the marine world, the seahorse must be one of the most revered yet neither that reverence nor their mythical, fantasy-like reputation protects them. They are so hard to find underwater and they are thoroughly and completely endangered.

With little in common with land horses, the seahorse genus, *Hippocampus*, is derived from the Greek 'hippos' for horse and 'campus' meaning sea monster. Closely related to pipefish and sea dragons, there are around fifty species worldwide. Adult sizes range from the latest in-critter, the minuscule pygmy seahorse, to the monster Pacific seahorse that grows to over 30 centimetres long.

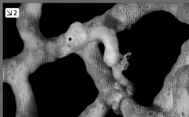

Seahorses live in both tropical and temperate waters and the best places to find them are in warm waters among seagrasses, mangroves, corals and estuaries. However, these are the most threatened of all marine habitats with man encroaching heavily and placing a lot of pressure on seahorse populations. Curiously though, these animals are highly proficient at establishing colonies in man-made environments. As their natural homes are destroyed, they adapt to whatever is around them – the mesh fence around a swimming pool, pylons of a jetty or the detritus of an artificial reef often reveal colonies lurking in the shadows. This is because all seahorses establish a small home patch with a central hold fast – a stick, sponge or piece of flotsam around which the seahorse wraps its tail. Although they don't seem to defend the patch from other seahorses, they are faithful to their hold fast, returning to it constantly after forays for food or to mate.

Not only are they faithful to their residences but also to their mates, forming monogamous pairs that last for quite some time, if not for life. Even if one half of the partnership disappears, the remaining partner is slow to seek out a new buddy. Pairs mate repeatedly, reinforcing their commitment with elaborate greeting dances soon after dawn each day. The female swims to the male, they both change colour, promenade and pirouette together for about ten minutes, after which the pair separates for the rest of the day. This ritual continues throughout the male's, yes male's, pregnancy until the day he gives birth.

And that is the most fascinating seahorse feature: male pregnancy. After the female has used her ovipositor to insert ripe eggs into the male's brood pouch, he produces sperm to fertilize them. The pouch seals shut and the male incubates the developing embryos. His pregnancy then has an almost human feel to it – oxygen diffuses from capillaries in the pouch tissue and hormones help create a placental fluid that bathes the eggs. This fluid changes as the pregnancy continues until it resembles the surrounding sea water, presumably to soften the blow of birth. It takes from ten days to six weeks (depending on the species and water temperature) for the male to go into labour, pumping and jack-knifing for many hours as he expels the young seahorses. The babies are miniature replicas of their parents and are able to fend for themselves immediately.

With all that romance and specialist care, you would think that seahorse numbers would be self-sustaining. However, their environments are continually under threat – sea grasses are dredged as the sea is filled for new land, mangroves are cut or inundated by freshwater run-off, corals are dynamited and estuaries are polluted. Yet it's a tribute to their ability to adapt that, despite all this, seahorses do survive and colonies expand.

1 The first pygmy seahorse found, *Hippocampus bargibanti* **2** and the smallest, *Hippocampus denise*. Other seahorses can be hard to identify as differences in their features in minimal: **3** Thorny *H. histrix* **4** a pregnant male Zebra-snout *H. barbouri* **5** Moluccen *H. moluccensis* **6** Tiger-tail *H. comes*

Andaman Sea

For many people a dive trip to Thailand means just one thing, the Similans, although in reality this has become a generic term for the narrow stretch of the Andaman Sea that parallels the coast of Thailand and up to Myanmar.

This long band of water creates the eastern border of the Indian Ocean starting from the southeast end of the Bay of Bengal, flowing past Thailand and then down to the Straits of Mallaca near Indonesian Sumatra. The Andaman and Nicobar Islands mark its westerly border. Although this may sound like a huge expanse, it is really a small sea about 1,200 kilometres long and 650 kilometres wide. It is also a surprisingly unexplored one – in dive terms anyway. The even narrower strip of sea that runs along the Thai coast and just over the border into Myanmar is the section that gets all the attention as access is straightforward and sailing to all these areas is not too time consuming.

Dive conditions are affected by the Indian Ocean's geological formation. The Andaman Sea drops away to over 3,500 metres and hovers over the meeting point of two tectonic plates. There is some volcanic activity way down at the bottom of the ocean and the constant movement of these underwater features ensures that deep water upwellings continually supply nutrients up to shallows. The second contributory factor to conditions are the actions of the annual monsoon pattern which restricts diving to just half the year.

Thailand and the Andaman Sea may not be inside the Coral Triangle, but the waters are biologically rich all the same.

Locations

There are three main destinations for divers: the Koh Similans Marine Park, the Surin Islands, including the incredible Richelieu Rock and further north the waters of southern Myanmar.

As you are more likely, and most sensibly, going to be on a liveaboard, the only destination choice you will need to make will be based on time and money. Itineraries vary from Similans-only cruises to combinations of all three areas. The further you go, the more time and higher the cost. Do you have enough of either to go all the way to Myanmar, or will one of those elements restrict you to travelling only part-way through this region?

Destinations

Similan islands

Probably the most visited of these destinations, the Similans are the closest to the main liveaboard departure point of Ao Chalong on Phuket although they can also be reached from Khao Lak on the coast a couple of hours to the north of Phuket airport. It is also possible to see and dive the Similans in a long day trip by speedboat from either but this isn't a great option as your time and dive numbers will be limited and if the water is rough, being on a speedboat is never pleasant. Plus the islands are so beautiful: do yourself a favour and book a liveaboard. These depart in the evening from Ao Chalong and you awake to find yourself moored in an incredibly calm and scenic bay ready to explore the underwater realm. You could stay on Similan No 4, Koh Mieng, where there is a small government-run guesthouse and campsite. Some dive operators from Khao Lak base overnight trips around this set-up but be aware it's all a bit on the rustic side. It's unlikely you'll want a lot of down time but when you're not diving you can admire the pristine views or walk on an idyllic, deserted beach.

Surin and Richelieu Rock

This isolated reef system is definitely a liveaboard-only destination with sailing time a further five hours north of the top of the Similans. Again, a few Khao Lak operators travel here in a speedboat but it can take as much as three hours each way and you only get two dives. It just doesn't seem worth it when a liveaboard travels at a leisurely pace and you get four dives a day and time to relax.

The Burma Banks

With the political temperament of Burma, diving has been slow to develop as an industry. However, for many years Thai operators have made special arrangements to cross the border between coastal towns Ranong and Kawthaung, again usually by liveaboard. Apart from a short delay when the immigration officials come on board and you get off to see the town, you would hardly know you had changed countries.

Places to stay and things to do at all these destinations are listed in Drying out on page 264

Thailand Andaman Sea

Similan islands

A legend for divers the world over, the Similans are ringed by perfect beaches and amazing coral reefs. Visibility rarely drops below 20 metres and can reach mythical proportions. Currents sometimes catch divers unawares but, from November to April, conditions are usually excellent with March and April the calmest.

Established as a national marine park in the 1980s, 'similan' means nine in Malay. What makes these nine islands so attractive are their two completely different sides. To the east the reefs have pure white sand floors with hard coral gardens that slope gently down to over 30 metres. Colourful soft corals and sea fans are plentiful, the diving is easy and the pace is calm. The west is much more dramatic, with currents that swirl around huge granite boulders creating spectacular swim-throughs. It's a bit like diving between skyscrapers that have been reclaimed by the sea.

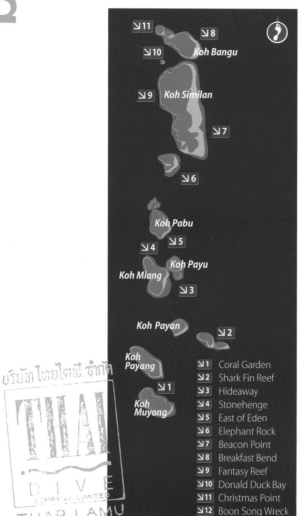

↘11

↘8

↘10   *Koh Bangu*

↘9   *Koh Similan*

↘7

↘6

Koh Pabu

↘5

↘4

Koh Payu

Koh Miang

↘3

Koh Payan

↘2

Koh Payang

↘1

Koh Muyong

↘1   Coral Garden
↘2   Shark Fin Reef
↘3   Hideaway
↘4   Stonehenge
↘5   East of Eden
↘6   Elephant Rock
↘7   Beacon Point
↘8   Breakfast Bend
↘9   Fantasy Reef
↘10   Donald Duck Bay
↘11   Christmas Point
↘12   Boon Song Wreck

↘1	Coral Garden	
💙	Depth	21 m
🔵	Visibility	good
🌊	Currents	none to mild
🔵	Dive type	liveaboard

This gentle and protected site is an ideal introduction to the Similans. The sheltered bay has a white sandy bottom leading to a hard coral plateau. Patches of staghorn are interspersed with plate corals and a small brain coral or two, all swamped by smaller reef fish like bright orange Antipas, blue chromis and damselfish. Soft corals give the bommies a splash of colour as do the anemones and clownfish. You can also see lionfish, puffers and titan triggerfish. The lionfish follow divers around as this area is also used for night dives.

Coral trout sheltering in the fronds of a soft coral

บริษัท ไทยไดฟ์ จำกัด

THAI

DIVE

COMPANY LIMITED

THAP LAMU

ⓢ2 Shark Fin Reef

🕐 **Depth**	26 m
◑ **Visibility**	good
🌊 **Currents**	none
🌐 **Dive type**	liveaboard

If you dive both sides of this reef, you can observe how the Similans have two very different profiles. Shark Fin Reef has a coral garden on one side while on the other is a dramatic slope with large square boulders looking like they have been dumped from a great height. Starting on the deeper side near the south – where the boulders are truly enormous – you can swim between and around them often disturbing big animals like leopard sharks. These are very wary and will swim away at the hint of a diver but they also often come back to the same spot. About two-thirds of the way along, you come to a channel between the rocks which leads to the far side of the reef and the reef gardens there. A lot of colourful fish take advantage of the soft corals to find shelter.

ⓢ3 Hideaway

🕐 **Depth**	17 m
◑ **Visibility**	good
🌊 **Currents**	slight
🌐 **Dive type**	liveaboard

The bays off the south point of Similans No 5 are often used as overnight stops by the liveaboards. The scenery is idyllic and there are a couple of good spots for night dives. You can go quite deep at Hideaway, but the shallower areas are great to explore after dark. The reef starts at about seven metres with patches of coral divided by sandy areas. This is easy night diving as you don't need to worry too much about what is around you while you inspect beneath the patches of staghorn for sleeping fish like the parrots who are blowing their mucous bubbles. There are a lot of shrimp, lionfish and hermit crabs.

ⓢ4 Stonehenge

🕐 **Depth**	25 m
◑ **Visibility**	good
🌊 **Currents**	slight
🌐 **Dive type**	liveaboard

This site must have been named by a Brit, although if you get an Aussie divemaster, references are made to Ayers Rock. You get the idea though – the granite boulder formations here are huge. They are also

ⓢ5 East of Eden

🕐 **Depth**	21 m
◑ **Visibility**	good to excellent
🌊 **Currents**	slight
🌐 **Dive type**	liveaboard

Off Similan No 7, this sloping wall drops to a secondary reef completely encrusted with big fans and rainbows of huge soft corals. Masses of glassy sweepers flit and dance in the light like sparkling stars. Tuna and schooling trevally swim above while the upper reef hides plenty of delicate small creatures like ornate ghost pipefish.

decorated with masses of gorgonians, pastel toned soft corals and many schools of fish. There are batfish, barracuda and jacks just off into the blue, while swimming between the rocks are angelfish, lionfish and white collar butterflies. It's no doubt to do with the currents moving between the rocks but you feel as if you are playing follow-the-leader with the fish sometimes as they follow you about. Or vice versa. If you have time to inspect the rocks there are also plenty of nudibranch egg rings.

You can even catch sight of the indigenous Similans sweetlips here. At night, the site re-ignites with nocturnal activity. Nestling in almost every crevice are cleaner shrimp or tiny pink crabs. Hermit crabs scramble everywhere, arrow crabs poke their noses up from a fan. Stay completely still, but divert your beams a little away from the wall, and you'll be rewarded with tiny, shy cuttlefish peeking out from matching crinoids. Heading back uphill to the sandy sea floor, decorator crabs are on the prowl, along with cowries and cone shells. A stealthy octopus will wait for the right moment to nip out for a quick meal.

Giant jellyfish with commensal fish; diving East of Eden

☻ Never count on the weather

Diving in Thailand was always something we wanted to do so we were thrilled when we arrived in Phuket on 25 April for a four-day liveaboard aboard the *Mermaid*, to the Similan Islands. We knew we were pushing our luck with the weather, arriving so late in the season, but this was the only time we could get away from work.

We were picked up at the airport by the Mermaid Liveaboards manager, who said that she hoped we weren't wishing for too much company on the boat because the only passengers were the two of us and one other guy from England! We were given the master cabin, which was quite lovely; however we realized in the middle of our first night that we wished the beds had been secured to the floor. We experienced an incredibly rough six-hour crossing to the Similan Islands, due to a major storm brewing near India; the ocean was so rough that our beds were slammed from wall to wall all night long! We both felt so bad after that night that we missed the entire first day of diving.

We got up the second morning, feeling terrific and ready to make our first dive of the trip! Unfortunately, due to the poor ocean conditions, we fought a lot of current and surge on practically every dive. The dive trip was not a total bust though – we got to see several types of fish that we had never seen before and we got to see manta rays on two dives. One particular dive stands out in our minds as one of the best; it took place at Koh Bon, a little north of the Similan Island No 9. During this dive, we had the privilege of being entertained by three large manta rays doing the 'manta dance'!

We hovered as motionless as we could in about 40 feet of water, while all three swooped close to our heads, did somersaults in front of us, and swam curiously and gracefully around us. One of the mantas swam within ten feet of us, stared directly into our masks for what seemed like an eternity, and then continued entertaining us with his presence. They are fascinating creatures and mesmerizing to watch. Our English friend had never seen a manta before, so he immediately swam over to us and gave us each 'high fives' with a huge grin on his face!

Because we travelled to Thailand at the end of the ideal diving season, we had fairly poor ocean conditions. However, the *Mermaid* was a nice boat, the crew was great and food was incredible, once we were able to eat! One day we hope to head back to the Similan Islands, and if we do, we will apply the valuable lesson we learned and visit during the middle of the season!

Suzanne and Steve Turek, conservation biologists for the Department of Fish and Game, Redding, California

⬂6	Elephant Rock	
☻	**Depth**	28 m
◑	**Visibility**	good to excellent
☁	**Currents**	can be strong
⬯	**Dive type**	liveaboard

This one of the Similans' most famous sites purely because of the series of unusually shaped granite boulders that reach up from invisible depths and emerge on the western side of the island. On land they are said to mimic the shape of an elephant's head. Beneath the water they tumble over each other to form a complex of arches and tunnels and some of the most dramatic swim-throughs in the entire chain. Small fans nestle into crevices for protection from the surge while critters crawl on the sheer rocky surfaces and slither in and out of burrows. Small tubastrea trees add a hint of green while hawkfish perch on their branches. Swimming over the sand, there are a lot of sea cucumbers. Check these for fantastic imperial shrimp, often with their smaller mate and juveniles. Tiny gobies will sit with them too. Mantis shrimp skitter about in the rubble with lots of blennies while gobies bob up from the rocks. Back up around the boulders there are groups of trevally and schools of small yellow grunts under a ledge. The site can get some quite strong currents as water rushes between the boulders but the action attracts reef sharks, rays and schooling fish. Snappers, butterfly and surgeonfish appear in hundreds rather than handfuls.

Yellowfin goatfish shelter in crevices

⬇7 Beacon Point

🕐	**Depth**	28 m
🕐	**Visibility**	good to excellent
🌊	**Currents**	can be strong
🌀	**Dive type**	liveaboard

At the bottom of Similan No 8 (this is actually Koh Similan) there are a few dive sites all named Beacon: point, reef and beach. It's a highly varied diving area but liveliest on the point to the south of the island. The drop-off is divided by ever-more granite boulders creating a dramatic backdrop to the marine life. The current can get quite strong so it's good to stay in the lee of the rocks when it does. This is what differentiates this site as the strong currents attract bigger fish like the massive schools of big eye trevally that are seen along with passing reef sharks. There are also some very good hard corals which support the usual range of fish – triggers, lionfish and surgeons are common plus you are likely to see the Similans angelfish. Just north of the point there is now a 27 metre-long wooden wreck on Beacon Beach that can also be dived.

⬇8 Breakfast Bend

🕐	**Depth**	31 m
🕐	**Visibility**	good to excellent
🌊	**Currents**	slight to medium
🌀	**Dive type**	liveaboard

At the very top of the Similans chain is Koh Banggu (No 9) and on her eastern side is this charming and easy dive. They say it got its name as diving here makes a great start to the day with sunrays penetrating down onto the gentle sloping reef. There is a lot of rubble but it's interspersed with hard coral patches and there are small soft corals in the shallows. The marine life is good with many nudibranchs, including chromodoris and phyllidia types, crawling over the uneven seabed. (Phyllidias are those ones with warty looking spots on their bodies.) Another far less peaceful creature is the titan triggerfish. Many live on this reef, but they are aggressive only when nesting and the rest of the time you can catch them being cleaned by shrimp. There are also morays, lobster, sweetlips, groupers and plenty of other small fish flitting about.

⬇9 Fantasy Reef

🕐	**Depth**	27 m
🕐	**Visibility**	fair to excellent
🌊	**Currents**	slight to strong
🌀	**Dive type**	day boat

Across on the western side of Koh Similan is this well-named reef which seems to encapsulate all things Similan. There are big boulders and small swim-throughs, plenty of fans and corals in between them and some very good visibility. There is also the chance of quite perky currents, which is probably what attracts so many fish to the reef. The list of species is extensive, with triggerfish – including the shy clown trigger – surgeonfish, rabbitfish, damsels and clownfish. There are a lot of moorish idols in groups and solitary gigantic groupers hanging about in a small cave, the cave itself swamped by tiny glassfish. Note that this site was closed to divers in 1999 to allow it to regenerate. Marine park officials felt it had been damaged by numbers but dive operators say it was illegal fishing. Rumour has it that it is due to reopen.

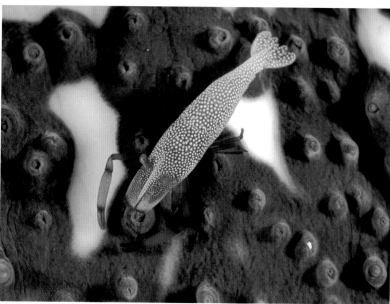

An octopus keeps a wary but curious eye on the photographer; imperial shrimp living on a sea cucumber

↘10 Donald Duck Bay

⬡	**Depth**	19 m
◔	**Visibility**	good to excellent
≋	**Currents**	none
⬒	**Dive type**	liveaboard

This is another site named for the shape of the boulders that sit above the point of a terribly pretty bay. It is also where the liveaboard boats can moor in calm waters so is used frequently for night dives. It's not the tidiest of places in the Similans as there is a campsite nearby and, sadly, quite a lot of rubbish ends up in the water. However, what that means is you almost get to do a muck dive. The usual seascape of boulders decorated with small corals gives way to a gully with a flat bottom. This is the spot to hunt about either by day or night. In the dark there are a lot of typical night-stalkers like curious octopus and giant cuttlefish out on the hunt plus snake eels with their noses just protruding from the sand. A particularly exciting find for good spotters is the almost invisible cockatoo waspfish.

↘11 Christmas Point

⬡	**Depth**	20 m
◔	**Visibility**	excellent
≋	**Currents**	mild to strong
⬒	**Dive type**	liveaboard

Wonder how this one got its name? The site marks the top end of the Similans chain and the visibility here can be very, very good, no doubt as it is swept by more open ocean currents. These can be strong at times and surface conditions a little rough, but below there is good reef with the classic Similans scenery of square cut boulders interspersed with bright hued fans. On one side of the dive, there are some large stony arches to swim through and these are mobbed by schools of fish. Trevally are quite common. Down on the rubble seabed are blue and black ribbon eels, spotted jaw fish and lovely, pure white egg cowries with their jet-black mantles. Occasionally you may find a leopard shark resting here. This is a good site to spot the Similans sweetlips, clown triggerfish, puffers and angelfish.

↘12 Boon Song Wreck

⬡	**Depth**	18 m
◔	**Visibility**	poor to good
≋	**Currents**	slight to mild
⬒	**Dive type**	liveaboard

Also known as the Bansak wreck as it sits just a little way from Bansak beach on the coast, this site is usually visited last and on the way back to port. Like most wrecks, the Boon Song is far more than it appears at first glance. The hull of a tin dredging boat, she is now a solid square of metal resting on the seabed. She sank in 1984 so the structure is very well preserved. You can even see some of the mechanical parts such as gear wheels and metal scoops. Visibility can be quite poor, due to the silty surrounds, but it really doesn't matter. Her real value is as a haven for a wealth of tiny critters. Circumnavigating the hull is like a nudibranch treasure hunt with many more shapes, sizes and colours than you are likely to see elsewhere. While focusing on these diminutive creatures, you also start to notice a whole lot more – estuarine stonefish, tiny flounders on the sand and unusual miniature spindle cowries that grip on to baby whip coral branches. There are honeycomb morays and blotched morays in crevices, lots of lionfish and tiny peacock flounders. Of course the wreck is also known for its resident leopard sharks that nestle on the sand and a school of porcupine puffers that hover constantly over the top deck.

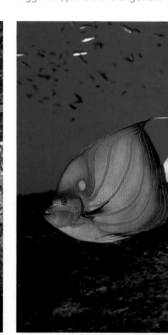

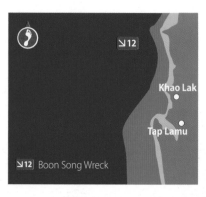

Boulders and fans; the blue-ringed angel, often called a Similans angel as there are so many here

We found this weird creature hanging nose down in the coral. We had no idea what it was, but our log books recorded it as looking a bit like a seahorse... much later we realised it was an ornate ghost pipefish.

Koh Bon and Koh Tachai

Head north from the Similans chain and the first major dive site you encounter is Koh Bon. Shortly after is Koh Tachai. Both islands are now included within the boundaries of the Similan National Park.

Koh Bon is just an hour north of Similans No 9 and has steep, grassy cliffs. It also has one of the most photographed scenes in the Andaman Sea. A cavernous hole perforates part of the island's steep walls so you can see right through to the other side. The main reef consists of a sharp wall that runs to a depth of over 45 metres. It is covered almost completely in soft corals while the deeper sandy parts are where you may see pelagics. A little to the side is the famous Pinnacle dive site.

Koh Tachai is another 25 kilometres further north and is a greener and lusher island. The beaches are pure white and utterly beautiful; this is a promising site for pelagic encounters. The best section of reef runs parallel to the south side of the island.

Koh Tachai ↘15

↘13 The Pinnacle
↘14 West Ridge
↘15 Koh Tachai

Koh Bon ↘13 ↘14

↘13 The Pinnacle, Koh Bon

Depth	35 m	
Visibility	poor to stunning	
Currents	generally strong	
Dive type	liveaboard	

The water around Koh Bon can be gloomy from suspended plankton. The sharp-sided pinnacle rises up from who knows where to about 20 metres. All the rocky surfaces are smothered by yellow soft corals, with clusters of golden toned fans surrounded by yellow snappers. The effect of all the sunny hues in the deep, dark water is rather surreal. Leopard sharks often rest on a ledge while a little way off in the blue are mingled schools of batfish and jacks. There could be as many as 200; perhaps more. The water can be as thick with fish as it is with plankton. The soup attracts a mass of animals to feed: it is a marvellous sight. Unfortunately, hovering at such depth for too long isn't all that wise and a safety stop on a nearby shallow reef is required. Although it will be hard to drag yourself away, you may be rewarded with a glimpse of a manta. They often make appearances, swimming swiftly through the small channel between the pinnacle and the nearby reef, no doubt attracted by the seasonal smorgasbord.

↘14 West Ridge, Koh Bon

Depth	25 m	
Visibility	good	
Currents	generally strong	
Dive type	liveaboard	

After diving the pinnacle, you could swim across to West Ridge but chances are you will do this as a separate dive. The western end of the island extends to an underwater promontory that leads down to well over 30 metres. At the very tip of the exposed promontory there can be some ripping currents that naturally attract bigger schools of fish – masses of snappers,

trevally and sweepers hover just below the divers. Coming back along the reef ridge, the rocks at the bottom are covered with really beautiful soft corals, in shades of blue, yellow and white. There are also big gorgonians and a lot of schooling fish. Starting to move back up to the shallows, the hard corals are in less good shape. The beds of staghorn have been damaged although there are still plenty of animals: sea snakes, grey angelfish and puffers are seen regularly. When you eventually make it up to the shallow, calm waters at about 10 metres, look in the rubble for playful mantis shrimp, flabellina nudibranchs and stealthy scorpionfish.

Leopard shark on the Pinnacle at Koh Bon

⏷15 Koh Tachai	
🌀 **Depth**	35 m
◐ **Visibility**	good to excellent
🔄 **Currents**	generally strong
🌊 **Dive type**	liveaboard

Southeast of the island lies a submerged reef made up of hard corals and scattered boulders. As the currents are nearly always swift here, a mooring rope leads down to where it's possible to shelter from the currents. There are soft corals coating the bommies and crinoids add a splash of brighter colour. At the bottom of the reef a resident school of batfish hovers around a cleaning station, a sea snake passes by and a gang of puffers stand off to the side. An unusual carpet anemone protects porcelain crabs and eggshell shrimp (these have white spots down the insides of their transparent bodies). Around the boulders are masses of swooping jacks; trevally and mackerel nip in and out to feed on glassy sweepers. To complete the complement of pelagic fish, a massive shoal of chevron barracuda swirls constantly above the dramatic pinnacle.

Surin islands

After Koh Bon and Koh Tachai, the Surin National Park islands are the final land masses before Burmese waters. These jungle-covered granite outcrops are enveloped by reefs that are exposed to deep ocean currents.

In total there are five islands in the marine park plus two underwater pinnacles. The islands are ringed by hard coral beds extending a fair distance from the shallow coastal waters. There are frequent pelagic sightings with turtles, reef sharks, Spanish mackerel and schooling barracuda seen on most dives. However, the inshore reefs generally are not as impressive as some of the others in this region so they are dived mostly as an overnight stopover.

The islands attract passing yachts, campers (there is a small campsite on North Surin) and snorkellers while divers target just one destination: 20 kilometres

⏷16 South Point	
🌀 **Depth**	20 m
◐ **Visibility**	fair to good
🔄 **Currents**	none
🌊 **Dive type**	liveaboard

A short distance from the jetty on North Surin, this bay makes a great night dive and is usually done at night as a precursor to arriving at Richelieu Rock as you cannot moor overnight there. The seabed is a mix of sand and coral rubble although there are some very good hard corals in patches.

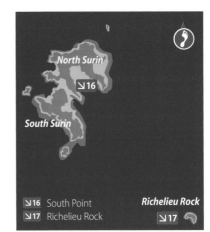

⏷16 South Point	⏷17 Richelieu Rock
⏷17 Richelieu Rock	

from Surin is the dive site that has it all – Richelieu Rock. An hour to the east, this isolated open ocean pinnacle rises from 40 metres and extends to the surface.

As a dive, it is completely, justifiably famous. In fact, if the gods are smiling on you and your dive buddies, this could be the one do-not-miss dive of your life.

The staghorns are alive with critters. It's easy to spot large grey morays as they poke their noses out to feed and the crustaceans are incredibly prolific. A torch beam highlights the reflective eyes of large, bright red crabs, tiny hermit and decorator crabs on the sand, coral crabs and green eyed shrimp up in the staghorn. Look in the crevices for young lobsters and saron shrimp. These hairy, highly patterned shrimp are never seen in daylight. The scorpionfish move out onto the sand to feed as well, so are hardly camouflaged as they would be during the day.

Chevron Barracuda at Koh Tachai; crabs and flounder on Surin

17 Richelieu Rock

🔷 **Depth**	32 m
◑ **Visibility**	medium to stunning
🌊 **Currents**	none to strong
⬇ **Dive type**	liveaboard

Describing the splendour that is Richelieu Rock in such a short space is more than a challenge – it's nigh on impossible. What's equally impossible is seeing this extensive site in just one underwater visit. It will take several immersions over the mound to be really sure you have seen it all and it seems every time you go, you discover more. This isolated, submerged hill is without doubt the dive site that has it all – from the tiniest of tiny critters to the ultimate in grace, size and beauty: the whaleshark.

The rock is only just exposed at low tide making it a danger for passing boats without navigational equipment. The reef is shaped a little like a crescent moon, positioned with it's tips to the south, and

is made up of a large mound with many smaller mounds scattered around its edges. Dives usually start with entry over the centre of the largest mound from where you can swim towards the east or west to the deepest points. These areas are absolutely smothered in soft corals and on the lip of the reef, before it drops off, you are likely to pass enormous coral groupers, giant potato cod, reef sharks, barracuda, snappers and even a manta on occasion.

Back on the slopes there are a wealth of smaller creatures to admire: lionfish, scorpions, cowries and seasnakes compete with trumpetfish, angelfish and butterflies for attention.

In between the smaller mounds and the main one there are many small channels and crevices to explore and it is in these that you will find seahorses, white-eyed morays, clownfish in their anemones, mantis shrimp, turtles and so much more.

Every surface seems to house yet another fascinating marine resident. What's more, these aren't isolated incidents: you won't see just one ornate ghost pipefish, but four in one crevice and then a few more in the next.

Sometimes, and far less often than you could wish for, you will hear the distant sound of manic tank banging. This is the signal that a whaleshark has been spotted and you should make a mad dash towards the sound. When the conditions are right, you may be really lucky and see several in one day. Both adults and juveniles are attracted to the rock and this is one of the few places in the world where you can still dive with them. On our last trip to Richelieu we were lucky enough to see four there on one day... it was the most amazing moment in time for all of us who were there – so we will let one of our buddies on that day tell the story!

" On one single dive we saw minute harlequin shrimp pairs and four enormous whalesharks, two curious turtles and several elegant seahorses. Not to mention the masses of morays, giant groupers, nudibranchs, ghost pipefish, schooling snappers... the list could go on and on. Suffice it to say, you could spend days here and still not see everything the Rock has to offer.

Lizardfish, saron shrimp and gigantic grouper all live around the Rock

Thailand Dive log Andaman Sea: Richelieu Rock

A first for everything

There were so many firsts: our first time in Thailand, first time on a liveaboard, first time diving on the Rock and the first time I'd achieved a lifelong ambition.

To set the scene, I'm halfway through the first of three dives planned on this world class site and I've already notched up leopard sharks, a huge potato cod, seasnakes and a turtle when I find myself with my head down a crevice trying to position my camera for a shot of two delightful harlequin shrimp.

Suddenly, I felt this hand grab my ankle and as I turn around, all my buddies are screaming, pointing and most of all grinning and I soon realize why. Out in the crystal clear blue water a shadow is emerging, not any old shadow but a shadow covered in white spots. It's one of those surreal moments when it takes your brain a few seconds to catch up with your eyes but then it hits you in a wave of euphoria. I realize that I'm about to have an up close and personal encounter with the one thing I've waited a diving lifetime to see, a whaleshark.

Back on the dive deck it's group hugs all around with the first whaleshark sighting for about half the divers onboard but what we didn't realize was that the Rock hadn't finished with us yet, not by a long way. After a surface interval that seemed like an eternity we're back in the water, sort of looking at the reef but with one eye firmly out in the blue. We didn't have to wait long and this time the four-metre baby from the first dive brought along its big seven-metre sister for a look, gliding past us as if they didn't have a care in the world. The pair swim past with a slow and graceful motion, allowing us to take photos and spend a few precious seconds swimming next to these amazing creatures whose beauty and presence is unsurpassed and only matched by the diversity and excitement of diving the Rock. In a few short hours this had become, and still is, my favourite dive site on the planet.

The Rock didn't let us down and the whalesharks joined us for our third and final dive of the day. I knew whalesharks were sometimes seen on the Rock, but never in my wildest dreams did I think it would happen for me. It was definitely a day of 'Dom Perignon' moments and a day of fulfilled lifetime ambitions.

Andrew Perkins, Manager, Retail Superstore, Telford, UK

Mergui Archipelago

These days most liveaboard operators extend their itineraries to include some time amongst the spectacular reefs in the south of Myanmar – and for good reason. The diving here is superlative. The reefs that abut the border with Thailand are very impressive – there are several marine sanctuaries and a wide variety of habitats.

Just a short sail north of Richelieu Rock you cross the border to Kawthaung. A visa is not required but some convoluted formalities take place on the boat, before it resumes its trip to the Mergui Archipelago, passing some incredible scenery along the way. The reefs are not significantly different to those that run north from Thailand but they are mostly pristine. Inshore sites suffer a little from silt run-off and boat traffic. Even so, there is plenty of exciting muck diving to be had just an hour or so from port, although the further out you head the better it gets.

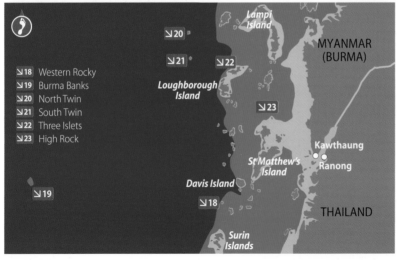

↘18	Western Rocky
↘19	Burma Banks
↘20	North Twin
↘21	South Twin
↘22	Three Islets
↘23	High Rock

↘18	**Western Rocky**	
🌀	**Depth**	25 m
◐	**Visibility**	excellent
🌀	**Currents**	slight
⬭	**Dive type**	liveaboard

How do you improve on diving Richelieu Rock? Simple, sail up to Burma's Western Rocky. This area was closed for quite some time to allow it to regenerate. Now it is a site that rivals her Thai neighbour. An enormous submerged pinnacle is ringed by sheer walls that plummet vertically from the surface. The sharp sides are covered in glistening cup corals and crinoids grip onto crevices. There is a splendid cathedral-like arch at the end of the south wall. Swimming through it and onto the next segment of wall you are surrounded by masses of stripy snappers. To the east of the arch is a tunnel that cuts completely through the rock. Its opening at the base on the south side sits at around 18 metres and you can swim in to find huge lobsters and (fingers crossed) a nurse shark. The tunnel runs for about 30 metres and you can just see the exits at the far side. There are two, but one is too narrow for divers to use easily. Next, fin to the western end of the rock, which has the prettiest soft corals.

Beside the main rock, further east, are a series of smaller pinnacles with more walls to explore. Reaching them requires passing over the most fantastic fan corals smothered in glassy sweepers. Banded sea snakes investigate tiny caves and porcelain crabs and eggshell shrimp shelter in carpet anemones. Schools of squid take refuge in the lee of a wall and more nurse sharks hide in the caverns. You may even be fortunate enough to encounter a whaleshark here.

❝❞ Jill and I rolled in and dropped to five metres to wait for the boys and next thing, I hear Jill rattling her shaker like a mad woman... a baby male whaleshark was right below us.

Burma Banks

Depth	25 m
Visibility	excellent
Currents	slight
Dive type	liveaboard

It's a great pity that when a site gets well known as the place to see sharks, it also gets a bit too well known to fishermen. A few years ago the Burma Banks were absolutely bereft – not a shark to be seen. However, more recently they seem to have returned and the area is once again a great shark spotting destination.

The Banks cover a large area and encompass several different sea mounds and a variety of dive sites. Silvertip Bank is the most visited for obvious reasons. The mound rises from 500 metres to about 15 and at the top a long plateau is carpeted with small fans and some pretty, soft corals. There's schooling snappers, trevally and queen triggerfish. The reef edge drops dramatically and if you peer down into the depths you're likely to glimpse some of the many whitetips that pass by. Back up on the flatter section, other species of shark make irregular appearances – reef sharks, nurses and even the large silvertips. They swoop around divers and seem quite curious but slide away just as easily.

On occasion, crews set up a shark attraction dive and although it may not be your thing, it is one of the rare moments when you get to see apex predators. The bait bucket always attracts a few wary young silvertips and the regular star of the show, Max, a resident nurse shark. She appears to be almost tame but should naturally be treated with respect. The rest of the site has more to see but that gets lost in the excitement. There are dogtooth tuna and octopus and smaller fish include rockmover wrasse, dartfin gobies and sand gobies with their commensal shrimp.

Scenes and creatures from Silvertip Bank: a silvertip; giant grouper; Max; and everyone at the bucket!

↘20 North Twin

🕐 **Depth**	24 m
🔆 **Visibility**	fair to good
🌊 **Currents**	mild to strong
🌊 **Dive type**	liveaboard

North and South Twin Islands sit about 20 kilometres apart, with North being the smaller of the two. The currents here can be quite strong and when they're not, the visibility goes way down. At the bottom of the island a pinnacle drops from just below the surface to about 30 metres.

↘21 South Twin

🕐 **Depth**	30 m
🔆 **Visibility**	fair to excellent
🌊 **Currents**	none to slight
🌊 **Dive type**	liveaboard

A little larger than her sister at a kilometre long, South Twin can be one of the more interesting of Murgui's sites plus the dives here are comparatively easy with gentle conditions around the bays to the south of the island. An enormous variety of marine life is found on these reefs which feel very similar to parts of the Similans. Granite boulders tumble down from the side of the island and onto a sloping reef. Visibility is usually good as you swim through the gullies past small soft corals and fans,

Around this outcrop, the underwater landscape is reminiscent of the Similans with large granite boulders creating swim-throughs and crevices that are thick with seafans and purple soft corals. The marine life displays a real contrast. One minute, a nurse shark appears, lazily swimming past then a few seconds later you notice two minute flabellina nudibranchs crawling along a hydroid, competing for the tastiest bits to chew on. Fish life includes angelfish, parrotfish, surgeons and if you pause to look at the fans you will catch the resident hawkfish staring back at you.

discovering many critters along the way. You can dive in several different directions – and at night – so the list of finds is huge. There are blue ribbon eels, honeycomb and yellowmargin morays. Shells are prolific with spider conchs and gorgeous cowries under tiny rocky overhangs. The tiger cowrie is easy enough to spot, but not the *Mauritia maculifera* cowrie, which has no common name but definitely lives here. There are so many nudis, it's a struggle to remember which species you have seen and even with a picture you can't identify some. Up in the shallows are substantial hard coral gardens. Young whitetip sharks are seen lurking beneath these, while flitting about above are the typical fish species like anthias and damsels, and small schools of rainbow runners pass by.

Fan corals on the pinnacle at North Twin; a pair of rare nudibranchs, *Dermatobranchus ornatus*, which eat gorgonians; a Tiger cowrie prowling the reef with his mantle extended

❽ Undercurrents

Myanmar: a message from the publishers

The diving in Burmese waters is superb but should divers visit a country with one of the worst human rights records in the world? While many contend that sport and politics should not mix, we feel it necessary to make an exception here. Human rights groups and campaigners, including Aung San Suu Kyi, the Nobel Peace Prizewinning, democratically elected leader who is held under house arrest by the government, argue that tourists should not visit the country because this lends moral credence to the regime as well as giving it financial support. Those against a boycott argue that visiting the country gives tourists the chance to financially support the local communities who rely on money from visitors, that international visitors act as a defence against further human rights abuses and that isolating the regime provides no incentive for it to change. Ultimately the decision as to whether or not to visit the country is a personal one. Footprint would advise all potential visitors to make themselves aware of the arguments on both sides in order to make a fully informed decision.

🌀 Big puppies?

From the second we dropped in on Three Islets, I knew that it was going to be one of *those* dives that's simply not going to go how it's meant to. First, we had been told it was a great dive for spotting all sorts of small creatures including the tigertail seahorses so I'd put the macro lens on the camera. Next, our buddies disappeared ahead of us into a canyon then, as we reached the swim-through, some rigid current hit. And Jill just hates current. All the same, we made our way through, and then the last straw: a whole gang of grey reef sharks appeared. Oh boy! now I really knew Jill wasn't going to be happy – this was the closest we had ever been to any sharks, and they are simply not her favourite creature. Yet these majestic beasts were swimming about in the current so playfully, it made me think of puppies jumping in and out of the waves on our local beach. They ignored us of course, we are just not interesting to them, while I sat there holding Jill with one hand and my useless camera in the other.

Sean and Jill Keen, Bexhill-on-Sea, UK

🅂22	**Three Islets**	
🕐	**Depth**	27 m
🌓	**Visibility**	poor to fair
🌊	**Currents**	slight to strong
🌊	**Dive type**	liveaboard

Also known as Shark Cave, this fantastic site consists of three small islands that only just break the surface of the water. The middle is the largest at about 100 metres long and is the main focus of most dives. A shelving area on one side leads down to a point where the rocky surfaces are covered in crinoids, tubastrea and other small corals that provide homes to many small creatures: orang-utan crabs nestle in a yellow coral, there are rare tiger-tail seahorses that are attached to finger sponges, lots of morays and even some fire urchins. Aggressive mantis shrimp crack open shells on the reef wall and will not be diverted from their task by divers. On the north of the island a murky cavern divides the island. To reach it you swim through a small cave between the rocks to find a channel that is home to grey reef sharks. The currents here can be hard to fight so you may just get a quick glimpse or come back on another dive to watch them patrol up and down the channel. They have been known to be aggressive so be warned that it's best to sit near the side walls. Swimming back out to the sloping part of the reef, there are long snout pipefish, jawfish in the sand, tiny octopus, several mantis shrimps and masses of lionfish out and prowling. More yellow long snout pipefish appear near a Crown of Thorns starfish. It's always sad to see these as are they are so destructive but they are also food for the minute boxer crabs that can sometimes be found hiding underneath.

A honeycomb moray standing guard over a cowrie shell; the tiger-tail seahorse (left)

🅂23	**High Rock, One Tree Island**	
🕐	**Depth**	33 m
🌓	**Visibility**	fair to good
🌊	**Currents**	slight to medium
🌊	**Dive type**	day boat

There's this rather comical but very pretty rock sitting in the middle of nowhere with a lone tree crowning it. Below the water, it transforms into a pinnacle that is divided in two with sheer sides forming a wall on the northeast and a rocky slope falling from the southwest side. Lively currents make it worth sticking close to the reef while hunting out some of the resident critters. For such an open water dive it's odd that small critters seem to grab most of the attention: 25-centimetre-long nudibranchs are covered in fronds and look just like a piece of seaweed; intricate ornate ghost pipefish sit on fans and more unusual long snout pipefish are on the seabed. Frogfish hide at the back of fan corals while a seahorse pair, one yellow, one dark brown and heavily pregnant, are be spotted with their tails gripping onto finger sponges. Toxic sea urchins with their commensal cardinalfish and squat lobsters decorate the sea floor. While gassing off at the top of the reef in shallow waters, there are masses of scorpionfish, urchins and gobies. You might even spot a barracuda or a school of trevally, although more likely is a titan triggerfish.

Drying out

Phuket, Phi Phi and Krabi have so many options for places to stay that you really are spoilt for choice. Make the most of it because all other Andaman Sea diving is, by definition, boat based. Although there are certainly plenty of those to choose from, too.

Phuket
Dive centres

Calypso Divers, T+66 (0)76 330869, calypsophuket.com. Located on Kata Beach this broad-ranging company conducts everything from novice PADI courses right through to 5 night liveaboards as far as Richelieu Rock. Their overnight trip to the Phi Phi Islands with land accommodation included is a great use of time and goes to the best sites in the area. Day trips from US$100, Phi Phi special around US$300.

EuroDivers, T+66 (0)76 280814, euro-divers.com. Day-trip dives run from a central reservations office in Ao Chalong plus bases in several top-class hotels around the island.

Sea Fun Divers, T+66 (0)76 330124, seafundivers.com. Day-trip specialists with schedules to all the sites outside Phuket and heading towards Phi Phi. Smart and spacious boat. Located at Kata Beach and also in the Meridien Hotel, Karon. Full range of courses available. Day trips from US$120.

Sleeping

$$-$ **Ao Chalong Villa and Spa**, T+63 (0)2 854 8888, aochalongvillaandspa.com. This small resort is tucked away in a lane a short distance from Chalong Jetty. (The walk is 20 mins but only when the tide is out.) Rooms vary but are great value and very comfortable. This is a quiet location, with some rooms fronting the bay, the rest are around the pool in delightful gardens. The onsite restaurant is superb and has authentic Thai food.

$ **Kata Minta**, T+66 (0)76 333283, kataminta.com. Cute, small boutique-style hotel just off Kata Beach. Good facilities, rooms are decorated in a Thai style and just a 5-min walk from the beach.

Eating

Restaurants include stalls in night markets (Patong's is amazing) to 5-star cuisine in the top hotels. The turnover of restaurants is frequent and what was good on one trip may not be the same on the next. For the best, up-to-date recommendations ask your divemaster or, if you like Thai cuisine, look for the places where locals are eating. A row of famous seafood restaurants lines the beach at Chalong. They serve well-priced, delicious fish under the palm trees.

Phi Phi
Dive centres

Phi Phi Scuba, T+66 (0)76 385 518, phiphi-scuba.com. Located on the front at Ton Sai Bay with a full complement of dive services.

Sleeping

$$-$ **Bay View Resort**, T+66 (0)75 601127, phiphibayview.com. Large resort with bungalows sitting along a tree-lined, terraced hill. Facing Laem Hin Beach, the hotel is 5 mins from Tong Sai Jetty on Phi Phi Don. The resort collects guests in a longtail boat and will arrange diving.

Ao Nang, Krabi
Dive centres

Aqua Vision, Ao Nang, T+66 (0)75 637415, aqua-vision.net. One of Ao Nang's newer and larger dive centres, works with many hotels including Wanna's and, at the other end of the price scale, the Sheraton.

Sleeping

$$-$ **Wanna's Place/Andaman Sunset**, T+66 (0)75 637484, wannasplace.com. Wanna's is on the front at Ao Nang beach in a very convenient location, although it is quite busy nearby. Good rooms in the main or cute bungalows. The restaurant should not be missed.

Eating

Similar to Phuket the range and variety of restaurants is wide. A special mention has to go to Wanna's Place as the Thai beef salads are simply amazing.

Other options

With the continuing spread of tourism development in the area around Phuket, there is no reason to be limited to staying on the island itself. Try Khao Lak for closer access (hence shorter day trips) to the Similans or Koh Lanta, south of Krabi, to get nearer to Hin Muang but still within sight of Phi Phi. Contact these companies if you fancy somewhere a little more remote.

Dive centres

Sea Bees Diving, T+66 (0)76 485174, sea-bees.com. This extensive business has a base in Ao Chalong on Phuket, but they are also well positioned on lovely Khao Lak beach, an hour or so north. They run day trips, courses and have 2 liveaboards, so there are masses of options.

Lanta Divers, T+66 (0)75 684208, lantadiver.com. Based on Koh Lanta, this Swedish operation can put together full packages and dive trips around the south.

Ao Chalong Villas and bay in the background

Thailand Drying out Phuket gulf

The Similans, Surin and Richelieu

The Similan Islands are 55 nautical miles northwest of Phuket and Surin is 110 nautical miles. Consequently, this is really liveaboard territory with very few options for diving this area as a land-based trip. The Thai royal family does have a rather lovely place on Similan No 4, but the only public accommodation (also on No 4) is a campsite with tents and a few simple bungalows – not really a place for divers toting loads of equipment with them. Likewise, there is limited accommodation on Koh Surin Nua.

Myanmar

Diving in Myanmar is limited to much the same system as diving the Andamans. Many better liveaboards include the waters just over the border in their routes and will handle all formalities. Immigration at the border between Ranong and Kawtheung simply means paying a 'Port and Park fee' of US$150 in clean notes and getting your passport stamped. The officials usually come on board to do this. A local guide/interpreter is then installed on the boat, and should you wish to disembark, there is enough time to admire the dazzling gold temples and tour the local shops.

Liveaboards

Arranging to dive the Andaman Sea is no great difficulty. There are many, many operators from budget to luxury but over the last couple of years there have also been some big changes to the local scene. Some of the better known liveaboards have gone and new ones have come in to take their place. Remember that those costing more will generally be of a higher quality and have added extras like en suite bathrooms and soft drinks included. Ask enough questions to ensure your choice has the right facilities for you (see page 8). Check out:

MV Black Manta, whitemanta.com
MV Jazz, mvjazz.com
MV Mermaid I, mermaid-liveaboards.com
MV Philkade, philkade.com
MV Queen Scuba, coralgranddivers.com
SY Siren, worldwidediveandsail.com

Phuket gulf

Phuket Town Mostly a retail therapy destination (and a very good one), there are also some lovely, old Sino-Chinese buildings in the Chinatown district.
Wat Chalong Temple South from Phuket Town, this is just one of 29 Buddhist monasteries on the island but the most important. The buildings are very ornate. Free, but dress modestly.
Thalang National Museum Just north of Phuket town, this contains ancient artefacts and exhibits on the famous Battle of Thalang when two Thai heroines repelled the Burmese Army. Entry US$1.
Phuket Aquarium This surprisingly good aquarium is sited on Cape Panwa. There are jellyfish exhibits, a hatchery, a walk through tunnel and nature trails outside. Great for families. Entry US$3.
Khao Sok National Park A few hours' north of Phuket, this protected lowland rainforest has animal conservation projects and entertainment such as canoeing and elephant treks. All-inclusive safaris cost US$75 for 1 day or 3 days, US$250.
Koh Tapu Now known as James Bond Island, this is a two-hour boat ride from Phuket and is incredibly pretty but also highly touristy. A day trip to the bay by boat, passing Nail Island, includes a stop at a sea gypsy village on the way back. Tours can be as much as US$100.
Phi Phi If you don't stay on the Phi Phi islands you can always retread Leonardo's steps for a day. Return ferry trips up to US$30, day tours substantially more.
Songkran If you're in Phuket in April you'll catch the Thai New Year water festival. It is heralded by masses of Thais filling plastic bins with water and ice, driving the streets and ditching it over the unwary. And they do love dousing tourists! The tradition behind this energetic event lies in the cleaning of hands and washing away any bad thoughts or actions. Scented water is also poured over the shoulder and slowly down the back while saying good wishes and words of blessing for the New Year. Great fun and completely harmless so join in the spirit of the day.
Krabi and Tiger Cave Temple The town has good shops and from here you can easily reach this temple with its nature trail and many shrines set in caves. Then climb the 1237 steps to the mountain-top statue of the Buddha.

Bangkok

Completely manic, outrageously noisy and entertaining beyond belief, 24 hours in Thailand's capital guarantees a high-voltage stopover.

Although you could spend a week there, a single day's itinerary will give a taste of the city's best features. Start by taking a three-wheeled tuk-tuk ride to the **Grand Palace**, a superlative example of traditional Thai architecture. Inside the complex is the Temple of the Emerald Buddha, **Wat Phra Kaew**, Thailand's most sacred temple. Next, walk the short distance to the **Chao Praya River**. If you have a good map, pass by the unusual **Royal Barges Museum** then go on to Tha Chang Pier. Hop on the Chao Phraya Express river boat to lovely **Wat Arun**, the Temple of the Dawn, which is directly opposite. If you started early, re-embark for a short cruise upriver and back, which will give a local's view of Thai river life. Hop off at Thra Phra Arthit jetty. From here you can walk to *the* place for cheap designer goods, **Khao San Road**. This travellers' hang-out is full of shops and cheap but good restaurants. Those along the river are a good lunch option too but more expensive. And finally for a touch of class, take a taxi ride to the museum at **Jim Thompson's House**. Credited for creating the silk industry, his home is now full of interesting exhibits.

Touring

If you have a second day, there are several interesting places within easy reach of Bangkok. The ancient Siamese capital is at **Ayutthaya**, an hour north by road. This World Heritage site has some amazing architectural ruins of temples and palaces. Go to Damnoen Saduak for the famous – but very touristy – **floating markets** where canals are packed with boats piled high with fruit and vegetables. And, of course, you can reach the **River Kwai** if you are interested in war history. All these can be achieved within a day, and some tours will cover both the markets and the River Kwai. Tours cost upwards of US$60.

Sleeping

$$$ **The Peninsula Bangkok**, T+66 (0)2 8612888, bangkok.peninsula.com. On the river for honeymoons and special events.
$$ **Holiday Inn**, T+66 (0)2 2384300, ichotelsgroup.com. Central location with easy airport access.

Eating

With everything from fast food to top-notch hotel cuisine, be bold and walk into any restaurant where you see locals eating something good. If the menu is in Thai, point at your neighbour's meals.

Transport

Tuk-tuks offer big-thrill rides through the city, but always negotiate the price before getting in. Taxis are less fun but metered and air-con. The Chao Praya Express river boats are cheap and stop at nearly all of the above places of interest.

Top: Wat Arun and Bangkok river ferry. Bottom: ancient Ayutthaya; one of the Royal Barges; the Grand Palace

Thailand Drying out Andaman Sea

Gulf of Thailand

There will be many who feel the Gulf of Thailand deserves more attention than is given here and, credit where it's due, there are plenty of reasons to visit this side of the country. The main one being that when the weather is off on the west, it's just delightful in the Gulf. However, as the east coast is not open to the rigours and influences of the Indian Ocean it has less in the way of prolific reefs.

Koh Samui is the main tourist island. It is very pretty with an excellent infrastructure and plenty of accommodation on picture-postcard beaches. For diving though, the small reefs around the island are not all that interesting and they tend to be murky. The gentle, shelving beaches are popular spots for taking a course and, once training is underway, most centres take divers to the nearby Ang Thong National Marine Park where hidden lagoons and sheer limestone cliffs reflect the style of the underwater scenery. There are 42 seperate islands in the park but the sea surrounding them is very shallow. While the Gulf does reach depths of up to 60 metres in places, the waters in Ang Thong are rarely more than 10 metres deep and the visibility is never crystal clear due to fresh water run-off from the mainland. However, these are ideal conditions for novices. The reefs are pretty, the diving is pleasant but not too challenging and it's great for snorkellers.

A little north, Koh Tao along with her near neighbour, Ko Nang Yuan, have recently become the epicentre of diving in the Gulf of Thailand. The reason is simple. Unlike Samui, where you really need to travel for an hour or more to reach better dive sites, these islands have diving just seconds from the beach. The reefs are ideal for beginners and there are many dive centres catering for them. There's plenty to see including resident green and hawksbill turtles. Koh Tao was named after the island's turtle-like shape, and the island is also a breeding ground although over-development has caused problems both for the turtles and the reefs.

There is some positive news though. Around Koh Tao, there are several deep water pinnacles that provide some of the best diving in the region. However, you must remember that conditions in the Gulf are highly variable which is why serious divers tend to stick to the west coast. Even in peak season visibility can be as low as three metres, but will clear to an incredible 40 metres in an instant. The shallow seabed and current patterns are such that sediment never has the opportunity to disperse to deeper waters.

Locations

The best diving and facilities are, without doubt, accessed from Koh Tao. There are a few liveaboards, but schedules are best described as flexible, meaning that if the boat isn't full it won't go. Be sure to check the operators' policy on this before making a trip just for that reason.

Destinations

Koh Samui

This island is a perennial favourite for those who want a typical sun, sand and sea holiday. And for good reason. The beaches on Samui are delightful and, compared to Phuket on the opposite coast, things are a little less manic. The most popular beaches are those closest to the airport. **Chaweng,** just to the south, is a long arc of perfect white sand with views of the rising sun. There are masses of hotels along the bay but most tend to focus on the package-holiday market. This feel spills over to a lively daytime beach-bar scene. Nightlife is popular and extensive but the majority of bars and restaurants (along with shops and banks) are along the main road to the rear of the beach stretch. A little further south is **Lamai Beach.** This is a little smaller and a little quieter but not all that different. The area was once a backpackers' hangout, so the feel is more laid-back than Chaweng although there are just as many facilities. **Bhoput** and **Big Buddha beaches,** sit together in a bay to the north of the airport. It is a more characterful part of Samui with the 'old fisherman's village' in Bhoput having a traditional feel. Big Buddha attracts families more than party animals although there are still plenty of those. Speedboats for Koh Tao leave from the jetty in the middle of the bay. *Distance from airport: up to 30 mins*

Koh Tao

Once Samui became a major destination, the traveller-set moved away and onto Koh Tao. The island was once a small fishing community, but is now one of Southeast Asia's most popular destinations, partly due to the novel, *The Beach,* by Alex Garland. It was here that his imaginary traveller came although the movie was filmed over on Phi Phi. The once almost deserted island as immortalized in the book, is now a fairly developed place with many rooms and restaurants. **Mae Haad** is where the boats arrive. It's a busy spot but charming enough with shops and a post office. There are a few resorts, but most people head up one bay to white-sand **Sairee Beach** which is only about 10 minutes' walk away. This is the most popular with bungalows and dive centres galore. There's also a small fishing museum and a temple. *Distance from airport: up to 2 hrs*

Places to stay and things to do at all these destinations are listed in Drying out on page 271

The lotus flower, used to pay homage to the Buddha; longtail boat; prow of a dive boat; Chaweng Beach

Thailand Gulf of Thailand

Koh Samui and Koh Tao

Beautiful white-sand beaches, lush green hills and turquoise-blue waters. You could hardly go wrong visiting these or any of the other scenic islands that pepper the Gulf of Thailand as they all have access to the same local dives.

Koh Phangan and Nang Yuan are just two more popular options but whichever island you stay on, you will need to travel to experience the more advanced dive sites as they are all a way off in exposed open ocean. Koh Tao, however, is the most central and has the best shore and local diving with sheltered bays making it ideal for novices or those who like peaceful dive days in between visits to the more uptempo ones.

↘1	Hin Bai (Sail Rock)	
🌐	**Depth**	30 m
◑	**Visibility**	good to excellent
🌊	**Currents**	mild to strong
🌅	**Dive type**	day boat

One of the most famous dive trips is to Hin Bai or Sail Rock. Jutting out of the water 18 kilometres off Samui's north shore, and about halfway between Phangan and Tao, this rock rises from 30 metres to just above the surface. It is covered in beautiful green and yellow corals and frequented by large marine animals like reef sharks and rays. Its unique feature, though, is the spectacular journey upwards through an underwater chimney that is flooded with beams of sunlight. It feels like ascending inside a cathedral spire. The entry point is at 19 metres and the exit at five, where you emerge to find yourself surrounded by carpets of anemones and their many resident clownfish. The outer walls are carved with lots of small holes with, it seems, a white-eyed moray in each. Visibility here is some of the best in the Gulf as the pinnacle is an exposed site and the currents keep plankton and sediment on the move.

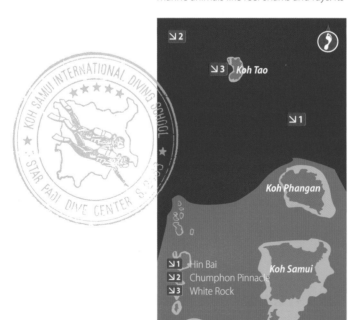

↘2

↘3 Koh Tao

↘1

Koh Phangan

Koh Samui

↘1 Hin Bai
↘2 Chumphon Pinnacle
↘3 White Rock

⌖2 Chumphon Pinnacle

⏱	Depth	36 m
◔	Visibility	fair to great
〰	Currents	none to strong
⬭	Dive type	day boat

The best dive in this area is undoubtedly Chumphon Pinnacle, where tales of big marine mammals have hit legendary status. A massive granite pinnacle soars from 40 metres to about 16 metres below the surface and is surrounded by a group of smaller ones. Diving here is a bit like a wander through an underwater mountain range. There are large plateaux covered in healthy hard corals, sponges and seawhips which lead back up the pinnacles to reveal a huge variety of life. Giant groupers and batfish are always hovering around while white-eyed morays reside amongst the colourful coral gardens. Not only are huge schools of jacks spotted regularly, but occasionally there are also whalesharks and sailfish. Even whales have been seen.

⌖3 White Rock

⏱	Depth	23 m
◔	Visibility	fair to good
〰	Currents	mild to medium
⬭	Dive type	day boat

Ko Nang Yuan is said to be the only place in the world where three islands are joined together by sandbars. The islands are ringed by a variety of shallow dive sites and there are some beautiful arches to swim through. The most exciting dive is probably White Rock, which is actually two submerged granite boulders sitting 12 metres apart. The site is a great place for finding all sorts of reef creatures like stingrays and butterflyfish. Being quite shallow, it also makes a good night dive. However, its main claim to fame is local personality, Trevor, the terrible triggerfish. This giant trigger is a chap with an attitude problem and, despite being a permanent resident on a fairly busy dive, has been known to nip at unwary divers' fins.

White-eyed moray saying hi; Trevor the terrible saying goodbye – hopefully

🐋 Whale of a time

Having finally managed to organize time off that coincided with a trip that the technical liveaboard *MV Trident* was doing, two of us set off from Phuket to drive across to the Gulf of Thailand and catch a ferry from Chumpon to Koh Tao before boarding the boat.

The incredibly bad weather on the ferry over was the first indication that the trip might not be going ahead as planned. Once on Koh Tao we headed off to meet the Trident guys – our luck was out and the four-day trip was cancelled, but in place of that they agreed to dive some of the wrecks closer to home. Once we were on the first wreck for the day we dropped down to 60 metres to find the visibility was only a couple of metres. We decided it was all a bit of a loss so we headed back towards Koh Tao then decided at the last minute to stop at Chumphon Pinnacle to see if we could see any sharks.

We dropped into the water with our twin sets as we had no recreational dive gear onboard and headed down to 30-odd metres. My buddy gets out the Evian bottle – he's got that in one hand and his camera in the other, and waits for the sharks to appear. At this point I look up to see a four-metre or so whaleshark cruising around us. Meanwhile, my dive buddy is still crinkling the Evian bottle hoping to attract black tips etc, and is completely oblivious to the huge whaleshark cruising above him.

After 30 minutes of whaleshark action we decide to move on and check out the rest of the pinnacle as it had been a year or so since we dived it. The whaleshark followed us part of the way round before heading off into the blue.

We never did get back to the wrecks that trip as the weather got a lot worse but at least we had the dive all to ourselves with a whaleshark.

Daniel Galt is a dive instructor
who lives and works in Thailand

Life in the deep
Masters of disguise

Swimming across the seabed, eyes scanning the barren view, you notice a small protrusion in the sand. It's a way off but it looks like a snake eel. As you approach, it disappears, then moments later a mantis shrimp pops up. Pause, think, check if your mask has fogged. Fin a little further and the critter drops out of sight; you glance away but moments later a striped sea snake appears in the same spot. You think you are going crazy, but no. It's the mimic octopus and he's just having a laugh at your expense.

There's no doubt about it, octopus and their relatives are some of the most intelligent creatures in the sea. Part of the cephalopod family, which includes squid, cuttlefish and the nautilus, their name comes from the Greek meaning head-footed, a pretty self-explanatory translation. There are over 100 species in the world including numerous ones that live in deep water. What sets them apart from all other marine invertebrates is a highly developed nervous system and a large centralized brain that makes them capable of many skills which seem almost human and some that we would have no chance of achieving.

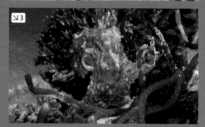

Octopus in particular are great learners, always watching what goes on around them then using the knowledge to solve tasks. In captivity they are known to do things like open bottles, which may seem a little pointless until you see ones underwater that have prised opened a tin or bottle and used it as a secure space for laying their eggs.

They also have fantastic eyesight with a lens at the front of the eyeball and a retina, much like ours. This transmits visual information to the brain but it does so in black and white. The transmission is via the alignment of light waves rather than differences in wave length, which is how we see in colour. Despite this, all octopus families have an incredible capacity to change their appearance using colour. Tiny chromatophores in their skin can be manipulated to change surface hue and patterns so that they match a background or, like the mimic, another animal. They can also change the texture of their skin to match what they see around them by contracting rings of muscle and causing flaps of skin to stand up. It's these features that combine in the mimic octopus to create those masterly disguises. Others adapt these characteristics to protect themselves by becoming almost invisible on the reef or to become a warning (the blue-ringed octopus flashes blue rings to scare off predators). Some even change colour as a greeting to both fellow octos and divers who they genuinely find curious and will sometimes approach.

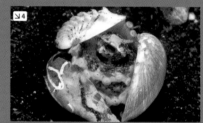

Octopus are soft-bodied creatures, with that huge head-body and eight long limbs extending from it. These form a circle that encapsulates their mouth. Their limbs are referred to as arms and they do have a shell, it's just not all that obvious, having evolved to become two rods inside the bulbous body. Octopus mate when the male passes sperm packets to his intended via a specially modified arm. Once her eggs are fertilized, the female attaches them to a secure surface. Depending on the species, this can be a coconut shell or inside a small cavern in the reef. She then tends them for three to six months before pea-sized babies emerge and the mother dies. The new generation quickly grow and mature until they reach adult size, and mate early the following spring or autumn.

⌐1 Up close and personal with a mimic octopus;
⌐2 A tiny octopus hatchling at just 25 mm long;
⌐3 Octopus use corals and sponges for camouflage;
⌐4 Grabbing three discarded shells to make a house;
⌐5 Common octopus using a tin to protect her brood;
⌐6 A blue-ringed octopus displays a warning.

Drying out

Koh Samui is the tourist heartland of this region and it is well developed. Koh Tao seems to be doing its best to catch up with an equally extensive selection of hotels, bungalows and dive centres but has a slightly more laid-back atmosphere.

Koh Samui

Diving

Samui International Diving School, T+66 (0)77 422386, www.planet-scuba.net. With several offices on Koh Samui including Chaweng and Lamai beaches, this company does everything from novice courses to full packages. They are also located on Koh Tao as Planet Scuba with offices on Mae Haad and Sairee beaches.

Sleeping

$$$ **Poppies Samui Resort**, T+ 66 (0)77 422419, poppies-samui.com. Part of the delightful group born in Bali, these large cottages are set in lush gardens. The onsite restaurant has excellent Thai food and a lovely ambience.

$$-$ **Eden Bungalows**, T+66 (0)77 427645, edenbungalows.com. Simple but pleasant, bungalow complex set near Bhoput Beach and within easy reach of the pier.

Koh Tao

Diving

Master Divers, T+66 (0)77 456314, masterdivers.co.uk. Located next to the Songserm Pier on Koh Tao, this company has several well regarded divisions with day-trip diving, PADI courses, a liveaboard (MV Trident) and a technical diving arm (techthailand.com).

Coral Grand Divers, T+66 (0)77 456431, coralgranddivers.com are on site at the Coral Grand Resort (see below) with full facilities from novice courses all the way up to IDC plus local and day-trip diving.

Sleeping

$$$-$$ **Koh Tao Coral Grand Resort**, T+66 (0)77 456431, kohtaocoral.com. On the northern end of Sairee, this decent, large resort has nice bungalows of differing standards and budgets plus restaurants, bar restaurant.

$$-$ **SeaShell Resort**, T+66 (0)77 456299, seashell-resort.com. Sitting right on Sairee Beach, this good-value small resort has beachside or garden bungalows and a popular seafood restaurant.

Koh Samui

The most populous of the Gulf islands, Koh Samui has some interesting cultural sites. If time is short, arrange a day tour through your hotel centre.

Wat Phra Yai Nicknamed Big Buddha Temple, this intricate structure boasts a 12-m high statue and has superb views over the island. Big Buddha Beach, free.

Wat Khunaram A bit of an oddity, this temple contains a perfectly mummified monk. Near Lamai Beach.

Nathon Samui's main town is full to bursting with shops and markets, ideal for some retail therapy.

Surat Thani To see a working Thai town and the regional capital, catch a ferry to Don Sak (45 km from Samui town). The crossing takes 1½ hours, US$1.30. This may seem a long day but is worth it in mid-October to see the Chak Phra Festival. This is literally 'the procession of hauling the Buddha image'. The lively festival marks the Buddha's return to Earth Land and waterborne processions are organized and include boat races on the Tapi River. Traditional long boats are manned by up to 50 oarsmen.

Thai kickboxing If you fancy watching some real Thai kickboxing, head for the stadium at Chaweng. Seats from US$12.

Koh Tao

The main attractions around all the Gulf islands tend to be nature orientated – walking, waterfalls, idyllic beaches and so on. On Koh Tao you can do all these at once by taking an around-the-island cruise, stopping at scenic hotspots to swim and snorkel. Many people like to hike in the hills, kayaking is popular and you can even go rock climbing.

Singapore

Singapore's emblem, the Merlion, represents the city's early days as a simple fishing village.

Few people would consider any major city as the ideal destination for a dive holiday, yet to reach Southeast Asia's tropical coral-rimmed islands, you will have to pass through a regional hub city.

And as you have to do that, you may as well make the most of it. You could travel through fiesty Kuala Lumpur, historic Hong Kong or brazen Bangkok, but Singapore is the most central, with great onward connections, some of the best facilities, and is a very easy city to get around. Its tone is one of easy adaptability. It has grown up around its Asian soul, while always keeping an eye to the west.

Spend a couple of days here at the start of a trip to acclimatize to the weather, the lifestyle and the psyche of Asia. It is a personal opinion, but this is the premier stopover destination for pre and post diving.

Getting there

Flying into Singapore is straightforward with masses of major airlines travelling this route. There are also excellent onward connections to all of Asia's dive-focussed regions. Incoming flights land at ultra-modern, well-planned Changi Airport where there are three calm and highly efficient terminals: Terminal 1 is mostly used by airlines based in other regional countries; Terminal 2 by Singaporean regional airlines; while Singapore Airlines use Terminal 3 for their long haul flights. All three are spacious, with internal gardens, entertainment zones (watch a movie, play a game, surf the net – all for free) and a good selection of shops, restaurants and cafés.

There are two on-site hotels (airport-hotel.com.sg), which are great for people with a long layover, and one external hotel (CrownePlaza.com). There is also a new budget terminal which is 5-10 minutes from Terminal 2 by free shuttle bus.

Getting around

Changi is on the northeast corner of the island and just 20 minutes or so from the centre of the city. There are several options for getting to and from the airport. Beneath the terminal is the Mass Rapid Transit train station: just a couple of dollars will get you all the way into the city centre. Taxis are not as cheap as they once were, but if there are two (or more) of you, these are quick, plentiful and conveniently drop you at your hotel door. There are also private transfer services with booking counters as you exit from the luggage hall. Once you are in the city, apart from the MRT and taxis there is also an efficient and frequent bus system. For all of these, pick up free maps when you arrive at the airport and consider buying a Tourist Pass for access to all public transport for SG$8 per day (thesingaporetouristpass.com). Self-drive car hire is available but, with limited parking facilities and such a good public transport system, this hardly seems worthwhile.

Touring

Organized tours are easy to come by and any hotel receptionist or concierge will assist. Singapore is also a great walking city. The official Visit Singapore website (visitsingapore.com) has details of both guided and self-guided walks. It's OK to wander about on your own: this is a safe city by western standards. If you're passing through to connect to another flight but have a few hours to spare, free city bus tours to and from the airport leave regularly.

Language

In such a multi-cultural society, where a plethora of Chinese dialects compete with as many Asian ones, you will be pleased to know that English is the language used officially and by all communities. However, even the locals say that they really speak Singlish, an amalgam of local languages and direct translations that rarely fail to amuse – and confuse – at times.

⬊1	Orchard Road	⬊5	Chinatown
⬊2	Little India	⬊6	Sentosa
⬊3	Singapore Flyer	⬊7	Singapore Zoo
⬊4	Riverside	⬊8	Jurong Bird Park

Local laws and customs

There is many a joke about the strict rules and regulations imposed on this small island nation. Some visitors find it ludicrous that seemingly harmless activities are outlawed. These include failing to flush the toilet after use, littering, jaywalking, and chewing gum. Actually, chewing the gun isn't illegal, but manufacturing, selling and dropping it is. However, this adds up to Singapore being one of the cleanest places in the world and one where you won't ever get gum on your shoes or on your trousers. Quite good really.

With such a broad mix of Asian communities, customs are highly varied yet people rarely take offence with foreigners. One thing to be aware of, however, is that you must never lose your temper. The Asian concept of never 'losing face' is strong here. If something goes wrong and you complain, whoever you speak to is unlikely to admit to any wrong-doing. Stay calm, be polite and friendly and you will get the situation resolved. A last note of caution: penalties for possession of drugs are severe and drug trafficking is punishable by death.

Safety and health

While Singapore's unusual restrictions may seem unwarranted, some of them ensure that this is one of the safest places on the planet. Likewise, the country has been ranked as having one of the best healthcare systems in the world. Should you fall ill, you will be well cared for. Ask your hotel for assistance.

Costs

In many ways, Singapore can be regarded as a cheap place to visit – except perhaps when it comes to hotels. Rates can be high, but the calibre of most is good and a little research will get you a room that is well-located, comfortable and not too pricey. Eating out is one of the nation's great treats and you can eat well for virtually nothing (or rather a lot) but there are plenty of options. Transport is cheap too, entry fees to tourist sites are often nominal and there are many things to do that are completely free.

Tipping is not the norm. Hotels and restaurants will have a set service charge but it is considered polite to leave some extra change for taxi drivers, stall holders and other services where you may have paid in cash.

❝❞ This is – in our opinion – Asia's most accessible city, especially for travellers who fly for up to 24 hours to reach one of the region's spectacular dive destinations.

 Tourist information → the official government website can be found at visitsingapore.com.

Fact file

International flights	AirAsia, British Airways, Qantas, Singapore Airlines/Silk Air, Thai Airways, United, Virgin
Departure tax	Included in your ticket
Entry	EU, US and Commonwealth - valid passport required for stays of up to 30 days
Ground transport	MRT, buses, taxis
Money	US$1 = 1.45 Singapore dollars (SGD)
Language	English is widely spoken
Electricity	220v, plug type B
Time zone	GMT +8
Religion	Buddhist, plus Christian, Islam, Tao and Hindu
Phone	Country code +65; IDD 001; Police 999

Sights

The majority of visitors stop in Singapore for just three days and although this may be enough time to get a brief overview of the city, you won't have time to scratch beneath the surface. Scratch beneath the surface of this fabulous amalgam of cultures to see what really makes the city tick. Getting around by bus or taxi is easy and cheap, you will see far more by walking. It is hot so a hat and water is vital, along with plenty of stops for cold drinks, snacks and air-con to cool down.

Chinatown

One the most historic parts of the city, this is an ideal walking area. Start at Mosque Street off South Bridge Road to see the **Jamae Mosque**, built in the late 1820s by South Indian Muslims. The **Sri Mariamman Temple** is around the corner. This ornate building is the city's oldest Hindu temple. Going south, South Bridge Road is marked by traditional pawn shops and medical halls. Next on the right are Pagoda and Temple Streets, their **street markets** and stores loaded with Chinese souvenirs that compete with high-end arts and crafts. The food court here is worth stopping at before turning into Trengganu Street and, on the corner of Smith Street, stopping for the old Cantonese opera house, **Lai Chun Yuen**. Back on South Bridge Road, walk a little further south to the turning for **Ann Siang Hill** and **Club Street**. Both are lined with old Chinese remittance (lending) houses and Colonial-style mansions which were mostly built in the 1930s. Look for the unusual use of Chinese decorative design. Nearby, but slightly east, Telok Ayer Street is the location of Taoist **Thian Hock Keng Temple** and the 1920s-built **Chinese Methodist Church**. If you are in Singapore during Chinese New Year look out for traditional festivities and dances.

Riverside

After all that culture, walk back north up South Bridge Road to the **Singapore River** for some cool air and to rest your feet. Divert to the riverside walkway beneath Elgin or Coleman Bridges and hop onto one of the traditional 'bumboats' that ply the river. There are kiosks all along the walkway and a short cruise will take you past **Clarke** and **Boat Quays** and the old Parliament Building complex. There are views to the skyscrapers of the business district towering overhead. The cruise will stop near the river mouth, where you will find the **Merlion** statue, Singapore's mascot.

Little India

This small pocket of the city demonstrates the other side of Singapore's multi-cultural lifestyle. From Little India MRT station walk to **Serangoon Road**, one of the oldest roads in Singapore, then to the **Little India Arcade**, a cluster of shop houses that was renovated and restored in the 1980s. There is a lively array of Indian businesses and trades: get your fortune told, have henna patterns painted on your hands or buy Indian sweets, Ayurvedic medicines or beautiful sari fabrics. Exit onto Campbell Lane for flower shops, handicrafts and the

famed Indian **PGP** supermarket, which has household items, incense and spice mixes. Walk along Dunlop Street, passing stores with textiles and cosmetics like kohl, henna and perfume oils, to the far end and the **Abdul Gaffoor Mosque** which has an ornate sundial denoting the names of 25 chosen prophets. The Anglican **Church of True Light** is on Perak Street, one block north. Built in 1850, this church has Bible verses in Chinese painted onto the pillars and walls. If you are hungry at any time, walk north to **Upper Dickson Road** were there are masses on Indian restaurants with food from all regions. Finally, return to where you started to see the **Tekka Centre**. This was the original produce markets still sell fresh fruit and vegetables, meat and fish. There is also a hawkers' food centre while upstairs are clothing, brassware and antique stalls.

Sri Mariamann Temple (top); Temple Street market; the Elgin Bridge and Clarke Quay festivals

Orchard Road

Synonymous with serious retail therapy, Orchard Road is famous for it's vast range of designer, clothing and electrical goods stores. The numerous multi-storey plazas are populated by a multitude of small stores and have a theme: all cameras here, all jewellery there. Competition is fierce and you can haggle; but beware, this is an enormous area. It pays to research in advance if you are after something specific. Start at the western end and finish in the east as this is close to Singapore's most famous landmark, **Raffles Hotel**. End your day in the bar and billiard room with a Singapore Sling and, if it's late, you could stay for dinner too. The evening buffet is incredible. Or if you're still raring to go, head back to the river where there is always some lively nightlife.

Attractions

Singapore Flyer Singapore's latest tourist attraction is perfect for an overview of the entire city. A spectacular ferris wheel lifts passengers 165 metres – that's 42 stories of a building – into the air. Hovering in a roomy capsule for 30 minutes, you can see over the Singapore F1 circuit and the new casino complex as it takes shape, across Marina Bay to the ocean, the skyscrapers of the business district, the Singapore River and the historical district. The views are quite breathtaking, so much so that it is really very tempting to stay on board for a second spin. It would be worth going at sunset for the cocktail flight. Flyer trips from SG$30, singaporeflyer.com.

Beneath the Flyer is a garden and a small collection of shops and restaurants, plus a rather unusual treat: the **Kenko Reflexology and Fish Spa** is the latest thing in wellness treatments and just wonderful for hot feet that have been touring all day. Dip your toes into a pool of 'doctor fish' – an eastern European Garra Rufa species – that away nibble at dead skin. This special exfoliating technique is a little ticklish but well worth it for those who are missing their daily encounter with some marine species. Fish reflexology from SG$30.

Sentosa Island 15 minutes from the city, and home to the aquarium, nature trails and reserves, 120-year-old Fort Siloso, and even golf courses. There is a hotel, cafés, beaches and many seasonal events.

Singapore Zoo Set in a lovely rainforest environment, the well-designed grounds house over 2,500 animals including some endangered species. Many roam free, their enclosures separated from the visitors by dry or wet moats. The educational sections and the night safari are great for children.

Jurong Bird Park This open air birds-only zoo has 8,000 residents. Equally impressive in its construction, fantastic atriums with jungles and forests house free-flying species you will never see in the wild.

Singapore Botanic Gardens This haven from the hustle and bustle is just west of Orchard Road. Explore the National Orchid Garden's many Asian and tropical species.

Museums and Galleries Take your pick from the Asian Civilisations Museum, National Museum or Maritime Museum. There are many others on subjects like toys, stamps and sports plus heritage centres and many galleries covering historic to modern works of art.

Listings for these are on visitsingapore.com.

Singapore Sighs

Reversing the trend: the fish eating Patricia and Beth's feet; the Singapore Flyer from the ground and the air

Diving

Yes it is possible, you just need to be a little creative in your thinking. The most interesting way to get wet, and without even getting your kit out of your bag, is to go down to the aquarium on Sentosa Island. This is a fun dive that will get you really close to some big animals as well as having the opportunity to see how an aquarium works behind the scenes.

You can also dive in local waters, as many trainees do, but this is less easy to organize. Approach a local dive store or school – these plan trips to the islands to the south of Singapore. Pulau Hantu, or Ghost Island, is a favoured area. Two small land masses are linked by a sand bar at low tide. The surrounding reef is regarded as being the best with a reputation for many nudibranchs and crustaceans. There are other islands: St Johns, Kusu and even Sentosa have reefs worth a snorkel at least, although the visibility is never very good. Also within striking distance of Singapore are the Bintan Islands, which are Indonesian but can be reached by ferry in an hour or so.

You can dive from Singapore by taking a mini-liveaboard to nearby Indonesian or Malay waters. This fantastic way to spend a weekend is so popular with locals and expats that getting on board requires forward planning. See page 169 for information.

⛵	Underwaterworld, Singapore	
🕐	**Depth**	4 m
◑	**Visibility**	good
🌊	**Currents**	none
🛢	**Dive type**	tank

Strangely, diving in an aquarium tank is hardly different from the ocean, at least when it comes to planning. On arrival at Underwaterworld, divers are given a full dive brief as to what will come and what is expected. You cannot use your own kit for hygiene reasons, so first you are assessed by your divemaster, given a wetsuit and weights (no buoyancy device required) then sent off to change. Next, you get a tour of the behind the scenes tanks, and get to see rescued marine creatures that are being cared for until they are ready to go on display. Finally, it is time to slide into the perspex tunnel that you normally see from below. Stepping in is weird as the first thing you see are the people watching you but you soon become attuned to the 'oohs' and 'ahhs' that you can't hear but can see as they look longingly or crazily at you. As the small group follows the divemaster, the rays and sharks return to their rounds of swimming up and over the perspex tunnel, and in and out of the fake caves and canyons. It is a curious feeling as you are far

closer to some predators than you will ever get in the ocean, but these animals are accustomed to their guests. For those who think of the poor creatures enclosed in the unnatural space, this aquarium (at least) rescues many animals from certain death after being caught in shipping lanes outside the city and the money you have paid to join them in the tank goes to helping others.   SG$120, underwaterworld.com.sg

⊙ Sentosa Island

Off Singapore's southern tip, this island was turned into a tourist playground by the government with many organized attractions such as museums and golf courses to spas and a flying trapeze. However, the island also plays a strong part in conserving Singapore's wildlife. There are nature trails through forest covered hills where you can see, birds, flowers, geckos and macaques and for marine lovers, apart from the aquarium, there is the opportunity to see the rare pink Indo-Pacific Humpback Dolphins. After you have visited these, head over to Siloso beach for beach games, lively music, fantastic sunsets and cocktails at Café del Mar.

Drying out

Accommodation options in Singapore are endless, with hotels ranging from trendy boutique and converted 'shop houses' to magnificent colonial. If you can afford that most famous of hotels, Raffles, there is nothing quite like it, but most divers will just stop there for an obligatory Singapore Sling. To keep your costs down monitor a booking service like wotif.com or if you already have a favourite hotel then watch their website for special offers.

If you are new to Singapore, choose by area: for nightlife and restaurants, it's a good idea to stay near Clarke Quay, if you want to shop, target Orchard Road. The following have been tried and tested.

Sleeping

$$$ Grand Plaza Park Hotel – City Hall, T+65 6336 3456. Well located with Clarke Quay, Fort Canning Park and museums near by. Large rooms with traditional decor.

$$$ Novotel, T+65 6338 3333, novotel.com. Newly restyled, modern rooms in a great location on the river at Clarke Quay. Easy walking distance to Chinatown.

$$ Albert Court, T+65 6339 3939, albertcourt.com.sg. Converted from pre-war shop houses near Little India, this small traditional-looking hotel is comfortable.

$$ Gallery Hotel, T+65 6849 8686, galleryhotel.com.sg. On the river but away from the Quays, über-trendy rooms were designed by art students and are bright and modern with free internet access.

🍴 Feeding frenzy

Chinese, Indian, Western, seafood, meats, vegetarian: you name it and you can have it. Singapore is quite justifiably described as culinary heaven, due to the huge variety of food styles you can get here and because, generally, eating out is cheap.

A trip to Singapore wouldn't be complete without at least one lunch at a hawker centre where masses of stall holders share premises. Find a table and peruse the activity, see what appeals. Order Indonesian satay for starters from one, a Chinese dish for a main course from another. It only gets complicated when you see so many types of food and you want to try them all. One stall may sell Hokkien dishes while the next has Cantonese staples. It's the done thing to pick and choose. There are hawkers centres at **Lau Pa Sat** in the business district (Raffles Place MRT) where you sit inside a Victorian style cast iron building, or go to the **Newton Centre** near Orchard Road and Little India (Newton MRT). Must-try specialities include chilli crab, Hainanese chicken rice, laksa (noodles in coconut curry gravy), bak kut the (spicy pork ribs in soup) and roti prata (a pancake served with thick curry). Try really hard and you will spend US$10 a head.

Of course, this is not fine dining. For that head to **Raffles**, their evening buffet is amazing and good value, even at US$40 per person, or go down to **Clarke Quay** where there is a variety of classy and trendy restaurants inside the newly renovated warehouse area. Along the river and all the way down to **Boat Quay** are an extensive selection of restaurants. There, the touts can be a little pushy but it's all done with good humour.

A favourite with locals and tourists is **Brewerks** with a microbrewery and wine bar, burgers, pizzas and other Western delights. That may seem a cop out but if you fancy a taste of home, this is the place to go. Otherwise, wander along the riverside walk and take your pick of every imaginable style of cuisine, from French and Belgian to Malay, then round off the evening with a drink in one of the waterside bars or clubs.

Sleeping	$$$ US$150+ double room per night		$$ US$75-150	$ under US$75
Eating	$$$ US$40+ 2-course meal, excluding drinks		$$ US$20-40	$ under US$20

Resources

Overshadowed by five full metres of awe-inspiring juvenile whaleshark, *Rhinocodon typus*

Marine biodiversity

When you consider that seven tenths of the planet is covered in water, it may seem curious that most divers' hit lists are confined to the equatorial belt. But there is good reason. This is where the majority of accessible marine life resides.

All oceans are teeming with life, but many seas are too deep and too cold to encourage the development of all but the most specialized species. These conditions also make many areas off-limits to sport diving.

The warm waters that surround the equator are known to have remained tropical for millions of years. High light levels and sun-heated waters encourage reef growth and provide time for marine species to diversify. This simple equation ensures that tropical waters are just that much richer than temperate waters. Yet nothing is ever really that simple. The world's oceans – and diving zones – are also influenced by deep water plates, ridges, submerged volcanoes and marine currents. It has been known for many years that the waters in the Indo-Pacific region, stretching from Madagascar in the west to the Galápagos in the east, are far richer than those of the Atlantic. However, Southeast Asia is the specific region that displays the highest levels of biodiversity.

This is due to it's position in the Pacific Ocean, a geologically complex region known as the Pacific Ring of Fire: a deep water string of submerged volcanoes encircle the Pacific and were a key element in the formation of the Earth's crust and many centuries later, resulting in an array of biologically unique island ecosystems and species.

The Coral Triangle

While scientific research has suggested that the area around the top of Indonesian Sulawesi was the Ring of Fire's epicentre, more recent studies have introduced the **Coral Triangle**. This is the area enclosed by Southern Indonesia, eastern Borneo, up to the Philippines, then across to Papua New Guinea and the Solomons. Studies conducted across this region have confirmed it is the global center of marine biodiversity. Covering an area of 5.7 million km² (about half of the area of the United States) there are over 600 reef-building coral species (whichis 75% of all species known to science) and more than 3,000 species of reef fish.

These figures vary by country with species numbers reducing the further away from the region you go. For example in Indonesia there are around 3200 species of fish including 123 damselfish. Papua New Guinea has 100 damsels, but by the time you reach Fiji there are just 60. Way over in the Galápagos the

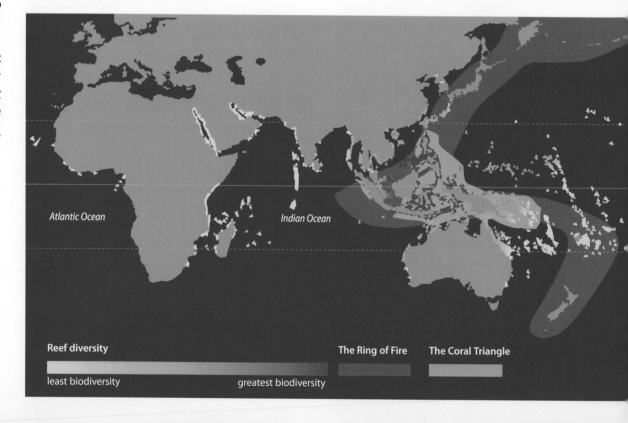

Atlantic Ocean

Indian Ocean

Reef diversity

least biodiversity   greatest biodiversity

The Ring of Fire   **The Coral Triangle**

number drops to 18 while the Caribbean has a mere 16 across its entire sea. Australia, always the exception to the rule, has the highest numbers of damsels at 132 as the continent covers tropical, temperate and cold waters.

Species diversity and discovery

The other reason for higher species diversity in the Asia-Pacific basin is the way in which ocean currents transport cold waters around the planet. The Indo-Pacific area is partly protected from arctic waters by the Russian and Alaskan land masses. As far back as the ice age, melting ice water flooded into the Atlantic, reducing its temperature enough to decimate the animal population, leaving just a small refuge in the area we know as the Caribbean. Ocean currents also distribute fish away from the Asian epicentre.

This information is by no means a reason to ignore one country or another. However, one thing you can be sure of, diving in Asian waters is more likely to be a journey of discovery than it is elsewhere. New species are discovered across the world on a regular basis, but none more so than in Southeast Asia. Just a few months ago an entirely new frogfish was found in the Ambon area (see right) while other examples from recent years include completely new nudibranchs in Thailand and several new pygmy seahorses in Indonesia.

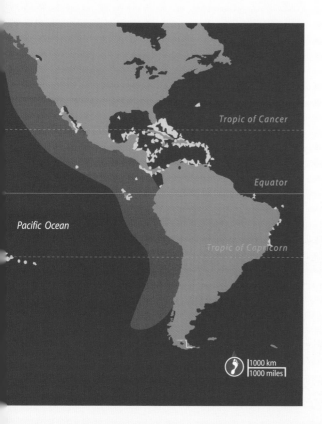

Tropic of Cancer

Equator

Pacific Ocean

Tropic of Capricorn

1000 km
1000 miles

🌀 Frogfish discovery

It's fair to assume that for most divers, discovering a species of fish would have to be one of the ultimate rewards of the sport. I'm no different and have spent endless dives searching for something new. I've never had much luck though, so you can imagine my surprise when my wife Fitrie, on her very first real open water dive, found not only a fish I had never seen before and the most unique one I had ever seen, but also a frogfish – my favourite - to top it off!

Fitrie had just completed her Open Water course and certificate in hand, asked if she could join my small group of divers going to Ambon's very special muck site, Laha. We were making jokes about it being her first dive and how she would be lucky to even spot a lionfish! Once we were in the water, the group were all spotting some incredible creatures and Fitrie, while still struggling a bit with her buoyancy, had sighted a good number of them herself. After 50 minutes, the current started to pick up and gently swept us towards the mouth of the bay so we decided to ascend. I moved closer to Fitrie to help her with her buoyancy but she tugged several times on my hand and pointed at the bottom. I didn't feel any real need to pay attention to what she was pointing at – after all, a novice surely couldn't have sighted anything I hadn't seen before – but as I gave the thumbs up signal, she kept tugging and a small brownish-orange face caught my eye. I really couldn't believe what I saw! In fact, I had no idea what we were looking at and could only be sure that I had never seen anything like it in all my years of diving.

On the surface, we realized we needed a photo of this unique fish to help identify it, so after grabbing a camera, our divemaster Toby and I returned to Laha. Later, Toby mentioned he might have seen something like it but many years ago so we circulated the photos around the world to friends and fish experts, trying to identify this curious creature. The answer finally came via the University of Washington. Studies are still ongoing, but it seems we have found a new species.

In the end, I finally had the good luck of being at the scene of a new fish discovery, and with a little jealousy I admit, I have to raise my hat to Fitrie whose keen eyes made it possible on her very first open water dive. Next time I'm having her buy the lottery ticket.

Buck Randolph, Owner, Maluku Divers

image © Buck Randolph

Resources Marine biodiversity

Conservation

A few years ago, Jean-Michel Cousteau spoke on Capitol Hill: "The ocean holds 97% of earth's water, drives climate and weather, generates more than 70% of the oxygen we breathe, absorbs carbon dioxide, supplies our fresh water through rain, provides food, and is a deep source of inspiration to our spirits."

Yet our seas are heavily endangered and coral reefs are one of the most threatened ecosystems on the planet. If destruction continues at its present rate, 70% of the world's coral reefs will disappear in a generation. And where will that leave us?

Most people (divers generally excluded) think nothing of how the fish arrives on their dinner plate, nor what happens to sewerage or the side-effects of many industries. Centuries of bad practices have led to the direct destruction of the world's coral reefs – some figures suggest that up to 30% have been lost already. Over time, few people realised they were literally killing the resource that supported them. Fishing practices, both commercial and small scale, are much to blame for the damage to many marine ecosytems. Drag-netting the ocean floor, for example, kills marine life indiscriminately while at the other end of the scale, poor local fishermen took to dropping chemicals to catch fish in greater numbers, never understanding that this kills everything, leaving nothing to support either the people or the fish. As a coral reef dies, so do other environments around it. With no reef paralleling the shore, mangrove nursery grounds become eroded and creatures that used these as a safe haven, no longer can. A once protected coast is open to the ravages of weather and may well collapse into the sea. Other man-made issues like pollution simply aggravate these problems.

There is a lot of publicity about how global warming is leading to rises in sea levels, but less focus on how this impacts on coral reefs and consequently on the planet as a whole. Corals

66 99 The diving community has an important role to play in helping protect rapidly degrading coral reefs around the world. As divers, we have a personal relationship with reefs and often see firsthand the damage sustained by reef ecosystems by changing global conditions. Project AWARE provides many opportunities for individuals to participate in reef monitoring, education and conservation locally. Volunteer divers are at the core of these monitoring programmes and are natural advocates for the protection of declining underwater ecosystems.
Suzanne Pleydell, Director, Project AWARE Foundation (International)

live inside a specific temperature range (around 25°-29°C) and it only takes an increase of one degree in water temperature for corals to start struggling.

Tiny individual corals feed on **zooxanthellae**, symbiotic yellow, green or brown-hued algaes, which live inside the corals, giving them colour and sustaining them via photosynthesis. But, as waters warm, the algae either dies, or the corals expel them, causing them to bleach. Water that is too warm also encourages the growth of harmful algae over the corals. This speeds up its demise as they block out the sun: the **zooxanthellae** cannot photosynthesise so they die, taking the corals with them. The marine realm has created an antidote to this problem – algae is usually eaten by fish, but due to overfishing, there are insufficient numbers to keep the balance. Other side effects are seen when corals get ill and predators move in. The Crown of Thorns starfish is a typical example as these both predate on and cause coral bleaching. Their natural predators are few and the ones that do exist are depleted by overfishing as well.

Right around the world, people depend on coral reefs for foods as well as a source of income. Despite their environmental and economic importance, new research indicates that more than half of the world's coral reefs could die in less than 25 years.

Coral destruction as caused by humans – a fin or an anchor; coral bleaching caused by three Crown of Thorns starfish

Divers and conservation

A diver's role may be a comparatively small one but remember one of the first rules of diving – look, don't touch. Sadly, there are people who genuinely don't care and you have to wonder what it is they are doing if they have only gone down to destroy.

- ▶▶ Do not touch corals, or any living organism, as your hands can leave harmful oils and pressure can damage protective coatings allowing destructive bacteria to penetrate.
- ▶▶ Don't wear gloves, unless absolutely necessary, as you will be too tempted to put your hands down without thinking.
- ▶▶ If tough conditions dictate that you must touch the reef, a single finger is enough to give you balance, and a carefully placed reef hook does less damage than two hands.
- ▶▶ Don't bring anything up from the seabed, not even a shell. It may seem to be dead, but you just don't know what tiny creature has crawled inside.
- ▶▶ Be careful to stay above the reef, good buoyancy is vital.
- ▶▶ Ensure all your gauges and equipment are either hooked to your BC or tucked in a pocket.
- ▶▶ Watch what you do with your fins; it's easy to misjudge what is behind you.

There are many organizations and bodies dedicated to looking after our seas and the animals that live within them. Look at the Marine Conservation Society (mcsuk.org), The Shark Research Institute (sharks.org), Reef Check (reefcheck.org), WWF (panda.org), and the International Coral Reef Action Network (icran.org). Contemplate getting involved by helping to monitor reefs. Ask your dive operator about PADI's Project AWARE activities (projectaware.org) or if you have time sign up for an expedition run by a body like Coral Cay Conservation (coralcay.org) or GlobalVision International (gvi.co.uk).

www.projectaware.org

Drag nets caught on coral bommie which will eventually smother it

🌀 Neptune's medical chest

While most people know that heart pills come from garden flowers (digitalis is derived from hollyhocks) few realise that there are also drugs being developed from marine sources. The list is growing along with the need to find cures for diseases that have become resistant to current solutions or to find something completely new.

Around the world, scientists forage plant-choked jungles and prolific coral reefs in a process that is tagged "bioprospecting". Although few natural substances show pharmaceutical promise, and less make it to full drug status, the possibilities are immense.

Several decades ago, researchers considered how running away from a predator is not an option for marine invertebrates such as sponges and corals. Instead, these creatures rely on other methods of protection like producing a potent toxin. With a little tweaking, these toxins may actually save human lives. One of the very first successes was over 40 years ago with the discovery of a group of compounds, called arabinosides. These were extracted from the sponge *Tethya crypta* and used to develop an antiretroviral drug which eventually developed into AZT for AIDS and a herpes treatment.

A number of marine derived drugs are being evaluated in human trials. Australian chemists found corals developed an internal 'sunscreen' to cope with exposure to ultraviolet radiation. A synthetic copy of the compound can be used to produce a sunscreen. In Japan and Taiwan, scientists found that a red algae called *Digenea* produces kainic acid which is being tested as treatment for diseases of the nervous system, such as Huntington's Chorea and Alzheimer's. The deadly venom extracted from some cone shells may help victims of a stroke or heart disease while at the far end of the scale, an anti-inflammatory and analgesic chemical, pseudopterosin, was extracted from the Bahamian soft coral, *Pseudoterigorgia elisabethae* and this led to the development of bioproducts which are now used in skin care cosmetics.

Something like 7,000 unique compounds have been discovered in marine species which may have potential in the medical field but out of the thousands of species tested, only hundreds are now referred to as 'drug leads'. Very few become serious candidates as there is concern in some quarters that damage caused by this type of research is not justified by the results. Scientists simply don't know enough about some of the areas they are delving into, yet careful bioprospecting may one day lead to a lifesaving drug. If the world's oceans and reefs are not cared for, many undiscovered compounds could remain that way.

Diver training

For many, the underwater experience starts on holiday. There you are, snorkelling over some exotic reef but watching the divers far below and wanting to join in. So it's over to the hotel pool for a try dive session followed by a quick resort course. For others, it can be the influence of friends at home who are so enthusiastic about their chosen pastime, they spend every waking minute talking non-stop about it. Either way, for those who discover that their blood no longer circulates without nitrogen in it, it's time to take things seriously and get qualified.

There are several ways to do this which should be considered carefully: you can train at home, abroad or even online these days, but the most important factor is to ensure that you get the best training possible from one of the world's major diving organisations. This is not a sport to cut corners over.

Training organizations

By far the largest and best known dive body is **PADI** (Professional Association of Diving Instructors, padi.com). You will see their signs right around the world, from your local dive store to resorts abroad, but they are by no means the only training organization. Other well respected international bodies include the **British Sub-Aqua Club** (BSAC, bsac.com), the **National Association of Underwater Instructors** (NAUI, naui.com) and **Scuba Schools International** (SSI, divessi.com).

Each of these has a range of comparative courses run via weekly club-style meetings, local day courses or residential courses either at home or away. All courses are well-structured, thorough and will cover the relevant concerns for each level. Courses are designed to be completed in a specific number of days and any training operation will do their best to ensure you meet that target. Before signing on the dotted line, do your research: get some recommendations, ask to meet your potential instructor then go with the company and person who makes you feel confident and relaxed within the training environment. Also bear in mind that you need to have a well-recognised certification. If your training is not internationally recognised you may find that another country will not accept your certification card and you have to start over.

Learning to dive

This should include three straightforward steps. Basic training is often called **Open Water** and builds essential skills to get you safely in the water but limits your depth and does not teach any rescue skills. An **Advanced Open Water** course will expand your knowledge and further in-water practice ensures competence in deeper water under differing conditions. Finally, take a **Rescue Diver** course. This may be included in one of the above stages but if not ensure you do it. It is important to learn how to save your own life, or someone else's, and is a vital addition to the initial training programme.

Where to learn

One option would be to go on holiday to somewhere lovely and, hopefully, qualify in warm waters under sunny skies. The downside of this is that you are giving up precious holiday time to sit in a classroom. There are several Asian hot-spots that regularly attract back-packers, gap-year travellers and those who just want to learn. Lombok's Gili islands and Thailand's Koh Tao are all well regarded and popular training destinations with PADI Open Water courses at around US$350. Bear in mind that anything too much cheaper indicates that your operator may be forced to cut corners somewhere. Many rock-bottom courses do not include

Pool training at Manta Dive in Gili Trewangan; first time in open water in Lombok; rescue training practice in Ao Chalong, Phuket

manuals and fees. Also make sure your chosen dive school has an instructor who can speak your language.

Alternatively, you could book into a school in your home country or join a club. These will have a range of options from more relaxed week-by-week training sessions to intensive long weekend options. If these are all going to put a dent in your schedule, you could learn at your own pace with an online course (padi.com/elearning) then register with a local school for your open water dives.

When you do choose to kick off your dive training, remember that you need to be in good health and reasonably comfortable in the water – no, you don't need to be an Olympic swimmer but you should be able to swim further than from the pool edge to the swim-up bar. If you have any known medical conditions, for example asthma or diabetes, get advice from a medical professional before you start.

Continued training

At this point many people stop training, and that's fine, but the half dozen or so dives taken to get you through a course will not make you a competent diver. Practice, as they say, makes perfect so try to get in some diving on a regular basis and consider doing either some speciality or higher level courses as they will help refine your skills. Ideas are on the right.

Continued safety

Finally, every time you are back in the water remind yourself again that this is not a sport to cut corners over. It's important to be healthy when you dive, continually check the state of your equipment and always dive in a buddy pair. Listen to every dive brief carefully: the divemaster is there to ensure his divers come back safely, not just lead them around, so the information he supplies is vital to both an enjoyable dive and a safe one.

Asnar at Maratua briefing on the complex Channel dive site

❽ The training ladder

There is a clear route that takes potential divers from novice to qualified, yet diving is a sport where you can, and should, keep learning. Improving your technical skills as time goes by means you will enjoy dives more, as will understanding the environment you are exploring and your impact on it.

The most interesting way to keep learning is by taking a few PADI speciality courses. Take one small course every now and then and you can build up to the ultimate non-professional accolade, Master Scuba Diver.

▸▸ Progress up through PADI Rescue Diver then concentrate on improving your own skills and levels of confidence in all situations with Deep Diver, Wreck Diver, Night Diver or even Ice Diver.

▸▸ Focus on specific interests like Digital Underwater Photographer and Underwater Videographer which will add to your camera equipment skills and can be combined with a Peak Performance Buoyancy Course which will make shooting, and diving generally, easier.

▸▸ Understanding the marine environment will also enhance your dives. Consider Coral Reef Conservation Diver, National Geographic Diver Project AWARE Specialist and Underwater Naturalist.

In addition to these great options, there are courses tailored for children: Bubblemaker can be taken at eight years old and Junior Open Water from ten. If you have family, get them involved. Or, if you want to teach there are several courses that cover instructor qualifications at varying levels, which should be augmented by plenty of in-water experience.

❝❞ Many people learn to dive while they are on holiday, just like I did. And it is a great way to learn – warm water, nice sunny days, easy conditions and no nasty distractions like work getting in the way. However, I really do like to advise people to continue their training back home. This keeps the knowledge fresh, develops skills by diving in very different environment and, of course, builds a great network of friends and professionals from local dive stores and schools.

Deborah Sutton, Marketing Manager, PADI International Limited

PADI
padi.com

Health and first aid

There are many healthcare issues involved in being a diver and most of the "can I, can't I?" stuff will be covered by your training. The following information is for guidance only. If you are unsure about anything at all to do with how a medical condition may affect your ability to dive safely, make sure you contact a doctor with specialist dive knowledge before you go away.

Before you go

There are a couple things to take care of before you depart:

Insurance Never underestimate the necessity of good, diver-specific medical insurance. Ensure that it covers repatriation in an emergency and check the depth limitations. Many policies will only cover you up to 30 metres while others confusingly say "covered to the depth you are qualified to."

Check up If you do have any pre-existing conditions, take a quick trip down to your doctor and ensure you have both sufficient medications and information to handle your own healthcare. It may be a good idea to get a certificate clearing you to dive in order to show operators. Remember to have your teeth checked every now and then as trapped air in a cavity is a very painful thing.

Vaccinations for the tropics

With most divers heading off to at least one distant destination every year it's worth getting a full set of vaccinations then having boosters as and when necessary. Ensure you allow plenty of time to get this done in advance of your trip. For the countries listed in this guide you will require some or all of the following:

- polio
- hepatitis A & B
- tetanus
- rabies
- typhoid
- yellow fever

Discuss your individual requirements with your GP/practice nurse or travel clinic as you may need something more than the above.

Anti-malarials

The best way to avoid getting malaria is not to get bitten. Yes, easier said than done, but the usual advice of a repellent lotion plus covered arms and legs after dusk will help enormously. However, because you can't avoid mosquitoes in damp environments such as kitting-up areas, you may need to take anti-malarial tablets. Which one to take is where it gets more complicated and the best advice is to research via your doctor, nurse or a travel clinic but make sure you tell them you are a diver as some have side effects such as nausea, diarrhoea and sun sensitivity. Some anti-malarials are not given to divers as they are said to cause panic or anxiety but these reports tend to be anecdotal. Good websites for current recommendations are fitfortravel.scot.nhs.uk and cdc.gov/travel.

Malaria drugs need to be taken for a period before entering an at-risk area and usually for four weeks afterwards so plan well in advance and don't forget to complete the course.

66 99 My travel medicine kit always includes ear drying agent but I make my own. It's heaps cheaper and works just as well. Mix half rubbing alcohol and half vinegar: the vinegar helps change the pH of the ear canal to inhibit the growth of fungi which are responsible for most infections. The alcohol does the drying so if it irritates a little, reduce the quantity – this varies from person to person so it takes a bit of experimenting. The trick though is to prevent rather than treat, so if you are subject to ear problems, try this at the end of every day. And I always like to remind people that for cuts and grazes, even insect bites, there is really is no substitute for a daily wash with plain old soap and fresh water.

Doctor Joann Gren, Emergency Medicine Specialist

What to take

First aid kit Most of what you will need to create a good first aid travel kit can be bought without prescription; just ask your local pharmacist to help you put together suitable items in small quantities. Consider including these items:

- an 'anti-itch' or steroid cream (eg, hydrocortisone) for use on insect bites, rashes and skin inflammation
- an analgesic, like paracetamol (acetaminophen) or ibuprofen
- antihistamine tablets for mild allergic reactions
- a small tube of antiseptic cream or antiseptic wipes
- lots of band-aids and a small pack of sterile bandages
- seasickness remedy
- sinus decongestant tablets
- rehydration sachets
- an anti-diarrhoea drug
- tweezers
- an ear drying aid (eg Swim-Ear)
- small scissors
- latex condoms
- and a good Swiss Army type knife.

Plus these antibiotic preparations that need to be prescribed:

- a broad spectrum antibiotic for general infections. Discuss ciprofloxacin with your doctor as it is particularly good for marine infections
- antibiotic drops for ear and eye infections
- an antibiotic ointment for skin infections

Most doctors are sympathetic to prescribing in advance if you explain why. Don't forget to get – and take – sufficient quantities of any medicines that you require on a daily basis, for instance if you are diabetic or use the contraceptive pill.

While you're there

The tropics are beautiful but they do throw up some health issues for travellers, especially those who arrive from colder climes. Here are some tips on ways to ensure your holiday isn't ruined but if in doubt always visit a local doctor. You may be reluctant to do this in some out-of-the-way village, but many doctors, even in the most remote countries, are highly trained. If you are unsure, ask a divemaster or hotel receptionist to recommend one.

Dehydration One of the most common ailments for divers. No one ever drinks enough water and being dehydrated can lead to many other problems, not least of which is the bends. Drink at least two litres of water a day. Sugary soft drinks do not aid rehydration, nor, sadly, does beer. Cramps in your feet at night is a classic indication. Use a sachet of rehydration salts to top up your levels quickly. Alternatively, add 8 level teaspoons of sugar and 1 level teaspoon of salt to 1 litre of water. Tastes foul though.

Sunburn and heat-stroke Perhaps the second most common ailment. Use factor 30 sunscreen to prevent sunburn and wear a hat while you are out on the water where there are reflected rays. Heat stroke arrives disguised as the flu (headaches, muscle aches and pains, fatigue) but with some stomach problems thrown in. If you suspect that's what you have, stay cool, drink lots of fluid and get some advice if you don't return to normal very quickly.

Mosquito bites Try not to scratch because if you do they may get infected by all the mini-nasties in seawater. Use an anti-itch cream and keep your hands in your pockets.

Seasickness Some people suffer, the rest are oblivious. If you suffer just a little, stay out in the fresh air and keep your eyes on the horizon until you get accustomed to the boat's movement. If you suffer badly, there is no doubt about it, drugs work the best. You will need to find a brand that doesn't make you drowsy and that may be a matter of trial and error. Some people swear by pressure bands, others by ginger as a natural remedy.

Ear problems Being immersed in salt water for hours at a time can cause a lot of trouble for ears. Always, always remember to clear your ears before you feel pressure, which will alleviate a lot of potential problems. However, do this gently as over-vigorous, repeated clearing can cause inflammation. People with recurring problems may want to use a steroid nasal spray a few days before a trip and continue once diving. This will cut down on inflammation caused by the normal barotrauma of diving. If your ears get sore, it may be best to rest them for a day. If you suspect you have an infection a good on the spot test is to press the hollow behind your ear lobe. If this is painful start the antibiotic drops.

Sinus problems Coming from cooler climates to the tropics can bring on a cold or flu-like symptoms. Many people swear by nasal decongestants as these often make equalizing easier. However, they can also wear off halfway through a dive and cause a reverse ear block, so be careful. Nothing clears sinuses as well as a good salt water sniff if it's just a case of clearing some city pollution but

anything that is very painful may indicate an infection. Again, take a day out, then start antibiotics if necessary.

Colds and flu A change in climate or the change from a busy life at home to a relaxed one somewhere nice and – wallop – you get a cold. Antibiotics will not help unless you have a specific infection so don't go swallowing the pills hoping for a miracle cure. Instead go back to mother's remedies – lots of fluid, vitamin C (oranges and lemons) keep warm and take a mild painkiller.

Allergies Many people have become intolerant to allergens such as dust mites and pollen or have food intolerances to things like wheat or tomatoes. These can cause discomfort but are not life threatening and can be easily treated with an oral antihistamine. Likewise, skin reactions to neoprene or plankton can be treated with a steroid ointment. However, if you have a serious allergy, ensure you are carrying any necessary drugs with you. Specific food allergies such as seafood or nuts are extremely dangerous especially if you are miles offshore so carry an epi-pen with you at all times. More importantly, make sure that someone else knows where that is and what to do. Either your dive buddy or the divemaster should be fully informed of any intolerances.

Women's issues There are few women who would choose to go diving when they have their period. You can delay them by continuing the cycle of your contraceptive pill but ensure you get good advice on how long you can safely do this. If you don't take the pill but suspect that your period will come in the last few days of a trip, you can delay it for a few days by using a progesterone-only pill. Pregnancy is a little more of an issue. There is no definitive research on how a foetus might be affected by diving. Many women have dived before realizing they were pregnant with no ill effects, but is it worth the risk?

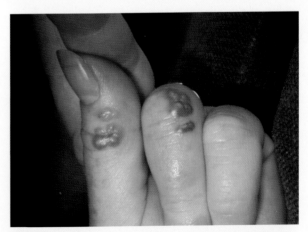

Ouch! The image above shows the effects of touching what you shouldn't. This is the result of brushing against a stinging hydroid while taking a photo, and the skin's reaction to the toxins in the hydroid.

The Bends We are all taught about decompression sickness when training and then most of us promptly forget what we were taught. Few divers would be confident enough to cope with a buddy with a suspected bend. That's why it's imperative to dive with a recognized and trustworthy dive operation who will ensure your divemaster is able to cope. All the same, it's as well to have basic knowledge of what is going on.

Symptoms can include joint or muscle pain, dizziness, difficulty breathing, extreme fatigue, skin rashes, unconsciousness and paralysis. Treatment will depend on how severe these symptoms are so first of all ensure that the person is in no immediate danger, is warm, can breathe and has a pulse. **Then get help.** If symptoms are mild (eg, fatigue, skin rash and itching) you will probably be advised to administer 100% oxygen and a litre of fluid. If symptoms are more severe, call for assistance. You will be advised if you should administer CPR, 100% oxygen or fluids until you can reach a hyperbaric facility.

Note that CPR is designed to keep someone going until they reach a tertiary care facility and will only be of use if you can reach one in 15-20 minutes. If there is no pulse within that time, stop.

Another thing to note here is that skin bends are becoming more common. Many divemasters suspect this may be because people are stretching their bottom time by spending extended periods at shallow depths then failing to do a safety stop as their computers are still well within limits. Research is on-going in this area, but always exercise as much caution as possible.

Bruises, sprains and broken ribs It would be an amazing dive trip where someone doesn't drop a tank on their foot, slip on a wet deck or trip en route to the RIB. If you can get to a doctor do, otherwise apply the **RICE** principle… **R**est, use **I**ce on the injured area, use a **C**ompression dressing, and **E**levate it.

Olive seasnakes are venomous but are nosy rather than aggressive

Nitrogen Narcosis Not an accident as such, except that narked divers often do silly things and can have one. To reverse the effects of narcosis, ascend to a shallower depth and allow enough time on slow, controlled safety stops to recover. It may be as well to take a day off.

Severe headaches Again not an accident but may lead to one if ignored. Many people suffer from extreme headaches underwater. There are many contributing factors to this but one way to control them is to ensure you breathe constantly and gently. Try not to hold your breath – ever.

Marine creatures

No matter how careful we all are in the water there are times when the marine world takes exception to us being there:

Fish bites It may not happen often but there is the potential for an unimpressed fish to dash out and bite a diver. Triggerfish are the best known aggressors but even cute little Nemos are known to take a nip. More frequent perhaps is when poor-sighted morays emerge from a hole and chomp on a finger that's too close. In all cases, clean out the wound thoroughly with clean water or vinegar then apply an antibiotic ointment. Large bites may become infected and need antibiotics and anti-tetanus treatment. So you should keep your jabs up to date.

Venomous animals Not that you would intentionally touch anything dangerous but should you happen to get too close, use one of these basic first aid treatments then seek professional advice. The venom of some marine animals is broken down by heat and the following treatment can be used for sea urchins, crown of thorns starfish and stingrays. It will also aid, but is less effective on, stone, scorpion or lionfish, cone shells and seasnakes.

▸▸ clean the wound
▸▸ immerse in hot water (50°C) until pain stops (up to two hours)
▸▸ apply pressure immobilization: wrap a broad, firm bandage over the bite quite tightly and extend as high as possible over the limb. Keep still, apply a splint and bind so that the limb cannot be moved.
▸▸ seek advice on whether the person needs an antivenom or injection of long acting local anaesthetic.

Snorkellers should be very careful and wear swim shoes as many toxic animals bury themselves in the sand. If you step on a ray or urchins remove obvious spines or barbs, use the hot water treatment and antiseptic creams as necessary. More commonly, fire corals, stinging hydroids and stinging plankton can be treated with acetic acid – vinegar or lemon juice – or an anaesthetic cream. Jellyfish stings can be treated this way but ensure you remove the tentacles using rubber gloves. Coral cuts are easily infected so wash the cut well with clean, soapy water or vinegar then apply an antibiotic ointment frequently. These will take a long time to heal unless you stay out of the water so you will need to repeat the treatment after each dive.

Marine nasties

Every time we dive, we descend into a realm where hidden dangers lurk in the form of unrecognized or misunderstood creatures. We are all familiar with more obvious nasties such as much-maligned sharks, seldom-aggressive barracuda and mildly stinging anemones. However, it pays to be aware of creatures you may encounter underwater that can be a less obvious threat.

Cephalopods The only nasty cephalopod is the Blue-ringed octopus. Rarely aggressive, this chap spends most if its life hiding from predators. But take heed if those blue rings are flashing – this fellow harbours tetrodotoxin, one of the most deadly poisons known to man.

Corals and hydroids These fragile organisms should never be touched as they are easily damaged, but also because some will retaliate. All hard coral skeletons are made of calcium carbonate, which is hard and sharp and can cut or scratch soft skin. Some, like fire coral, also contain stinging nematocysts (a microscopic cell containing a poisoned barb) which can penetrate skin then burn or itch for some time. Swaying, fern-like hydroid clusters are seen all over reefs and are often mistaken for harmless plants. However, hydroids (or seaferns) have a sting in their 'fronds'. They contain hundreds of stinging cells in their tentacles.

Crustacea Cute as a puppy scampering about the reef floor, the mantis shrimp is deceptively dangerous. Two types are fondly described as thumbcrackers and spearchuckers depending on the shape of their modified front claws. When hunting or attacked these claws shoot out with enough power to crack a thumb or spear a hand.

Fire or Bristle Worms This caterpillar-like critter may seem innocuous and uninteresting but the ultra-fine spines can easily penetrate gloves and wetsuits. Once embedded in the skin, the spines break and cause a burning sensation, swelling or rashes. Scrubbing with pumice may help.

Fish All fish have some form of defence, even if it's just one like the razor sharp caudal blade that sits in front of the surgeonfish's tail fin. Triggerfish are perhaps the most dangerous as both titan and yellowmargined triggers are incredibly aggressive. They will chase off sea creatures and landlubbers alike when they are nesting and think nothing of nipping at a fin or an ear. Many forms of jellyfish sting, ranging from the deadly Australian box jellyfish to ones that are almost harmless. Balls of lined catfish rolling across the seabed are very entertaining, however, highly venomous, razor-sharp spines in their fins can inflicting serious wounds, the venom has been known to cause death. The scorpionfish family are one of the reef's most contrasting, with some very beautiful species and some really ugly ones. They all employ the same form of defence – a ridge of venomous spines runs along their bodies which can inject varying strengths of venom into the attacker. Generally, lionfish stings are less serious than those of scorpionfish. More dangerous is the false stonefish, then the devilfish whose venom is almost as potent as the potentially deadly stonefish. Many divers confuse these species so take care to avoid them all.

Seasnakes and eels These animals suffer from a reputation they don't really deserve. Many snakes are venomous but they are mostly just curious. If a snake appears to be taking too much interest, offer it your fin to 'taste' and it will soon leave. Likewise, a morays' reputation for aggression is due to poor eyesight and the way they search for food – head poking out of a hole, mouth gaping, teeth bared. If your hand is too close they will snap, thinking it's a fish.

Sea urchins Put an unwary foot down on a sea urchin and you are unlikely to forget it. The brittle, needle-sharp spines easily penetrate skin and neoprene. The common, long-spined urchin is not toxic but others have potentially fatal poisons. Take care over those with swollen tips on the spines – these are poison sacs. The Crown of Thorns starfish is part of the same species group as sea urchins, but are better known for their ability to destroy large swathes of coral. At up to half a metre across, their thick rigid spines have sharp points. A sting has similar effects to those of sea urchins but severe cases can cause paralysis.

Shells Only a handful of shells are dangerous. These are mostly within the cone shell group which have a venom filled, harpoon-like radula dart or tooth. Injected into prey, its venom will paralyse and is toxic enough to kill humans.

Clockwise from top left: fire coral, ball of catfish, sea urchin, coneshell, stonefish, bristleworm.

Indonesia

www.
dive-the-world
.com

- **Resorts, courses and worldwide liveaboards**

- **Up-to-date local knowledge**

- **Prices to suit every budget**

- **Last minute deals and special offers**

- **Lowest prices guaranteed**

Choose your
diving adventure!

Thailand · Fiji · Burma
Malaysia · Indonesia
Maldives · Australia
Red Sea & more ...

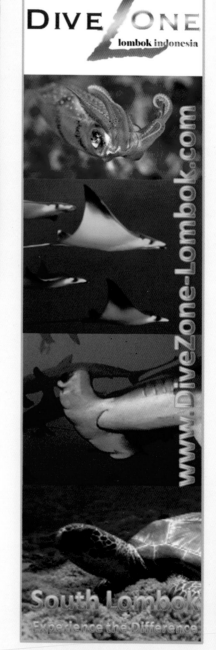

Cocotinos,
a small beach resort
situated in Wori Bay and
overlooking the world-famous
Bunaken Marine Park

www.odysseadivers.com
info.desk@odysseaasia.com

Cocotinos Lombok,
Opening 1st Quarter 2010!

OdysseaDivers
Your Passion · Our Journey

DISCOVER ONE OF BALI'S
BEST KEPT SCERETS

A Unique Hotel Experience

THE WATERGARDEN
Hotel and Restaurant
EAST BALI

" You'll find it hard to leave! "

Jalan Raya Candi Dasa
Bali - Indonesia
Tel: (62-363) 41540
Fax: (62-363) 41164
E-mail: waterg@dps.centrin.net.id
URL: www.watergardenhotel.com

AquaMarine
Diving - BALI

experience
theBESTDIVINGin
Bali

Photographs courtesy of Tierney, Ferrari, Fatherree

**AquaMarine only offers
Bali's best diving sites, including:**
Nusa Penida - drift-diving
Tulamben - wreck- & reef-diving
Padangbai - sharks and pelagics
Menjangan Island - wall-diving

**Muck Divers &
Macro Photographers:**
Book one of our dedicated spotter
guides to Secret Bay, Puri Jati, Seraya
Slopes & other (newly-discovered)
critter havens

T : +62 361 730107
F : +62 361 735368
E : info@AquaMarineDiving.com

www.AquaMarineDiving.com

Directory

Equatorial Diving in
Gorontalo
Sulawesi, Indonesia

Dense coral growth

Diverse marine life

New and
endemic species

Caverns, muck, pinnacles,
walls and wrecks

Waters crowded only by fish

Access by air

www.miguelsdiving.com
Photo: William Tan

Dive THE BEST
of both worlds

**North Sulawesi's finest
resort combination**

Bunaken National Park

KIMA BAJO
RESORT & SPA

KIMA BAJO
RESORT & SPA
Manado
www.kimabajo.com

Lembeh Strait

FINE DIVING
KUNGKUNGAN
BAY RESORT

KUNGKUNGAN BAY
RESORT & SPA
Lembeh
www.kungkungan.com

info@ecodivers.com
www.ECO-DIVERS.com

---

the elysian
boutique villa hotel

**Villas with private pools set in
a leafy Balinese garden -
a haven in the heart of
Seminyak.**

P. +62 361 730999 | F. +62 361 737509
E. reservations@theelysian.com
www.theelysian.com

HIPHOTELS   member of
design hotels

SANGALAKI DIVE LODGE
BORNEO

THE MOST EXCLUSIVE + DIVERSE
DIVING IN BORNEO

* UNIQUE CONSERVATION ISLAND *

* SIMPLE ECO-FRIENDLY RESORT *

* AWESOME DIVING! *

*"Come to where the Mantas play
and the Turtles lay"*

PROJECT
AWARE

PADI
5 Star
Instructor
Development
Center

www.sangalaki.net
email: jeremy@sangalaki.net

Also check out: www.divevietnam.com

THE WORLD

www.dive-the-world.com

- Resorts, courses and worldwide liveaboards
- Up-to-date local knowledge
- Prices to suit every budget
- Lowest prices guaranteed

Thailand · Fiji · Burma · Malaysia · Indonesia
Maldives · Australia · Red Sea & more...

Worldwide

dive:tours

South East Asia

Thailand Borneo Manado
Raja Ampat Bali Lombok
Komodo Philippines

for package deals, liveaboards
& tailor-made itineraries

email: us@divetours.co.uk
www.divetours.co.uk
+44 (0)1244 401177

YOU CAN DIVE IN THE WORLD'S N° 1 MARINE PARK...

...OR ENJOY A LOT MORE.

15 elegantly furnished Villas...
PADI Diving Center...Spa...Pool...
Gourmet Restaurant...Boutique...
Exclusively located in the Heart of
the Bunaken National Marine Park

Siladen
Resort & Spa

Pulau Siladen, Bunaken National Marine Park
North Sulawesi

Indonesia

Tel./Fax: +62 431 856820
e-mail: info@siladen.com
Chill out at: www.siladen.com

archipelago
e x p e d i t i o n s

Komodo • The Banda Sea
Raja Ampat

www.archipelago-fleet.com

Unique dive experiences
exploring Indonesia's
richest reefs and critter sites

MALUKU DIVERS
Ambon, Maluku

www.divingmaluku.com

Directory

Malaysia

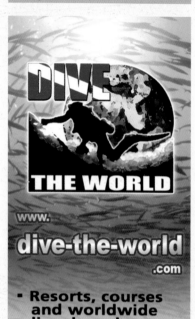

DIVE THE WORLD

www.
dive-the-world
.com

- **Resorts, courses and worldwide liveaboards**

- **Up-to-date local knowledge**

- **Prices to suit every budget**

- **Last minute deals and special offers**

- **Lowest prices guaranteed**

Choose your
    diving adventure!

**Thailand · Fiji · Burma
Malaysia · Indonesia
Maldives · Australia
Red Sea & more ...**

Malaysia

Sipadan-Kapalai Resort
Lankayan Island Resort

The top diving resorts in Borneo
Lankayan - a new diving frontier in the Sulu Seas
Kapalai - macro heaven in the Celebes Seas and
Sipadan - possibly the best diving in the world
www.dive-malaysia.com

Worldwide

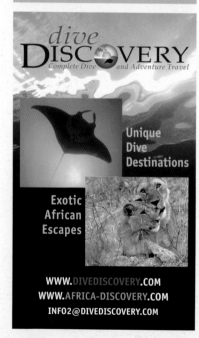

dive **DISCOVERY**
Complete Dive and Adventure Travel

**Unique
Dive
Destinations**

**Exotic
African
Escapes**

WWW.DIVEDISCOVERY.COM
WWW.AFRICA-DISCOVERY.COM
INFO2@DIVEDISCOVERY.COM

Philippines

BOUNDLESS
JOURNEYS
AWAIT...

Tubbataha Reef

Apo Reef

Anilao, Batangas

Puerto Galera

Apo Island, Dumaguete

Bohol

Ticao / Donsol, Sorsogon

▶ PHILIPPINES
DIVE COURSES | DIVE TOURS
LIVE ABOARD TRIPS

Adventure Bound

www.adventurebound.com.ph
info@adventurebound.com.ph

M/Y OCEANA MARIA | M/Y VASCO
OCEANA RESORT, PUERTO GALERA
CRYSTAL BLUE RESORT, ANILAO

300 BAR ◆ ◼ DIVE SHOP

www.300bar.net
info@300bar.net | T: (632)8132067

D.O.T. ACCREDITED

Probably one of the best reasons
for diving with us.

LoveStory

Sea Bees Diving
Phuket & Khao Lak

Sea Bees is the multiple winner of the "Tauchen Award" for "Best Dive Centre in South-East-Asia" and the only dive centre in
Thailand with a 5 Star ISO / EUF certificate. Sea Bees Diving is also a " Go Eco Operator" and member of Quality Divers.
Sea Bees Diving • 1/3 Moo 9 Viset Road • Chalong • Phuket 83130 • Tel: +66-76-381765 • www.sea-bees.com • info@sea-bees.com

Acknowledgements

Credit where it's due

This is the second time around the block on producing one of these guides for Footprint and more than ever, we have to acknowledge that we could never have done it on our own.

This time we knew it wasn't going to be simply about relating our dive experiences over dinner or drinks, but rather, 12 full months of jumping on and off planes followed by long sessions of being glued to the Apple Macs! Yes, there was some diving, too. Once again, our efforts were aided and abetted by a support network of good friends, those who became friends along the way, and colleagues. Many people went above and beyond the call of duty by sharing their real-world dive tales and being constant bouncing boards, keeping us focused on what it is that divers really want.

Our sincere thanks for simply being there when we needed you: Andy & Sue, Jill & Sean, Dave & Jo, Phil & Patricia, Steve & Suz, Roy & Di, Jacquie & Rick, Bruce, Sue Laing, Estelle, Mike & Sam, Annabel Thomas and Andy Shorten. Extra thanks to Cindi La Raia for keeping us up to date with dive travel and Doctor Joann Gren who ensures we don't make any serious medical clangers.

For sharing their tales: Carole Bellars, Bruce Brownstein, Helen Brunt, Nana Enerio, Daniel Galt, Sean & Jill Keen, Sue Laing, Cindi La Raia, Andrew Lok & Carlene Cheong, Gavin Macaulay, George More, Mike and Samantha Muir, Paul O'Toole, Andrew Perkins, Buck Randolph, Andrew Shorten, Jeremy Stein, William Tan, Phil Tobin, Steve and Suzanne Turek, Clare Vincent-Silk & Spike Brown and Estelle Zauner.

A round of applause to all those who came away with us as we researched: the Irian Jaya, Banda and Maratua groups. And to all the people who responded to our research, supplied a name, dropped a tip... we wish we could list you all.

And always in memory of Larry Smith.

Many colleagues across the world have been supportive, making sure we got to the right place at the right time, helped ensure our memories weren't muddied and details were up to date, even when our queries had nothing to do with them:

In the UK Domingo Ramon Enerio and Rosario Afuang/Philippines Department of Tourism; Simon Chance, Suzanne Pleydell and Deborah Sutton/PADI UK; Bettina Walsh/Singapore Tourism Board; Richard Hume/Hume Whitehead; Michelle, Jazz and Nuala/Singapore Airlines; and Jon Cohen and Fujifilm UK (fujifilm.co.uk).

In Indonesia Annabel Thomas/AquaMarine Diving – Bali, Andrew Shorten/Archipelago Fleet; Jonathan Cross/Blue Season Bali; Lisa Crosby/Kararu Dive Voyages; Antony, Harriet and Ben/Manta Dive; George More/Dive Zone; Andrew Lok/Odyssea Divers; Simone Gerritsen/Thalassa; Jeremy Stein/Sangalaki, Bill Quinlan/Waka Resorts; Rudynald Baihaqi/The Oberoi Lombok.

In the Philippines Alex Floro & Conz Paz/Adventure Bound; Paul O'Toole and Goto Alparce/Atlantis Resort Puerto Galera; Michael Andersen/Jysk Travel; Maria Ravanilla, Christie Navarro and Amy Detera/Philippines Department of Tourism.

In Malaysia and Singapore: Gavin Macauley & Sheldon Hey/Dive-the-world; Vincent Chew & Michael Smith/Black Manta; David Espinosa/Australasian Scuba diver; Serene Ong/Singapore Flyer.

In Thailand: Ingo Siewert/Dive-the-World; Steffan Kochan/Calypso divers; Rene Balot/SeaFun Divers.

Bali's life would have gone into meltdown without the TLC supplied by Fiona, Kirk and Steve who helped run our lives, and hers, when we weren't there to do so ourselves. Thanks from all of us.

Finally, many thanks to the entire team at Footprint but especially to Patrick Dawson, Liz Harper, Catherine Phillips and, as always, Alan Murphy – the non-diver who somehow manages to wade through 300 or so pages of dive chatter without losing the plot, his good humour or our respect.

Resources

Research and reference

The following were our principal forms of reference, although there were more:

Reefbase (reefbase.org), Earthtrends (earthtrends.wri.org), The CIA World Factbook (cia.gov), Starfish (starfish.ch), The World Atlas of Coral Reefs (Spalding, Ravilious and Green)

Marine Identification

Reef Fish Identification (Allen, Steene, Humann & DeLoach); World of Water Marine Publications (Neville Coleman); IKAN Reef & Fish guides (Debelius, Kuiter, Norman, Halstead); Fishbase (fishbase.org)

Photography

Cameras Nikon F90/Nikon D200 SLRs in Sea and Sea housings; Nikonos V; Nikon Coolpix 5200 digital; Fuji Finepix F50D

Flashes Ikelite Substrobe 50's; Sea and Sea YS90 duos; Inon Z240

Lenses Nikkor 17-35 zoom, 12-24 zoom, 60mm micro, 105mm micro, 16mm, 20mm

Film Fujichrome Velvia 50 & 100 and Fujichrome Provia 100F (fuji.co.uk)

Suppliers Kevin Reed at Aquaphot (aquaphot.net); Cameras Underwater (camerasunderwater.co.uk); Steve Warren at Ocean Optics (oceanoptics.co.uk); B&H Photo Video (bhphotovideo.com); Fujifilm UK (fujifilm.co.uk);

Dive kit Amphibian Sports, London

Additional Images

Thanks to Suzanne Turek for that great portrait of us; Buck Randolph for the new frogfish; and to anyone – but especially Estelle and Phil – who ever clicked a camera then sent us a picture that has ended up on this page.

Acknowledgements

❝❞ It's not all about fish, you know.

Credits

Footprint credits

Text editors: Alan Murphy, Tim Jollands, Alice Jell
Layout and production: Beth Tierney
Picture editor: Shaun Tierney
Maps: Kevin Feeney, Shane Feeney, Beth Tierney
Chapter maps produced by Compare Infobase Ltd, New Delhi, India

Managing Director: Andy Riddle
Publisher: Patrick Dawson
Commissioning Editor: Alan Murphy
Editorial: Sara Chare, Ria Gane, Jenny Haddington, Felicity Laughton, Nicola Gibbs
Cartography: Robert Lunn, Sarah Sorenson
Sales and marketing: Liz Harper, Hannah Bonnell
Advertising: Renu Sibal
Business Development: Zoë Jackson
Finance and administration: Elizabeth Taylor

Design: Mytton Williams, Bath

Photography credits

Cover images:
© Shaun Tierney/SeaFocus
Inside Images: © SeaFocus/www.seafocus.com

Print

Manufactured in Italy by Printer Trento
Pulp from sustainable forests

Footprint feedback

We try as hard as we can to make each Footprint guide as up to date as possible but, of course, things always change. If you want to let us know about your experiences – good, bad or ugly – then don't delay, go to www.footprintbooks.com and send in your comments.

Publishing information

Footprint Diving Southeast Asia 1st edition
© Footprint Handbooks Ltd
March 2009

ISBN 978 1 906098 50 6
CIP DATA: A catalogue record for this book is available from the British Library

® Footprint Handbooks and the Footprint mark are a registered trademark of Footprint Handbooks Ltd

Published by Footprint
6 Riverside Court, Lower Bristol Road,
Bath BA2 3DZ, UK
T +44 (0)1225 469141
F +44 (0)1225 469461
www.footprintbooks.com

Distributed in the USA by
Globe Pequot Press, Guilford, Connecticut

All rights reserved. No part of this publication may be reproduced, stored in a retrieval system, or transmitted, in any form or by any means, electronic, mechanical, photocopying, recording, or otherwise without the prior permission of Footprint Handbooks Ltd.

Disclaimer

We have, of course, tried to ensure that the facts in this guidebook are accurate. However, travellers should note that places change, owners move on, properties and companies close or are sold, and our opinions are subjective. So it is not possible to guarantee absolute accuracy or that our opinions will always coincide with yours. Travellers should obtain advice from consulates, airlines etc about travel and visa requirements before travelling. The authors and publishers do not accept responsibility for any loss, injury or inconvenience resulting from the information provided in this guidebook. This does not affect your statutory rights.

Life in the deep

butterflies in the sea 194
hey dude – let's talk turtle 142
hitchiking on a fire urchin 44
marine voyeurs 158
masters of disguise 270
not even a pretty face 68
stealth predators 123
wild horses 245

Bunaken, Manado and Lembeh Straits
North Sulawesi - Best diving in Indonesia

TW🐟FISH
Divers

Friendly, relaxed atmosphere and NO crowds!

Small guide ratios of less than 4 divers

PADI

5 STAR
INSTRUCTOR
DEVELOPMENT
DIVE RESORT
★★★★★

Tropical island resorts at TWO fantastic locations
Tel. +62 811 43 2805   www.TwoFishDivers.com